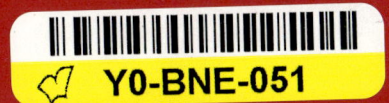

SCANDALS AND FOLLIES

First Edition September 2000

Copyright©2000 Lee Davis

All rights reserved under International and Pan-american copyright Conventions.
Published in the United States by Proscenium Publishers Inc., New York.
Manufactured in the United States of America.

Library of Congress Catalogin-in-Publication Data

Davis, Lee.
    Scandals and follies: the rise and fall of the great Broadway revue / by Lee Davis
    p. cm.
    Includes bibliographical references and index.
    ISBN 0-87910-274-8
      1. Musicals--New york (State)--New York--History and criticism. 2. Musical theater--New York (State)--New York--Reviews. I. Title.

ML1711.8.N3 D38 2000
792.6'09747'1--dc21

                                                                                               99-088656

The author is grateful for permission to reprint copyrighted material as detailed in the Acknowledgements

SCANDALS AND FOLLIES

The Rise and Fall of the Great Broadway Revue

LEE DAVIS

LIMELIGHT EDITIONS · New York

To the memory of James Heineman

A longer than lifetime friend and nurturing advisor whose wit, charm, intelligence and love of the theatre were a glowing, portable reflection of this book's subject.

Table of Contents

Acknowledgements   9

Introduction   13

1. Boisterous Beginnings;
The Pastorizing of Broadway   20

2. From Six-A-Day to Two-A-Day to One-A-Day   47

3. Finally, The Follies   69

4. The Door Opens   89

5. Clash of the Titans   111

6. The Real War   137

7. The Great Challenger   153

8. Say It With Music   177

9. Less Is More   197

10. High Times   225

11. We're Out of the Money   269

12. Bad Times, Thoughtful Times   299

13. The War Effort   339

14. Death by Electronics   358

Selected Bibliography   377

Endnotes   381

Index   385

Acknowledgements

There's a warm and concentrated comfort in devotion. It possesses a single focus, and so it gives back an instant and manageable gratification.

Next to the abiding allegiance I have to those I love and have loved, my most abiding and indestructible devotion, since I was an early and impressionable adolescent, has been focused, with the intensity of a key light, upon the musical theatre. And the two men who were responsible for installing that passionate veneration in me were the master librettist Guy Bolton and the producer/choreographer Russell Markert.

Guy and Virginia Bolton were the first, because they provided my family and me with house seats for my first Broadway musical, the 1943 revival of Rodgers and Hart's *A Connecticut Yankee*. It was a gift that was as fatal as it was vital, for I was hopelessly, eternally smitten that evening. I was besotted with every detail of that experience from the moment I entered the theatre until the last note of the playout died. And from that moment forward, I've never fallen out of love with the theatre, and particularly the musical theatre.

The second kindler of the flame, Russell Markert—at the time the associate producer of the Radio City Music Hall stage spectacles and founder and choreographer of the Music Hall Rockettes—filled our home on weekends with the likes of Dixie Dunbar, Mitzi Mayfair and other dancing stars of the Broadway revue, which was in full flower at the time. These performers taught my awestruck friends and me the periphery of their routines; we reveled in their talent and in Russell Markert's mesmerizing memories of George White and Florenz Ziegfeld, and his own adventures with the *Scandals*.

And so to them, I give continuing and eternal thanks for setting me upon a path that had to include, at some time or other, the writing of this book, as I also give thanks to the writers and composers and performers of *Make Mine Manhattan*, *Call Me Mister*, *Inside U.S.A.*, *Two on the Aisle* and *New Faces of 1952* in whose audiences I once sat, awash in the delight of the Broadway revue during its final years of popular acceptance.

I'm equally grateful to the comedy dance team of Helene and Howard, for whom I once worked and with whom I once traveled. They gave me the opportunity to be slightly in on the workings of the very last gasp of this glorious entertainment invention, the final, ill-fated *Ziegfeld Follies* which never made it to New York.

All of this came together, in 1996, in "Where Have All the Girls and Gags Gone?", a two part article in *Show Music Magazine* which formed the basis of this book. For their enthusiasm and graciousness and help, I'm eternally grateful to *Show Music*'s editor, Max Preeo, and its indefatigable and ceaselessly helpful publisher, John Pike.

John's bailiwick, the Goodspeed Opera House, under theë leadership of Michael Price, is responsible, also, for both inspiration and information, in great abundance. Lisa Viall, Goodspeed's astonishingly efficient and knowledgeable librarian, gave me great and necessary help, as did her predecessor, Kristin Johnson.

My son Chris was likewise indispensable in searching the internet for information that books and interviews sometimes didn't provide. Bob Klineman was a faithful and invaluable advisor, and John Meyer, whose encyclopedic mind and giant musical talent are boundless, supplied some juicy, on target, show-biz tidbits.

Thanks also to the following, who were unstintingly generous in supplying me with memories, material and information obtainable nowhere else: Richard Adler, Mary Ellin Barrett, Peggy Bolton, Irving Caesar, Betty Comden and Adolph Green, Martin Gottfried, Mary Cleere Haran, Kitty Carlisle Hart, Anne Kaufman Schneider, Steven Suskin, Douglas Watt, Ethel Watt and Deborah Grace Winer.

The collecting of the illustrations for this book was a thorough, exhausting and fascinating search, impossible without the gracious help of the following people: Bobby Horowitz, who led me to Pat Timberg, whose mother, Rosemarie Sinnett (stage name: Collette Ayres), was one of Ziegfeld's beauties. Pat, in turn, guided me to the Ziegfeld Club, where vice president Paula Lamont and administrator Nils Hanson awaited and magnanimously threw open the club's archives.

Much appreciation to Mary Ellin Barrett, Irving Berlin's daughter, and Bert Fink, Mike Dvorchak and Tom Briggs of the Rodgers and Hammerstein/Irving Berlin Organization, who made available to me a treasure store of Berlin memorabilia, information and photos.

Great thanks are due Anne Kaufman Schneider, George S. Kaufman's daughter, for making some of his revue sketches available to me and for directing me to the Max Gordon collection at the Princeton University library, where archivist Mary Anne Jensen and photo-duplication coordinator AnnaLee Pauls couldn't have been more helpful.

Great gratitude to Reagan Fletcher, Maryann Chach, Mark Swartz and Sylvia Wang for their hours upon hours of considerate and irreplaceable help in searching through the delectable riches of the Shubert archives.

And, finally, a warm thank you to Ron Mandelbaum for the resources of the staggeringly vast library of Photofest.

Great gratitude to my agent, Kay Kidde, and her enthusiastic support in dark days and bright, and to my far sighted publisher, Mel Zerman.

And always, always, an enormous expression of eternal gratitude for the remarkable generosity of spirit and time and information given to me by Robert Kimball, that great gentleman, two-legged reference library and dean of musical theatre. And the same goes to the ghost of the man whose mantle Bob Kimball inherited, Stanley Green. When times get tough, Stanley still stands at my shoulder, repeating the words of advice he once gave me. "Go ahead," he said, with his usual pixyish smile. "Write about the musical theatre. You'll never make a living doing it, but you'll have a hell of a lot of fun." And he was, as always, right.

Lee Davis
WESTHAMPTON, NY
SEPTEMBER, 1998

Introduction

It was a grand and glorious and circumscribed moment, a sumptuous space of time in which the reassuring presence of an unfolding plot was nudged offstage by bevies of beauties, clans of clowns, infinitely ascending staircases and miles and miles of gauzy drops. Variety was its identity and a third of its ancestry. Humor was its staple, music its underpinning, spectacle its clothing.

I refer, of course, to the lifetime and particularity of that unique and delicious invention, the Broadway revue, whose time onstage was fleeting but undeniable, abbreviated but unforgettable. For a mere 50 years, from 1907, when the first Follies premiered, to 1957, when the last, shadowy representation that dared, with as much audacity as its namesake, to call itself *The Ziegfeld Follies* flopped on the road, the true, fully realized Broadway revue held more than its own as an essential, basic ingredient of every New York season.

Although its influence extends, like its staircases, interminably, its stay on Broadway was brief. And, even then, it had times of visibility and times of near invisibility. It came and went like its multiple sets, was now abundant, now nearly indefinable—like the costumes of its showgirls. But it was always, even during its leanest times, essential.

In fact, no self-respecting Broadway season from World War I through World War II could or would have existed without its healthy quota of revues. And there were few Broadway musical stars from the turn of the century through the 1960s who hadn't either spent vital portions of their schooling or some of their most illustrious moments in a revue.

The best revues were composed of a balance of form and facts. The form could be sumptuous, as realized by Florenz Ziegfeld; sophisticated, as by George White; slightly sleazy, as by Earl Carroll; or relentlessly sleazy, as by Jake Shubert.

The facts were in the sketches. Whether they were sending up, in the best burlesque tradition, current fare on Broadway, or probing the mores of the masses, poking fun at the fashions and foibles of the very well-off, or satirically skewering political chicanery, social injustice and the less admirable appetites of nations and their leaders, revues dealt with the identity of the age in which they were written.

And so, the Broadway revue at its best was a musical mirror of its times. It was closer to and more reflective of the periods in which it existed than anything else on musical Broadway, then or now. But, because of the nature of its material and the material of its sketches, it was also more vulnerable to time's caprices and fashions than its sometime competitor, sometime companion, the book musical.

There was also a distinctive, digestible quality in the structure of the revue. Like the life it mirrored, it contained moments that were memorable and moments that invited forgetting. Mountains, but plenty of plains. And yet, if something didn't work, what followed it usually did, and somewhere, sometime in the evening, there would be a savory reward for just about everyone. And so, when the tyrannical time demands of radio and television began to nibble away at the regency of Broadway, it was logical that the revue would be most vulnerable to the nibblers. Its fragmentation, its unevenness and its often deliberately anti-organic form made it easily divisible.

Eventually, its trappings would be entirely consumed by television—ironically, at the hands of creators, directors and performers who had learned their lessons in and from the very show business form they were destroying.

But hardly any of these refugees from revues took with them the revue's heart and essence. Max Liebman learned and transferred some of the revue's internal techniques to the tube, and Sid Caesar and Imogene Coca and their cohorts and progeny practiced these techniques brilliantly. But what most of the creators of television variety failed to take from stage to studio were the abiding lessons of the masters of the revue.

And masters there were, as there are in any art form. There was Ziegfeld, who took a feisty but primitive collection of show biz gimmicks and invested them with taste and a subtle unity, and thus really invented the form; there was a select group of others, among them Charles Dillingham, John Murray Anderson, George White, Leonard Sillman, Mike Todd, Billy Rose and, yes, more times than not, Earl Carroll, who balanced precariously somewhere between the sophistication of George White and the exploitativeness of Jake Shubert and Harold Minsky.

The American masters were met and sometimes bested by the two great British overlords, Charles B. Cochran and Andre Charlot. All, on both sides of the Atlantic, were thoroughly aware that despite the apparent informality of a revue in its truest manifestation, it was conceived as carefully and thoughtfully as any successful book show.

Intriguingly, it was Charles B. Cochran who set his methods to paper; the others preferred to keep their secrets to themselves or leave them up to colleagues or biographers to discover.

But Cochran, in 1926, revealed his recipe for revues, thus preserving a standard of measurement that, when met by his contemporaries and followers, produced hits—and, when ignored, more often than not produced disasters.

"When a revue is in preparation," he wrote, "I invariably bombard my authors with suggestions, because a revue has first to be built, and then written. In any successful revue many scenes and interludes, upon which considerable time has been spent, are sacrificed before the first performance. Often ideas that seem good at birth do not mature well. For this reason revues put together hurriedly, with little time for substitution and rewriting, often fail. My experience has been that I have seldom failed with a revue if there has been plenty of time for preparation." [1]

Good advice, ignored regularly and catastrophically. It was a method reduced to a science by the great Andre Charlot. Noel Coward had the good fortune to observe Charlot at work while the impresario was working on Coward's *London Calling* in 1923, and Coward recorded it:

"He [Charlot] would have the names of all the numbers in the revue printed on separate cards, place them on his desk and then, as though playing Patience, juggle with them and go on moving them about, shifting them again and again until he was satisfied that they were in the right running order. The finale of the first half would already have been agreed upon, but all the numbers leading up to it had to build, and built to the number *before* the finale and that number, whatever it was, had to be sure-fire. The second number in the second half was, still is, and always will be, terribly important. It has to be so strong, or so funny, or so spectacular or whatever, that the audience, including by then the stragglers from the bar, will settle back comfortably in their seats, happy in the knowledge that the second half is going to be ever more brilliant than the first.

"All this can be settled with the cards fairly amicably. Then the fun begins. 'You can't possibly change the set from So And So straight into So And So.' 'Gertie couldn't possibly make the change from tweeds at the end of the sketch into deep evening dress for the beginning of her big number.' And so on and so on; more juggling of the cards until all is set and will run smoothly.

"This can still be done, present day directors please note, with, first, good material—songs, sketches, and dances; then, stars or star personalities if you are lucky enough to find them; taste, tact and endless patience from the director and never forget, the right running order."[2]

And that was the way it was when the revue was right and glorious.

But those days have, alas, passed, and what parades as a revue today is a shadow of the real thing; often a pleasant enough pastime, but no more like the shows of the Great Broadway Revue Period than *Grease* is to *Show Boat*. True, some of the best of the Broadway revues of that age were united by themes. As *Thousands Cheer* and *Pins and Needles* come easily to mind. But today, a revue *must* have a unifying theme or, in far too many cases, a unifying composer. We don't trust the form to remain as it once was, reeking of variety, vaudeville, minstrelsy and burlesque, but manifesting, through a mastery of, as Coward put it, "the right running order," a unique, satisfying evening of memorable and varied entertainment.

Ironically, although television killed the revue, present-day economics prevents it from resurrection. The television variety show that interred the Broadway revue in the 1960s has all but departed from the living room or bedroom screen. What remains of it, in tattered reflection, is relegated to late nights and is so overwhelmed by commercial breaks that any sense of form is forever fragmented. Nay, annihilated. But the economic problem, the gigantic cost of mounting the spectacle that once dazzled and delighted us still looms large, as it does more and more over all of contemporary Broadway.

And so, the revue's golden days and nights have passed, probably forever. All the more reason then, that, before it fades into the stuff that archaeologists unearth and interpret, a definitive review of the revue is in order, a resurrection, if only on paper, of the trip it once took, over rocky roads and smooth, from a raucous and fragmented beginning, through unsteady adolescence, first flowering, maturity, magnificence and downfall. The trip forms the framework of a splendid story, full of variety and color and heartbreak and passion and foolishness and irony and truth. Like life itself. Curtain up, then, on confusion.

1

THE PASTORIZING OF BROADWAY

Boisterous Beginnings
The Pastorizing of Broadway

Everything has a beginning. Everyone has ancestors, even on the musical stages of today, where what seems to be often attempts to mask what is.

And the Broadway revue has not one, but three ancestors: minstrelsy, variety and burlesque.

Telling that to the well-heeled, well-dressed theatregoers of 1915, debarking from cabs and hansoms before Klaw and Erlanger's miracle on 42nd Street, the New Amsterdam Theatre, would probably invite dismissive confusion. The printed claims were there and obvious: the latest edition of *The Ziegfeld Follies*, that lovingly balanced, thoughtfully created, opulently mounted big Broadway revue, was something brand new. Wasn't it?

Well, yes. In a sense. But not really new, for, despite the producer's claims, this was not a unique creation, but the dramatic moment when a theatre form that had been developing for a long time was finally brought to its majority.

More confusion. It would probably be useless to tell this glittering audience that just as some of the scions of New York, passing under the undulating waves of the New Amsterdam's marquee, and on into its foyer of friezes, had struggled up from wretched poverty to disposable riches, so had the revue begun humbly and haltingly before arriving at this bejeweled and beknighted state.

And not only that. The ladies who, in the fashion of the day, took their time in taking their seats, parading back and forth through the Grand Promenade to show off their finery, were a far cry from the female denizens of the dives that housed variety.

Well, perhaps it was just as well that most of the gowned and white-tied opening night audience that took its seats in the mammoth auditorium, with its balanced boxes embraced by whiplashes of Art Nouveau filigree, didn't wholly comprehend or care about the long and winding and sometimes tortuous journey the revue had made from minstrelsy before finally arriving on this night at this palace of pleasure.

Nor would the youngest of the 100 performers, comfortably tucked into the dressing rooms that were wrapped, in a seven story tower, around the auditorium and the stage on the 41st Street side, behind the iron staircases that ran up to the roof garden and down to the mainstage, completely comprehend the trial and error and struggle that the older performers and those who had come before them had endured. Navigating the multiple phases of burlesque, these veterans had brought this, one of the musical theatre's most distinctive and exhilarating means of expressing itself, to its present, august state of being. To understand this, these younger performers would have to quiet their own anticipatory excitement and listen to the memories of the oldtimers. Or, better yet, utilize the magic of the theatre, and crank up a time machine so that it reversed itself, and recreated the popular musical entertainment tastes of the raucous and rambunctious years of a Republic that had just emerged from a Civil War:

The curtain rises. A burst of banjo music, and the crowd roars in rightful expectation. The company, spread from wing to wing in a giant arc, a ragtag rainbow of mismatched costumes, advances on the apron and sings:

O some will shout den take a rest
    Down on de campground
But when I shout I shout my best
    Way down on de old campground
Ole Satan tried to mek me hush
    Down on de campground
Wid my gospel gun I run him in de brush
    Way down on de ole campground!

Wild applause. Whistles. Cheers.

"Gentlemen! Be seated!" intones the immaculately white-tie-and-tailed interlocutor, and as the cast sits, four blackfaced men, in outrageous, checkered outfits, their expressions locked in eternal amazement, their mouths the overdrawn ovals of clowns, their repartee shot from interior gattling guns, tumble on.
    The bragging match begins.
    "Mistah Bones?"
    "What dat, Mistah Tambo?"
    "I say, Mistah Bones, I wants you to know dat las' night I wup de Lion of de West."
    "Huh. I wup mah weight in wildcats."
    "Nuthin. Ah et a alligator."
    "You what?"
    "You hear me. Ah et a alligator."
    "You use a fork or a spoon?"
    "Fork."
    "Dat don' count. I et mah last one wit no utensils. Jes mah teeth."
    The interlocutor intervenes, with intonation.
    "Gentlemen! Gentlemen! Be seated! It is, you will agree, to our mutual benefit that we all practice a little decorum, a little civility, a few of the gracious, gravitative and grammatically correct behaviors that separate us from the primeval primates."

(Hoots and whistles from the gallery.)

"Say what?" asks Mr. Tambo.

("You tell 'im nigger!" yells a voice from the gallery, followed by more cheers and louder hoots.)

"Never mind," says the interlocutor, airily. I can tell by your phrenology that you don't understand."

"Wha—"

"Never mind. You don't even know the word."

"Ah most suttenly does," counters Tambo, rising to his full height. "An de wuhd is frenologism."

"Phren—"

"Ah learned dat on a ferry ride ah took when ah was home last summah. When ah got out a little piece from the shore, de man who drove de ferry axed me if I knowed anyting about frenologism. I told him no. Ah, says he, den one quarter of your life is gone. Finally, he says, does you know anyting about gramm'r? I told him no. Ah, says he, den one half ob you life am gone. He axed if I knowed anyting about dickshionary. I told him no and he say tree quarters of your life is gone. Den we hit a rock, and I axed him if he knowed how to swim. He said no. Den say I, de whole four quarters of your life am gone—shure."

The house erupts.

In the second act, the interlocutor asks Tambo to explain transcendentalism. Tambo obliges:

"Transcendentalism is dat spiritual cognoscence ob psychological irrefragibility, connected wid consicentient ademption ob incolumbient spirituality and etherialized connection—which is deribed from a profound contemplation ob de irregability ob dose ineccesible divisions ob de more minute portions ob subdivided particles ob invisible atoms dat become ana-tom-catically tattalable in de circumambulatin commotion ob ambiloquous voluminiousness."

The spectacle is breathtaking: A shipwreck, a seamstress rescued from a burning building, acrobats who build and destroy human pyramids, singers who sing on key, comedians who skewer the greats of the day: John D. Rockefeller, J.P. Morgan, Anthony Comstock, Stanford White, Harry K. Thaw, and Evelyn Nesbitt, swinging provocatively out over the audience on a ravishing, red velvet swing.

But it's the burlesque of the latest hit operetta that the audience, knowing, wealthy, spiffily dressed and studiously aware of it, anticipates.

And it comes, just before the olio: The Parisian Widows, a romp through the alleyways and artists' salons, the garrets and garages of Gay Paree, featuring Barney McCann, alias Isie Smooth; Tony Sparrario, alias Isie Rough; Barking Dog, King of the Grafters; and Sure Lock Holmes, a real detective.

The sketch clears, and the girls come on, scandalously dressed in bloomers, but somewhat more decorous than their sisters in the other burlesque, further downtown, where the bloomers are scantier and the humor, in the courtroom scenes, more direct:

"I'm justice," says the judge.
"Justice what?" asks the plaintiff.
"Justice good as you are."
Rim shot from the pit. Bang, the bladder comes out and socks the plaintiff over the head.
"Sorry," says the plaintiff.
"That's better," says the judge.
"Now then, your horror—" begins the plaintiff.
Squirt. The seltzer bottle soaks the plaintiff.
Next quick scene: A street-corner. A bum asks a gaudily dressed chorus girl who can't stop undulating: "Will you give me a nickel for a cup of coffee?"
"Sorry," she moans, still undulating, "All I have is a ten dollar bill."
"Fine," says the tramp, "I can change that."
Blackout.

Next quick sketch: Two comics wearing squashed down derbies and checkered suits eight sizes too big pause in front of a painted drop.

"What's the difference between mashed potatoes and pea soup?" asks one.

"I don't know the difference between mashed potatoes and pea soup," answers the other. "What IS the difference between mashed potatoes and pea soup?"

"The difference," says the other, "between mashed potatoes and pea soup is that you can mash potatoes but you can't..."

Rim shot. Blackout.

The air is gray with cigar smoke, a super-heated fog that tears the eyes and tickles the sinuses. The noise is thunderous, at least for a pre-electronic time: top-of-the lungs, bottom-of-the-diaphragm conversation, clattering music, shrill singing, determined shouting, frequent animal squeals, intermittent laughter, nascent anger. No hush falls over this crowd when the first act enters. It's hard to tell where the show is located, on the stage or in the house. It's entertainment, certain enough. And its venue resembles that of a convivial parlor when your parlor is full of actors, musicians, drunks and prostitutes.

The name attached to this last bit of mayhem is variety, an export direct from England that found a boisterously receptive home in late eighteenth and early nineteenth century New York, and one of the three major ancestors of the Broadway revue. The previous two, minstrel shows and burlesque, occupy equal bragging rights and claims to star billing on the revue's family tree.

But first things first, and since variety predated both burlesque and minstrelsy, it receives first billing here.

Its roots reach back to eighteenth century British taverns, which grew annexes their owners called, variously, music halls, music rooms or, if they were especially plush, musickhouses.

If England's music halls were noisy, America's were raucous beyond redemption. The program of comic songs, acrobatics, conjuring, juggling and dancing fought with and usually lost out to the roar of the drinking, shouting and sometimes object-throwing crowd. The stench of beer fused with the stink of cigar smoke. Ladies of the demimonde strolled through the haze, stopping at whatever table contained a few gentlemen in need. The ancestors of today's B-girls, these strollers-cum-waitresses were tough ladies; no tea for whiskey or water for gin for them. Since they were the real thing, they drank the real thing and stayed far more alert than most of their clients.

Their activity was, after all, as old as the world, and the entertainment that spun on the stage at one end of the music hall had its own long and colorful history, too. Variety had been the staff of theatre life of Shakespearian times; the bear-baiting that had gone on outside of the Globe had been designed as part of an entire day of entertainment—a tradition begun by the Greeks—that included *Hamlet* or *Twelfth Night*. Simultaneously, in seventeenth century Italy, the *a soggetto, all'improviso* harlequinades of the *commedia dell' arte*, were the ancestors of England's pantomimes and Punch and Judy shows, and their very wordlessness made them just the thing for the early nineteenth century music halls of the American frontier—east or west.

And so, in early America, variety was particularly tough, probably because America in the eighteenth and early nineteenth century was a tough place, full to overflowing with divergence, diversity, rigorousness and rowdiness. And proud of it. The dancehalls and music halls in New York City not only had their hostesses who sold them-selves selves between acts, but stag lines in the shadows, waiting for a patron to pass out so that he could be robbed. Or, if he was young enough and a sailor, dragged out of the place and sold to the captain of some short-handed ship. It was a chancy life.

On the other hand, burlesque, the second resident of revue's family tree, came from far more genteel and literary soil. That it would develop into the most raucous form of all is instructive and part of the spontaneity that only live theatre, of all the arts, possesses. But in its pure form, it certainly had a respectable heritage, flourishing on both page and stage in England from the moment that Buckingham parodied Dryden and the heroic drama in 1671's *The Rehearsal*. Restoration comedy was rife with the nonsense and satire that were the twin legs upon which this, the classic style of burlesque stood; in 1728, Gay's *Beggar's Opera* took on the traditions of opera and drama; Fielding did in classic drama with his 1730 *Tragedy of Tragedies, or the Life and Death of Tom Thumb the Great*; and Sheridan, taking his cue from Tobias Smollett, skewered sentimental drama and literature in 1779 with a play appropriately called *The Critic*.

The two early nineteenth century masters of the form had their roots at the Drury Lane. James Robinson Planche and William Mitchell ground out parodies by the yard, Planche mostly for Mme. Vestris and her troupe, Mitchell for anyone. Their form was the "burletta," a type of burlesque that, in order to qualify for its title, had to contain at least five songs in each act. Planche subtitled one of these "A Most Extravagant Extravaganza, or Rum-Antic Burletta." And so, spectacular effects, designed to produce gasps of pleasure, were wedded to the mix, and the entire package was exported to America.

In 1823, Pierce Egan arrived from England with *Tom and Jerry, or Life in London*, a sort of musical travelogue in which the two leading characters' adventures were lighthearted excuses for stage trickery and a succession of singing, dancing, juggling and comedy acts. George Odell, in his *Annals of the New York Stage*, described it as a melange of "...rapidly shifting scenes, great diversity of city types of character, and a large amount of consequent spectacle, song and dance..."[1]

An extravagant success if there ever was one, and a year later, in 1824, a Negro company burlesqued the burlesque in a production titled *The Death of Life in London, or Tom and Jerry's Funeral*. That was the way it went with the form. No success could open without the reward of an almost instant parody of it. And the more outlandish, the better. Comic tastes ran to the immediately recognizable and the terminally silly in the American theatre of the mid-nineteenth century, although a knowledge of Greek myths and their casts of characters didn't hurt. Planche's *The Deep, Deep Sea* for instance, featured takeoffs on Rossini arias and a penultimate quarrel between Amphitrite, Andromeda, Cassiope and Perseus.

That was for the boxes. But the pit wasn't ignored in this new democracy. At the other end of the scale, one of the greatest hits of this time introduced the purely American figure of Fireman Mose, the Bowery B'hoy Triumphant. Mose was actually patterned upon Moses Humphrey, a fireman of the Lady Washington Company who, through the regency of his muscles and his girth, reigned as the king of Five Points, the brawlingest, most dangerous part of lower Manhattan, until 1836. That year, in a near riot that involved over a hundred firemen and members of the homicidal Five Points gangs, he was deposed of his kingdom by one Henry Chanfrau, the elder brother of an actor.

Dethroned, he departed for self-imposed exile in Hawaii. But his memory lived on in *A Glance at New York in 1848* and its immediate sequel, *A New Glance at New York*, followed closely by *Mose in California*, *Mose in France*, *Mose in China* and *Mose in a Muss*. *A Glance at New York*, then, introduced a character who would reprise himself for the rest of the century. A thin thread of a plot that established the American-country-cousin-coming-to-the-city-and-outwitting-the-sophisticates theme was just the wrapping twine that strung together a parade of extravagant scene changes (Chatham

Square, the Chatham Theatre, the Old Dutch Church, a soup house, city hall, and the Catherine Fish Market) and spectacular special effects, such as Mose rescuing a child from a burning building. Sandwiched in were specialty acts, and one of the specialties involved six lovely members of the Ladies Bowling Saloon attempting to dance. Voila. The first recorded chorus line on the American stage kicked up its toes.

John Brougham, an Irish actor and playwright who wrote 162 produced plays, made his own debut with a burlesque of a burlesque, an Americanization of the Tom and Jerry form, *Life in New York, or Tom and Jerry on a Visit*, which had a finale lit by fireworks. By 1861, he'd established himself as the American master of the burletta/burlesque form with *Pocahontas, or The Gentle Savage*, followed closely by *Hiawatha, or Ardent Spirits and Laughing Water*. The "Gentle Savages" bore names such as Cod-Livr-Oyl, Kal-O-Mel, Kross-As-Kan-Bee, and Lump-A-Sugah.

Meanwhile, Planche and Mitchell, realizing the potential of a new market, brought their burlettas to America. Mitchell, particularly, utilized the production possibilities of Niblo's Garden to spoof the currently popular ballet *La Bayadere, or The Maid of Cashmere*, with *Buy-It-Dear, 'Tis Made of Cashmere*.

Pure burlesque, then, with its spectacular effects and its spoofs of contemporary literature, people and issues became a stage staple in New York at the beginning of the nineteenth century.

But America added another, more impure dimension to the original; and it, combined with its purer part, became one of the richest training grounds for some of the Broadway revue's shiniest lights. The dimension: lightly clad girls, sometimes dancing, sometimes posing, and usually the major reason for male attendance.

Like any revolutionary movement, this seamier development, which emphasized and eventually became known mostly for its sex and nudity, had tentative beginnings. In 1833, at the Bowery Theatre, a certain Mlle. Francisquay appeared in a legitimate play titled *The*

Ice Witch, wearing a decolleté costume that was simultaneously hissed by the boxes and cheered by the balcony and gallery, a sure indication of where this sort of daring would play best.

In 1861, Adah Isaacs Menken created the role of Mazeppa of Byron's poem, strapped, the publicity said, "nude" to the back of an "untamed stallion." The stallion was no stallion and Ms. Menken was no nude. She wore, according to historian Irving Zeidman, "baggy trunks...enough for three bathing suits, a sash and fleshings."[2] But the costume, or lack of it, caused a stir in both gallery and boxes and possibly paved the way for the arrival, in 1866, of *The Black Crook*, that famous entertainment that introduced not only the American musical, but American burlesque to the theatregoing American public.

More of that in a moment, after some time well spent with the third branch on the revue's family tree, the minstrel show:

Until one February night in 1843, the word minstrel was distinct and separate and reserved to describe the descendants of the professional, strolling players of the Middle Ages who matured into the court poets and musicians of fifteenth century England and France. But all of that changed for good in America when Billy Whitlock, Frank Pelham, Dan Emmett and Frank Brower, billing themselves as the Virginia Minstrels, roared onto the New York theatrical scene.

Each of the four had applied burnt cork to their white faces to perform blackfaced in circuses, but they'd been known then as "delineators." Now, in 1843, they were out of work and down on their luck. But they were showmen and had heard about a group of Swiss performers named the Tyrolese Minstrel Family, who had toured America triumphantly during the previous season.

The ambitious and desperate quartet adopted the name, appending it to a Southern state in which slavery was a recognizable fact. *Ipso facto*, their role as "Ethiopean delineators" would now be translated into minstrelsy.

What the paying audience didn't expect, and what delighted

them, was a new form of musical and comedy entertainment that resulted from the improvisation of four imaginative actors. The Virginia Minstrels arranged their chairs in a semicircle; the two men on each end used elementary clackers: the tambourine and the bones that would become endmen's trademarks. They mixed their songs and dances with funny sayings and skits; they ended the first part of the evening with a "stump speech" loaded with malapropisms, and they climaxed the show with a plantation production number that supposedly gave a flavor of the life and actions and amusement of the Southern Negro.

The form was so natural, it seemed improvised—and, in fact, much of the evening, because of the talents of the four, was. But most of all, there was exuberance and excitement. The minstrels, in their wide-eyed, large-lipped, ragged- costumed absurdity, rolled onto the stage in a thundercloud of energy which hardly ever dissipated. They insulted each other, they baited each other, they made mincemeat out of the language, they took the audience into their confidence and their fun, and, in one night, they added a new form to show business in America—in fact, the world.

The gallery and the balcony went wild. "The b'hoys and their seamstress sweethearts", as the *Literary Digest*[3] put it, now had not only Mose, but minstrels who spoke in their voice, which was also the voice of the frontier. Not only this. The seeming anarchy of the minstrel form represented some of their core values. It was they, after all, who, in the Astor Place Riots in 1849, had stood up to the guns of the militia and driven the English Shakespearean actor James MacReady out of New York and the country.

There was something, in other words, particularly and peculiarly American about the Virginia Minstrels whose antics would be downright repulsive to the audiences of today. But for the next 40 years, minstrel shows would be the most popular form of theatre for the new nation. The Virginia Minstrels left for England in late 1843 for a tour of that country, then disbanded, since each of the original actors thought of himself as a single performer and chafed at submerging his personality into that of a troupe.

But the ground had been broken. There was now, because of the Virginia Minstrels, a minstrel-mad public, and a growing group of larger and larger minstrel troupes. In 1844, the Ethiopian Serenaders played the White House, "For the Especial Amusement of The President of the United States, John Tyler." And minstrels entertained the next four administrations of presidents Polk, Taylor, Fillmore and Pierce. It's possible to assume that President Lincoln was less amused than they by blackface humor, although not necessarily. After all, it was he who decided to attend a production of *Our American Cousin*, featuring the Mose/Brother Jonathan character, at the Ford Theatre on the fateful and tragic night of April 14, 1865.

No, frontier humor, or at least the remainder of the country's perception of it, was in. Groups like the Buckley Serenaders toured the South; San Francisco claimed five professional minstrel troupes; Boston had Ordway's Aeolians. Carncross and Dixey's Minstrels ran for nine straight years in Philadelphia; Sanford's ran seven.

But it was in New York, where it all began, that minstrel shows ran rampant. Hooley's Minstrels held sway in Brooklyn; E.P. Christy's Minstrels filled houses for an uninterrupted ten years in Manhattan. From mid-1840 to mid-1850, there were never less than five major companies playing on Broadway, and during the 1850s, ten major minstrel houses did capacity business, three of them on the same Broadway block. The Chatham, the Bowery, the Old Park, Barnum's American Museum, churches, synagogues, even a show boat on the Hudson filled their seats and their coffers with minstrel shows. It was entertainment for the masses, and the masses responded with wild enthusiasm.

New, exuberant stage dances, evolved for the plantation production numbers with such strained titles as "The Virginia Jungle Dance," "The Nubian Jungle Dance," "The African Fling" and "The African Sailor's Hornpipe." As the craze continued,

Stephen Foster, who had starred as a blackface singer with an amateur theatre group when he was nine years old, churned out a continual stream of songs for the most popular of all of the minstrel troupes, the Christy Minstrels.

By the 1850s, the form was firmly established: there was a white interlocutor who sat in the middle of the extended semicircle, serving not only as master of ceremonies, but orchestrator of the pace and the content of the show. The interplay between performers and audience, begun with the Virginia Minstrels, was an expected mainstay of every company. The interlocutor, with his faultless command of the language, was also an object of mockery by the endmen, Brudder Bones and Brudder Tambo. And that delighted the bowery b'hoys no end, too.

With the addition of Stephen Foster's sentimental ballads, a romantic tenor became a necessary adjunct in the first part, sandwiched between the puns, malapropisms, riddles and non-sequiturs of the endmen.

The second part, or "olio," was pure variety, including song and dance men, acrobats, comb players, porcupine quill players or glass players, and always, at the end of the olio, the stump speech begun by the Virginia Minstrels. More often than not, this impassioned oration poked fun at contemporary politics or social ills. And so the ancestors of the monologues of Will Rogers in the *Ziegfeld Follies* were born, and began their buoyant childhood.

After the olio, a one-act sketch ended the show. It began with the plantation number, then, borrowing from pure burlesque, evolved into satirical farce, ladled on with malaprop-dialect, and a finale that, again borrowing from burlesque, almost always included a combination of beatings with inflated bladders, bombardments of cream pies and sometimes even firework explosions.

For a while, at the end of the 1850s, Dan Bryant's Minstrels continued with the plantation finale, but the satirical sketch, blurring the space between burlesque and minstrelsy, now began to establish itself as the forerunner and begetter of the revue sketch.

And so it started. The three branches of the family tree of the Broadway revue formed an essential, life-giving centerpiece in the mix that made musical Broadway what it was at the dawn of the twentieth century. Variety provided the succession of acts. Pure burlesque provided satire; impure burlesque presented girls in various states of dress and undress. Minstrel shows provided a form, reliance on mass-oriented comedy and a refinement of burlesque into satirical sketches.

And all of this finally converged at the corner of Broadway and Prince Street on September 12, 1866, at Niblo's Garden with *The Black Crook*.

Much has been written and rewritten about this poor (in multiple ways) show, about the collision and consequent elision of two companies at one time in one place—one of them a classic troupe of actors, the other a stranded French ballet company. And all of it is fundamentally true.

The background was straightforward enough: William Wheatley, the general manager of Niblo's, had committed himself to the production of a tortured melodrama by Charles M. Barras modeled upon Carl Maria von Weber's opera *Der Freischutz* : the story of Hertzog (otherwise known as the Black Crook), who must deliver a human soul every New Year's Eve to an evil "Arch Fiend." The rest of the convoluted plot involved a painter named Rudolph, who's duped by Hertzog into wandering through a forest in search of a cache of gold. Along the way, he saves the life of a dove who turns out to be Stalacta, the Queen of the Golden Realm. She undupes Rudolph, takes him to Fairyland and unites him with his true love, Amina.

Wheatley, faced with this melodrama of melodramas, probably welcomed the plight of impresario Henry C. Jarrett,who had imported a French ballet troupe to perform *La Biche au Bois* at the Academy of Music.

The problem was that the Academy of Music had burned to the ground while the ballet troupe was en route. (Fire, incidentally, was a recurring problem for both casts and theatregoers in the nineteenth century. The lethal combination of gas lamps and inflammable scenery, few stairways and fewer exits, combined to make playgoing before the invention of electricity and asbestos adventurous, to say the least. Two surveys, one in 1878 and one in 1882, concluded that one out of every four theatres burned within the first four years of its construction, and the average life of a theatre in New York before it was charred to the sidewalk was 12 years. One theatre historian of the period noted sardonically, "One of the pleasures of old-time theatregoing was speculating on the chances of being incinerated before the close of the performance.")[4]

At any rate, the ballet company was without either home or return fare, and, upon meeting, the two impresarios reasoned that, since the melodrama contained a forest scene and the ballet took place in a *bois*, why not combine the two and add a few songs for good measures?

Why not indeed, and so, a goliath of a show that ran five and a half hours was born. And in its sprawling, patched together wanderings, it contained the seeds of the American musical, particularly the American revue.

Forget the book. Most critics wished they could, and most audiences did. What mattered were four elements, three of them from variety, minstrel shows and old-time burlesque, and one that would firmly and forever establish new-time burlesque as a permanent fixture on Broadway: from variety and minstrelsy, there were songs that came out of nowhere and often disappeared before the next performance. Only one, "You Naughty, Naughty Men," a comic relief song for Carlina, Amina's maid, has survived in printed form, and its relation to the rest of the plot is tenuous at best.

From burlesque, there was spectacle aplenty. Interiors gave way to grottos that gave way to forests that gave way to Fairyland. Niblo's head carpenter, the 400-pound, six-foot-six giant, Benson J. Sherwood, worked his crew mercilessly to spend much of the show's astronomical $50,000 production budget on scenic effects.

To populate the sets, there were ballet dancers, doing their *Biche au Bois* routine in the forest. And—and here was a revolutionary and ticket-selling stroke of genius, borrowed from new-time burlesque—there was a chorus line of tall, voluptuous girls in tights, billed as "Amazons" doing "Amazon Marches" lightly choreographed by David Costa.

They were a sensation, for this was the age of sexual arousal from a mere glimpse of a well turned ankle. These hussies showed not only ankles, but calves, knees and thighs. Wow. A bombshell had hit the city, and when the dust settled, *The Black Crook*, no doubt refueled by the repeat attendance of its many, many male patrons, ran for 16 months, and took in over $1,000,000. And this was in an age when runs of more than a couple of weeks were considered phenomenal.

And so, the stage was set for the beginnings of the American musical, the flowering of variety, the sustenance of the minstrel show and the birth of burly-cue. In fact, if nothing else, *The Black Crook* was a defining moment for all of these forms. It tapped into and solidified post Civil War audiences' taste for variety. It cemented their passion for minstrelsy. Its spectacle satisfied their need for opulence, the girls their more carnal preferences, and the show's spinoffs satisfied their appetite for pure burlesque. Immediate take-offs tumbled after the original; within months, a string of parodies permeated the city: *Black Crook Jr., White Crook, Red Golden Crook* far outlasted *The White Fawn*, the orthodox sequel which opened and closed swiftly.

And the original established a new branch of burlesque devoted mainly to the female form. Two years after *The Black Crook*, Lydia Thompson and Her Imported English Blondes arrived in New York, and although they might be mistaken for a beef trust or a female wrestling team today, they matched perfectly the male idea of female proportions and protuberances in 1868.

The blondes entered the back door of Broadway, opening at Woods' Museum and Menagerie on 34th Street, in the guise of the mythological creatures of a play titled *Ixion* by a mercifully forgotten playwright named F.C. Burnand. But it soon became apparent that the semi-covered vixens were the only attraction that sold tickets to the play, and within a couple of weeks, they moved to Niblo's to fill the space lately vacated by *The Black Crook*. And so Lydia Thompson, her hefty but lovely star Pauline Markham, and her blondes settled in for a long run in New York, and a longer run nationwide. They established not only the girlie revue, but also furthered and refined the show girl, a tradition established by *The Black Crook's* Amazons. Her main job, an 1877 *New York Times* critic observed, was to join "...a half a score of pretty girls exhibited in an unending walk around...they really have nothing to offer but their persons..."

The consequences of the success of both *The Black Crook* and Lydia Thompson's Imported Blondes resulted in a burst of burlesque theatres, featuring, as one advertisement put it, "New wardrobes, bright, catchy music and pictures, Amazon marches, pretty girls and novelty specialty acts."

Within months, burlesque "wheels" or combines that booked shows nationwide became the natural outgrowth, and, in defiance of them, rural "turkey" companies, one-nighters from whence the name for a theatrical flop originated, were born.

This last, country cousin of girlie burlesque survived into the 1940s, in hundreds of county fairs: a scene or two involving the phallic possibilities of pickles or frankfurters, a clown or two and a couple of cooch dancers who, for an extra quarter, would retire to a smaller tent behind the stage in which the dance became more and more explicit and the costume less and less in evidence, until it disappeared altogether.

Certified strippers didn't appear in theatre burlesque until the 1920s, but their ancestors set the stage in the nineteenth century turkey shows, while their more refined sisters went on to decorate the stages of the yet-to-be invented Follies, Scandals, Vanities and Artists and Models series.

It was a lowdown beginning. But then again, the origins of musical theatre in America were anything but polite. True, there were responsible, respectable American playwrights performed in legitimate theatres from the late eighteenth century onward—Royall Tyler, Dion Boucicault, William Gillette, Clyde Fitch, even, pseudonymically, Washington Irving. And there were fine actors performing integral productions of Shakespeare.

But there was also a rowdy and rough population of New York who regarded themselves as the true Americans, and they preferred their entertainment basic and raw, like their lives. That was the way it was on the streets and in the theatres of mid-nineteenth century New York, and particularly in Five Points, the waterfront district that housed not only many of the theatres of the time, but a wild assortment of cutthroats, prostitutes, ragpickers, waifs and members of the score or more street gangs—the Dead Rabbits, Bowery B'hoys, Plug Uglies, Whyos, Shirt Tails, Cadets and Short Boys, among them. It only got worse as the decade spun on; the old, abandoned Dutch brewery in Five Points was a breeding farm for crime, venereal disease, incestuous offspring and juvenile delinquency. Of 600 children in the area in 1870, only nine attended any kind of school.

But beyond the mayhem and danger, there were just plain bad manners and ignorance in staggering abundance. In his reminiscence of the world and work of Harrigan and Hart, E. J. Kahn Jr. notes that "The post-Civil War years in New York were so conspicuous for ill-mannered behavior that one historian of that era, who survived its brawls to write of it, declared, 'Had anyone said "I'm sorry" in those-days he would promptly have been locked up as irresponsible.' "[5]

This sort of behavioral anarchy naturally spilled from the streets into the theatres located upon them, and it was a rare performance that wasn't interrupted by the shenanigans in the audience. In the music halls and burlesque theatres and minstrel houses, these eruptions sometimes threatened to topple over into mayhem. Silence was unknown, and the very best of patrons chatted during songs and dialogue alike. General William Tecumseh Sherman spent the last years of his life in New York and most of his nights in New York theatres, so much so that the managers reserved a seat solely for him. His applause, some said, resembled cannon fire, and one newspaperman wrote, "When his hands are idle, his tongue wags gleefully with a running commentary."

And so, three hour performances sometimes stretched to five while performers interrupted the plot to exchange remarks with audience members or make a speech about something contemporary. Some remarkable performers silenced audiences momentarily by the sheer force of their artistry; others felt it was better to join than fight, and thus the expected repartee between performer and audience, begun in minstrel shows and raised to a fine art by Al Jolson in the 1920s, arose out of a survival instinct in the mid-nineteenth century.

Well into the 1870s, when Ned Harrigan and Tony Hart had established their theatre for and about the common man, the din was sometimes terrific. What was mere murmuring in the boxes and the orchestra was shouting in the gallery. This airless aerie, smelling variously of sweat, cabbage, beer and horses, contained no reserved seats, but long wooden benches. The doors opened at 7:30; the patrons paid between 15 and 25 cents apiece, and the strongest, swiftest and earliest got the best places.

Songbooks were sold for ten cents apiece, and if the show had been in for a run, the gallery could be counted on to join in the singing of some of the choruses with lusty enthusiasm.

There were certain rules of etiquette that were enforced. Even though ladies weren't welcome in the gallery, no man could keep his hat on during a performance. If he forgot, ushers with long bamboo poles knocked it off. And the poles were swung with gusto. The ushers wielding them were beefy men with eagle eyes. They kept watch over tobacco chewers, who were allowed to spit freely on the floor and each other, but not over the rail and on the orchestra patrons below. An infraction got either an eviction or a whack from a pole, as did the throwing of spitballs at the dudes in the stalls.

And that was just the civil condition in the theatres. The whole clattering combination was raised to another decibel level in the music halls. In 1877, John Sparks, half of the Sparks Brothers, appeared nightly in Owney Geogheghan's Saloon at 103 Bowery. In addition to his singing chores on Geogheghan's small stage, Sparks was expected to serve drinks, dance jigs and put on the gloves with any patron who wanted to fight and who didn't outweigh him too much.

Theatres and music halls and their neighborhoods at mid century were, then, no place to bring your maiden Aunt Edna. The times were ripe for reform and enterprise, and into this approximation of bedlam strode or, rather, waddled a most unlikely reformer.

Corpulent of body, short of stature, abundantly endowed with mountainous mutton chops and a tidal wave of a moustache, always and religiously attired in tall boots, a high hat and a floor length black coat, Tony Pastor was, eternally, a theatre manager, performer and showman whose motivations were probably equally distributed between his wallet and his heart. Although he was a hard bargainer, he loved the theatre well enough to virtually live in it and was famous for standing at the door at every performance, greeting his regular customers by name.

Born in 1837 in Greenwich Village, Pastor was introduced to show business as a child by his father, a theatre violinist. By the time he was nine, he was singing as an infant prodigy at Barnum's American Museum, and as a teenager, he was a performer in the minstrel olios of several traveling circuses.

Along the way, he wrote about 2,000 songs, some of which he performed in his first appearance in variety in April of 1861, at the American Theatre at 444 Broadway. History doesn't recall his assessment of the vulgarity and mayhem of the variety theatres of the day, but it does note that four years later, he opened his own Opera House at 199-201 Broadway with what he advertised as a "clean bill."

It featured, no doubt, some of his own tunes about such topical subjects as Edison's phonograph, or one of his ballads praising home, mother and the simple life—possibly the one about the son who didn't have time to write, but did, in the end, find the time to come home and die.

But it also added to the variety mix three revolutionary, "clean" situations: the beginnings of the taming of variety audiences, jokes that were relatively free of double and quadruple entendres, and headliners—well known actors, actresses and singers who would, because of the relatively civilized atmosphere, appear and draw the crowds.

And build audiences Pastor did, first from the expected roughneck pack that ordinarily frequented variety, and then, gradually, as word spread, from the carriage trade which was able to spend much more money in far shorter periods of time. There was, clearly, profit in presenting shows to which you could bring your maiden Aunt and, at matinees, your children. And Tony Pastor proved it.

Gradually, he began to change the proportions in the mix of Bowery mayhem and uptown genteelness at 199-201 Broadway. By 1875, he'd left the Bowery behind and moved uptown to 585 Broadway. And by 1881, when he opened his last and best theatre in Tammany Hall at 14th Street, he felt confident enough to shut down the barroom during the performance, prohibit smoking in the audience and eschew vulgarity on the stage.

His first bill included the French Twin Sisters, character comic

Dan Collyer, a girl instrumentalist, a knockabout comedy team, headliner Ella Wesner (a male impersonator who sang English ditties and delivered a comic monologue) and Tony Pastor himself.

It was a tough go; because the theatre was small, he had to charge 50 cents for matinees and $1.00 at night for the best seats, which had the advantage of attracting the carriage trade. He took to presenting "Ladies Matinees" since, even in the 1880s, the streets of New York's theatre district were still relatively unsafe at night. His further intent was to prove that ladies could enjoy his bills, and to get them there in the first place, he offered door prizes including whole hams, bags of flour and sacks of potatoes to the first 25 women patrons. The lure didn't work at first; Pastor was obviously appealing to the wrong class of women. When he began to give away silk dresses as door prizes, the trickle of women, whose husbands he really wanted at night, rapidly turned into a torrent.

The form of his shows was borrowed from minstrelsy; in fact, when Pastor closed down his theatre during the summer, he frequently took to the road in his own company, Tony Pastor's Minstrels.

The first third of the show was devoted to a series of variety acts; the second was an olio; the third was an after-piece, usually a burlesque of a currently popular operetta.

And it was for an after-piece burlesque of Gilbert and Sullivan's *Pirates of Penzance* that Pastor hired a 19-year-old inexperienced and innocent singer from Iowa, by way of Chicago, named Helen Louise Leonard. In her memoirs, published under the name Lillian Russell—the new and lasting identity that Tony Pastor would give her—she described her audition:

> "One afternoon," she wrote, "while mother was out, a friend of ours named Mrs. Rose (who lived in the same house) said she had a caller for whom she would like me to sing. I consented. I never needed much coaxing to perform—whatever the time or place. So I went up to her suite and met a soldierly-looking lit

tle Italian who listened critically while I sang my little repertory of songs. Then he suddenly turned to me and said: 'How would you like to sing those songs every night in my theatre for seventy-five dollars a week?'

"...I decided that mother must know nothing of the venture until it succeeded and I lay awake all night planning a lifetime of song and success. And the next day I went to Tony Pastor's Theatre to have my voice tried."[6]

Her voice was gorgeous, as graceful and satisfying as her dancing, her transfixing eyes, her abundant but hourglass figure, her clear and youthful skin. She was accepted, and Pastor pressed a $50 bill into her hand so that she could buy the signature white gown with "bugles" that would become her hallmark. "Everything in Pastor's was clean and fresh and new," she recalled. "There was no smoking permitted in the theatre and the audience was usually in full dress. In an age when 'variety' was considered just a little too daring for women to attend, Tony Pastor's Theatre set a standard that was unique and drew as many women as men. Every act was scrupulously clean and free from any suggestiveness, the performers were fine men and women and great artists did not hesitate to appear there..."

Pastor billed the American-born singer as "Lillian Russell, the English Ballad Singer," and for the first several months and regularly thereafter, the clear and rounded soprano of Lillian Russell rang through Tony Pastor's Theatre. Her mother discovered that her daughter was singing on the stage a month later, when a reporter from *The New York Times* who boarded with the Leonards remarked that there was a singer at Pastor's who was a dead ringer for her daughter Helen.

But by that time, Helen Leonard had ceased to exist, and Lillian Russell had become popular enough to join the Four Cohans, the Three Keatons and Nat Goodwin as a repeat headliner at Pastor's. And, from all accounts, she had matured quickly, particularly after meeting Tony Pastor's orchestra conductor, Dave Braham, a bespectacled, professorial-looking man with a floppy mustache and an abundant head of red hair, who wasted no time in impregnating Lillian Russell. They married, the child died in infancy, and soon after this, Lillian Russell scandalized New York by running off to London with Edward Solomon, a comic opera composer. In 1883, Braham sued for divorce, received it, and Lillian Russell married Edward Solomon.

Braham, meanwhile, left Tony Pastor's for Ned Harrigan and Tony Hart's Bowery Theatre. They were busily enjoying their seemingly inexhaustible run of the *Mulligan Guards*—three satirical soldiers who won world wide fame when Kipling immortalized them, without checking his sources. A month or so on the premises, and Braham found a home as the Sullivan to Harrigan's Gilbert.

The Mulligan Guards had been marching on since 1879, in their first variety presentation *The Mulligan Guard Ball*, which was followed that same year by *The Mulligan Guards' Chowder*, *The Mulligan Guards' Christmas*, in 1880 with *The Mulligan Guards' Surprise*, *The Mulligans' Picnic*, *The Mulligan Guards' Nominee*, and *Mulligans' Silver Wedding*.

The old and rowdy tradition of the variety theatre still survived, and, in fact, thrived with Harrigan and Hart and their bottomless store of Mulligan Guards extravaganzas. But eventually, Harrigan, too, taking a cue from Tony Pastor, realized the changing times, and his productions became more and more extravagant and increasingly stuffed with special effects. Although the characters were in the tradition of Mose the Fireman, and the sketches within them traditionally ended with their trademark "smash finish," their content evolved, as the character of musical entertainment, moving steadily uptown, began to acquire more and more civility and spectacle.

Harrigan and Hart opened their Theater Comique in 1881, a venue that was built for special effects such as burning buildings, fireworks displays, aeroplanes that circled the audience and chorus girls on swings. The titles of his variety/extravaganza/burlesques became more imaginative: *The Major, Squatter Sovereignty, Mordacai Lyons, McSorley's Inflation* or *The McSorleys, The Muddy Day, Cordelia's Aspirations, Dan's Tribulations, McAllister's Legacy* and the last, an 1885 production with his partner Tony Hart, *Investigation*. Hart's departure didn't, however, mean the last of Ned Harrigan, who brought in Dan Collyer to replace Hart and eventually built yet a newer, bigger, more uptown theatre, the Harrigan Theater, which opened in 1890 with *Reilly and the Four Hundred* and introduced Ada Lewis as a tough, gum-chewing Bowery girl.

Still, the times were accelerating and spinning past Ned Harrigan and Tony Pastor. By 1890, the two had become reminders of a rough and unhewn musical theatre past. And the final piece in the puzzle, the child of variety and the immediate ancestor of the Broadway revue, was waiting to be born a mere year after Pastor opened his final theatre. Its name could have easily been applied to Tony Pastor's entertainment, but Pastor refused to attach it to his bills, calling it "sissy and Frenchy."

Nevertheless, vaudeville was about to be born, and it would be heard, loudly and insistently.

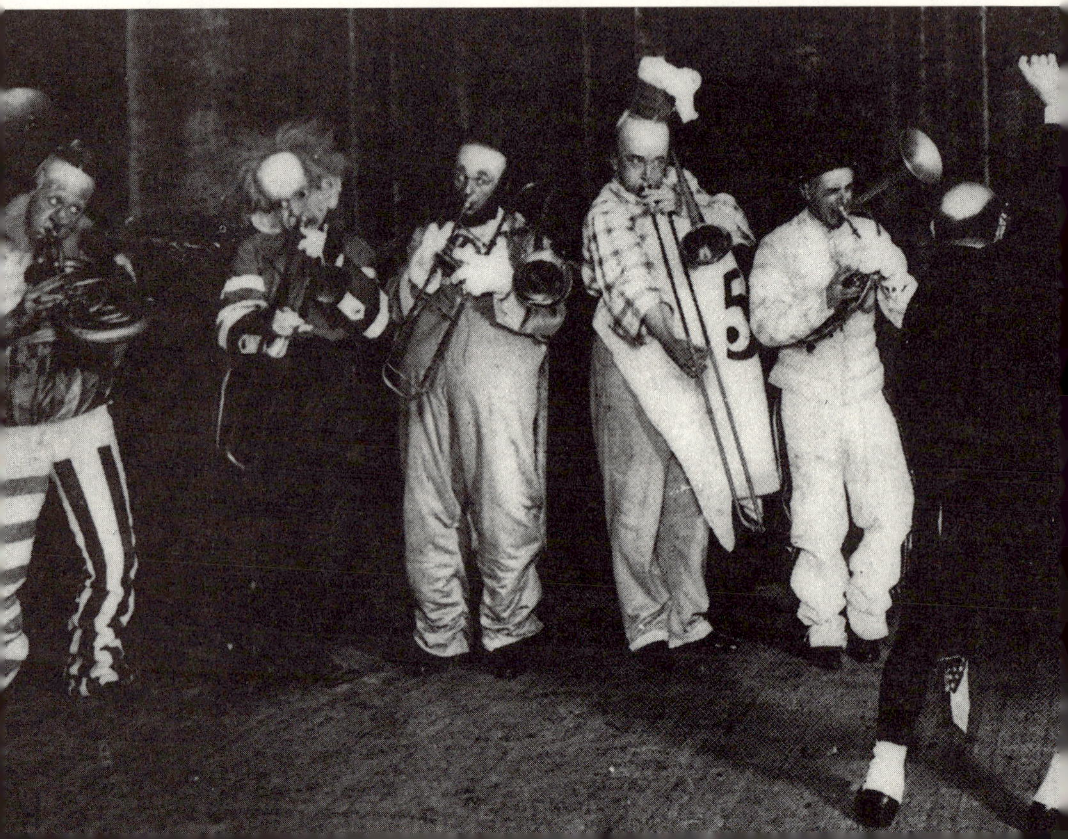

2

From
Six-A-Day
to
Two-A-Day
to
One-A-Night

From Six-A-Day to Two-A-Day to One-A-Night

❦

The musical theatre in New York, encouraged by Tony Pastor's successful venture in attracting women and big money to "clean shows," had become steadily more sophisticated and expensive. A $2 top was an expected extravagance by 1882, although there were still plenty of 50-and 25-cent seats in the gallery. Comic operas and operettas were the preferred entertainment of the knowledgeable; Gilbert and Sullivan, Offenbach and Strauss were the preferred composers. The Americans, Reginald DeKoven, Julian Edwards, Victor Herbert, Gustave Kerker, John Philip Sousa and John Stromberg, were just warming up.

But a Bostonian businessman named Benjamin Franklin Keith wasn't interested in such fine distinctions. Not a newcomer to show business (he was rumored to have worked as an office manager for Barnum and for several other circuses, although there are conflicting stories, none of them official, about his background), he was aware that Tony Pastor had revolutionized and, to a certain extent, democratized musical entertainment by making it not only respectable, but accessible to a large audience. And yet, the rest of the theatrical profession was slow to take the old master's cue. By 1883, two full years after Pastor proved that his formula worked, there were only three "high class" variety theatres in the East: Pastor's in New York, Hyde & Behman's in Brooklyn and the Howard Athenaeum in Boston.

In fact, according to Elbridge T. Gerry, the grandson of the Elbridge Gerry who originated the practice of "gerrymandering" in politics, and the man who founded the Gerry Society which protected the rights of child actors whether they liked it or not, there were really only three types of theatres in America's large cities in the 1880s.

"[These] theaters...are divisible into three classes," he wrote in 1905 in *The New York Observer*, (1) reputable, where only the legitimate drama is exhibited to audiences composed of cultured and intelligent people; (2) semireputable, where the stage is devoted to spectacular exhibitions, vulgarity, appropriately termed 'leg drama,' [and] the scanty costumes which barely evade the prohibition of the Penal Code on the subject of decency; (3) disreputable, where both dialogue and performances fester with indelicacy, and the audience, composed of the lowest and most degraded class of society, engage [sic] in smoking and drinking and as an adjunct of their enjoyment of the exhibition."

If this is so, thought Keith, why not improve upon the second category—admittedly a Puritan's look at Pastor's—and present clean,family-style variety, not merely at twice a week matinees and nightly shows, but on a continuous basis? And why not charge considerably less than Pastor's, Hyde & Behman's and the Howard Athenaeum? Why not deal old-time variety, Gerry's third category, the death blow it deserves?

And so, in 1882, Keith, who had been running a dime museum that featured a freak baby on Washington Street in Boston, took the profits and poured then into the Bijou Dream, the first continuous performance house. And, having no compunction about French names, he called the performance vaudeville, after either the satiric songs of the fifteenth-century Norman, Olivier Basselin, who dubbed them *chansons du Vau de Vire* (songs of the valley of Vire), or Paris's city street songs, the *voix de villes*. History is vague about the origin of the word, but precise about the fact that Keith was the first to use it.

He charged from 15 to 50 cents admission and established a grim and grueling routine that would form the pattern of small time vaudeville for the next 35 years.

He, himself, described it neatly: "It is designed to run twelve hours during which period performers appear two or three times, as it would be manifestly impossible to secure enough different acts to fill out the dozen hours. The best class of actors appear twice, just as at a matinee and evening performance in a dramatic theatre, and the balance do three turns.'"[1]

The acts would be an amalgamation of variety singers and so forth—a little something for everybody except, perhaps, the more demonstrative patrons of the old variety saloons. Vaudeville would be—and would forever remain—scrupulously clean, as the signs tacked up backstage at this and later vaudeville houses would trumpet to the actors:

> You are hereby warned that your act must be free from all vulgarity and suggestiveness in words, action, and costume...and all vulgar, double-meaning and profane words and songs must be cut out of your act before the first performance...
>
> Such words as Liar, Slob, Son-of-a-Gun, Devil, Sucker, Damn, and all other words unfit for the ears of ladies and children, also any reference to questionable streets, resorts, localities, and bar rooms, are prohibited under fine of instant discharge.[2]

As his power grew and his holdings increased, Keith modified this even more, adding to the lexicon of banned expressions, and, furthermore, overturning some of the timeworn technique of variety comedians. Over the callboard in each of his theatres, the following foreboding warning was posted:

NOTICE TO PERFORMERS

Don't say "slob" or "son-of-a-gun" or "hully gee" on this stage unless you want to be cancelled peremptorily. Do not address anyone in the audience in any manner. If you have not the ability to entertain Mr. Keith's audiences without risk of offending them, do the best you can. Lack of talent will be less open to censure than would be an insult to a patron. If you are in doubt as to the character of your act, consult the local manager before you go on the stage, for if you are guilty of uttering anything sacrilegious or even suggestive, you will be immediately closed and will never again be allowed in a theatre where Mr. Keith is in authority.[3]

That this frequently resulted in what one critic of the time described as "bilge water in champagne glasses" was apparently okay with the public. They came by the hundreds, then the thousands. Keith became rich and famous, opened theatres in Philadelphia and Providence, and in 1893, he came to New York and leased the venerable Union Square Playhouse.

It and its million dollar imitators—and there were many at the turn of the century—proliferated in modern or refurbished splendor, and a hierarchy of vaudeville houses began to develop. The old ones, which once housed burlesque or variety, remained picturesque out front and squalid backstage. But the new, first-class ones set a standard not only of performance but comfort. The Union Square Theatre boasted 20 dressing rooms, each with a private bath. Not even the first class playhouses of the 1880s and 1890s could boast that, although the vast building boom on Broadway when the new century dawned would make 20 seem as nothing.

And so, as the last decade of the nineteenth century matured, vaudeville took the country by storm, and for the next 35 years, it would be far and away America's most popular form of entertainment. At its height, there would be over a thousand theatres devoted exclusively to vaudeville in the United States. In the 1890s, and in the early decades of the new century, Keith became bigger and more powerful by the month, eventually controlling the two major vaudeville circuits, Keith's which controlled all the houses east of Chicago, and the Orpheum, managed by Martin Beck, which was responsible for houses in Chicago and the West. For years, practically every big time vaudeville house in America—and there were literally hundreds of them—was controlled by either the Keith or Orpheum Circuit.

The others, the small time vaudevilles, which featured split weeks and six-a-day (the big time eventually became two-a-day), and which were either proving grounds for new acts or last stands for older ones, were parts of smaller, independent circuits, some of which endured, like the Loew's and Pantages circuits in the West, while others, like the Sun and Sheedy Agencies were gradually absorbed into the Keith-Orpheum empire.

Everything was controlled from Keith's opulent office in the Palace Theatre building on Broadway, where, eventually, he would take on Edward Albee as a partner and, ultimately, as his successor.

Meanwhile, Tony Pastor struggled. None of the vaudeville houses charged more than 75 cents for the best box seats; most of the orchestra went for 50 cents, and a seat in the back of the gallery was usually ten cents. Pastor couldn't charge that sort of price and begin to pay his performers, even at the depressed salaries he was offering. His little theatre wasn't big enough.

But the vaudeville houses were, and they were making average profits of $250,000 a year. In 1907, *Variety* reported that vaudeville theatres in the United States made a combined profit of $30,000,000. And this was the age before the income tax.

The salaries of headliners continued to climb, too. Lillian Russell, who had once worked for $75 a week for Tony Pastor, was commanding $3,150 a week in vaudeville, and little Elsie Janis and her multiple imitations was close behind with $3,000.

Pastor tried valiantly to hold out; Lillian Russell played there every now and then for sentimental reasons, as did the Four Cohans and the Three Keatons. Young Buster was only five years old on his return visit and the Gerry Society threatened to close Pastor down if he appeared. The gentlemanly and honorable Italian gent blithely signed an affidavit stating that Buster Keaton was definitely seven years old, and the Gerrys went away.

It was fortunate, for Tony Pastor had hit upon a popular embroidery for the Keatons' act. For five dollars a week, he hired a skinny East Side kid named Izzy Baline to sing ballads from the gallery during the Keatons' turn. The kid was an instant hit; he'd be an even bigger one after he changed his name to Irving Berlin.

But Tony Pastor's days as an impresario were numbered, as were both the concept of old time variety and the days of the actor-manager. High-powered producers with dreams of becoming as rich as Benjamin Franklin Keith were beginning to establish themselves, and variety was dimming to black as fast as vaudeville was coming up full. By 1903, Tony Pastor would be out of business.

Vaudeville continued to grow, and became not only the model (along with burlesque and minstrelsy) for the coming of the Broadway revue, but its greatest reservoir of talent. When the time came, as it would in 1894, for the first Broadway revue to debut, that reservoir was already being fed. By the 1920s, it was overflowing. Although W.C. Fields, Fanny Brice, Leon Errol and Bert Lahr came from burlesque, vaudeville supplied, among many, Al Jolson, Eddie Cantor, Frank Tinney, Jesse Lasky, the Dolly Sisters, Will Rogers, Carl Randall, Grace George, Henry Miller, Fay Templeton, May Irwin, Raymond Hitchcock, Douglas Fairbanks, Henry Dixey, Fred Stone, Lillie Langtry, Ina Claire, Elsie Janis, Marilyn Miller, Ernest Truex, Nora Bayes, Emma Trentini, Marjorie Rambeau, Alla Nazimova, Rudolph Valentino before he was Rudolph Valentino, Rosa Ponselle, Isadora Duncan, Ruth St. Denis, Fred Astaire, James Cagney, Fred Allen, Bob Hope, Ed Wynn, Willie and Eugene Howard, the Marx Brothers, Joe E. Brown, Eddie Foy, Milton Berle— the list goes on seemingly forever.

Even the royalty of the legitimate stage, the Barrymores, Eleanora Duse and Mrs. Patrick Campbell among them, did olio versions of great plays in some of the better, two-a-day houses.

Alfred Lunt, recalling in *Billboard* in 1936 his 26 weeks on the Orpheum circuit with Lillie Langtry, remembered fascinating times in the wings watching the other acts, and a mystifying 15 minutes onstage with the Jersey Lily. "Our sketch was called 'Ashes,'" he wrote. "I played the role of the man with whom Mrs. Langtry was in love. Inasmuch as Mrs. Langtry, at that time, was 63 and I was 21, audiences were inclined to be somewhat bewildered. Usually they began by thinking that I was her son, so it must have seemed a little odd to them when I suddenly began to make violent love to her. But they were really very nice about it all."[4]

That was the way vaudeville audiences were. Nice. And for that, they had Tony Pastor to thank. Tony Pastor and their parents.

These same audiences, able to fairly fearlessly venture out after dark on the streets of New York at the end of the century, were also frequenting the legitimate theatre. Radio and motion pictures, the twin forces that would bury vaudeville, and television, which would change the character of the Broadway musical, hadn't arrived yet, and business on Broadway was booming.

The extravaganza was in particularly healthy condition. It was healthy enough to stimulate the interest of Edward E. Rice, a clerk in the Boston Cunard Line office. Convinced that audiences, who, without a murmur of complaint, settled into their seats at *The Black Crook* at 8:30 p.m. and were still able to roar approval when the final curtain fell at 1:15 a.m., and were there for more than the periodic leg shows, Rice decided he could write and produce a show considerably better than what he perceived as a marathon of a monstrosity.

He joined forces with J. Cheever Goodwin, a Harvard graduate and reporter on *The Boston Traveler*, and the two came up with *Evangeline*, a marriage of extravaganza and burlesque—which was hardly a new idea. What was new was its original score, the first by an American. Rice, its composer, was a self-taught pianist, and his music was serviceable, as were the lyrics and sort of book by his partner, J. Cheever Goodwin.

Opening on July 27, 1874, at the same Niblo's Garden that had housed *The Black Crook, Evangeline* lasted a mere two weeks in New York. But, as a host of other shows after it proved at the end of the nineteenth and halfway through the twentieth century, the road saved it. It would run there for a decade, one of the most often played musicals of its time.

Rice had locked into one of the major tastes of his time. Although audiences' allegiances were scattered, among operetta, opera boufe, burlesque, minstrel shows, the last gasps of variety via Harrigan and Hart and Tony Pastor, and vaudeville, these audiences were increasingly interested and intrigued by extravaganza. For this reason, possibly, the waning days of the great but, ultimately, insane pantomime artist George Lafayette Fox, were concerned with a hybrid between British style pantomime and American extravaganza. Much the same as James O'Neill, Fox became locked into the character of *Humpty Dumpty*, following the riotous success of his first production featuring the character in 1868, at the Olympia Theatre.

From *Humpty Dumpty Abroad, Humpty Dumpty at School, Humpty Dumpty at Home* (all in the 1873–74 season), to *Humpty Dumpty in Every Clime* during the following season, Fox performed the role over a thousand times. He began to deteriorate as this lock on his talents spun on, and, finally, during the run of the final *Humpty Dumpty* in the 1876–77 season, he began attacking audience members. He was relieved of the role in November, was committed to an insane asylum, and died there shortly thereafter.

Meanwhile, pure extravaganza took a quantum leap upward with *Around the World in Eighty Days*. One of two shows by the same name that opened within two weeks of each other in September of 1875 (the first, at the Grand Opera House, opened on the 16th and closed on the 28th), this production, at the Academy of Music, featured its scenery and special effects equally with its players, and so became a key ancestor of the *Ziegfeld Follies*. In fact, the Kiralfy Brothers, three Hungarian acrobats and pantomimists turned producers, were generally lauded as the Joseph Urbans of their day.

Realism was their stock-in-trade, and they replaced the hanging one-dimensional forests of *The Black Crook* and its imitators with round representations of, among 11 varied scenes, the Suez Canal, the Taj Mahal, Calcutta, the "Great Religious Festival of the Suttee" and the "Wreck of the Henrietta", depicting "the total disappearance of the steamer under the waves."

A year later, they were back, this time at Niblo's, with a five-hour extravaganza titled *The Deluge*, a recreation of the Old Testament, and eight years later, again at Niblo's, with a bloated Parisian confection titled *Excelsior*, which drew crowds by its "spectacular electric lighting effects under the personal supervision of Thomas A. Edison."

It was only natural that an edifice to extravaganza be built, and on the night of October 21, 1882, after a number of numbing delays, the Casino opened. It was, for most of its early life, dubbed "Aronson's Folly" because, while the theatre district was centered around Union Square, Rudolph Aronson, its owner, located his pleasure palace on the southwest corner of Broadway and 31st Street, nearer pastureland than the Great White Way.

While its outward appearance as a Moorish palace couldn't be disputed, its interior really wasn't ready for the public in November of 1882. The heating didn't work; carpets hadn't been installed; there were still unpainted walls. After opening night, the inaugural production of the Johann Strauss operetta, *The Queen's Lace Handkerchief*, was shut down for two months while the theatre was fine-tuned.

When the Casino reopened on December 30, it was pronounced, with some justification, "America's Handsomest Place of Amusement." But its importance in the ancestry of the Broadway revue centered, in addition to its space for extravaganza, upon two brand new details: first, in addition to its other alluring accoutrements, it featured the first open-air roof garden in the United States, replete with rich Oriental tapestries, giant palms, tables at which patrons could drink and dine, and a fully equipped stage upon which to present a show for their late night tastes.

Second, the financial backing for the Casino was provided by a consortium of some of the wealthiest, most respected financiers in New York: Cyrus W. Field, William K. Vanderbilt, Chauncey Depew, Tom Platt, Pierre Lorillard and J. P. Morgan. Musical entertainment had come a long way in a short time from the smoky, disreputable dives of its infancy.

And it would go further still, just as rapidly. As the 1880s unfolded, John Brougham continued to crank out his burlesques, a prodigious output that would eventually total 162 productions and earn him the title, via critic Richard Moody, of "...a mid-nineteenth-century combination of W.C. Fields and George S. Kaufman." Ned Harrigan was increasingly letting his dramatic after-pieces expand, until they became the dominant portion of his varieties. Minstrelsy endured, and vaudeville grew.

But the times were ripe for change. When the Kiralfy Brothers revived *The Black Crook* for two weeks in April of 1890, *The New York Times* defined it as "probably the stupidest stage play ever invented." And although the hit of the 1890–91 season—in fact of the decade—was the extravaganza *A Trip to Chinatown*, which remained at the Madison Square Theatre for 697 performances, the real news of the season, at least for theatre historians, was the arrival of a modestly noticed operetta, part of the repertory of the Boston Ideal Opera Company which decided to stop for a while at the Standard Theatre. *Robin Hood*, with music by the eccentrically attired Reginald DeKoven (his taste ran to silk hats, sable-lined overcoats and an English attitude) and the first of the 300 libretto and lyrics combinations by the astonishing Harry B. Smith, was its name. It was the first operetta written by Americans as a contemporary musical, even if its story was, to put it mildly, legendary.

Robin Hood didn't remain in New York any longer than *Evangeline*, but its hit drinking song "Brown October Ale" made the Variety Circuit for years, and its other enduring ballad, actually an interpolation, still echoes from various cathedrals and country churches wherever and whenever traditional weddings are performed. The song, "O Promise Me" was actually plagiarized by DeKoven from an old Italian folk melody, and its lyric was not by Harry B. Smith, but by the English critic Clement Scott.

The story goes that none of the singers in the show liked the song enough to sing it, and it was about to be chucked when Jessie Bartlett Davis, a contralto playing the trouser role of Alan-a-Dale, found herself humming it in her dressing room, an octave lower than it had been presented to the cast. W. H. MacDonald, the Little John of the piece, passed by, heard her humming and cried "Jessie! If you ever sing that song as you're singing it now, on the low octave, it will make your reputation!" She did, and it did, and so one of the less tenuous ties between church and stage was forged.

Meanwhile, back on the extravaganza/variety/burlesque/vaudeville front, no clear pattern had emerged. The Casino's foray into vaudeville, an attempt to battle the major circuits, failed, and only the last minute booking of Lillian Russell in an old French operetta, *Girofle-Girofla*, kept the theatre open. A full-length burlesque of *Lady Windermere's Fan* was only moderately successful, and in the extravaganza department, *The Voyage of Suzette* and *A Trip to Venus* sputtered and died. *1492*, an import by impresario Edward E. Rice from Chicago's Columbian Exposition, with female impersonator Richard Harlowe's show-stopping delivery of a song called "Isabella," became the hit of the 1892-1893 season.

But beyond Broadway, the nation was undergoing one of its periodic economic crises, the 17th since 1790. The Panic of 1893, brought on when National Cordage, a high ranking speculative stock took a precipitous nosedive, dealt the financial markets a body blow. Wall Street went berserk; times went overnight from tranquility to turmoil, unemployment became so widespread that a number of "Industrial Armies" marched on Washington D.C., and a series of strikes—notably the walkouts of 150,000 coal miners in Pennsylvania,

Ohio, Indiana, Illinois and Michigan and the Pullman Car Company strike that tied up the mails and brought on federal troops—reverbrated through the country.

It was, as history had already proved and future history would confirm, just the right sort of atmosphere for experiment in the arts. And, on this larger stage, the last piece in the puzzle that, fitted together I would form the Broadway revue, was set in place.

The Passing Show, the first true Broadway revue, opened at the Casino on the night of May 12, 1894, with a suitable amount of advance hoopla. It would be, *The New York Times* noted on the Sunday previous to the opening, "...a review, in dramatic form, of the chief events of the past year—political, historical and theatrical."

And there it was, altogether: the core of the revue that would remain, sometimes emphasized, sometimes diminished, sometimes embroidered, sometimes all but buried, but, nevertheless, at the center of this particular genre of the American musical. Its needs and necessities would form its advantage and its disadvantage, providing it with its life and its modernity but also dating it and often locking it, as surely as if it were in isolation, in the precise time—the decade, and often the year—in which it was first produced.

Some elements—ironically, most of them the legacy of *The Black Crook*—would transcend time. But the Broadway revue would be, typically, topical. And that would, in turn, be both invigorating and antiquating.

The Passing Show didn't emerge at the Casino like Venus from the seashell. It wasn't a purely American invention, although it certainly owed its form to variety, the minstrel show, burlesque and vaudeville. But its immediate and most obvious model was the current Parisian revue, a vogue which was a variation on vaudeville, which in turn was already waning in popularity in the far away city of fashion and light. Like vaudeville and variety, it consisted of a succession of acts and sketches, but instead of one performer or group of performers doing one act or one sketch, the same performers appeared, over and over.

Furthermore, a wisp of a plot, which, in the manner of nineteenth century romantic ballet, disappeared almost entirely before the finale, gave the production an appearance of form.

The sketches were straight out of burlesque, and *The Passing Show*'s sketches, by George Lederer and Sydney Rosenfeld, tweaked the current legitimate taste for Arthur Wing Pinero by sending up his *The Amazons* and *Sowing the Wind*, and kidded Grand Opera with "Round the Opera in Twenty Minutes," which created a mulligatawny of such disparate characters as Tannhauser, Escamillo and Pagliacci. There were acrobats and Amazons, a ballet, "living pictures" in which magazine covers and other mythical and contemporary happenings were frozen in three-dimensional place, comedy by the Tamale Brothers, singing choruses, love songs, and satiric ditties, such as the popular,. and often cited "Old Before His Time," in which contemporary acting and playwriting came in for a skewering:

"The modern school of acting's
    such a thing of pure delight [is],
The heroine has consumption,
    the hero meningitis.
The villain, yellow jaundice:
    oh, his sufferings are fearful.
The scene's laid in a hospital,
    to make it nice and cheerful;
And the happ'nings, tho' abnormal,
    are supported by statistics.
It's a school of realism,
    and endorsed by realistics..."[5]

The lyrics were by Sidney Rosenfeld, the music by Ludwig Englander, and that was another consistency that vaudeville and variety didn't possess, nor would subsequent revues always enjoy. Still, the "main scores" of revues, before the inevitable interpolations, were almost always credited to one set of composer/lyricists, and Englander, who came to the United States in 1882 from Vienna and remained on Broadway until his death in 1914, was the first. After *The Passing Show*, he turned his talents to operettas, writing with, among others, the ubiquitous Harry B. Smith.

The Passing Show disproved its title by remaining at the Casino for four months, attracting crowds even in the heat of summer. From there, the cast of 100 (performers, except the stars, were paid little in these pre-Equity days, and casts of 200 were not uncommon) minus its two stars, Adele Richie and Jefferson de Angelis, took to the road, first to the Harlem Opera House for a week in September, back to the Casino for 24 performances, then a circle back to New York for a week in March at the American Theatre and, finally, a farewell week in September, 1895, at the Grand Opera House.

The producers of *The Passing Show*, evidently taking their cue from the xenophobia and phraseology of Tony Pastor, steadfastly avoided the French spelling and referred to their show as a "review," as would other producers for the next decade.

But the next step in the refinement of the Broadway revue was already on its way across the Atlantic. From *The Black Crook* through *The Passing Show*, hefty Amazons were the chorus lines and showgirls of American musicals. But on September 18, 1894, English producer George Edwardes, in collaboration with Augustin Daly, brought his *A Gaiety Girl* to Daly's Theatre. And his girls were far from Amazons, although not exactly the twentieth century ideal of litheness.

Still, they were a clear move away from the frankly sensual and decidedly beefy appearance of Lydia Thompson and her Imported English Blondes. *These* imported blondes, brunettes and redheads had class to augment their curves and distinct evidence of dieting.

Not that the nation's corset makers would be driven out of business the following Monday. Lillian Russell, alone, would see to that, and, besides, all change is incremental. But a new, more svelte and sophisticated silhouette arrived on Broadway with the Edwardes girls.

And so *A Gaiety Girl*, which was one of the three shows (the others were *In Town* and *The Shop Girl*) that established Edwardes as the originator of British—some said all—musical comedy, arrived. The wisp of a plot, by Owen Hall, dealt with the trials and tribulations of a group of girls from Edwardes's flagship Gaiety Theatre in London. Ignored by society at a posh party until they perform, their honesty is later challenged when an expensive diamond comb is planted on one of them. A handsome young officer falls in love with the lovely victim and clears her name.

And that was about it. The rest of the show consisted of production numbers and interpolated specialties, with music by Sydney Jones and lyrics by Harry Greenbank. It was all very up-to-date and stylish and therefore, a fine, upstanding excuse for the establishment of a long-lasting theatrical tradition: the congregating, outside the stage door, of wealthy admirers and thus escorters of the gorgeous girls onstage. The New York press coined the phrase "Stage Door Johnnies" for the nightly crowd of well-dressed and well-heeled men milling outside *Gaiety Girl*, and the phrase stuck. By the time *Florodora* arrived at the Casino in November of 1900, the tradition had become set in diamonds.

Interestingly enough, *A Gaiety Girl* remained in New York for only 79 performances. Beginnings aren't always as spectacularly successful as, say, *The Black Crook*. But once the experimentation began, the century played itself out with daring novelties.

The Casino, buoyed by the success of *The Passing Show*, a series of summer "reviews," and in the summer of 1898, the complementary variety that occupied the roof-garden that Edward E. Rice had added to his Moroccan Palace was titled Rice's *Summer Nights*. The show ran a bit short, and on July 5, he added an extended after-piece titled *The Origins of the Cake Walk, or Clorindy* (transposed, in some sources, to *Clorindy, or The Origins of the Cake Walk*).

Whatever the billing, it was something revolutionary and new: an all black production that wasn't a minstrel show. Its up to date, ragtime score was by Will Marion Cook, and its not-so-articulate lyrics and hint of a libretto were by Paul Laurence. Embarrassingly stereotypical in terms of today, it was a sensation and a delight for the wealthy white audiences of the 1898–99 season who, the next day at lunch, cheerily whistled its hit song, "Who Dat Say Chicken in Dis Crowd?" It ran for the rest of the summer and established the pattern for the black revues that would thrive on Broadway into the 1930s.

And so, the last decade of the century was a time of change, absorption and experiment for the American musical. From the chaos and conflict that had come from the distinct rift between native American products and imports, European acting styles and American ones, and the definite duchies of variety, burlesque, minstrelsy and vaudeville, a blurring of differences now began to take place. And, while American producers persisted until the last gasp of the century to refer to their revues as reviews, nobody who knew was being kidded. The revue was a new and exhilarating theatre form that incorporated all of these elements.

At the same time, a new crop of American composers, most of whom were born elsewhere, established themselves, united by their dependency upon native-born (Buffalo, N.Y.) Harry B. Smith for their libretti and lyrics. In the tradition of one G. Operti, who was the conductor at Niblo's, and who took credit for the overture, ballet music and some of the original songs of *The Black Crook*, most of these composers began their careers as conductors in the major musical houses: Gustave Kerker, who came from Westphalia, Germany, occupied the pit at the Casino while writing operettas; Ludwig Englander, from Vienna, did the same; William Furst, whose origin is murky and who eventually wrote mostly for Lillian Russell and her company, conducted the Garden orchestra; John Philip Sousa, of Washington, D.C., was the Marine Corps bandmaster before and while he took to writing operettas at the turn of the century, and Victor Herbert, of Dublin, Ireland, was first cellist with the Metropolitan Opera orchestra and later the conductor of the Pittsburgh Symphony while simultaneously eclipsing, handily, DeKoven's melodic wanderings and establishing a niche as the originator of the first valid and musically important American operetta.

Herbert was, in physical as well as musical ways, the most impressive figure of the musical theatre of the last decade of the nineteenth and the first decade of twentieth century, although he ventured full force into the revue format only once, in 1917. Legend has it that he wrote his first operetta, which was never produced, for Lillian Russell in 1893. But from 1894's *Prince* to 1924's *The Dream Girl*, he wrote the music for 42 produced operettas, many of them for contemporary counterparts of Lillian Russell: Emma Trentini, Fritzi Scheff and Alice Neilsen, among them. He worked with an army of librettist/lyricists and called upon the indefatigable Harry B. Smith for 13 of his productions.

So much for the immortality that operetta afforded. Revues, with their contemporary character, sometimes attracted lesser talents. The most important composer for the Broadway revue at the end of the century was the usually and, perhaps, mercifully forgotten John Stromberg, the pit conductor at Weber and Fields Music Hall. It was pure serendipity, for Joe Weber and Lew Fields, who were the two men who did more to first sustain, then develop the pattern and the pace of Harrigan and Hart, likewise sustained the concept of American burlesque and helped mightily in moving the Broadway review toward its final identity as the Broadway revue.

Like Harrigan and Hart—who had by now separated (Hart was in ill health and Harrigan had been forced to sell his theatre to Richard Mansfield, who rechristened it the Garrick) —Weber and Fields had fought their way up and out of the teeming streets and aromatic alleys of the Bowery. Sons of impoverished Jewish immigrants, they joined forces at the early age of nine, corking their faces and doing minstrel routines in beer gardens and dime museums.

By the time they'd reached their teens, they'd traded the blackface for what was referred to as a "knock-about Dutch act," which combined slapstick with their immigrant background. Audiences in the circuses in which they appeared were convulsed with their mangling and apparent incomprehension of the English language. Fields, the tall, thin member of the duo, grew the name of Myer, and Weber, who was short and squat, became Mike. The names and their padded suits and shallow derbies became their trademarks from then until they parted company, temporarily in 1904 and permanently in 1912.

Weber and Fields touched all the bases. Leaving the circus, the story goes, after the townspeople of David City, Nebraska, reacting to one of their own being cheated by a three card monte dealer, raided the circus and burned down the main tent, they proceeded to a stint in Adah Richmond's Burlesque Company and with Gus Hill's Stars, another burlesque outfit.

It was here, and later, in vaudeville on the Orpheum Circuit that they honed their "travesties" which would become the staples of the shows they would mount when, in 1896, they bought the 665-seat Imperial Music Hall at the corner of Broadway and 29th Street. Only three years old, the Imperial had suffered the same fate that was slowly driving Tony Pastor out of business: with a stage only 16 feet deep, 665 seats, and a $1.50 top, shows mounted there, even with the minimal 1890s salaries, couldn't make money.

But the two had a mission, and that was to introduce their own brand of slam-bang satire to a public whose taste had been whetted by *The Passing Show*. Strictly speaking, Weber and, Fields's productions owed more to the classic burlesque and the Harrigan and Hart celebration of the underclass of the mid-century than anything else. But, like the writers and performers of revues, they cast about constantly for new contemporary targets to lampoon.

And when Julian Mitchell took over the staging of their shows in 1897 with *The Glad Hand*, or, *Secret Servants*, which twitted the Gold Rush and William Gillette's extraordinarily successful drama *Secret

Service, the girls became as important as the gags. In fact, the chorus line at Weber and Fields rivaled, for successive seasons' "Stage Door Johnnies", those at the Casino. Small wonder that Ziegfeld later hired Julian Mitchell to stage his first Follies.

Weber and Fields mounted new burlesque/spectacles in their postage stamp theatre each season. In September of 1898, it was *Hurly-Burly*, starring svelte singer/actress Fay Templeton and, straight from Belasco, David Warfield. In November, it was *Cyranose de Bric-a-Brac*. On January 19, 1899, Fay Templeton returned in *Catherine*. In April of that year, it was *Helter-Skelter*.

But it was with their new September show that Weber and Fields really hit their stride and began to turn a profit. Lillian Russell joined their productions as a $1,250-a-week headliner in *Whirl-i-Gig*, and their previous attempts at staging book musical/parodies underwent a final change. The burlesques became second-act olios, while the first act was set as extended vaudeville, starring Lillian Russell. First-night seats for the show were auctioned to the highest bidder; Jesse Lewisohn snapped up two boxes for $1,000, Stanford White and William Randolph Hearst paid $750 for their seats, and the rest of the orchestra went for $100 a seat. The extraordinary success of *Whirl-i-Gig* drew other headliners to the Weber and Fields Music Hall. Bessie Clayton and DeWolf Hopper joined the mix in 1900, in *Fiddle-Dee-Dee*, in which *Quo Vadis* was burlesqued as *Quo Vas Iss?*. 1901's entry for the company was *Hoity-Toity*. 1902's was *Twirly Whirly*. In 1903, it was *Whoop-Dee-Doo*.

But in 1904, despite the crowds, the Weber and Fields balloon burst. From as far back as 1901, the two had been on increasingly angry terms, sometimes not speaking to each other offstage for weeks, then months. During rehearsals for *Hoity-Toity*, their trusted composer/conductor, John Stromberg committed suicide. The next year, their stock company began to come apart. Lillian Russell, DeWolf Hopper and Bessie Clayton all departed; by 1903, Lew

Fields was gone, too.

But *Higgledy-Piggledy*, the 1904 offering, possessed three new talents: the young comedienne Marie Dressler, the gorgeous chanteuse Anna Held. And, as co-producer with Joe Weber, Ms. Held's brash and energetic husband, Florenz Ziegfeld.

3

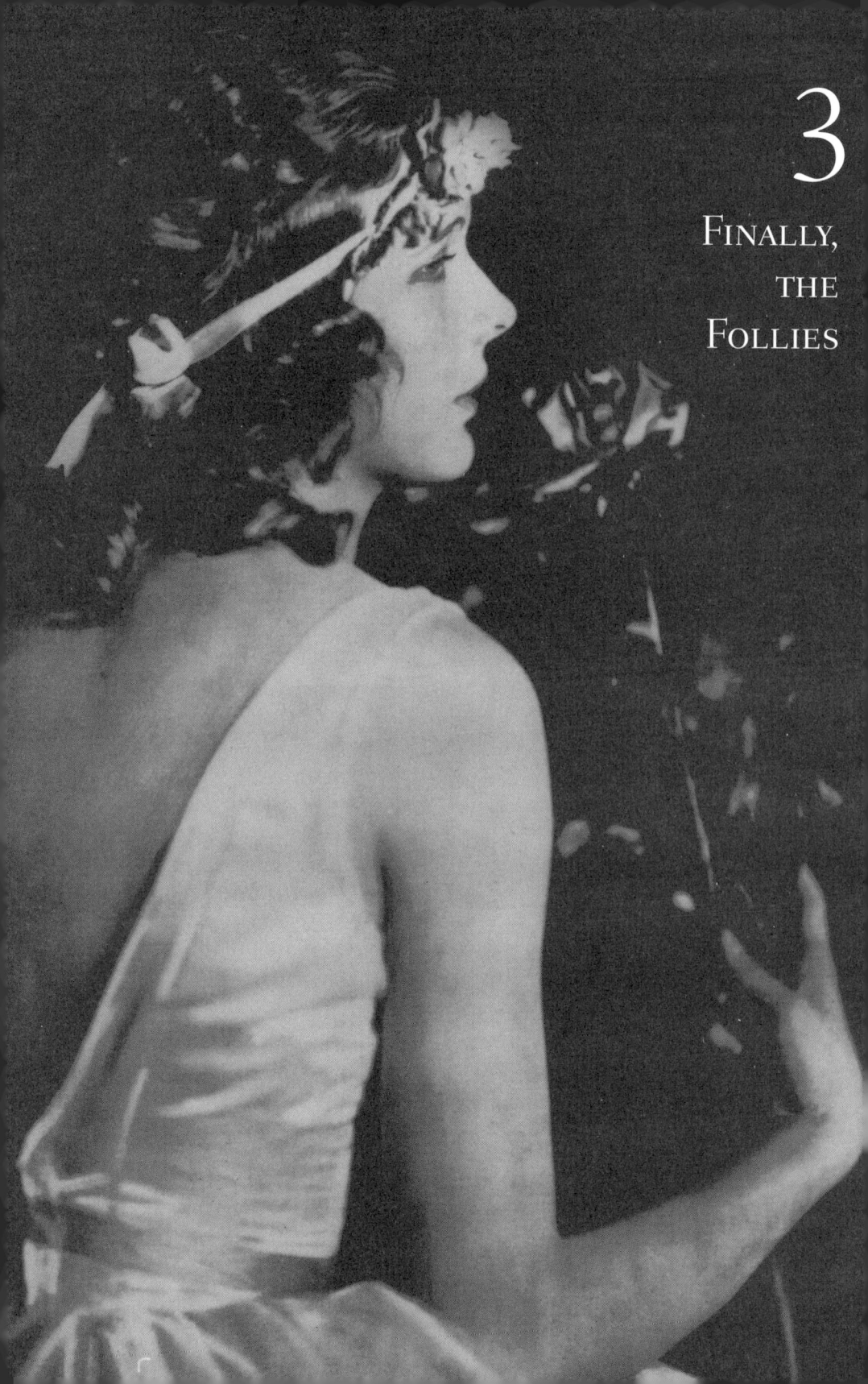

Finally, the Follies

Finally, the Follies

※

By the turn of the century, the "busiest mile on Broadway," described in great and loving detail by music publisher/author Edward B. Marks in his memoir, *They All Had Glamour*, had moved considerably uptown from its 1880s location between Number 1 Broadway and the junction of Broadway and Park Row. The "roar of passing traffic" that he recalled had extended northward to Longacre (now Times) Square where Oscar Hammerstein had just opened his elegant Victoria Theatre. You could still see and hear, as Marks word-painted them, "...[the] bright yellow buses with landscape pictures rumbl[ing] over the paving stones as ironshod hoofs beat their tattoo on them..."

The stage coaches that, a mere ten years ago, had made the two-mile run to Greenwich Village and the ten-mile run into the fields of Harlem had disappeared. The Fulton Street overpass, which, Marks recalled "...raised a storm of disapproval [from] the prevailing moral citizens [who] claimed it corrupted youth, as youngsters with advanced ideas got under the bridge to watch the hoop-skirted, petticoated, white-stockinged, tassel-booted ladies as they unwittingly exposed their hidden charms on their way over the bridge..." had been left downtown.

So had the gangs of Five Points. And so had Tony Pastor. The neighborhood had crumbled around him. Gone, as Marks described them were "...the private coaches of the wealthy, the barouc victorias...the spenders and gilded youth." Gone, in other words, were his customers and his profits. The neighborhood had deteriorated; the carriage trade had taken their custom to Hammerstein's, and the Keith Circuit had gobbled up the nearby Union Square Theatre, refurbished it, dressed its ushers and doormen like operetta military men and charged its customers from 10 to 30 cents admission.

Even Lillian Russell was too busy and famous to pay her periodic, theatre-filling visits. At the end of the 1908 season, Pastor closed his theatre for the last time. Early that August, a *New York Times* reporter found him in his barely furnished office over the theatre. The not all that venerable actor/manager explained that he came in to check his mail and read the newspapers. A week later, on August 15, 1908, he died, leaving an estate of $9,000.

And with him, the era of the actor/manager departed. It had been gasping ever since 1896, when the notorious Syndicate had been born. During that boom year, a new breed of ruthless men, headed by manager Charles Frohman and two former Midwest booking agents, Marc Klaw and Abe Erlanger, would change the face of the Broadway theatre and curb the freedom of its performers forever.

Until that moment, players could move freely from playhouse to playhouse. But when Frohman, Klaw, Erlanger, and three lesser lights, Al Hayman and Philadelphians Samuel Nirdlinger and J. Frederick Zimmerman fused their resources and their theatres into a monopoly, freedom died. In one swift stroke of a pen, they formed the Syndicate, a merciless force that bought up and therefore controlled the vast majority of the playable playhouses in New York and on the road.

Oh, some actor/managers fought back at first. David Belasco was one; Mrs. Fiske, Richard Mansfield, Joseph Jefferson and James O'Neill played in tents and sports arenas rather than meet the demeaning demands of the Syndicate, particularly those of the terrible team of Klaw and Erlanger.

Anything, they said publicly. Anything but work for Klaw and Erlanger. And they had a point. Klaw was a retiring man, chiefly remembered for his observation about Broadway, which he said was populated by "theatre habitues and sons of habitues." But Abe Erlanger was another matter entirely, one of the most hated and egomaniacal men in show business.

Guy Bolton and P.G. Wodehouse recalled him in their suspect memoir *Bring on the Girls*: "We were quite fond of Abe," they began, slyly, then lapsed into their form of reality, "He ate broken bottles and conducted human sacrifices at the time of the full moon, but he was a thoroughly good chap, heart of gold beneath a rugged exterior and all that sort of thing..."

But battling the Syndicate was an exercise in frustrating futility, and by the turn of the century, Klaw and Erlanger owned eight theatres in New York—Erlanger's, the Liberty, the Gaiety, the Frolic, the Fulton, the Avon, the Belmont and the Windsor.

And at the dawn of the new century, they planned the construction of their flagship theatre, one to rival Hammerstein and the Shuberts and anyone else who dared to challenge their supremacy in theatrical real estate. It didn't hurt that the Syndicate had bought up a goodly number of the lots vacated when the area from 40th to 45th Street, west of Broadway and along Longacre Square, was turned from a quiet residential neighborhood, bereft even of streetlights, into a bustling commercial center.

Of course, there was Oscar Hammerstein, who had established much more than a beachhead in the area. In January of 1895, when the only other theatre in the vicinity was the two year old American, Hammerstein had taken over several lots, including the charred remains of an old armory between 44th and 45th Streets on Broadway. Ten months later, the Olympia, a veritable palace of entertainment, filled every inch of the space.

There were two main auditoriums, the huge, 2,800-seat Music Hall, which would be devoted to vaudeville, and the 1,700-seat Lyric, devoted to musicals. But that was just the beginning. To round out the complex, there was a concert hall, and overhead, spanning all three theatres, an enclosed roof garden which seated over a thousand. Cooled by water cascading over the glass in summer and heated in winter, it was a venue for all seasons. Besides this, the complex sported an Oriental cafe, a billiard parlor, and, below street level, a bowling alley.

Its creation and sustenance demanded enough to bankrupt a small country, and it temporarily ruined Hammerstein. In 1898, the Olympia was repossessed by the New York Life Insurance Company and chopped up into three theatres. One of them—the Lyric—was leased by the Syndicate through Charles Frohman.

Hammerstein, undaunted, set out to build another theatre, the Victoria, on the site of Gilley Moore's Market Stables, in the heart of Longacre Square at 42nd Street and Seventh Avenue. The Victoria began life as a legitimate theatre, but soon traded this for a variety format which featured the big stars of the time—the Seven Little Foys, the Keatons, the Four Cohans, Bert Williams, Houdini, Charlie Chaplin and, after 1906, Evelyn Nesbitt.

But most of all, the Victoria was noted for its own, integral roof garden, named by the showman the Paradise. Both open air and covered, it rambled across the Victoria roof and spilled onto the nearby Republic (now the Victory), also owned by Hammerstein. And on this portion of the roof garden, strollers, drinkers and audience members could amble through an actual Dutch dairy farm, outfitted with a windmill, a live cow, chickens, a goat, ducks in a pond and a milkmaid, serving warm milk from the cow. Who could ask for anything more?

Klaw and Erlanger, that's who. Their flagship theatre, the New Amsterdam, slated to be built on the lot that extended between 41st and 42nd Streets, west of Broadway, would not only represent the finest of the Art Nouveau that was the rage of the 1900 Paris Exposition, but sport the best climate-controlled roof in the city.

All of this time spent with architecture had a purpose: the turn of the century was a time of high extravagance, the atmosphere that gave the phrase The Gay Nineties its validity. The productions of the time reflected and energized this, and made the times right and ripe for a producer to seize upon them, intertwine their disparate parts, and build upon a shaky structure to create one coherent musical theatre form.

Florenz Ziegfeld was the man whose time had come.

What had been clumsily patched together in *The Black Crook* and refined through *A Gaiety Girl*, vaudeville and the Weber and Fields Music Halls, was growing and thriving, but it still existed in its separate parts. *The Passing Show* had, it seemed, for all its stir at the time, been a passing fad, although it survived in bits and pieces and influences, as did *Gaiety Girl's* girls.

The Casino continued to offer operettas during the season and reviews on its roof in the summer. In 1897, Koster and Bial's vaudeville house hauled in Harry B. Smith and Ludwig Englander to write a main score for their latest bill, thus, through verisimilitude, taking a giant step out of vaudeville and toward revue. Wallack's mounted *Miss Manhattan*, a giant extravaganza, which came in for kidding at Weber and Fields *Mister New York, Esquire*

In 1898, *Hotel Topsy Turvy*, a London and Paris hit, billed as a "vaudeville operetta," opened at the Herald Square, starring Eddie Foy, Marie Dressler and Aubrey Boucicault. In 1899, the extravaganza *The Man in the Moon* at Hammerstein's Olympia and the Herald Square's equally extravagant *An Arabian Girl and Forty Thieves* battled the bicycle craze and each other for seekers of spectacle. In November of 1900, the Victoria's *Star and Garter*, although billed as vaudeville, contained all the elements without the form of a revue; singers, dancers, jugglers, and sendups of contemporary dramas existed, but in no particular balance or order. And in that same month, the "Stage Door Johnny" craze hit a new high of dedication and the *Gaiety Girl* concept was ratcheted up considerably with the arrival at the Casino of *Florodora* and its immortal sextette, whose personnel, shortly after opening night, began to change monthly, as member after member departed on the arm of one millionaire or another.

It was into this atmosphere that Florenz Ziegfeld and his moderately talented, moderately beautiful but remarkably imaginative and energetic common law wife, Anna Held, arrived.

Ziegfeld was the son of the president and founder of the Chicago Musical College, but his tastes and talents ran to discovery and production, not music. Legend has it that he was bitten by the bug of theatre in 1883, when Buffalo Bill and Annie Oakley roared into Chicago with their Wild West Show. At the age of 17, Dr. Ziegfeld had consigned his son to a ranch in Wyoming to break him of his love for show business. The budding impresario reportedly turned the skills he learned on the ranch to joining Buffalo Bill's show.

From there, the young Ziegfeld, leaning more toward P.T. Barnum than William Cody, presented "The Dancing Ducks of Denmark" which was shut down when it was discovered that he was creating the illusion of a dance by employing an assistant to turn up a series of gas jets on a heated iron grid. The poor ducks had no choice but to lift their feet.

Undaunted, he followed this disaster with a worse one, when he attempted to fool the public with an illuminated bowl containing, he said, the "Invisible Brazilian Fish." There was nothing in the bowl but water, and by the end of two days, there was nothing in the till, either.

In 1892, Dr. Ziegfeld was given the task of providing the musical talent for the Chicago Columbian Exposition, and he sent his son to Europe to gather talent. Apparently, the array that young Florenz returned with was disastrously terrible, but, hardly discouraged, he caught a train to New York and came back with strongman extraordinaire, Sandow. The Great Sandow became greater through Ziegfeld's promotion pranks, including the luring of Chicago socialite Mrs. Potter Palmer backstage to inspect Sandow's muscles. Ziegfeld continued to promote Sandow after the fair, until an unfortunate match in San Francisco between Sandow and a lion. Sandow lost, and Ziegfeld lost his meal ticket.

Ever unbowed, he sailed for Europe, and at London's Palace Theatre saw, met, and was conquered by Anna Held. She was a match for him in cleverness, showmanship and daring, and the two established a personal and professional relationship that would, ultimately, change the face of musical theatre in America.

When they arrived in New York in 1896 as titular man and wife, Ziegfeld had already expanded their relationship into that of producer/promoter and star. Still, Miss Held's first appearance in September of 1896, at the Herald Square, in a revival of Charles Hoyt's *A Parlor Match*, caused barely a ripple along Broadway.

But in the next three years, Ziegfeld embarked on a concerted campaign to create a public image of a petite, naughty and up-to-the-minute Frenchwoman who rode a bicycle, raced in the new danger to life and her gorgeous limbs—the automobile—and took daily baths in grade A milk. Ziegfeld even arranged to have the milk supplier sue him when he refused to pay for a shipment that arrived sour.

By 1899, he convinced Harry B. Smith and Reginald DeKoven to come up with a confection for Anna Held titled *Papa's Wife*. It featured its star stopping the show nightly with the racy tune "I Wish I Really Weren't, But I Am," and making a grand exit in an 1899 automobile.

And it introduced the first line of Ziegfeld girls.

Calling him a true "connoisseur of pulchritude," Smith, in his memoirs, recalled that "There were only sixteen girls in *Papa's Wife*, but they were all highly decorative and in their costuming, economy was not considered."[1]

So, the pattern that Ziegfeld would follow was established. His eye for beauty was unassailable; his taste for elaborate and expensive costuming was admirable, and from then on, Anna Held would appear in a constantly ascending series of dresses that were fashioned from such disparate elements as real flowers that drifted petals behind her when she walked to velvet creations punctuated with scores of real diamonds. "If you dress like a queen, you feel like a queen" was his philosophy, and it would soon pay off. Of course, these early shows were, nominally, book shows. But by 1901, when, once again with Harry B. Smith and Reginald DeKoven, Ziegfeld opened *The Little Duchess* at the Casino for Anna Held, notes in the program later in the run read "Owing to the length of the performance the plot has been eliminated." The audiences that kept the show running for four months, breaking Lillian Russell's old house record, really came to see Anna Held in a bathing suit, and girls in rosebud dresses or in a sextettte, removing their stockings.

But the road to success for Ziegfeld wasn't smooth, nor would it ever be. Although *The Red Feather*, his musical without Anna Held at the Lyric in November of 1903, was hailed for the "dazzling splendor of superb costumes, and an abundance of handsome young women," it flopped, and the same fate awaited *Mam'selle Napoleon* a month later, despite Anna Held's presence.

When Weber and Fields went their separate ways in 1904, Ziegfeld took Lew Fields's place as co-producer, with Joe Weber, of *Higgledy-Piggledy*, starring Anna Held and featuring Marie Dressler, who walked off with the best reviews. But the Ziegfelds and Weber never did experience a comfortable fit, and they parted company quickly and unamicably.

Meanwhile, innovations were occurring on Broadway. Victor Herbert was entrenching himself on the well deserved plateau he would occupy as America's foremost operetta composer, but the young and brash member of the four Cohans, George M., was wowing audiences with a new and popular sound. The arrival of *Little Johnny Jones*, *Forty-Five Minutes from Broadway* and *George Washington Jr.*, all produced in two seasons, was to many like the twentieth-century equivalent of the output of Harrigan and Hart.

And the goliath among giant theatres, the Hippodrome, opened in April of 1905. Located on Sixth Avenue between 43rd and 44th

Streets, it ginned up the definition of spectacle exponentially. The triumvirate of Frederic Thompson, Elmer S. Dundy and "Bet-a-Million" Gates, who had built Luna Park on Coney Island determined that they would erect the largest, most fabulous theatre in the world. Seating 5,200, with a stage 12 times that of the average Broadway house, and a proscenium 40 feet high and 96 feet wide, it was large enough to accommodate two full-sized circus rings. Not only this, it rivaled the New Amsterdam's hydraulic equipment, and added an apron that could be lowered 12 feet and flooded by three centrifugal pumps discharging 8,000 gallons of water per minute. Thus was born the famous Hippodrome tank, which could change in a matter of minutes from a swimming pool for an aquacade of young swimmers, to white water rapids, to a tidal ocean.

This leviathan of a place demanded a huge staff, and in 1905, it was possible; the payroll numbered 1,000, including 78 electricians, 22 engineers, a ballet of 200, 400 chorus girls and 100 chorus boys. *A Yankee Circus on Mars* was the opening show, and it was a formless monster, part-circus, part-vaudeville, part-"tableauxdrama." Elephants, horses and people paraded before an awed public, whose taste for extravaganza kept the Hippodrome filled for years to come.

That its ruling triumvirate was unable to really run a theatre became, however, apparent in its first year of operation, and it was taken over in early 1905 by a new and powerful force, Sam, Lee and J.J. Shubert. By all accounts, Sam was the only likable brother, and he was killed in a train accident in late 1905. The other two were perfect matches for the Syndicate, with whom they sat down in 1900 to work out a partnership. Abe Erlanger reneged on the deal, thus becoming the brothers' eternal enemy, and they his. When the Shuberts took over the Hippodrome with *A Society Circus*, with its dancing waters, its "Motoring in Mid-Air" tribute to flying machines and its 596-performance run, the battle was truly joined. It was time for Klaw and Erlanger to top the Shuberts.

But it was clearly not going to be with spectacle. What, then? By

June of 1906, another avenue suddenly opened up to Klaw and Erlanger, who were well aware of the ingeniousness of Florenz Ziegfeld.

The avenue took the form of a Columbia varsity show titled *Mamzelle Champagne*, which opened on June 26, to the customary society fanfare on the Madison Square Garden Roof. It was a pathetic show, but it was cheap, and roof garden audiences, thankful for healing breezes in those pre-air-conditioning nights, were less demanding than their downstairs counterparts.

On one particular night, as the second act began, with a trifling tune called, ironically, "I Could Love a Million Girls," Harry K. Thaw, the beleaguered and mentally unbalanced husband of musical comedy starlet Evelyn Nesbitt, worked his way to the table of famous, revered and fun-loving architect Stanford White, who had designed Madison Square Garden, the edifice upon whose roof *Mamzelle Champagne* was unfolding, and who was dallying, nearly daily, with Evelyn Nesbitt. As the chorus warbled on, Thaw drew out a revolver and pumped three shots into the back of Stanford White's head. The performance came to a violent close.

But not the run of *Mamselle Champagne*. A show that should have closed in one night, it continued for 60 packed performances (the demand for seats near White's table was delirious) and upped the general popularity of roof garden reviews several fold.

Klaw and Erlanger didn't trust Ziegfeld with the New Amsterdam roof. Not yet. But they read the papers, and they knew how to make money. They had a decidedly third rate roof over the New York Theatre. It was nearly disreputable, really an open walled shed with a corrugated iron roof and a canvas tarpaulin to keep the rain off the customers and the lighting system, and a pagoda over the elevator entrance to shelter the higher paying customers, who enjoyed softer seats in contrast to the folding chairs that surrounded most of the roof's tables. It was a little like what would become summer stock, but in the city.

Klaw and Erlanger had lost a considerable amount of money with the New York's last tenant, *The Land of Nod*, with music by Joe E. Howard and Victor Herbert, an extravaganza by any standards except those set by the Hippodrome. The show, which had opened on April 1, had lasted 17 performances, and the New York had been dark ever since.

Nevertheless, the two canny producers were willing to sink $13,800 into the production of a new revue (they were even willing to jettison the American "review" title and utilize the French spelling, and, for good measure, change the roof's name to the Jardin de Paris), but they were only willing to pay the young and moderately tried producer Florenz Ziegfeld $200 a week, and warned him that weekly running expenses should not exceed $2,000.

No matter. Ziegfeld and Anna Held had spent some time in Paris at the *Folies Bergere*, and the approach of its producers appealed to them. Ziegfeld contacted Harry B. Smith and Julian Mitchell, with whom he had staged *Higgledy-Piggledy at* Weber and Fields Music Hall. One legend has it that Anna Held suggested that he use the name "Follies" for his new revue, in suggestion and imitation of the *Folies* they had so lately admired. Partly true. She certainly encouraged him to use the Paris spectacle as his model.

But another legend has it that the *Folies* had nothing at all to do with the naming of the revue. Instead, Anna Held suggested that he appropriate the title of a popular newspaper column of the time called *Follies of the Day*, and name it *Follies of the Year*. Maybe, although the usually omitted fact that the column was written by Harry B. Smith, who claimed that he suggested the title to Ziegfeld, casts this into a certain amount of doubt.

What is certain is that Ziegfeld, throughout his entire career the epitome of the superstitious showman, insisted that the show's title have exactly thirteen letters. Thus, its final form: *Follies of 1907*. For the evolution of the Broadway revue, no title could be more appropriate, for it telegraphed the news that the show would have satirical moments and that the subject matter would be contemporary.

It would also have girls, gorgeous girls gorgeously dressed, gorgeously presented, and in satisfying abundance. Since that was already Ziegfeld's trademark, he hired 50 beauties and billed them as "The Anna Held Girls." As would be his pattern for the rest of his 21 *Follies*, he also hired an army of composers and lyricists: Edgar Selden, Vincent Bryan, Gertrude Hoffman, Matt Woodward, Silvio Hein, E. Ray Goetz, Will Cobb, Gus Edwards, Paul West, Alfred Solomon, Billy Gaston, William Jerome, Jean Schwartz and Seymour Furth.

It was a jumble of jollity, pulchritude and naughtiness, all right. Annabelle Whitford was featured as the Gibson Bathing Girl in stockings and bloomers, Mlle. Dazie dazzled with a "Ju-Jitsu Waltz," if that's imaginable, which was danced (fought?) with Prince Tokio "straight from Japan." Later in the two acts and 13 scenes, Mlle. Dazie became a convincing Salome. Grace La Rue sang the Billy Gaston song "Miss Ginger from Jamaica", and comedian Dave Lewis stopped the show nightly with his rendition of the up-to-date "I Oughtn't to Auto Anymore" by Vincent Bryan and E. Ray Goetz.

Ziegfeld, having understood early the value of commercial endorsements to help along a restricted budget, fashioned an interlude titled "Budweiser's a Friend of Mine" (music and lyrics by Vincent Bryan and Seymour Furth). In another sketch, Harry B. Smith chose to imagine Pocahontas and Captain John Smith being introduced to modern life as a way of satirizing Theodore Roosevelt (who, according to Smith's autobiography, "was in the audience one night and laughed louder than anyone"). Other sketches focused on Chauncey Depew as the head of the Misinformation Department; an operatic duel with Oscar Hammerstein and Heinrich Conried fighting in court, supported by their respective opera companies in court; and, in various situations, an assembly of characters stretching from Anthony Comstock, Commodore Perry and Andrew Carnegie to John D. Rockefeller and Edna May.

Probably partly because of the restricted budget, partly because of Ziegfeld himself, the acts and the sketches differed from performance to performance. Nora Bayes came and went, as did Annabelle Whitford and her Gibson Bathing Girls. What remained were the Anna Held Girls and the spectacular production numbers, including one in which the girls, marching up and down the aisles among the audience, banged on drums.

The Follies of 1907 raised a few journalistic eyebrows, but always with qualification. While one review questioned the propriety of some of its numbers, dialogue and costumes, it concluded, "The auditor resigns himself to fate, and at the conclusion of the performance departs, like a passenger on one of those switch-back devices which provide thrills at summer resorts, conscious that he has been scared now and then, but not irreparably shocked, and tempted to try again."[3]

"Tempted to try again" was the key phrase, and although the New York run at the New York Roof/Jardin des Paris lasted only a disappointing 70 nights, the *Follies* moved to the Liberty for a few extra performances and then went on to successful runs in Washington and Baltimore. Its $120,000 profit convinced Klaw, Erlanger and Ziegfeld that the temptation to try again should be heeded.

But not quite yet. They were all busy elsewhere. The New Amsterdam had received rave notices for its decor, but little else. After four years, it still hadn't housed a hit. There was a Viennese Operetta called *The Merry Widow* that Colonel Henry W. Savage was trying to sell them, and his offer sounded interesting.

Elsewhere, the Follies had caused hardly a ripple on the face of musical theatre in the 1907–08 season. Two "reviews" (American producers were still studiously avoiding the French spelling, as well as Ziegfeld's production techniques) opened within three days of each other. The first, more successful one was the Casino's opening attraction of the autumn, produced by Sam S. and Lee Shubert. *The Gay White Way*, with a thin excuse of a book by Sydney Rosenfeld and J. Clarence Harvey that sent comic detective Jefferson de Angelis wandering through several Manhattan landmarks in search of the identity of the missing head in a photograph. But more importantly, it featured enough variety and burlesque sketches—particularly one with de Angelis and Blanche Ring sending up the famous sawmill scene in *Blue Jeans* to keep it running for a healthy 105 performances. Ludwig Englander provided the main score, but as was the practice in this era, an increasing number of acts insisted on interpolations by composers and lyricists of their choice. One of the interpolators in *The Gay White Way* was a young composer who had penned his first addition to others' scores at the Casino, in an English import called *An English Daisy* (1904). Earlier in the 1907-08 season, he had interpolated no less than seven songs into a Charles Frohman import, *The Dairymaids*. But in *The Gay White Way*, Jerome Kern's melody, with lyrics by Michael Rourke, of "Without the Girl—Inside!" was his first song for a revue. Pardon. Review. It wouldn't be his last.

The other review of the month, which opened on October 10, put Julian Mitchell back to work at Weber's Music Hall. *Hip! Hip! Hooray!* had Bessie Clayton's legs and Valeska Suratt's hats and Joe Weber's German accent, but audiences missed Lew Fields, just as they missed Joe Weber at the Herald Square, where Fields had established himself. The show closed after 64 performances.

But everything else was eclipsed when, on October 21, *The Merry Widow*, trailing a comet tail of advance word of its European triumphs, opened at the New Amsterdam. From that moment on and for years thereafter, American musical theatregoers traded their allegiance to British musicals for those of Austria. The waltz became the dance of the moment. Merry Widow hats became the rage. A new type of ladies' undergarment was invented. But most of all, sophisticated, grownup, believable entertainment had reached the American stage—the sort of entertainment that Florenz Ziegfeld had tried, tentatively, on the roof of the New York Theatre, on a budget that was a fraction of the one that Colonel Henry W. Savage had spent on *The

Merry Widow.

Colonel Savage, a man who shared the detestation trophy on Broadway with Abe Erlanger, was a tall and imposing figure, who walked with a limp, induced possibly, Guy Bolton and P.G. Wodehouse later opined, from being "shot in the foot by some indignant author."[4] Later, when the mild-mannered Klaw retired from the business, Savage would enter into partnership with Erlanger, but for now, he was on his own and at the top of the Broadway heap. *The Merry Widow* was not just a success; it was a sensation that begat a craze. The reviews were scarcely written when Vincent Bryan and E. Ray Goetz interpolated a song titled "The Man Who Wrote the 'Merry Widow' Waltz" into *The Dairymaids*. On January 2, 1908, Joe Weber, with the help of Julian Mitchell and the permission of Colonel Savage, presented *The Merry Widow Burlesque* at Weber's Music Hall, and it played for over 150 performances. "Lehar's operetta made a fortune for Colonel Savage," recalled Harry B. Smith in his memoirs "Eventually it cost American managers a number of fortunes, because, for several years afterward, they produced every German and Austrian operetta they could get, in the vain hope of finding another 'Merry Widow'"[5] The Savage original, starring Donald Brian and Ethel Jackson, lit the New Amsterdam for a record 416 performances, then spent decades on the road. It was, for the history books, another *Black Crook*, but with class and substance.

And so, in a sense, Ziegfeld's hand was strengthened. His sophistication might play during the season, and downstairs. And since *The Merry Widow* was making money, Klaw and Erlanger were willing to lease the New York Theatre for an in-season variation on their summer success. The result was a compromise. Gathering together his *Follies* creative team, Harry B. Smith (shadow of a book), Herbert Gresham (staging of the book) and Julian Mitchell (ensemble staging), Ziegfeld, in deference to the times, had Smith write some twaddle about Mephisto visiting a lovesick sculptor, betting him he can't be faithful for a year, and tempting him with all sorts of international dancing, singing and performing beauties. In the end, they all go off to the Bal Tabarin. But this was a mere excuse for the young producer to put to use some of the more successful experiments he had tried in his first *Follies*, while working with Mitchell to evolve new ones.

Adelaide Genee, a highly respected dancer, touted characteristically by Ziegfeld as "the world's greatest dancer," was the headliner, performing in the midst of four swirling production scenes or, as they were described in the program, "divertisements," and particularly in a hunt scene with real hounds. Surrounding her were her "Dancing Girls from the Empire Theatre, London," as replacements for the Anna Held Girls, and a huge cast of various singers, dancers, acrobats and aerial artists, their "Evolutions arranged by Herr H. Schultz."

The music was mainly by Maurice Levi, but Paul Luncki, Addison Burkhardt, Matt Woodward and Louis A. Hirsch added interpolations, most notably and successfully, a now obligatory reference by Levi and Smith titled "Since My Mariutch Learned the Merry Widow Waltz." Ziegfeld was obviously still shaking the sawdust of his days with Sandow off his feet, but he was learning. *The Soul Kiss*, with its foolish but lavish loveliness, stayed at the New York for 122 performances and made a profit.

Despite this and the hoopla over the New Amsterdam's waltzing, Austrian resident, the past continued to dominate the remainder of musical Broadway with vaudeville, minstrel shows and extravaganzas. *The Top of the World*, the Majestic's extravaganza of the season, replete with Aurora Borealis, Queen of the North, dancing fairies, and a chorus of collies, being sung to by chorus girls ("How'd You Like to Be My Bow-wow-wow?"), opened two nights before the *Merry Widow* debut and lasted for a healthy 156 performances.

And the Hippodrome, its productions now under the money-making control of the Shubert Brothers, tapped into another current craze with *The Auto Race*, which included just that, plus a naval battle, a ballet, a garden party and a circus. The Hippodrome's 5,000 seat girth remained pretty well-filled, twice a day for 312 performances.

And, finally, the past was given a touching recognition in the context of a brashly American form of "musical play", written by the equally brash and American George M. Cohan. In *Fifty Miles from Boston*, an obvious follow-up to his successful *Forty-five Minutes from Broadway*, presented at the Garrick, which was originally the Harrigan, Cohan paid tribute to the old trouper, who attended opening night, by naming a character after him and featuring a song that long outlived the show: "H-A-Double R-I-G-A-N."

But the future clearly belonged to Ziegfeld. On June 15, he opened his second *Follies* in the shed on the roof of the New York Theatre. Shed or not, the Jardin de Paris was now the place to be, at least in the spring and summer of 1908.

Even Ziegfeld wasn't courageous enough to venture into the revue without at least the ghost of a book. This time, Harry B. Smith turned to Adam and Eve, worrying about their progeny, and Herbert Gresham moved the principals through the book whenever it surfaced. Julian Mitchell again created the ensembles which were varied and various, including a preview of a trip through the Holland Tunnel, currently being dug between Manhattan and the Jersey Marshes (the marsh's mosquitos were Ziegfeld girls in body stockings, wings and bobbing antennae), a patriotic Navy number, and the girls parading as taxis with meters on their shoulders flashing ON and OFF.

Mlle. Dazie was back with her dazzling dances, as was Nora Bayes, who joined the 1908 *Follies* partway through its run, and whom Ziegfeld had promoted, as he had Anna Held, through planted press stories that she sucked lollipops every three hours to keep up her strength. Now, she was a star of vaudeville, the first of many that Ziegfeld would hire, and married to Jack Norworth, with whom she was to perform, fight publicly and write furiously popular songs for years. Probably the most famous of them was introduced in the 1908 *Follies*:"Shine on, Harvest Moon" (credited to them but actually written by Edward Madden and Gus Edwards). It eventually became a fixture on the music stand of every parlor piano in the country.

The expected naughtiness was supplied by Lucy Weston, an English songstress specializing in double and triple entendres. Contemporary tastes were titillated by the military drills, Mae Murray as the popular cover girl of the day, Nell Brinkley, and sketches set at the Chicago convention, in which most of the major political figures of the day were satirized. The 1908 edition far outdistanced its predecessor, running 120 performances. The staircase of ascension was plainly in place for Ziegfeld.

Or was it?

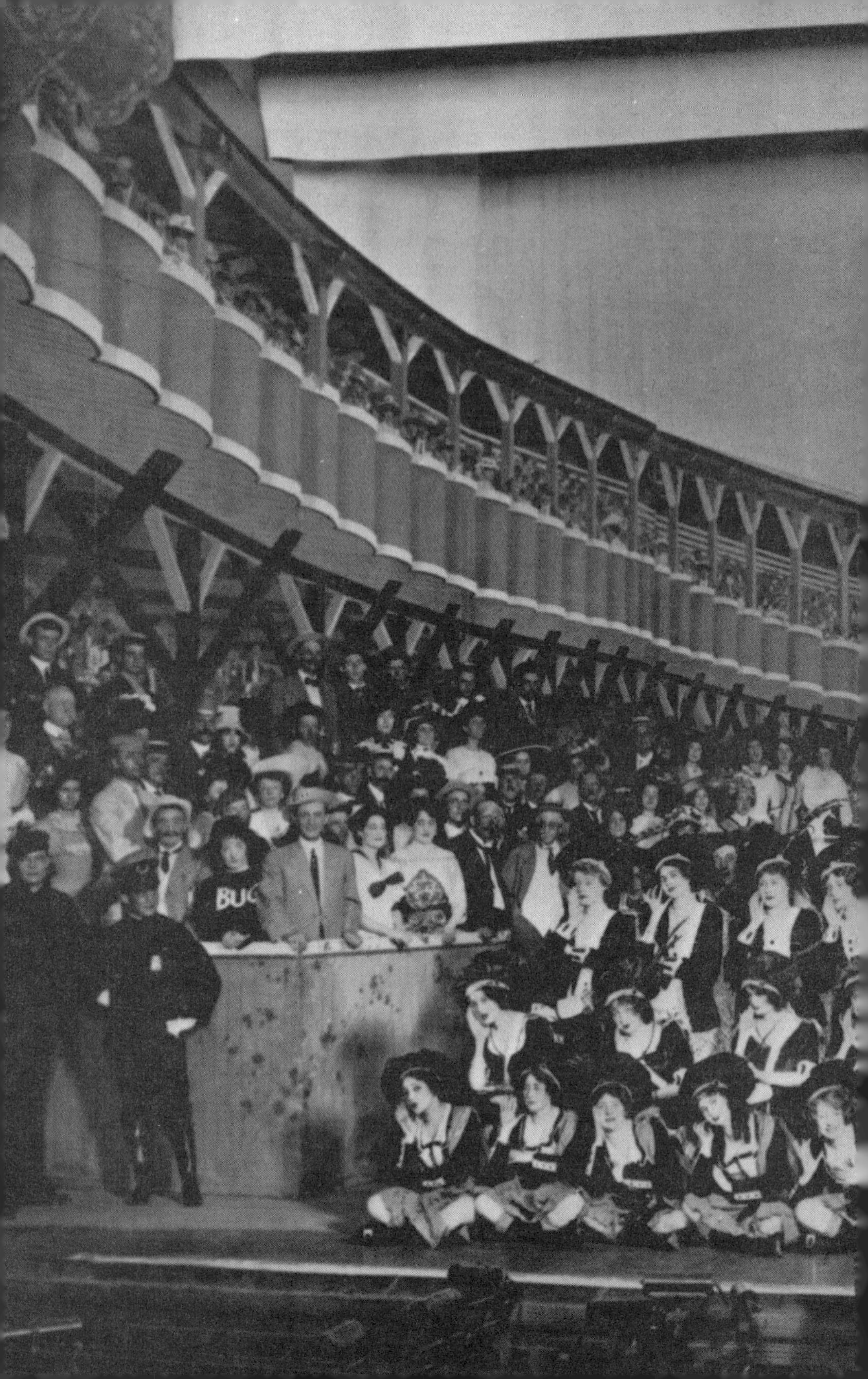

4
The Door Opens

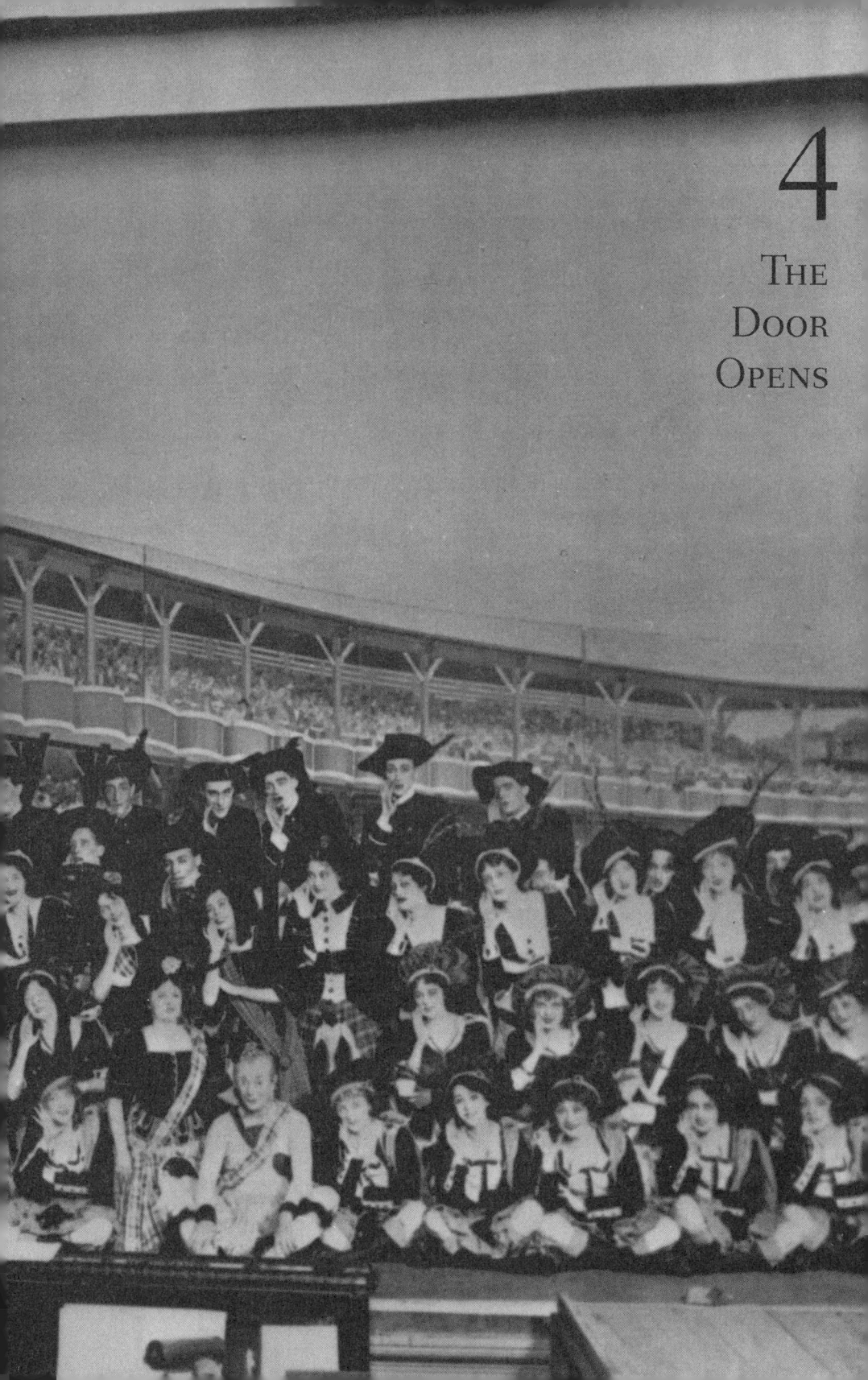

The Door Opens

❦

The past dies hard, particularly in show business, with its tradition of superstition beyond reason and undying reverence for fading stars and styles. The Shuberts, in tandem with Lew Fields, challenged Ziegfeld in July with *The Mimic World*. It introduced some new talent: singer Charles King, dancer Vernon Castle and director Ned Wayburn, a contender to Julian Mitchell, plus one halfway up-to-date interpolation by Louis A. Hirsch, "Ragtime Minstrel Man." As one critic noted, it "hasn't even the semblance of a plot and makes no pretense of any,"[1] and that was certainly another step on the way to the pure revue.

The Mimic World was, at heart, classic burlesque, sending up most of the hit plays of the season, and covering the scene changes between the sketches with such Seymour Furth-Edward Madden-Addison Burkhardt numbers as "When Tetrazinni Sings High F," "When Johnny Comes Marching Home from College," and "Madamoiselle," and a bevy of predictable production numbers whose titles told it all: "All the Stars and Stripes Belong to Me," "Monte Carlo Town" and "Ambassador's March." It was, nevertheless, popular and kept the Casino occupied for most of the summer.

The Shuberts began the new season on September 5, with their annual Hippodrome spectacular, this time titled *Sporting Days*, and featuring races, a sky war and the expected circus. It was all hugely successful and ran in its customary two-a-day format for 448 performances. Cartoon characters from the daily papers made it to the musical stage with *Fluffy Ruffles* (much music by Jerome Kern) and *Little Nemo* (music by Victor Herbert) while George M. Cohan continued to sustain the popular taste of, as he put it, "the factory worker and his girl," begun by Harrigan and Hart and fine-tuned by Weber and Fields. And there were Viennese operettas aplenty.

Even Ziegfeld fell back into the book show format (although it was billed as a "musical entertainment") for a vehicle for Anna Held. Sensing, possibly, that the show might not fill the New York Theatre on its own merits, Ziegfeld again embarked upon a massive publicity campaign.

Miss Held, the newspapers breathlessly reported, would wear a $35,000 sable coat and a new $30,000 dress onstage. A scandalous six foot square photo of her, wearing only a few clothes, was displayed in the theatre lobby for a day, then removed by the police as flashbulbs flashed.

The largest electric sign in American history, 80 feet long and 45 feet high, containing 32,000 square feet of glass, 11 miles of wire and 2,300 gas globes, went up over the New York.

Miss Innocence was the satiric title of the object of this nonstop hoopla, since audiences came to be titillated by the flip side of innocence from Ms. Held. And they received it, with an interpolation into the Ludwig Englander score by Harry Williams and Egbert Van Alstyne, provocatively titled "I Wonder What's the Matter with My Eyes."

Fortunately, partway through, Ziegfeld and Julian Mitchell ignored Harry B. Smith's book and brought on Nora Bayes and Jack Norworth's stalwart "Shine on, Harvest Moon" (which was treated as a new song by some critics) and a bevy of beauties in a burst of production numbers, elegantly costumed and presented. The song's singer was a tall, striking, voluptuous, promiscuous and hard-drinking beauty who had long ago discarded her real, nearly unpronounceable name of Eulallean De Jacques for the more marquee-friendly one of Lillian Lorraine. Ms. Lorraine's continued presence would signal the beginning of the end of the Held-Ziegfeld common law marriage. But not yet. *Miss Innocence* kept the New York lit for 176 healthy performances, further cementing Ziegfeld's reputation as a producer of opulent hits.

And yet, for some reason, this didn't hold true with the return of the *Follies of 1909* on June 14, at the Jardin de Paris. For all of its sophistication and taste and production values, it would interest theatre historians more than its patrons. It ran for a mere 64 performances. Only the 1921 edition would have a shorter stay.

But Ziegfeld and Julian Mitchell couldn't foresee this, as they plunged into an ever ascending series of theatrical experiments. By now, Harry B. Smith had abandoned any attempt at a book and devoted his considerable talents to lyrics, while his wife Irene spent ever more time consoling Anna Held, who, besides having a mysterious miscarriage in a hotel room, was becoming increasingly aware of the deepening affair between Ziegfeld and Lillian Lorraine.

The music for the 1909 *Follies* was ostensibly by Maurice Levi, but the interpolators were legion and included Edward Madden, Gus Edwards, E. Ray Goetz, Lewis Muir, A. Seymour Brown and Nat Ayer, Irving Berlin, and Nora Bayes and Jack Norworth (who added five songs for their stints and whose personally claimed "By the Light of the Silvery Moon" became the show's hit.)

Along with Bayes and Norworth, Bessie Clayton, Harry C. Kelly, Mae Murray, Gertrude Vanderbilt and Annabelle Whitford were allumni of earlier *Follies*, but this edition would introduce three new leading ladies, a sure way to produce problems with the tempestuous Ms. Bayes. First, there was the hiring, by Marc Klaw, of the overweight (even for 1909) and ungainly young singer Sophie Tucker. Ziegfeld, furious at not being consulted, ignored her through most of the rehearsal period. During the opening week in Atlantic City, where all *Follies* from that year forward would try out, he threw an idea at

Smith and Levi: a jungle scene involving Teddy Roosevelt. Because there was no principal available for the spot in which he scheduled the scene. Sophie Tucker was given the song by default.

The story goes that Smith and Levi stayed up all night and delivered "It's Moving Day Down in Jungle Town" the next morning. By that afternoon, Julian Mitchell had staged the number, with chorus girls in various animal outfits scurrying into the upper reaches of trees at every entrance of Teddy Roosevelt. Meanwhile, Sophie Tucker, as a lumpy leopard, delivered the song with incredible bravado—and stopped the show.

Nora Bayes threw a tantrum and the gauntlet: it was either Sophie Tucker or she. Ziegfeld compromised and removed the full throated young singer from everything except the jungle number. Bayes was only partly mollified, and when, after the week's vacation their contract allowed them in July, she and Norworth failed to return, Ziegfeld had them slapped with an injunction preventing them from appearing under any other management until their contract expired. The Norworths counter-sued, claiming that the new electric fans installed in the Jardin de Paris's roof and the noise of waiters serving drinks distracted Miss Bayes and interfered with her artistry. Ziegfeld eventually won the suit.

Meanwhile, he hired an even more tempestuous star, Eva Tanguay, to replace Nora Bayes. Tanguay, the "I Don't Care Girl", who frankly admitted that she had little talent except for self-promotion, did her scandalous turn from vaudeville, a writhing depiction of Salome lusting after John the Baptist. Audiences forgot Nora Bayes quickly.

The show itself was replete with the Court of Venus, featuring Annabelle Whitford as the goddess and Mae Murray as Cupid, and a satirical scene in the Manhattan Opera House with an actor portraying Oscar Hammerstein quarreling with his associates while a riotous *Tosca* is being performed.

Lillian Lorraine was extremely visible in a bubble bath, singing, in her not altogether pleasing voice—but who cared?—"Nothing But a Bubble." She posed as a Maxfield Parrish *Life* magazine cover girl, had the solo spot with "By the Light of the Silvery Moon," and later in the second act, appeared above the audience's heads in a Wright Brothers model airplane suspended from a circling ceiling monorail, while a group of Anna Held Girls dressed as planes sang "Up, Up, Up, in My Aeroplane."

The production numbers grew more and more elaborate. Forty-eight girls wearing battleship headdresses paraded as the states of the union, then retired behind a screen, pressed some buttons which ignited lights within the ships' portholes, and bobbed about as 48 illuminated battleships floating on the waves of New York Harbor. In the finale, the Polo Grounds appeared, with Lillian Lorraine on a pony, and the cast tossing 500 multi-colored baseballs into the audience.

The *Follies* lasted the summer, then departed for the road.

And now an intriguing situation developed. Although vaudeville prospered and the Hippodrome continued to delight huge audiences with its mega-spectacles—in the 1909–1910 season it was *A Trip to Japan*, which, adding melodrama to the mix, ran for 447 performances—no new reviews were staged. In August, 1909, *The Cohan and Harris Minstrels*, the last traditional minstrel show, opened on Broadway and closed quietly after a disappointing two weeks. It was the end of minstrelsy in New York, although not in the hinterlands.

It seemed as if other producers were waiting, watching a brave and brash showman develop the form he had begun to claim as his own. Ziegfeld delighted in the role and dipped into the twin reservoirs of burlesque and vaudeville for two more stars to light the *Follies of 1910*.

A seamy and second-rate burlesque show titled *College Girls* featured a gangly, not very pretty young girl who, unable to dance, had been fired by George M. Cohan from the chorus of his 1907 show *The Talk of New York*. Irving Berlin, however, caught her act in burlesque, became enchanted with her comic, Yiddish approach to songs (both had grown up on the Lower East Side and knew whereof they sang), and wrote "Sadie Salome," a hilarious sendup of Eva Tanguay for her.

Ziegfeld, at Berlin's urging, caught Fanny Brice's act, hired her for the *1910 Follies*, and comissioned Irving Berlin to write her an equivalent song. The young composer obliged with "Goodbye Becky Cohen," which, along with Will Marion Cook and Joe Jordan's "Lovie Joe," stopped the show cold. Legend has it that Fanny Brice received no fewer than 12 encores on opening night—a great shock to Abe Erlanger, who was less than enchanted by the singing comedienne and, had, in fact, also fired her, in Atlantic City.

Now Ziegfeld had hired her back and, according to her memoirs, as she came offstage after her eighth encore of "Lovie Joe," Erlanger met her in the wings, brandishing a straw hat with a broken rim. "See, I broke this applauding you," he said and handed her the hat, which she kept for the rest of her career.[2]

Later on, audiences' hats went off to the other new personality Ziegfeld introduced, on June 20, 1910, at the Jardin de Paris: Bert Williams. The extraordinary black actor had only recently and involuntarily parted from George Walker, his partner, who succumbed to paresis, the final stage of syphilis. Williams had created a sensation in *Mr. Lode of Coal,* a short-lived minstrel-style musical produced by F. Ray Comstock uptown at the Majestic in November of 1909.

David Belasco, recognizing the dramatic scope of this light skinned black who used blackface to unmistakably identify himself onstage, planned to hire him, marking the first time an African American would appear on Broadway in an otherwise all-white play. Ziegfeld realized what Belasco saw, but he also perceived the rich comic talent that Williams exhibited in the meandering monologues he was given in *Mr. Lode of Coal*. The producer hired him from under Belasco's aristocratic nose, thus adding yet another enemy to one of the longest lists in the business.

Bert Williams, like Fanny Brice, turned out to be a show-stopping star, particularly in a Jean Havez-Harry Von Tilzer tune called "I'll Lend You Everything I've Got Except My Wife." The last line of the lyric, delivered after a pregnant pause, was: "I'll make you a present of her."'

Once again, the score was ostensibly by Harry B. Smith and Gus Edwards, but the interpolators were legion. Aside from the debuts of Fanny Brice and Bert Williams, audiences for the *Follies* were treated to marching girls, led in the opening number by a Dutch band headed by comedians George Bickel and Harry Watson Jr. Lillian Lorraine was dazzlingly in evidence; Julian Mitchell put her on the first of the many swings she inhabited in subsequent *Follies*. In this, the show's inaugural number, she swung her long legs from a flower-bedecked perch and sang "Swing Me High, Swing Me Low," while eight lesser girls dangled behind her and an army of others controlled the swings from below with ropes strung with glittering and jingling bells. For the tired businessman, there was a bathing beauty scene and a brand new, short-lived dance craze, "The Pensacola Mooch."

But the most spectacular effect of all for 1910 audiences was the ability of Ziegfeld to feature not only his mistress, but his wife in the same show at the same time. While the entire cast warbled the Harry B. Smith-Gus Edwards song "Mister Earth and His Comet Love," the upstage curtains parted to show a motion picture of a comet crossing the sky. And there, glowing from the heart of the comet, was the smiling face of Anna Held.

The Follies of 1910 enjoyed a comfortable run into the autumn, and the mere fact that Ziegfeld was able to repeat and improve upon his formula and fill the Jardin de Paris for three summers in a row was not lost upon Broadway's other producers, particularly Klaw and Erlanger's lifelong rivals, the Shubert Brothers. They made a tentative try in the medium in July of 1910 at the Casino with *Up and Down Broadway*, a show that Gerald Bordman has dubbed "a revue that insisted on calling itself a musical comedy."[2]

The plot had to do with a campaign by Apollo and his fellow gods,

The producers: Top l: Jake (J.J.) Shubert appropriately posed; r: Lee Shubert. *(Shubert Archives)*

Center l to r: Irving Berlin with daughter Mary Ellin *(Mary Ellin Barrett)*; Oscar Hammerstein. *(Photofest)*

Below: The Act I gun drill from *Wars of the World* at the Hippodrome (1914). *(Shubert Archives)*

Follies foolery, etc.: Top: Lillian Lorraine and Florenz Ziegfeld, quietly. *(Zeigfeld Club)*

Left: The irrepressible, irresponsible Eva Tanguay. *(Photofest)*

Center right: The "Metropolitan Squawkette" (Trixie Friganza, Eugene Howard, Willie Howard, Ernest Hare) from the 1912 *Passing Show*. *(Shubert Archives)*

Bottom: A dramatic moment in *Stop! Look! Listen!* (1915). *(Courtesy of The Rodgers & Hammerstein Organization)*

Top: In the publisher's office at the 1910 *Follies*: Billie Reeves, Grace Tyson, Fanny Brice. *(Photofest)*

Center left: Leon Errol and Lillian Lorraine in a tangle in the 1912 *Follies*. *(Zeigfeld Club)*

Bottom right: The classy Castles, Irene and Vernon. *(Photofest)*

THE PASS SH

(Shubert Archives)

Above: Vera Maxwell is tempted by Walter Percival and the girls in a street scene from the 1911 *Follies*. *(Photofest)*

Bottom left: Willie Howard in drag as Trilby is about to be hypnotized by brother Eugene as a bumbling Svengali in the 1915 *Passing Show*. *(Shubert Archives)*

Bottom right: Anna Held. *(Ziegfeld Club)*

Top: The showgirls of the 1915 *Follies*. *(Photofest)*

Center: The famous cavalry charge in the 1916 *Passing Show*. *(Shubert Archives)*

Bottom left: Will Rogers and Marilyn Miller in the 1918 *Follies*. *(Courtesy of The Rodgers & Hammerstein Organization)*

Bottom right: Eddie Cantor in the 1923 *Follies*. *(Ziegfeld Club)*

Top: They're off to France in the finale of *Yip-Yip-Yaphank* (1918). *(Courtesy of The Rodgers & Hammerstein Organization)*

Center left: Marion Davies in *Follies* apparel *(Photofest)*; right: The separable Dolly Sisters. *(Ziegfeld Club)*

Bottom: John Steel and Grace Moore sing "An Orange Grove in California" from the 1923 *Music Box Revue*. *(Courtesy of The Rodgers & Hammerstein Organization)*

Top: George White challenges Ziegfeld opulence in his 1921 *Scandals*. *(Ziegfeld Club)*

Center left: Solly Ward, Phil Baker, Ivy Sawyer and Joseph Santley at the ticket agency in the *Music Box Revue of 1923*. *(Courtesy of The Rodgers & Hammerstein Organization)*

Center right: Ann Pennington and her dimpled knees. *(Ziegfeld Club)*

Bottom: Bobby Clark woos Fanny Brice in a Kalmar and Ruby sketch from the 1924 *Music Box Revue*. *(Courtesy of The Rodgers & Hammerstein Organization)*

Top: The fans aren't all in the audience in an uncharacteristically clothed scene from *Artists and Models* (1924). *(Shubert Archives)*

Bottom: Etta Pillard and the ensemble in the Jackie Coogan number from the 1923 *Artists and Models*. *(Shubert Archives)*

Top: Jake Shubert's concept of an artist's studio in the 1925 *Artists and Models*. (*Shubert Archives*)

Center left: the inimitable Ina Claire. (*Photofest*)

Center right: Ziegfeld beauty Dorothy Knapp. (*Ziegfeld Club*)

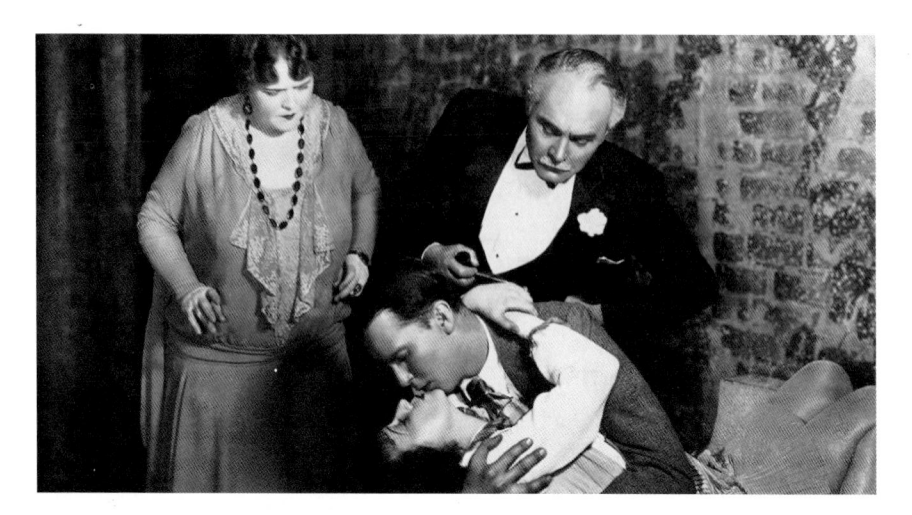

Top: Passion flowers in the *Garrick Gaieties* (1925). *(Courtesy of The Rodgers & Hammerstein Organization)*

Center left: Sterling Holloway sings "Manhattan" to June Cochran and a few other streetcar passengers. *(Courtesy of The Rodgers & Hammerstein Organization)*

Center right: Richard Rodgers and Lorenz Hart as momentary unknowns. *(Courtesy of The Rodgers & Hammerstein Organization)*

Bottom: Youngsters Philip Loeb, Sterling Holloway and Romney Brent as *Garrick Gaieties* musketeers. *(Courtesy of The Rodgers & Hammerstein Organization)*

Top: The unity of place is violated in the Egyptian scene from *A Night in Paris* (1926).
(*Shubert Archives*)

Bottom: It's off to an undesignated jungle in *A Night in Spain* (1927).
(*Shubert Archives*)

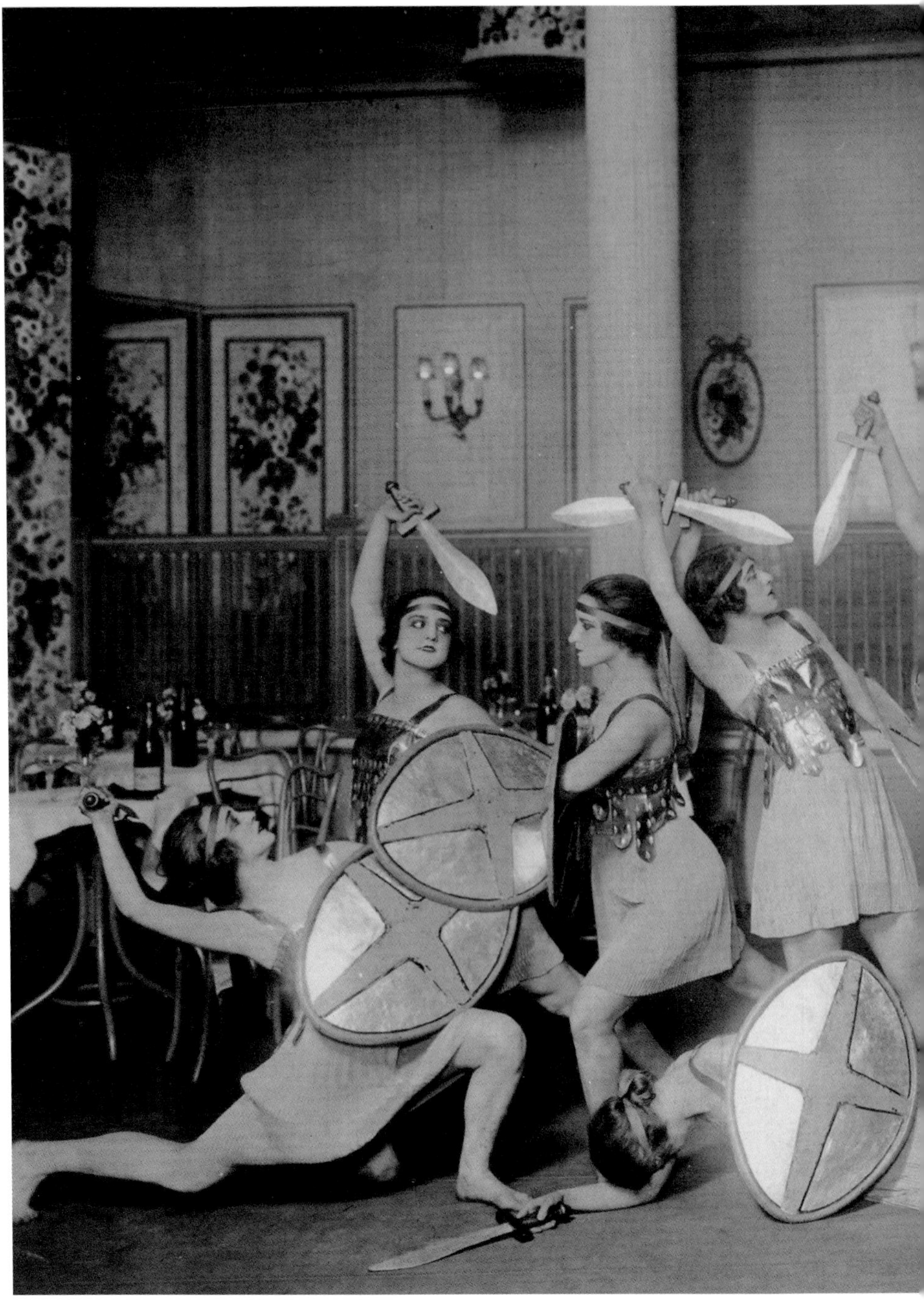

Miss Rolanda's Neo-Classical Dancers give patriotism a boost by depicting the glory of war in the Gladiator Ballet from *Over the Top* (1917). *(Shubert Archives)*

Sophistication makes an entrance to the Broadway revue with the appearance, in *Andre Charlot's Revue of 1924*, of Noel Coward and Gertrude Lawrence. (*Photofest*)

attended by their comic janitor, played by Eddie Foy, to reform contemporary theatrical taste. It was an excuse for a string of musical numbers, illustrating why Broadway should remain as it is. The Shuberts, true to their pugnacious and pilfering form, appropriated Irving Berlin not only to supply interpolations to the main score by Jean Schwartz and William Jerome, but to appear onstage with his vaudeville/variety partner, Ted Snyder. The two not only wrote but performed two up-to-date delights, "Oh, That Beautiful Rag" and "Sweet Italian Love." *Up and Down Broadway* remained at the Casino for the rest of the summer.

But with the return of the regular season, the producers played it safe. Klaw and Erlanger turned their attention to operetta (the importation of *Madame Sherry*), and the Shuberts filled the Hippodrome with *The International Cup, The Ballet of Niagara and the Earthquake*. In November, Oscar Hammerstein leased the New York Theatre from Klaw and Erlanger for Victor Herbert's newest operetta, *Naughty Marietta*. And the Syndicate turned to England to bring in the season's biggest hit, *The Pink Lady*, who reigned at the New Amsterdam for 312 performances.

It would be late in March of 1911, before something approaching another revue opened, and this was a nearly indefinable production, titled *La Belle Paree* and dubbed, rightfully, "a jumble of jollity" by the Shuberts. It was an experiment, as was the theatre in which it appeared. The brand new Winter Garden, located far uptown on Broadway between 50th and 51st Streets, on the site of the old Seventh Avenue horse car barns, was a hybrid, a crossbreeding of a legitimate theatre with an enclosed roof garden. Patrons could eat and drink while the show ran, and usually did, thus moving the atmosphere backward in time in the direction of Tony Pastor's.

The evening began with a one-act pseudo-"Chinese opera," presumably in the interest of legitimacy and culture, then gave over to a succession of acts and songs minus the production values that Ziegfeld had given his revues. In other words, it was expensive vaudeville, featuring the inevitable Mlle. Dazie, Grace Washburn, Florence Tempest, and Marian Sunshine doing a turn titled "Goblins," and Mme. Clarice and the chorus introducing yet another new dance, "The Edinburgh Wriggle."

Still, *La Belle Paree* was an important show for two lasting reasons: first, it contained a larger collection of songs by the young Jerome Kern than any other show so far, and second, it contained the first appearance on Broadway of a young singer who had made his way up from the circus to Dockstader's Minstrels to vaudeville. Al Jolson, in his blackface makeup from Dockstader's, was given a throwaway Jerome Kern-Frank Tours song, "Paris Is a Paradise for Coons," late enough in the show to perform it on opening night before half an audience and few critics.

But those who saw it remembered it, talked about it and wrote about it. Within a few weeks, Jolson and his song were moved up to the number five spot and given a production framework. And Jolson began his 15-year residency at the Winter Garden.

La Belle Paree had some of the trappings of a Ziegfeld show: girls in elaborate and usually pink costumes, opulent sets and strutting showgirls. What it didn't have was the Ziegfeld touch: the distinctive eye of the master, the willingness to spend thousands of dollars upon one scene, to dress his girls in real furs and real diamonds because, as he put it, "it makes them feel like royalty," to outfit a drugstore scene with real French perfume, to have an unerring eye for beauty, a tin ear for music, and hardly any noticeable sense of humor.

No, Ziegfeld had the touch, all right. And all the imitators never quite got it right. Perhaps it was his insatiable love for women that eventually allowed him to truly glorify the American Girl, and to make his life one long series of melodramas. By 1911, he was insanely in love with Lillian Lorraine and would remain so, to one degree or another, for the rest of his life, despite her erratic, irresponsible, often senseless behavior, her multiple marriages to other men, his own two marriages, and his need for all of his adult life to constantly sleep with the best of the beauties he hired.

By 1911, Ziegfeld was important enough for Klaw and Erlanger to allow him to put his name on his annual revue. And so, in 1911, it became, for the first time, *The Ziegfeld Follies*. And it was the most opulent production yet. Harry B. Smith was unavailable, so Ziegfeld turned to George V. Hobart for the sketches and Maurice Levi and Raymond Hubbell for the main score, with interpolations by Jerome Kern and Irving Berlin. As in the previous *Follies*, he introduced new talent, culled from the inexhaustible and constantly refilling reservoir of vaudeville. Bessie McCoy, his old standby, had dipped into six-a-day to bring the Dolly Sisters to Broadway in her 1910 show, *The Echo*, a short-lived effort that featured the only Broadway score by Deems Taylor.

The two sisters, whose real names were Janszieka and Rozsika Deutsch, and who became Jennie and Rosie Dolly in vaudeville (Wodehouse and Bolton vowed that they were also known as Jake and Heim) were born in Budapest and noted for their dancing and their ability to wear unusual costumes. Ziegfeld, on the advice of Bessie McCoy, caught them in *The Echo* and hired them in for their one and only *Follies*, in 1911.

Considerably longer lasting was Leon Errol, an Australian medical-student-turned-comedian who had perfected his droll delivery and rubber-legged gait first in legitimate productions in Australia, then in beer gardens in San Francisco and, finally, in New York burlesque. Erlanger saw him in a long sketch that Errol both wrote and directed, titled "The Lilies," and hired him for a projected musical called *The Primrose Path*. The show collapsed during its planning stages, leaving Erlanger with Errol's unfulfilled contract. Naturally, he put him to work in the 1911 *Follies*, whereupon Ziegfeld teamed him with Bert Williams, and Errol was launched. He would work for Ziegfeld almost annually until 1925.

The third face and form belonged to Vera Maxwell, one of the most stunning beauties ever to grace the *Follies*, and not a bad dancer, either. In fact, this edition, with its abundance of dancing, was an appropriate showcase for her. She and Lillian Lorraine handled the glamorous dancing and singing; the Dolly Sisters poured into one costume to dance as Siamese twins in one number, and Fanny Brice, tearing up a cabaret, supplied the comic dance routines.

Satire ruled the waves in a sendup of HMS Pinafore, titled "HMS Vaudeville" and featuring such seagoing salts as Sir Glassup Pilsener and Capt. Headliner. Klaw and Erlanger's own *The Pink Lady* was satirized in a sketch that featured comic Harry Watson Jr. in drag, and another hit of the season, Walter Browne's serious morality drama *Everywoman* became "Everywife," whose leading lady was matched with Bert Williams as "Nobody."

But the sketch that stopped the show and gained fame as one of the most hilarious revue routines of all time began life as four lines handed to Williams and Errol. The two improvised around them, eventually lengthening the sketch to 22 minutes.

It involved Errol arriving at Grand Central Station in the midst of the construction of the subway connection to the terminal. In order to get to his destination, he's guided higher and ever higher, across a maze of girders, by a tall and taciturn redcap, played with side-splitting understatement by Bert Williams. The two are attached by a safety rope which gets its first test when Errol, doing his customary rubber-legged walk, falls from a girder, to which is attached a sign reading "160-Foot Drop."

Williams pulls the dangling Leon Errol up, but just as he's about to bring him aboard the girder, Errol asks for a match. Williams fumbles for it, loosens his grip, and Errol, with a chromatic yell, disappears again.

Rescued, Errol joins Williams in a trek to a higher level, and in a burst of generosity, reaches into his pocket for a tip and produces— a nickel. Williams stares at it in disbelief, and when Errol inevitably falls again, this time from 288 feet, Williams lets the rope play out, unhooks it from his wrist and tosses Errol's luggage after him. In a grand finale, Errol lands offstage in the middle of a dynamite blast, and Williams describes to the audience his flight through the air, past the Metropolitan Tower, which he reaches for but misses.

Bessie McCoy sang "Be My Little Baby Bumblebee," by Stanley Murphy and Henry Marshall, and the lone Jerome Kern interpolation, "I'm a Crazy Daffydill," which was not one of the master's immortal melodies. Irving Berlin's two contributions went to Bert Williams, one, a dialect piece, "Ephraham," and the other an appeal to once again save Williams from his wife. "Woodman, Woodman, Spare That Tree," he sang, trying to preserve his last hiding place.

The new dance craze was the "Texas Tommy Swing," with Vera Maxwell, Fanny Brice and Lillian Lorraine heading up the Anna Held Girls, who were annually increasing in number.

The edition was a spectacular success, remaining at the Jardin de Paris for 88 performances, then departing for the road, where it again brought in a handsome profit for Klaw, Erlanger and Ziegfeld.

It was obvious that the revue, shaped into what was beginning to resemble a predictable form by Ziegfeld, was on Broadway to stay, and the Shuberts, once they had *Around the World*, their new and biggest extravaganza at the Hippodrome, safely launched, turned their attention to a revue that would challenge the Klaw-Erlanger-Ziegfeld creations.

The only previous challenge during the summer of 1911 had been a "revuette," titled *Hello, Paris*, at Henry Harris and Jesse Lasky's Follies Bergere, a dinner theatre reminiscent of Tony Pastor's. The show had some intriguing staging by a young director named Ned Wayburn, but it was a pallid enterprise otherwise, and barely lasted for a month, after which the Follies Bergere lost its tables and its name and became the Fulton Theatre.

The Shubert's enterprise was another story. They filled their Winter Garden stage on September 27 with *The Revue of Revues* (Broadway's aversion to its French spelling had finally been abandoned). The music was by the up-and-coming Louis A. Hirsch with lyrics by Melville J. Gideon. It was a hopeless hodgepodge whose only real contribution to the American musical or entertainment in general was the American debut of Gaby Deslys, the girlfriend of King Alphonso of Spain, in a dance-sketch in which she portrayed a gaminish, petite Parisian waif, willing to sell everything, including herself, for a chance at stardom. Satire received its due with a Japanese operetta, and the rotund blackfaced comedian Frank Tinney entertained with a series of monologues. The public stayed away in large quantities, and the show shuttered after 55 disastrous performances, to the delight of Ziegfeld.

But the Shuberts were far from discouraged, nor did Ziegfeld feel that he could rest on his accumulating laurels. The Great Glorifier, his reputation growing, involved himself in two book shows in 1912, in concert with Charles Dillingham. Both were successes, due in no small part to the presence of Ziegfeld who, as usual, masked an abundance of nothingness with genuine glamour and tasteful glitz. Although *Over the River* which opened at the Globe on January 8, 1912, was ostensibly based upon *The Man from Mexico*, an 1897 straight play about a man in jail which, itself, borrowed heavily from *Die Fledermaus*, it really was, for all intents and purposes, an amalgam of vaudeville and revue.

Its ads trumpeted "A Real Cabaret on Stage!" in which dances "From Turkey Trot to Tango" were danced. And most of the entertainment did take place in an approximation of Sherry's opulent establishment transferred to the Globe stage. Although John Golden composed the main score, interpolations abounded. Jean Schwartz, in person, played the piano for his "Chop Stick Rag," danced, naturally, in Chinese costumes by Lillian Lorraine and a bevy of beauties. Elsie Janis's "For de Lord's Sake, Play a Waltz" was a big hit, as were the contortionist dances of the Marvelous Millers and the comic antics of Eddie Foy.

The presence of Fritzie Scheff and Geraldine Farrar as patrons in the cabaret on opening night added to the general celebrity atmosphere, and the show ran for a healthy four months.

It was, in fact, a season that favored familiar names. Nostalgia reigned in February at the Broadway with the reuniting of Weber and Fields, in *Hokey-Pokey*. A recreation of the burlesque/variety of the pair's heyday, it brought back Wiliam Collier, Ada Lewis, Bessie Clayton, Fay Templeton and Lillian Russell, who resurrected "Come Down, Ma Evenin' Star" for her now constant escort, a beaming Diamond Jim Brady, who occupied an orchestra seat for most of the three month run.

But the most significant show of the season as far as the history of the Broadway revue is concerned was the second Dillingham-Ziegfeld collaboration, *A Winsome Widow*. Klaw and Erlanger had renamed the New York Theatre the Moulin Rouge and offered it to Ziegfeld for *A Winsome Widow*. Ziegfeld marshaled all of his *Follies* forces for this one: Julian Mitchell was hired to stage it; Raymond Hubbell, probably the busiest Broadway composer of the teens on Broadway, was responsible for the majority of the score; Frank Tinney, the Dolly Sisters and Leon Errol (as Ben Gay, the model for the ointment) headed the cast and a young singer named Mae West, who, at the age of 17, had turned down a chance to be in the *Follies* because she felt that it wasn't "intimate enough" for her particular talents, appeared as La Petite Daffy, a child vamp. She reportedly stopped the show, as did the spectacular Ziegfeld-Mitchell production numbers.

Notable among them were two: a masquerade carnival scene, described by *The New York Times* as "full of glowing color and beauty seldom excelled," and an ice palace scene in which a hundred multi-colored globes flung a rainbow of colors on show girls, skating behind enormous black and lavender windows. Day changed to night as the skater/dancers appeared before the windows, and moonlight suffused not only the stage but the entire theatre, as the skaters spun out into the audience.

It was breathtaking and a monster hit, so big a hit, in fact, that when late spring and the customary date for the new edition of the

Ziegfeld *Follies* arrived, a decision had to be made: the show had outgrown the confines of the New York Theatre roof; closing *A Winsome Widow* in order to free the space and the stars for the *Follies* would be a foolish financial risk. And so Ziegfeld decided to postpone this *Follies* until *A Winsome Widow* had run its profitable course.

It was all the Shubert Brothers needed. They rushed eagerly into the space of time left by the absence of a spring *Follies* by shamelessly appropriating the title of the enormous 1894 success, *The Passing Show*. Its 1912 reincarnation opened, with great fanfare, at the Winter Garden on July 22.

Despite the presence of Ned Wayburn as director and an embarrassment of riches in talent, the first, new *Passing Show* was a pretty pale confection. Borrowing from themselves (and possibly even *The Black Crook*) the Shuberts devoted the entire first act to "The Ballet of 1830 (as played for eight months at the Alhambra Theatre, London)." It was an old-fashioned artists-and-models-in-a-garden concoction with a scenario by Maurice Volney, and it was more pretentious than entertaining.

Act Two was a seven-scene almanac of songs and burlesques of current shows of the season, interspersed with a few political and social comments, augmented by frequent appearances of a chorus line—a *Follies*-type approach, in other words.

The Shuberts assembled a strong cast: Willie and Eugene Howard did their stand-up routine from vaudeville, and Eugene sang "The Ragtime Jockey Man," the Irving Berlin interpolation in an otherwise Louis A. Hirsch score; Shirley Kellogg satirized Bunty in the hit *Bunty Pulls the Strings*, Anna Wheaton became a winsome *Quaker Girl*, Charlotte Greenwoood was Fanny Silly, and Trixie Friganza was Nancy Sykes in a sendup of *Oliver Twist*; Daniel Morris became Mutt and George Moon Jeff in a satire on the hinterland's constant musical versions of the popular comic strip, which had had a brief stay at the Grand Opera House in November of 1911; Willie Howard played *Peter Grimm* in a capsule production directed by David Belasco, who was portrayed by Eugene Howard; Clarence Harvey satirized Andrew Carnegie, and Jobyna Howland was Lady Fluff-Bored 'Un, a sendup of Lady Duff-Gordon, who would eventually design the costumes for the *Follies*.

It was pleasant enough summer soda pop, good enough to play for a solid 136 performances and convince the Shuberts that they had a yearly challenge to the *Follies*, but not enough to discourage Ziegfeld, who had a sign prepared for the lobby of the Moulin Rouge, to wit:

> ZIEGFELD FOLLIES
> Series of 1912
> (Now in preparation)
> Will follow
> A WINSOME WIDOW
> at the
> ZIEGFELD MOULIN ROUGE
> Note: The wonderful chorus now appearing in "A Winsome Widow" is a permanent feature of the Ziegfeld Moulin Rouge and will therefore be prominent in the forthcoming production of
> ZIEGFELD FOLLIES

Ziegfeld had more than the Shuberts to keep him busy in 1912. First, there was the inevitable decision by Anna Held to end their marriage. Concluding a long run out of town with a revival of *Miss Innocence* in the summer of 1912, she filed suit for divorce, naming two specific counts of adultery, one at the Ansonia Hotel (where they had maintained an apartment) on April 1, 1910 with "Mary Ann Brennan," and one on April 2, 1909, on a railroad train in Nevada with "D.E. Jacques." Both co-respondents were, of course, Lillian Lorraine.

And then there was the continuing problem of Lillian Lorraine herself, who, in early 1912 married a rich wastrel by the name of Frederick Gresheimer, unmarried him and married him again, while still sleeping regularly with Ziegfeld and appearing equally as regularly with the producer in public. It all came to a head one summer evening when Gresheimer, coming upon the couple in a posh restaurant, caned Ziegfeld to the floor.

As much as he exercised power over his casts and his opponents, Ziegfeld melted before the women he bedded.0 And particularly Lillian Lorraine. Her antics escalated year by year; she showed up late for rehearsals and shows, drank ever more heavily and seemed to revel in humiliating Ziegfeld in public and private. And he took it, just to be with her.

Still, he was no match for his partner Erlanger, who detested Lillian Lorraine. When, in the out-of-town tryout of the 1912 *Follies*, she failed to appear onstage for the runthrough of "Daddy Has a Sweetheart (and Mother Is Her Name)," a new song by the young team of Dave Stamper and Gene Buck, Erlanger erupted.

"Where's Lorraine?" he shouted at Julian Mitchell.

"In her dressing room, I think," was the reply.

"Tell her she's fired," yelled Erlanger, getting up and jamming his straw hat on his head. "And the number is out of the show."

"But you spent $5,000 on it," reminded the 26-year-old Buck.

"Don't matter," fumed Erlanger, charging up the aisle. "And you're fired, too."

Ziegfeld remained silent throughout the entire scene. Both Lorraine and Buck were dropped from the show. They took the number to Oscar Hammerstein, who put it and Lillian Lorraine into his Olympia vaudeville. It was a huge success, drawing cheers for four solid weeks. Neither Ziegfeld nor Erlanger were fools. They hired both Lillian Lorraine and Gene Buck back.

That was the way it was in the stormy, roller coaster existence of Florenz Ziegfeld and his productions, and the result, on October 21, was the newest edition of the *Follies*. Out of the *sturm und drang* came a true revue, a succession of disparate parts that flowed together into a production that was more opulent, more tasteful, sophisticated and successful than any that had gone before. Harry B. Smith was back for his last collaboration with Ziegfeld, and the music was mostly by Raymond Hubbell.

Now that the Shuberts were in open competition with him, Ziegfeld replied in characteristic style. He stole Bernard Granville, a golden voiced tenor, from the Winter Garden to sing the songs that introduced the girls. And he pushed his production team to experiment with ever new and escalating effects.

"*The Follies of 1912* began in what was then a rather novel fashion," wrote Harry B. Smith in his memoirs. "Before the curtain rose, people in the audience started an argument, the subject of the dispute concerning the kind of entertainment those present expected and preferred. The disputants were actors in the cast placed in various parts of the auditorium. Harry Watson was a gallery god vociferously demanding the sort of show he liked. Charles Judels was a Frenchman who from his orchestra seat decried all American theatricals."[4]

The stars of the 1911 edition were all back and in place: Bert Williams and Leon Errol had a hilarious few moments as, respectively, the driver of a broken down hansom cab and a formally dressed drunk who is about to be taken for a ride, in both senses of the phrase. Topical satire was served in other sketches satirizing *The Pink Lady* and Teddy Roosevelt and William Taft arguing over the income tax, trusts, The Philippines, tariffs and Cuba.

The production numbers increased in opulence as some of the costumes decreased in fabric. The one that drew the deepest gasps was a "Palace of Beauties" in which each showgirl, as a beauty from mythology and history, paraded solemnly and gorgeously across the stage in an individual spotlight, led by a harlequin in nearly sheer black lace. The finale was a "Society Circus Parade" complete with a soaring circus tent, a pony chorus as ponies circling the main ring, and Lillian Lorraine posing in the middle of it all, wearing a black headpiece and a lemon-colored dress topped with a flaming orange cape.

The musical numbers not given to Granville were distributed

among Vera Maxwell, Bert Williams and Lillian Lorraine, who sang the most popular song from the show, an interpolation by William Jerome and Jimmy Monaco for a nautical number titled, appropriately, "Row Row Row."

It was Ziegfeld on his way to his zenith, and audiences and critics were delighted. The 1912 edition remained at the Moulin Rouge for 88 performances then took to the road. Percy Hammond, in Chicago, who had been grudgingly positive in 1911, admitting that "Mr. Ziegfeld in this manifestation of his genius remains supreme as our most expert of frivolous showmen," dropped all pretense and pronounced the 1912 version "The best of the series. By 'best'," he added, catching himself somewhat, "is meant the biggest, cleanest, most colorful, and almost the funniest of the spectacular shows."[5]

The remainder of the regular season contained only four revues that could even begin to rise above the level of vaudeville, which was content to go on succeeding without experimentation. Nostalgia was served by the last of the Weber and Fields burlesques in the new Weber and Fields Music Hall, built by the Shuberts on 44th Street. Besides the two comedians appearing for their final season in slapstick sketches, one of which, "Without the Law," kidded Bayard Veiller's successful thriller *Within the Law*, *Roly Poly* brought back the stars of the turn of the century: Marie Dressler, Bessie Clayton, Hazel Kirke, and Nora Bayes and Jack Norworth. It ran for a mere 60 performances, after which the Shuberts changed the name of the Music Hall to the 44th Street Theatre. It was there, in October of 1913, that Lew Fields presented a sorry try at matching vaudeville to burlesque in *A Glimpse of the Great White Way*. It came and went in 12 performances.

The other two revues were essentially personality pieces. The first, *Broadway to Paris*, was a pleasant enough series of musical numbers built around the slightly scandalous Gertrude Hoffman, who appeared in a series of elaborate but daringly abbreviated costumes and wriggled her way through a ten-week run.

The other, barely qualifying as more than vaudeville, was *Marie Dressler's All Star Gambols*. The All Stars were Ms. Dressler and Jefferson de Angelis, sending up *Camille* and leading a chorus through "The Evolution of Dancing." It closed after eight performances.

The taste of the musical-going audiences still ran to operettas by Gilbert and Sullivan in revival, Victor Herbert, Franz Lehar, Oscar Strauss, Jerome Kern and Ivan Caryll. Apparently, although the door to the Broadway revue had been opened by Ziegfeld, only he and the Shuberts had dared to decisively step through it.

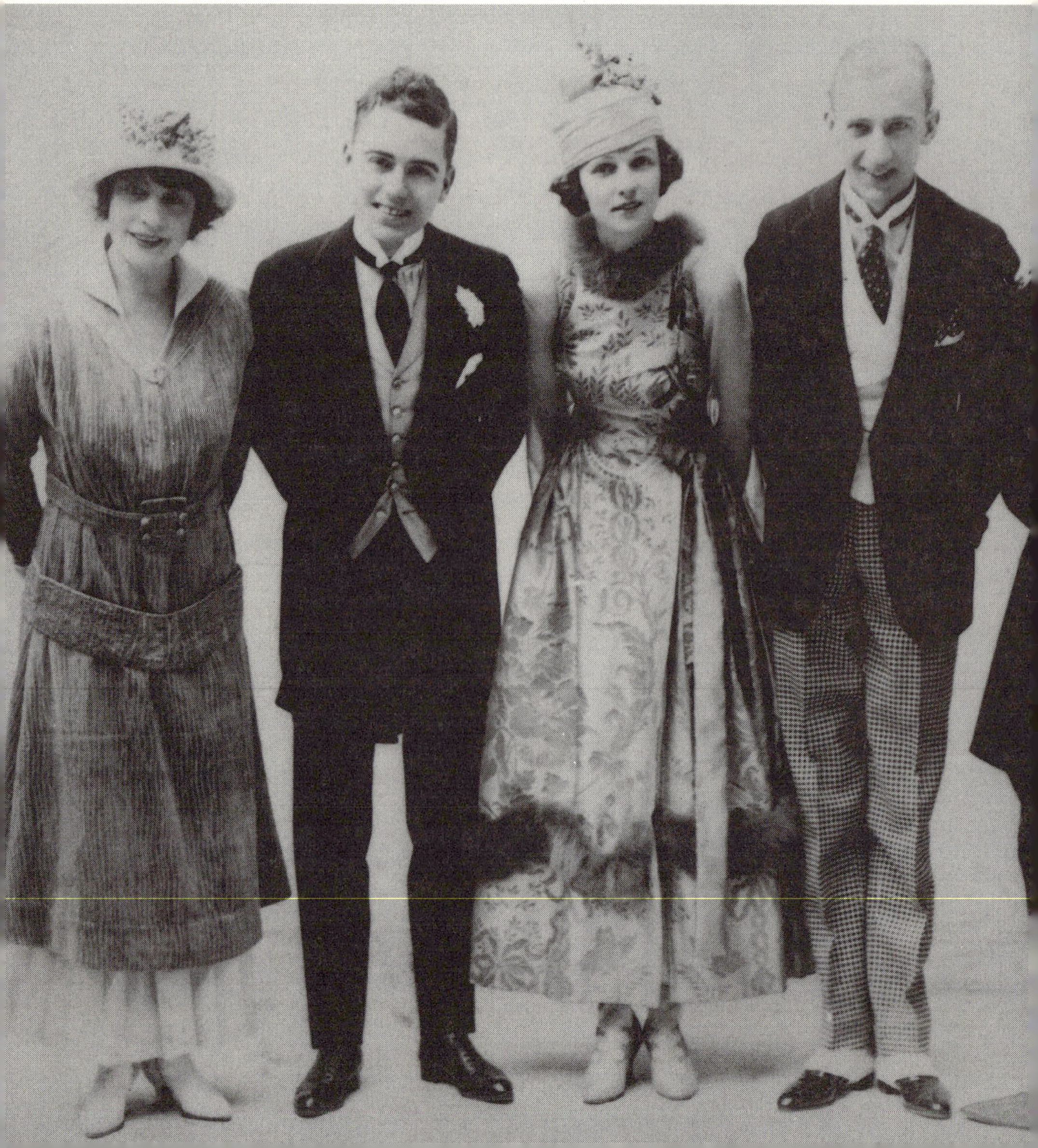

5
Clash of the Titans

Clash of the Titans

～

It was summer again. Time for the dueling producers to mount their warm weather revues. Ziegfeld, back on his customary schedule, was first, and he was determined to bury the Shuberts in splendor. Erlanger, an even more profound enemy of the Shuberts than Ziegfeld, helped by moving this edition of the *Follies* into the sumptuous and exquisite New Amsterdam, where the revues would remain for the next 15 years. It was a far cry from the tin shack on the New York Theatre roof, and Ziegfeld made the most of the move.

Although his continuing antics with Lillian Lorraine had cost him the friendship and the talents of Harry B. Smith, he still had Julian Mitchell and one of the most active—if only minimally talented—Broadway composers of the decade, Raymond Hubbell. This time it was George V. Hobart who supplied the lyrics and a skeleton framework involving Indians peering down at Manhattan from the roof of the Hotel McAlpin and asking the musical question, "New York, What's the Matter with You?"

Nothing, apparently, that some comedy and girls and opulence couldn't cure. And so, the *Ziegfeld Follies of 1913* unfolded, headed by Leon Errol, Frank Tinney, Elizabeth Brice and Nat M. Wills, but minus Bert Williams and Lillian Lorraine, who were spending the year in vaudeville. The new face and form for this Follies belonged to Ann Pennington, a passable dancer and dazzling charmer with long brown hair, flashing eyes and shapely legs that included, as the Ziegfeld publicity machine noted, dimpled knees. Her nickname of Tiny was chosen for logical reasons: she was a mere four-feet-eleven-and-a-half inches tall in the high heels that seemed to be sewn upon her; she weighed 100 pounds and wore a size one-and-a-half shoe.

But she would light up seven *Follies*, *Miss 1917* and the coming *Midnight Frolics*, and, when George White began his *Scandals* in 1919, she would ignite the chorus of his fledgling revues for several seasons.

The resources of the New Amsterdam were as new to Ziegfeld and Mitchell as they were to audiences of the time; it would be two years before Ziegfeld began to adequately utilize them. But Frank Tinney, appearing first in blackface, then joining Leon Errol as a pair of bumbling subway thieves, provided predictable humor. Errol, in one of the show's more popular scenes, joined dancer Stella Chatelaine and, eventually, the entire chorus in a sendup of the current dance craze, the Turkey Trot. Errol's attempts to teach the dance to the cast were constantly inhibited by his pants, which fell down at important moments.

Suffragettes were lampooned in "The Ragtime Suffragette," and the current craze for late dining at Rector's opulent restaurant provided Nat Wills with the only worthwhile song in the Hubbell/Hobart score, "If a Table at Rector's Could Talk." The score was so lacking in quality, in fact, that Ziegfeld brought the young duo of Gene Buck and Dave Stamper in to write three new songs, and he borrowed the already popular "Peg o' My Heart," "A Little Love, a Little Kiss," and "Rebecca of Sunnybrook Farm" from Tin Pan Alley to liven the proceedings. The big and talked-of production number saluted the opening of the Panama Canal with a huge array of beautiful girls in Ziegfeld-style sailor outfits. A passable edition, the *Ziegfeld Follies of 1913* ran a respectable 96 performances before leaving for the road, thus proving that even with the Shuberts opening their second *Passing Show* a mere month after the *Follies* premiered, the crowds didn't diminish. *The Passing Show* borrowed some of the same material that Ziegfeld used at the New Amsterdam, sending up the Turkey Trot, and turning the Peg of "Peg o' My Heart" into the focus of its thread of a plot. In it, the innocent Peg comes to America and falls in love with the far-from-innocent Broadway Jones, and they tour the big town and its multiple production numbers.

Billed in its ads as "A Kaleidoscopic Review of Some of the Past Season's Successes, Topics and Events," *The Passing Show of 1913* dropped the Act One ballet of the 1912 edition and added what would become the innovation of the *Passing Show* series and, later, the staple of American burlesque: the runway.

Actually, the runway that J. J. Shubert installed in the Winter Garden was a variation on an invention of the great German director, Max Reinhardt, who, in *Sumurun*, a wordless nine-tableaux presentation at the Casino in 1912, had convinced a protesting Lee Shubert that the production required the removal of several rows of seats to accommodate an apron built beyond the footlights and around the orchestra.

Jake Shubert's plan was to bring some of his Eighty-Girls-Eighty into closer proximity with the wealthy "Stage Door Johnnies" who occupied the front seats of the orchestra. It was a valid idea that gathered more validity and popularity as the years progressed and the costumes became briefer.

Satirical sketches sent up a large segment of the hits and some of the stars of the 1912–13 Broadway season: *The Sunshine Girl*, *Broadway Jones*, *Oh! Oh! Delphine* and poor old *Within the Law*. Gaby Deslys, Laurette Taylor and Billie Burke came in for their lumps. Charles King, Charlotte Greenwood and John Charles Thomas, making his Broadway debut, sang the songs of Jean Schwartz and Albert W. Brown; Mlle. Anne Dancrey and her company, imported from Paris's *Folies Bergere*, provided an international flair, and the long-and nimble-legged Ms. Greenwood and Bessie Clayton took care of some of the American style specialty dance turns, such as the "Florodora

Slide," the "Good Old-Fashioned Cakewalk," the "Tango Footed Monkey"and "The White House Glide." The last was part of the finale, a Ned Wayburn creation involving the show, pony and chorus girls—one of whom was soon to be the infamously loquacious Texas Guinan—ascending and descending the Capitol Steps in Washington D.C. This *Passing Show* was a profitable success, running for 116 performances before it departed for the road.

And so, the Battle of the Titans was joined. Aside from a throwback production by Lew Fields, titled *A Glimpse of the Great White Way*, which played a disappointing 12 performances in October at the 44th Street Theatre, no other musical producers dared to depart from the comfort of operetta until the very end of 1913.

Then, on December 10, the season's biggest hit, *Jinks*, opened at Hammerstein's Lyric Theatre. Produced by Arthur Hammerstein, the logical talent to challenge the supremacy of the Shuberts and Ziegfeld and Erlanger, it was advertised, not so originally, as a "musical jollity." Its book, by Leo Ditrichsen and Otto Harbach, was merely a framework upon which to hang a succession of vaudeville acts, into which the book now and then intruded. It inhabited, then, a twilight zone between operetta and revue, but the music by Rudolph Friml was a step above the scores so far for either the *Follies* or *The Passing Shows*, and that, plus the Hammerstein touch, kept it alive, first at the Lyric, then the Casino, for 213 performances.

And that, except for a New Year's *All Star Jubilee*, an eight-performance vaudeville produced by John Cort at the Casino and starring Anna Held, was the extent of producers' ventures into the new musical form in 1913.

Hammerstein dared; the other independent producers on Broadway would wait to see if the Titans stumbled. The Shuberts began 1914 with *The Whirl of the World*, a solid Winter Garden revue with some expected veterans and some surprising new stars. Willie and Eugene Howard were back, spoofing grand opera. Walter C. Kelly did some secondary comic turns; Ralph Hertz played an overbearing marquis in Harold Atteridge's semi-book, and—surprising and disturbing to Ziegfeld—Lillian Lorraine and Rosie Dolly, half of the Dolly Sisters, who had been with her sister in the 1911 *Follies*, appeared, doing a furious Maxixe. She was Rose Dolly in the *Follies*; in *Whirl of the World*, she was Rozsika Dolly. But no one, least of all Ziegfeld, was fooled.

The show was billed as "the dernier cri in dance craze," and the Shuberts' new in-house composer, Sigmund Romberg, made his Broadway debut writing castle walks, fox trots, a "Zulu hop" and no less than three rags—"Twentieth Century Rag," "Ragtime Pinafore" and "Ragtime Arabian Nights." It was a far cry from his later operetta waltzes and marches, but he was young and game and untried. The sheer enthusiasm of the show, directed by William J. Wilson, kept it at the Winter Garden for 161 performances.

But again, that was it until the dueling summer revues of the Titans appeared. Ziegfeld was busy becoming married again, this time to Billie Burke, whom he had met on New Year's Eve, 1913, at a party that included Lillian Lorraine and a new beau, Harry and Irene Smith, Lillian Russell and Diamond Jim Brady, and Anna Held. Entirely the opposite in looks, demeanor and brains from Mlle. Held, Billie Burke became his last and enduring and real wife, and the preserver of both the man and his memory.

Over in the Shubert camp, all was chaotic, as usual. If Florenz Ziegfeld's behavior was disreputable and Abe Erlanger's was obnoxious, Jake Shubert's was monstrous. He spent a considerable amount of time in the company of Willie Klein, the Shubert lawyer, settling assault and battery cases with some of the young girls he had slapped around during rehearsals.

That year, he had decked Helen White, a chorus girl who dared to serve him with a summons for breach of contract. A month later, backstage at the Winter Garden, he entered into an argument with Peggy Forbes, a show girl, and also drove her to the floor with two roundhouse punches that left her with a black eye, a cut lip and scratches on one cheek.

This encounter made the newspapers, since she was the great-granddaughter of former President of the United States Zachary Taylor. But, since none of the army of Winter Garden employees, who obviously witnessed the incident, could recall its happening, Klein was able to once again settle the matter out of court.

And so it went in Shubertland. It was possible to believe, in 1914, that the spirit of Bowery variety was still alive.

Meanwhile, back at the New Amsterdam, Ziegfeld was having his own altercation, this time with Julian Mitchell. The dispute was purely professional, but it was important enough for Mitchell to resign from the *Ziegfeld Follies of 1914.* Leon Errol took over the direction of the numbers Mitchell hadn't finished and received program credit for directing the entire production.

Capitalizing on the current dance craze, Ziegfeld included three tangos; one, a jungle production number called "Tangorilla," the second, a repeat of Leon Errol and Stella Chatelaine's encounter with the Turkey Trot in the 1913 edition, this time titled "Because I Can't Tango," and a third, a romp in a Tango Palace, in which Ann Pennington did a wild buck and wing.

The comic chores were handled by two established comedians and one making his *Follies* debut. Leon Errol, because of his other chores, only did the tango, came on in a rubber-legged solo routine and performed in two sketches, one in which he played a golf novice being taught the game by his caddy, played by Bert Williams, and another set on the 1313th floor of a building under construction from which he predictably fell off.

Williams, himself, hit a high point in his career with a masterpiece of pantomime, in which, after singing "Darktown Poker Club," the doleful, mobile-faced performer pantomimed an entire poker game with multiple players.

Ed Wynn, the third comedian, who was a goofy hit in vaudeville, made his *Follies* debut by opening the show as Joe King, the Joke

King. The setting was a version of Hades that contained girl devils wearing very little and Vera Michelena as a singing Satan. Later on, Wynn served as a tango instructor in the Tango Palace sequence, in which Leon Errol, as a drunken pupil, had the chorus staggering and rolling around the floor in imitation of him.

The wacky vaudevillian was an instant hit and never went back to vaudeville; for the next decade, Ziegfeld and the Shuberts would keep him active on Broadway, after which he would take charge of his fame and future.

And now it was time for the Shuberts to mount their yearly challenge to Ziegfeld. Nine days after *The Ziegfeld Follies of 1914* opened, *The Passing Show of 1914* lit the Winter Garden. This time, Romberg was elevated to primary composer, adding his eclectic melodies to Harold Atteridge's lyrics and giving way for four interpolations by Harry Carroll.

There were three debuts in this edition. One was the appearance of a new, slimmed-down showgirl, the logical, modern evolution from the beeftrust Amazon image that the Gaiety Girls first challenged on Broadway. Henceforth, beginning with *The Passing Show of 1914*, both the runway girls at the Winter Garden and the Ziegfeld beauties at the New Amsterdam would present dramatically slimmer silhouettes to the eager male occupants of the first few rows of the orchestra.

Secondly, the movies, a new invention that had become a serious but, because of its silence, a merely moderate challenge to the theatre, came in for several roundhouse sendups. In one, comic George Monroe appeared wearing the long curls of Mary Pickford and singing "Working for the Pictures." In another, the girls did "The Moving Picture Glide." The grand finale, a spectacular recreation of San Francisco, with Chinatown, the Palace Hotel, the Panama Pacific Exposition and even the earthquake, featured a brand new teenage dancer, singer and impersonator making her Broadway debut. Marilynn Miller, flashing her trademark smile and gorgeous legs, tipping up on point as she impersonated Mme. Adelaide Genee, then warbling in different octaves as she did takeoffs on Bessie, McCoy, Fritzi Scheff and Sophie Tucker, established herself immediately as a major musical star, who would, within a very short time, be stolen away by Ziegfeld.

Meanwhile, asserting herself in no uncertain terms, Lillian Lorraine again appeared for the Shuberts, as did Jose Collins. Both were given the major singing chores, while the eighty-member chorus was given plenty of other things to do, such as playing football with the men in the audience, doing yet another dance craze, "The Eagle Rock", with Bernard Granville and Aethel Amorita Kelly, taking off in a mock aeroplane, and marching up a sloping stage into the flies. The flashiest *Passing Show* yet, this edition stayed at the Winter Garden for 133 performances.

Once again, as the regular 1914–1915 season got underway, it became apparent that only the Shuberts and the Ziegfeld-Klaw-Erlanger combine dared to put their production money into revues. The big breakthrough hadn't occurred yet, although it wasn't far off.

In September, while real war rumbled in Europe, the Shuberts presented their last Hippodrome extravaganza, *Wars of the World*. Faced with ambivalence in the public about the entertainment value of war and the ability of the new motion picture to present spectacle beyond even the Hippodrome's abilities, it ran for a disappointing and money-losing (for the Hippodrome shows) 229 performances.

It was time for another producer to enter the Shubert-Ziegfeld-Erlanger fray, and Charles Dillingham was that producer. Dillingham had a long record of responsible and reputable productions but only two solid hits prior to this—Victor Herbert's *Mlle. Modiste* in 1905, and *The Red Mill* in 1906.

Now, in 1914, he brought back Dave Montgomery and Fred Stone, who had made their mark on Broadway in 1903, in *The Wizard of Oz*. The show in which he featured them was a childhood fantasy titled *Chin-Chin,* with a score by Ivan Caryll and lyrics by Anne

Caldwell. It was the hit of the season, and it gave Dillingham the cash and the courage to rent out the New Amsterdam for an audacious, contemporary, ragtime pseudo bookshow that was really a revue (Harry B. Smith's credit in the program was "Book (if any).")

Its name, *Watch Your Step,* was derived from the new rash of street signs that had lately appeared, in concert with the rush of building and movement uptown of a fast-growing New York City. Its composer, getting his first big chance with his first full score, was Irving Berlin, and he was given free rein to power the show with as much ragtime as he could create. This he did, with "The Syncopated Walk," "Metropolitan Nights," "Show Me How to Do the Fox Trot," "Look at Them Doing It!" and the enduring tune and countertune of "Play Me a Simple Melody," in which the past and the present overlayered each other. Nothing could have been more encapsulating of the year.

The cast was headed by the dancing Castles, Vernon and Irene—imported from Paris by Dillingham. The country would never be the same again. With the Castles, the dance craze of the time rose to a frenzy (Vernon Castle kidded it in *Watch Your Step* with "I'm a Dancing Teacher Now," set in one of the ubiquitous dancing schools of the period). And so did ladies' fashions, with Irene Castle's shockingly bobbed hair and her glorious gowns designed by Lucille, Lady Duff-Gordon.

It was dance, dance, dance, even in the names of the book's characters, which included Willie Steele, a Tango Lawyer; Silas Flint, a Maxixe Lawyer; and Estelle, a Hesitating Typewriter. Estelle was played by an imposing, learned, statuesque, blindingly beautiful model for most of the leading photographers of New York, Justine Johnstone. The very next year, she would become one of Ziegfeld's most glorious beauties.

She, however, wasn't the only transfer to the *Follies.* The other never appeared in New York. Dillingham had wired the eccentric and hilarious juggler, W.C. Fields, who was appearing in Australia, to join the show, which Fields did eagerly. But during the Syracuse tryout, prior to Broadway, Fields was dropped. In one of the collisions of fortune and propinquity that make reality fun, Sime Silverman, *Variety's* editor, and Gene Buck, who had joined the Ziegfeld staff as not only a lyricist, but a talent scout, heard the news, encountered Fields in a Syracuse restaurant and signed him for the 1915 *Follies.*

The comic duties of the Dillingham show were assumed by Frank Tinney and Harry Kelly, and the vocal ones by Charles King and Elizabeth Brice. An exciting innovation, *Watch Your Step* filled the New Amsterdam for 175 nights, then went on the road.

It was enough to inspire other giants, and George M. Cohan was inspired. On Christmas Day, 1914, he opened *Hello Broadway,* a pure revue that broke important new ground. As Gerald Bordman notes in his essential study of the American musical, Cohan had the courage to jettison the book entirely. A hat box, supposedly containing the plot, turns up empty. "What became of the plot?" asks one character. "There never was a plot," answers the other.

Since it was a Cohan show, it featured Cohan as star, writer, director, composer and producer; but it also featured William Collier, whose background was in pre-girlie burlesque, Louise Dresser, Peggy Wood and Rozsika Dolly, still dancing without her sister. Like *Watch Your Step*, it had its share of ragtime, including the "Barnum and Bailey Rag," and it declared such shows as *The Merry Widow* and Sousa operettas "all through..." The first-act finale was a tribute to Irving Berlin. But there was standard George M. Cohan material, too, including an "Old Fashioned Cakewalk" and a "Jesse James Glide," and a minstrel treatment of "Down By the Erie Canal" that eventually opened up into a Venetian scene. *Hello Broadway* kept the Globe Theatre occupied for a respectable 123 performances.

In February, the Shuberts were back with a Winter Garden revue, *Maid in America,* which traded upon rising patriotic fervor. Continuing the movement away from even token books, the program listed Harold Atteridge's contribution as "song cues," and Sigmund

Romberg and Harry Carroll's musical ones as "all kinds of music rewritten." As for the sketches, the credits read "Words by the actors and their friends."

The cast was a combination of old and new, including the slightly venerable by now Mlle. Dazie, Nora Bayes, Harry Fox, Hal Forde, Blossom Seeley, Lew Brice, Joe Jackson, Yansci (the other half of the Dolly Sisters), and plenty of chorus girls. It ran for a barely respectable 103 performances.

Not so the formless, if expensively mounted vaudeville that Klaw and Erlanger slapped together with Julian Mitchell for their Knickerbocker Theatre. Calling upon composer Raymond Hubbell, who seemed to be out of work with the Shuberts' abandonment of the Hippodrome shows, and matching him with Glen MacDonagh, who wrote some outlandish sketches, their *Fads and Fancies* collapsed of its own inferiority after 48 performances.

But 1915 was a watershed, a year of development for the American musical. On 39th Street, at the 299-seat Princess Theatre, Jerome Kern, Elizabeth Marbury, Ray Comstock and Guy Bolton were inventing the modern American musical comedy, in which book and music and lyrics would eventually be intertwined in equal importance into one organic creation.

Uptown, at the same time, the Shuberts (who were also part owners of the Princess) would be refining a form that was totally opposite and equally valid. What was termed the best of the *Passing Shows* so far opened on May 29, 1915, at the Winter Garden.

The Shubert stock company was in place, headed by Marilynn Miller, Willie and Eugene Howard, John Charles Thomas, George Monroe and ballerina Maria Baldina. The dance craze of 1915 was the hula; very well, choreographer Jack Mason brought the girls onto the runway in grass skirts which delighted the male patrons down front. Current fads and creations, both on and off Broadway, were lampooned: the Howard Brothers did in *Hamlet* and *Macbeth*, George Du Maurier's novel *Trilby*, Svengali and the Valentino of the stage,

Lou Tellegen, who, in their lexicon, became Lou Telegram. Marilynn Miller made her second *Passing Show* appearance as an endlessly curly Mary Pickford playing opposite Willie Howard as Charlie Chaplin and later dressed in male drag to impersonate Clifton Crawford, another matinee idol, while George Monroe, in various dresses, appeared as Lily, a nymph in search of the Song of Songs.

Extravaganza received its due with Marilynn Miller, Maria Baldina, Theodore Kosloff and a corps de ballet dancing an ode to springtime at the end of Act One, and the entire cast sweating out the "Panama-Pacific Drag" in a homage to the San Francisco Exposition. John Charles Thomas did what he could with the inferior score by Leo Edwards, W. F. Peters and J. Leubrie Hill.

For all its appeal and advancement over past editions, *The Passing Show* could only claim a chronological advantage over *The Ziegfeld Follies of 1915*. 1915 was the year in which the *Follies* reached their rightful majority and began their long run as the elegant, unbeatable best of the big Broadway revues. The magic ingredient that, mixed with the taste and genius of Ziegfeld, brought this about was mostly attributable to the manic temper of Jake Shubert. Arthur Voegtlin, John Wilson and Mannie Klein, the artistic directors/general managers of the Hippodrome under the Shuberts, had felt the wrath and left hook of Jake Shubert and were now working for Ziegfeld. But the two Shubert alumni who proved most valuable to the *Follies* and its creator were Dave Stamper and Gene Buck. Gene Buck would join Channing Pollock and Rennold Wolf in writing the lyrics and the sketches for this and succeeding *Follies*; Dave Stamper would join Louis Hirsch in supplying the music that would continually outclass *The Passing Show*'s thumping scores.

But the crowning, magical ingredient was a decision by Ziegfeld, after repeated encouragement from Gene Buck, to hire Joseph Urban, the great Viennese set designer whose work on Edward Sheldon's 1914 flop *The Garden of Paradise* Ziegfeld had openly admired. The entrance of Joseph Urban to the Broadway revue in

1915 was directly akin to the entrance of Agnes DeMille to the Broadway musical in 1943. It was the last piece in the puzzle, the finishing, absolutely necessary touch that would make it what it ultimately became. Urban's sets gave the revue the verisimilitude its material didn't. By the simple yet difficult device of being given an overall theme of color and design, the revue now seemed to be of a piece, seemed to have a grand and eloquent plan. That plan was also breathtaking in its beauty and its imagination, and, coincidentally, it conformed with Ziegfeld's own personal taste in color. He now had a designer who could translate his preference for white, gold, pink and blue into stage actuality, and from that limited palette, Urban created worlds that seemed to be lit from within, that moved without moving and soared not only to the flies onstage but into the auditorium itself. Blue was the unifying color of the *Ziegfeld Follies of 1915*, and audiences literally gasped in delight as the curtain rose on the opening underwater sequence, in which Kay Laurell, as the Channel Belle (or Aphrodite, depending upon your mythical preferences), swam within rippling, watery blue lights, and which gave way to the "Gates of Elysium" in which enormous gold elephants, their trunks uplifted, spouted real water.

Ziegfeld's stock company was growing, and, to the already established presences of Ann Pennington, Ed Wynn, Mae Murray, Bert Williams, Bernard Granville and Leon Errol, he added W.C. Fields, Ina Claire (who replaced swimming star Annette Kellerman at the last minute) and, as focal points of the Ziegfeld beauties, Olive Thomas and Justine Johnstone.

Ann Pennington paired up with a young dancer named George White—a name Ziegfeld would grow to disdain—as two dancers representing the Navy, and Mae Murray and Carl Randall hoofed on as the Army, in a patriotic pageant that featured Kay Laurell as the Dove of Peace and Justine Johnstone as Columbia.

Ed Wynn played a goofy film director in a comic scene that integrated film into the *Follies*, and was beaned by newcomer W.C. Fields with a billiard cue when Fields perceived that he was stepping on his laughs. The famous billiard scene that followed became a Fields classic. Ina Claire, beautiful and whimsical, did a sendup of a David Belasco production of *Marie Odile* (a number that Irving Berlin advised Ziegfeld to drop in Atlantic City because it was too highbrow; audiences loved it). The hit song of the show was, the legend goes, suggested by Ziegfeld to his composers and lyricists after frustrating telephone calls on the new transcontinental phone system to Billie Burke in San Francisco. "Hello Frisco Hello" was sung by Ina Claire and Bernard Granville before a drop in which various beauties appeared as various cities were named.

And the famous Ziegfeld parade of the 1915 edition consisted of girls appropriately accoutred as seasons of the year.

Leon Errol was seldom seen onstage; Julian Mitchell was back, but Errol was an equal partner as director.

It was a monumental and memorable evening that passed like a dream, which belied the chaos that always permeated the creation of a *Follies*. Revues are built, not written, and Channing Pollock and Rennold Wolf recalled in print in later years the particular madness of this edition. Fifty pounds of jotted notes from Ziegfeld arrived as they began work; daily bombardments of telephone calls and telegrams followed; the two appeared on the first day of rehearsal with 20 sketches and discovered that, upon Ziegfeld's orders, Joseph Urban had designed sets that bore no relationship to their creations. "We wrote a library," Pollack recalled, "and produced a pamphlet."[2]

Still, that pamphlet, expanded and ornamented, became the standard by which all large scale revues would henceforth be measured. Although it chalked up 41 fewer performances in New York than the *Passing Show of 1915*, *The Ziegfeld Follies of 1915* would far outdistance it in both road life and influence.

But this wasn't all that Ziegfeld accomplished in 1915. He set out to not merely bury the Shuberts, but entomb them. He had not only the mainstage of the New Amsterdam at his disposal now, but the enclosed roof garden too. Well-versed in utilizing this type of space, he had experimented in 1914 by fashioning the *Danse de Follies*, an eating, drinking and dancing establishment that opened after the *Follies'* final curtain fell.

It was Gene Buck who suggested that he add entertainment; after all, the space seated 480 on the floor and 280 in the balcony. It could be a source of revenue for after the *Follies* and a space for other shows when the *Follies* wasn't in residence. Ziegfeld agreed, asked Urban to design a series of sets for one end of the room, where the entertainment would take place, and the *Midnight Frolics*, a year round dinner and entertainment venue, was born.

Some of the stars from downstairs would appear in the *Frolics*, but, fundamentally, it would be an entirely different show, with new acts and new music (the first edition, which opened on January 5, 1915, had lyrics by Gene Buck and music by Dave Stamper and Louis Hirsch). Ziegfeld hired Ned Wayburn to stage the first 1915 edition; Leon Errol directed the second, titled "Just Girls," which opened in August of the same year.

It was the *Follies* in miniature and up close; girls and comedians appeared at tables and interacted with those onstage; an elevated glass walkway was fashioned, and 24 Ziegfeld beauties marched on it while wind machines lifted their skirts.

But the most interesting event of the second 1915 edition was the appearance of a young comedian who twirled a lariat and told stories, and who was hired by Gene Buck out of a Shubert hodgepodge called *Hands Up*. Ziegfeld took one look, hated Will Rogers, told Buck to fire him, and went out of town for a week.

Buck went to Rogers with the news, but Rogers's wife had already advised him to add to his lariat twirling some observations about what he read in the papers. He asked for a $50-a-week raise and a second chance. Buck gave both to him with some trepidation.

When Ziegfeld returned, he asked Buck how Rogers had taken the firing. Buck replied that Rogers was still in the *Frolics* and if

Ziegfeld would catch the show that night, he'd see why.

Ziegfeld did, and although he still didn't particularly like the act, it was obvious that the audience did. He raised Rogers's salary to $225 a week, and thus began a long and fruitful friendship.

Meanwhile, downstairs on Broadway, the revue was beginning to rise to, if not equal partnership, at least second billing to operetta. *Hands Up*, the Shubert's latest, a "musico-comico-filmo-melo-drama", minus Will Rogers, but with an E. Ray Goetz and Sigmund Romberg score and an interpolation titled "Esmerelda" by an unknown lyricist/composer named Cole Porter, limped through the summer.

Ned Wayburn, now a rising force as a stager of revues, produced his own, elaborate one titled *Ned Wayburn's Town Topics*. He brought Will Rogers over from the *Frolics* to twirl a lariat and comment upon town and world topics, and featured such established and up and coming stars as Blossom Seeley, Clifton Webb, Bert Leslie and Trixie Friganza. There was the novelty of a revolving stage and a parade of multiple beauties, and it was all mounted with the taste and panache for which Wayburn was justly noted. But despite some clever dialogue and lyrics by Harry B. Smith, Thomas J. Gray and Robert B. Smith, the music by Harold Orlob was singularly undistinguished, and to make matters worse, the very long show (it ran from 8:30 until midnight) was housed at the Century at 63rd Street and Broadway, considerably out of the Broadway orbit (Lee Shubert would eventually buy it and demolish it to make way for an apartment building). It would take a Ziegfeld to make the Century a paying house. And he would. But more of that later. *Town Topics* expired after 68 money-losing performances.

The second successful revue of the season, behind the *Follies*, was the first extravaganza produced by Charle Dillingham, who had taken over the Hippodrome from the Shuberts. Dillingham added class to the carnival atmosphere the size of the place demanded. He fired the resident hack composer, Manuel Klein, and installed his own hack composer, Raymond Hubbell, kept on the Scotch marvel

Richard H. Burnside as dialogue writer, company manager and director, and hired some identifiable talent that, although they could be scarcely seen, much less identified, from the back rows, did add a certain dimension of know-how that had been heretofore missing.

Nat Wills and Al Grady provided old-fashioned humor; there were views of New York by night from the vantage point of the roof top of a skyscraper; Jack and Jill got married; skiers slid down a prop mountainside and made spectacular leaps across a "bottomless chasm;" there was the obligatory patriotic pageant (since World War I was moving ever closer); and to top it all off, John Philip Sousa appeared, in person, with his famous band.

Hip-Hip Hooray, Dillingham's first production at the Hippodrome, was its biggest hit so far—running, matinee and evening, for 425 performances.

The Shuberts offered their Winter Garden revue, *A World of Pleasure*, in October. Still unwilling to do away entirely with a plot, they insisted upon Harold Atteridge's evening-long courtship gimmick to mask the vaudeville. Sigmund Romberg cranked out another insignificant score which utilized up-to-date terminology in its titles ("Girlies Are Out of My Life," "I Could Go Home to a Girlie Like You"), kept ragtime kicking ("The Ragtime Pipe of Pan" and "Ragtime Carnival"), tried to introduce yet another dance craze ("The Jigaree"), stirred the hearts with a patriotic pageant number ("The Greatest Battle Song of All") and resurrected the past ("Reminiscent Rosy-Posy"). The only outstanding moments in the revue were the comic turns of Lou Holtz and the interpolated "Pretty Baby," by Gus Kahn, Tony Jackson and Egbert Van Alstyne. Since *A World of Pleasure* only remained at the Winter Garden for 116 performances, Jake Shubert was able to salvage the song and insert it into his next *Passing Show*.

Not to be outdone, Klaw and Erlanger filled the New Amsterdam with a revue in November. They now had both Julian Mitchell and Joseph Urban in their camp, and they put them to work on a "musical globe trot" titled *Around the Map*. A throwback from the innovations Ziegfeld had introduced only months before in the same theatre, it clung to a silly plot line, threw in meaningless, tuneless tunes by Herman Finck and C.M.S. McLellan, and generally wasted the talents of the up-and-coming Georgia O'Ramey, Mitchell, and Urban, who designed some stunning settings, including the now grossly overused San Francisco Exposition, a Wagnerian Garden, the *Unter den Linden* in Berlin, and a traffic-stopping "Red Hot Stove Cabaret." *Around the Map* stayed in business for 12 performances fewer than those of *A World of Pleasure*.

It would take Charles Dillingham and Irving Berlin to restore revue to its rightful ascending path with their December entry at the Globe, *Stop! Look! Listen!* Once more, traffic signs provided the springboard for a jazzy, up-to-date, imaginative revue that, nevertheless, showed a streak of timidity by including a plot by Harry B. Smith about touring the world to find the right girl to star in a musical show.

It had the bewitchingly gorgeous Justine Johnstone and a brand new beauty named Marion Davies, Harland Dixon and James Doyle to dance the comic dances, Gabby Deslys and Harry Pilcer to perform the ballroom turns, Blossom Seeley to belt out the ragtime uptempos and Joseph Santley to appear as a philanthropist named Van Courtlandt Park.

But most of all, it had the substantial, original and take-homeable music and lyrics of Irving Berlin. From the very first moments, a sequence of rhymed, ragtime dialogue, through the sweeping sophistication of Harry Fox singing "The Girl on the Magazine Cover" to the big production number, staged by R. H. Burnside with six white pianos, to the strains of the immortal "I Love a Piano", it was Berlin's music that gave *Stop! Look! Listen!* its distinctive substance and its feeling that, as one of its song titles stated in no uncertain terms, "Everything in America Is Ragtime Crazy."

So much for the banquet year of 1915. 1916 began with *The Cohan Revue of 1916*, from whose stage the old master was missing, but whose fine hand was present in music, lyrics, sketches and just about everything else. He used his lead character, the bartending evangelist Billy Holliday, from his 1915 hit *Hit-the-Trail-Holliday* in a spoof of *Major Barbara*; burlesqued, in song, Julia Sanderson, Donald Brian and Joseph Cawthorn, the stars of Jerome Kern's *The Girl from Utah* with the clever and tuneful "Julia, Donald and Joe;" and combined a sendup of the popular Cleves Kinhead drama *Common Clay* with a no-holds-barred broadside at "42nd Street's gods, K. and E. and Jake and Lee." Ziegfeld, on the other hand, was treated with affection in the "Ziegfeld Rag." *The Cohan Revue of 1916* delighted audiences and outstayed both Dillingham and Klaw and Erlanger's revues that year.

And that would be it for that season until June, and *The Ziegfeld Follies of 1916.* Ziegfeld and Ned Wayburn had kept the flame burning between productions with a new edition of the *Midnight Frolics* which had opened on January 24, 1916. Featuring the music and lyrics of Gene Buck and Dave Stamper, Will Rogers, the Dolly Sisters (alive and well and together again), Oscar Shaw, Allyn King and Genevieve Warner, it had created a stir with a production number titled "A Girl's Trousseau." In it, a singing underwear salesman displayed life-size drawings of beautiful women in progressively less and less lingerie. As each drawing lit up, a live girl stepped through the illustration, wearing whatever it depicted. Finally, the salesman produced a nude sketch, the lights came up, the music swelled—and Will Rogers stepped through the picture.

Now, with the full-fledged *Follies* approaching and the battle of the revue giants in full force, Ziegfeld hired Wayburn as his full-time—for the next seven years—director. In addition, he engaged Lucille, Lady Duff-Gordon, as his costume designer with orders to use whatever lavish silks and accoutrements she wished, just so long as she made the girls look and feel more elegant and gorgeous than any other girl alive, and on any other producer's stage.

The score for this edition was composed by Dave Stamper, Louis

Hirsch and, for the first time, Jerome Kern, who had begun to become as visible and audible a force on Broadway as Irving Berlin and Victor Herbert.

If there was a unifying theme in the 1916 *Follies*, it was Shakespeare, although after half an act, the bard disappeared under a soft avalanche of roses and chiffon. *Romeo and Juliet* was spoofed; *Antony and Cleopatra* became an excuse for an Urban landscape of desert sands punctuated by an enormous silhouette of the Sphynx; Bert Williams mugged his way through *Othello*; later on, he became a laconic Pancho Villa.

The cast of 118 included practically all of Ziegfeld's expanding stock company. Ann Pennington and Bernard Granville did a hot hula, Ina Claire was back with more parodies, this time of Irene Castle, Geraldine Farrar, and Jane Cowl. Fanny Brice, back from vaudeville, was a loose-limbed Theda Bara, and, in an elaborate number that comprised some of the most famous moments in all of the *Follies*, she dynamited the current Russian ballet craze by doing a truly dying swan, flatfooted. Leon Errol and W.C. Fields were missing, but Will Rogers made the trip downstairs from the *Frolics* and began his long and hilarious run in the *Follies* with pithy observations that skewered the politics and problems of the day and neatly covered the extensive scene changes needed for Urban's gigantic creations.

Ned Wayburn moved the girls through a panoply of panoramas: they danced in a black and white number on electrified mats that shot sparks from their shoes; they dribbled roses from enormous urns; they danced and paraded through the obligatory patriotic number, which this time involved a warship sailing through troubled waters while a dirigible and an airplane circled overhead. The ship sank, a submarine surfaced to take its place, and the audience cheered.

The beauties of the evening were led by Olive Thomas, Marion Davies and Justine Johnstone, who managed to stay regally alone and aloof. Marion Davies would soon succumb to the charms and the power of William Randolph Hearst who, smitten beyond reason, occupied the same orchestra seat every night for eight weeks just to be in her presence.

Olive Thomas had equally grand ambitions. By the end of the run, she and Ziegfeld were as involved as Lillian Lorraine and Ziegfeld had once been, and, like La Lillian, she attempted to publicly control the Great Glorifier. But he had grown since the Lorraine days and nights. He ruled his growing army of girls like a strict father. When, the story goes, during one dress parade, in which Lady Duff-Gordon's creations appeared on the girls and under the lights for the first time, Olive Thomas complained bitterly about her costume to Ziegfeld, who was sitting in the darkness of the auditorium, asserted his hierarchy of behavior in no uncertain terms.

"Ziggy, I hate this dress," she whined. "It's too long Ziggy. The zipper doesn't work. Ziggy, I don't—

"A high pitched, stentorian voice pierced the darkness."Mr. Ziegfeld in the theatre," it said. "Ziggy in bed."[3]

Back at the Winter Garden, Jake Shubert toiled on in his crusade to better the master of the New Amsterdam. But from now on, it would only be a case of catch up. Still, he poured money and talent into *The Passing Show of 1916*, baldly stealing Ed Wynn, who came willingly when Jake dangled a proper amount of money before him. Wynn began the show by criticizing the opening number from a box in the audience, then walking onstage and redirecting the show.

Topicality ruled; there were parodies of Charlie Chaplin, Woodrow Wilson, Charles Evans Hughes, Teddy Roosevelt and, yes, Pancho Villa. And, not to be outdone by Fanny Brice and Ziegfeld, Jake Shubert leaped aboard the Russian ballet wagon by staging "An Olympian Ballet, featuring Thamara Swiskaia and Adolph Bolm." A patriotic pageant featured William Harper as Uncle Sam, and a treadmill, stretching from far upstage to the tip of the apron, allowed a cavalry charge to threaten the first rows of the orchestra.

As usual, Harold Atteridge was responsible for the lyrics;

Sigmund Romberg, with Otto Motzan, turned out yet another undistinguished score. The show's only musical highlights were three interpolations: "So This Is Paris," by Harry Tierney, "Pretty Baby," lifted bodily from *A World of Pleasure* (and just as big a success as it had been the first time around), and "The Making of a Girl" by the very young and very untried George Gershwin.

Both the *Follies* and *The Passing Show* were hugely successful, proving that the formula worked, and the taste for big, girlful revues had grown enough to assure solid success for both producers.

And for Dillingham, too, as he proved in August at the Hippodrome, when, instead of offering pale imitations or parodies of Russian ballet, he presented the real thing in the person of the great Anna Pavlova, dancing a pocket "Sleeping Beauty." *The Big Show*, as the 1916 entry was titled, delivered, with ice skaters, a circus with elephants, and Raymond Hubbell's only lasting standard, with lyrics by John Golden, "Poor Butterfly." The only drawback: it was badly introduced on opening night by a Chinese vaudeville performer, who was hastily replaced when Dillingham realized the enormity of the song's appeal. It became the hit of not only this Hippodrome show, but all others up to Rodgers and Hart's grandiloquent last one, *Jumbo*, in the 1930s. The 1916 edition ran a very healthy 425 performances.

Ziegfeld opened his second 1916 edition of the *Midnight Frolics* on the New Amsterdam roof at the beginning of October, and introduced yet another young comedian named Eddie Cantor. The young man would eventually become the nearest thing to a son that Ziegfeld ever had and, as such, pursued a love-hate relationship with the producer from that moment forward.

The Shuberts, too, were back in October with *The Show of Wonders*, a Winter Garden spectacle with an embarrassment of riches in the onstage talent department and the usual lack of creativity elsewhere. It didn't seem to matter; audiences were in the habit. They loved the extravagant revue and flocked to see Willie and

Eugene Howard's dialect antics and Willie Howard's sendup of Jack Norworth, minstrel veterans McIntyre and Heath in blackface routines, and the comic sensation of the Keith Circuit, Walter C. Kelly, in his hardy and popular turn as the eccentric and bigoted Virginia judge.

And most of all, they came to see the dancing of Marilynn Miller, featured this year in, of all things, a "Burmese Ballet."

But the finest revue of the year besides the *Follies* was a joint effort by Dillingham and Ziegfeld, the two men who, realizing that neither the Shuberts nor Klaw and Erlanger would ever possess the taste to nudge the extravagant Broadway revue into higher achievement, pooled their talents and their resources—and their courage—to present *The Century Girl*.

Ziegfeld brought Joseph Urban, Leon Errol and Julian Mitchell with him, and their presence was clearly felt, especially Urban's. Besides designing 12 giant panels for the lobby whose subject matter was—naturally—female beauty, Urban poured his genius onto the Century stage and emerged with, among much, Grand Central Station, an exotic forest glade bursting with flowers and weeping trees, and Tenniel's drawings for *Alice in Wonderland* at several times life size. But his greatest and most long-lasting creation was the famous Ziegfeld staircase, appearing for the first time in *The Century Girl*. A celestial set of steps that disappeared upward into violet and pink clouds, it formed the setting for a parade of beautiful showgirls, each representing great women of history, descending, while the ravishing Hazel Dawn, as the Twentieth Century Girl, ascended through a trapdoor.

No expense was spared. (Although, to be fair, chorus girls were making $25 a week and showgirls $40, while some of the headliners commanded $1,000 a week. Most of the expense was poured into the sumptuous sets and costumes and the multiple $15,000 props they utilized.)

The cast, besides Errol, featured Elsie Janis, Gus Van and Joe

Schenck, Vera Maxwell, Harry Kelly, Frank Tinney and Lilyan Tashman. Dillingham added Edward Royce to the production team and Lucille, Lady Duff-Gordon, as the designer of costumes. And since Ziegfeld's tin ear rivaled that of Jake Shubert's, it was probably Dillingham who decreed that the music should be composed by Victor Herbert and Irving Berlin, a combination not exactly made in heaven.

The two were represented in an argument of styles onstage by Arthur Cunningham portraying Herbert, and John Slavin playing Berlin, but their joint output of music was of no great note. Nothing survived except perhaps the historical curiosity of a Berlin tune included in the show at the last minute and written especially for another, different sort of production enterprise by Ziegfeld. The song was titled "You've Got Your Mother's Big Blue Eyes," and it was dedicated to Florenz Patricia Ziegfeld, the new daughter of Ziegfeld and Billie Burke.

Both projects were successful; Patricia momentarily distracted Ziegfeld from his philandering ways and *The Century Girl*, running for 200 performances, proved that, given the right kind of show, audiences would gladly venture north of Times Square.

With *The Century Girl*, it seemed as if the form of the Broadway revue was cemented in place: comics, satirical sketches, lavish production numbers, huge casts and armies of beautiful girls. But nothing endures forever, particularly in show business, and the cement would be scarcely dry before a profound and reverberating happening far beyond Broadway would modify what had just been solidified.

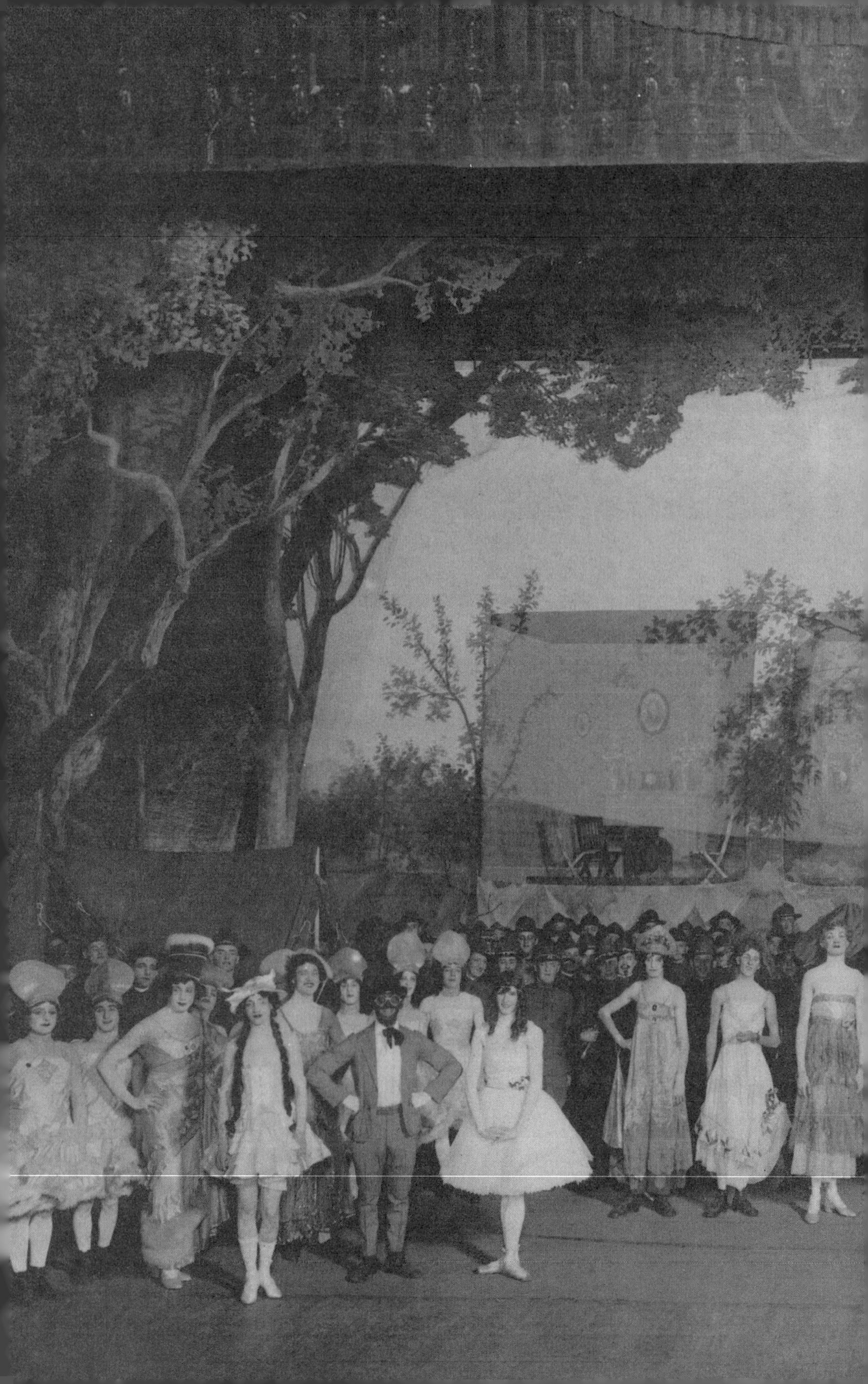

6

The Real War

The Real War

❦

For at least a decade, Broadway revues had featured, with increasing frequency, patriotic numbers. Now, in 1917, the subject matter gained solidity. Even Broadway was not immune to World War I. Possibly the only other producer who might have challenged the proprietary hold that the Shuberts, Dillingham, Ziegfeld and, at times, Cohan and Harris had on revues had been one of the first show business casualties of the war. In 1915, Charles Frohman had gone down with the *Lusitania*, sunk by a German U-Boat as it headed from New York to England.

Now, young men who played on Broadway on Saturday night were in uniform by the following Tuesday. And the entertainment that would follow them near the battlefields had to be, out of necessity, considerably smaller than the shows they left. And so the intimate revue was born.

But it would be a while before it came back home. Meanwhile, the grand revue, whose survival would not be threatened one bit by the coming of its smaller cousin, thrived, as entertainment and big business always thrive in wartime.

Sensing the dollars aching to be spent by audiences enjoying a boomtime economy, the Shuberts decided to mount a second *Passing Show* in April, just in case the war ended before the summer.

It wasn't much of an edition. Sigmund Romberg and Otto Motzan, with some help from the lyrics of Harold Atteridge, ground out yet another forgettable score.

The cast included the imposing Irene Franklin, the venerable, by now, Jefferson de Angelis and DeWolf Hopper, and the new, rough and tumble comedians Chic Sale and Ray Dooley. Chic Sale's cracker-barrel monologues, an obvious challenge to Will Rogers, caught on, and he became a Shubert staple.

By 1917, costumes had become less of a hindrance to the appreciation of the bodies of the girls on the runway, and, led by Wanda Lyon, they bounced and cartwheeled around as football fans in "College Boys, Dear," a production number recreation of a Harvard-Yale football game. The dance craze number busied itself with what couldn't really have been the latest step of 1917, "That Peech-a Reeno, Phil-i-Peeno Dance." In another production number, the girls emerged as tables, set for two.

There was flag waving aplenty, including "America's Fighting Jack," marched by 60 uniformed chorus girls, a stirring finale titled "Ring Out Liberty," and the only lasting song from the score, an interpolation by C. Francis Reisner, Benny Davis and Billy Bashette with the spirited title, "Goodbye Broadway, Hello France!"

It all added up to popular entertainment, reflective of the times as all revues were and would be, and audiences filled the Winter Garden for 196 performances—only four less than the far more tasteful, tuneful and substantial *Century Girl*.

In June, Raymond Hitchcock, the lanky, raspy-voiced comedian who, from the turn of the century forward, had made a meaningful name for himself as the star of a string of book musicals, decided that, as he told one newspaper reporter, "...restlessness of American life has brought a demand for speed and the quality best described as 'Zippiness' in stage productions, and the revue is the type of entertainment in which these qualities are best expressed."[1]

The result was the first of a series of Hitchcock revues, titled, in the babytalk parlance of 1917, *Hitchy-Koo*. Devoid of the huge amounts of money that Dillingham, the Shuberts and Ziegfeld were pouring recklessly into their productions, he produced scaled down imitations of the masters that were, by the force of his own personality and the presence of Leon Errol and Julian Mitchell to stage them, comfortably popular. None were nearly so successful as the first, which opened on June 7 and played for 220 performances.

Leon Errol appeared, doing his trademark, rubber-legged drunk scene, Irene Bordoni sang naughtily, sketches poked fun at contemporary figures like Billy Sunday, who was identified as "the P.T. Barnum of the hymnbook," and gaggles of girls paraded, in one scene, out of the pages of wedding albums of bygone Junes. The score, by E. Ray Goetz (who was also Hitchock's co-producer), Harry Grattan, Glen MacDonagh and Goetz, was singularly undistinguished, and two interpolations were the only memorable songs of the evening: "M-I-S-S-I-S-S-I-P-P-I," with music by Harry Tierney, was the novelty hit, and Lew Brown and Albert Von Tilzer's "I May Be Gone for a Long, Long Time," struck a responsive contemporary and patrioic chord.

Five nights after *Hitchy-Koo* opened, *The Ziegfeld Follies of 1917* arrived at the New Amsterdam. It was yet another example of the continuing ascension of the master of tasteful excess. Joseph Urban dazzled anew with nightscapes of New York, one of which was framed in flower-dripping urns; another featured three sets of red and gold ladders, lit from within, and climbed, over and over and rhythmically, by 50 girls in Chinese dress.

The expected flower number involved Edith Hallor sprinkling seeds on the stage after which showgirls in full flower appeared through trapdoors, and after that the stage changed into a glittering sky, lit by the reflection of glowing beads—actually horse pills painted silver—and against which Allyn King and Eleanor Long appeared in two gigantic bubbles.

The famous Ziegfeld stock company was assembling and was in full force in this edition. Will Rogers joked about the Senate; W.C. Fields embellished his pool-playing routine; Fanny Brice was the centerpiece of a Middle-Eastern number in which she portrayed an exotic dancer named Rebecca who was "Egyptian in everything but her nose" and Bert Williams delivered his understated monologues. And two new comedians joined the ranks: Walter Catlett, who originated, through his homespun delivery, the saying "Hot diggety dog!" and, from the *Frolics* upstairs, Eddie Cantor, making his debut in blackface, singing "That's the Kind of Baby for Me," an interpolation by Alfred Harrison and Jack Eagen.

There were other new faces: the dancing duo of Dorothy Dickson and Carl Hyson, direct from *Oh, Boy!*, the Bolton and Wodehouse and Kern musical at the Princess, did a dazzling turn, and the exquisite beauty, Dolores, made her first *Follies* appearance.

The main score, by the indefatigable team of Raymond Hubbell and Dave Stamper, was serviceable and made way for some major interpolations, one by Jerome Kern ("Because You're Just You") and one with interesting punctuation by Ring Lardner ("Home, Sweet, Home"). But the most obvious and credited musical addition was the patriotic Act One finale, complete with a Ben Ali Haggin tableau of Paul Revere on a treadmill (Haggin's *Follies* debut, also), the "Star Spangled Banner" and advancing battleships. Victor Herbert supplied the music, which was never played again.

It was Ziegfeld at his best, and in the midst of his best years, and it would play for the rest of the summer and into the fall, its only true competition Sigmund Romberg's sentimental operetta *Maytime*, which was the runaway hit of the season.

In August, Charles Dillingham opened his customary Hippodrome extravaganza, this time a patriotic exercise with the cautionary title *Cheer Up*. The musically ambidextrous Raymond Hubbell supplied the music to John Golden's lyrics, and a gigantic cast made way for diving horses, cornfields transformed into poppy fields, and an astonishingly realistic locomotive, complete with hoboes. It was one of the Hippodrome's most successful extravaganzas, running a record 456 performances.

The Shuberts climbed aboard the patriotic bandwagon in October of 1917, with *Doing Our Bit* which dressed up Ed Wynn, Frank Tinney, scores of girls and the Winter Garden in khaki. It, and its forgettable Romberg score, survived a bombardment by the critics, but the audiences came anyway, a profit-making 130 times.

Better taste was expected of Dillingham and Ziegfeld's next big revue at the Century. Utilizing the same production team as they had for the phenomenally successful *The Century Girl*, with the substitution of Jerome Kern for Irving Berlin and the retention of Victor Herbert as co-composer of the score, and the addition of Guy Bolton and P.G. Wodehouse—who were fast becoming the most sought after libretto writers on Broadway—to write the sketches, the two producers set out to better themselves. With Joseph Urban designing the sets and Ned Wayburn as director, *Miss 1917* was sure to be a monster hit.

Its cast would dwarf that of any revue so far, including the *Follies*. Its headliners would include Lew Fields, Andrew Tombes, Vivienne Segal, Harry Kelly, Elizabeth Brice, Charles King, Bessie McCoy Davis, Gus Van and Joe Schenck, Irene Castle, Bert Savoy and Lew Fields's son, Herbert.

The dancing feet of Ann Pennington and George White would head up the specialty numbers; the beautiful girls department would star Marion Davies, Vera Maxwell, Peggy Hopkins (later Peggy Hopkins Joyce) and Dolores (listed in the program as "Mlle. Dolores").

But perhaps its size and ambitions were the culprits that caused chaos from the beginning of rehearsals to the opening night curtain. "It was a little like threading an elephant through the eye of a needle," observed Bolton and Wodehouse, recalling the tumult that included the following, titanic confrontation between two massive egos:

At the end of a long sequence which began outside a stage door, melted into an Urban landscape of memory, supported by Kern and Wodehouse's exquisite "Land Where the Good Songs Go," and featured the superannuated entertainers delivering their signature songs, the young and relatively untried Vivienne Segal was to sing a song. Kern wanted her to do "They Didn't Believe Me;" Herbert wanted

"Kiss Me Again."

Ms. Siegel blanched as the two composers argued. Finally, Herbert turned to her and said, "Take both songs home. Come back tomorrow, and decide."

The eighteen-year old singer went to Charles Dillingham for shelter and advice. "Stick by your guns," he said, "and I'll stick by you."

She picked the Herbert melody, and, when the spot arrived in the following day's rehearsal, she began "Kiss Me Again."

Kern, furious and red-faced, stopped her. She explained that "Kiss Me Again" was more in her key than "They Didn't Believe Me."

"What do you know? You're just a singer!" he shouted.

"But Mr. Dillingham—"

"What does he know? He's just a producer!" was the rejoinder, and now the rumbling presence of Victor Herbert, lumbering down the aisle, complicated matters.

Dillingham, ever the conciliator, tried to mediate, but the feisty Kern was like a fighting rooster, determined to scratch on to the bitter end.

Finally, his patience exhausted, Dillingham decreed that Ms. Siegel would sing "Kiss Me Again." Kern stormed out of the theatre, vowing to take his music and his person out of the show.[2]

It was a one day emigration, but indicative of the way things were going with *Miss 1917*. When the show finally opened, on November 5, it was a staggering four hours long. Much of this gargantuan length resulted from a string of spectacular numbers in the mold of "The Land Where the Good Songs Go" extravaganza which, as the stage door flew out, featured Marion Davies singing *The Belle of New York's* "Follow On," Cleo Mayfield and a chorus swaying to "In the Good Old Summertime," Cecil Lean, Emma Haig and Yvonne Shelton following with "Dinah," Van and Schenck gamboling through "Under the Bamboo Tree," Bessie McCoy Davis and 12 girls warbling "The Yama Yama Man," a swan curtain descending before which Harry Kelly sang "Sammy," and Vivienne Segal, as Fritzi Scheff, singing "Kiss Me Again."

144 ∞ Scandals and Follies

At this point, the curtains parted to reveal a Ziegfeld-Urban staircase, upon which all of the principals and several score dancers strutted to Herbert's "March of the Toys" and Kern's "Toy Clog Dance." Borrowing from himself, Ned Wayburn then had the company disappear heavenward.

It was enough to bring cheers from critics and audiences alike, and it did. But, for one of the odd non-reasons that makes theatre the business it is, ticket-buyers stayed away; Miss 1917 collapsed, a gigantic loss, after 48 performances.

Before November, the season would see a revue of an entirely different character. A mixed grill, barely above vaudeville, Odds and Ends of 1917 was nevertheless one of the first full-fledged attempts on Broadway at an "intimate" revue. Jack Norworth, one of its producers, described it as "chummy," and that it was, much like an old time burlesque performed by friends for friends. Its cast consisted of relative unknowns, headed by Norworth and, in what turned out to be a sad comedown, Lillian Lorraine. The music and lyrics, by Bide Dudley, John Godfrey and James Byrnes, were as undistinguished as the show. But boomtimes and a novelty appeal kept the show in the tiny Bijou for 112 performances and a profit.

December brought two major, extravagant revues. The first, Over the Top, was a Shubert creation designed for the 44th Street Roof, and for the talents and beauty of Justine Johnstone. Ms. Johnstone's position on the marquee seems to be an odd sort of star billing, until the backstage details emerge.

Lee Shubert was, to put it plainly, besotted with Justine Johnstone. He had seen her from afar; now he wanted her up close and personal, and in his own show. The not quite twenty but eons wise Ms. Johnstone was not about to turn down star billing for herself and her Justine Johnstone Girls, and so she acquiesced. Up to a point. That point apparently was reached one evening when Shubert, in an avalanche of honesty and bad taste, reached across a table, took her hand and advised her to get out of the business, because, he said fervently, she lacked the one abiding quality necessary for success in show business.

"What is it you think I lack, Lee?" she asked.

"Greed," he said softly, then went on with rising emphasis. "It's what makes some people successful. It's what makes some actors stars, and the rest just actors. You have to want something more than anyone else wants it. You have to want it so much, you can taste it. You have to feel greed!"[3]

Shortly after this, Justine Johnstone stopped seeing Lee Shubert and married Walter Wanger.

Over the Top, which also featured the Broadway debut of Fred and Adele Astaire, flounced back and forth between frilly, feminine confections and scenes in the trenches, all of it set to another insignificant Sigmund Romberg score. It expired after 78 performances.

A worse fate awaited *Words and Music,* a Raymond Hitchcock-E. Ray Goetz pastiche staged by Leon Errol and featuring Marion Davies, Elizabeth Brice, the Dooleys and Richard Carle, the tall comedian who spoke through his adenoids and navigated a running gag that forced him to break a lot of crockery throughout the entire revue. It lasted for an embarrassing 24 performances.

And now, as war raged in France, 1918 dawned on Broadway, beginning on an elevated series of notes supplied by Irving Berlin and George M. Cohan for *The Cohan Revue of 1918.* The show actually opened at the New Amsterdam on New Year's Eve and advertised itself as "a hit and run play batted out by George M. Cohan." Despite its promises, it was, critics agreed, a mostly tired affair, enlivened somewhat by a delightful sendup called "Polly of the Follies." Two tunes, one by Cohan titled "When Ziegfeld's Follies Hit the Town" and one by Cohan and Berlin, "Polly, Pretty Polly with a Past," united the *Follies* with Belasco and his hit production of Guy Bolton's *Polly with a Past,* starring Ina Claire in her first major dramatic role.

Ms. Claire, herself, came in for further spoofing by Nora Bayes, who also did—or, rather, did in—Florence Reed and, as was her custom, insisted on singing interpolations by her own stable of composers and lyricists, in this case Ed Moran, James Brockman, Grant Clarke and Cliff Hess. Charles Winninger added his own mimicry, and the whole creation limped along for 96 performances and lost Cohan and Harris a moderate amount of money.

Let's Go was a suitable, if inaccurate title for the second revue of 1918. Although it only remained for a merciful 25 performances at the Fulton, this creation, advertised as "a costless, castless, careless revue," nevertheless promulgated the concept of the intimate version of the genre, which gained "legs," as they say in the corporate world, in May with another intimate cross between vaudeville and revue, staged by and featuring sailors from the Pelham Naval Training Station. A 16 performance resident of the Century Theatre, it was the first of a number of service revues that, because of the necessity of mobility, were also forced to be small. This, merged with the experimentation of Jack Norworth in his *Odds and Ends of 1917*, and, most particularly, the now established success of the small, revolutionary book musicals that had begun at the Princess in 1915 with *Nobody Home* and would end in 1918 with *Oh, Lady! Lady!!*, would finally set, in as much concrete as show business allows, the long lived form of the intimate revue.

The pocket revue was also given justification by the production necessities brought about by the war, just as the Princess shows came about because of the necessities of working with a small budget and a 299-seat theatre.

In 1918, and for decades to come, however, there would be room on Broadway for both big and small revues, both of which were on the verge of muscling onto equal footing with book shows in the musical world of the Twenties, Thirties and Forties.

June brought *Hitchy-Koo of 1918*, with Leon Errol directing and starring, and Raymond Hubbell and Glen MacDonagh supplying yet another evening of forgettable music. The second of Raymond Hitchcock's answers to Dillingham and Ziegfeld was a promise that failed to deliver. "Drammed jammed with hokum and jazz" said the advance material, and hokum there was, but the only jazz was contained in two interpolations, "Jazz-Ma-Tazz" by Ned Wayburn, and slightly, "You-oo Just You" by George Gershwin and Irving Caesar. The rest was a combination of nostalgia (Hubbell's "Lily of Longacre Square") and patriotism (Ned Wayburn and Harold Orlob's "Here Come the Yanks with the Tanks"), delivered by a game cast that included Hitchcock, Errol, Irene Bordoni and Ray Dooley. It occupied the Globe for a disappointing 68 performances—not even an entire summer.

Everything brightened on June 18, with the arrival at the New Amsterdam of *The Ziegfeld Follies of 1918.* All of the usual comics except Fanny Brice, who, nevertheless, appeared upstairs in the *Frolics*, were present. Eddie Cantor abandoned his blackface for the first time to appear as an army enlistee and a store clerk. Joe Frisco came downstairs from the *Frolics* and delivered a cigar-chewing monologue. W.C. Fields abandoned his pool cue for an equally tortured and creatively bent golf club. And Will Rogers had plenty of world affairs upon which to comment.

The Urban sets had a wartime, international dimension this time: the show opened with an enormous revolving globe with Kay Laurell as the "Spirit of the Follies," draped provocatively over the Arctic and parts of North America. Beneath her, Europe burned, and the Folly of Dance, the Folly of Fame, and other immaterial symbols danced on.

Lillian Lorraine, making her final *Follies* appearance, was in evidence in most of the big numbers, including an Urban masterwork, "The Garden of Your Dreams," with music and lyrics by Louis A. Hirsch and Gene Buck. The garden was shaped in the form of a stage-consuming Japanese bowl containing oversized bonsai, a bridge, and Ms. Lorraine in a kimono. She was a centerpiece star while 32 lesser stars paraded up and down the staircase; she sang "When I'm Looking at You" while the Fairbanks Twins did a mirror dance in a boudoir. She was most in evidence, however, in a patriotic pageant with interpolated music and lyrics by Irving Berlin. The production number began with Berlin's "I'm Gonna Pin My Medal on the Girl I Left Behind," then segued to a depiction of the Blue Devils, a French military unit. Lillian Lorraine was their leader, and, once the show had opened, she delighted in blacking some of her teeth and flashing her glowing and incomplete smile at important moments. Ziegfeld saw this one night and broke precedent by charging backstage and loudly berating her in front of the rest of the cast.[4]

Ann Pennington was on hand as usual to flash her dimpled knees in the dance numbers, but this year she was overshadowed by a Ziegfeld triumph: the stealing, from the Shuberts, of Marilynn Miller, who wowed audiences, as she would for all of her short career, this time in a silver ballet.

The Follies of 1918 ran into October at the New Amsterdam, then transferred to the Globe, where it remained through the Armistice.

In 1918, the Shuberts' *Passing Show* didn't appear until the end of July. The brothers were justifiably furious at Ziegfeld and Marilynn Miller. Confident that they had her under an ironclad contract, they were outsmarted by her attorney, who discovered that when the Shuberts had imported the Columbian Trio, of which she was one-third, to play the Winter Garden, she had been underage. The contract was nullified by a court decision; Ms. Miller went into the *Follies*, and the Shuberts went into a tantrum.

In retaliation, they poured a major amount of energy into their 1918 large scale revue, which featured their own stock company of Willie and Eugene Howard and the rising stars of Fred and Adele Astaire, whose lithe forms were hidden within chicken outfits for a big Birdland production number.

Lew Clayton and Frank Fay were on hand for further comic routines; the Sigmund Romberg-Jean Schwartz score included a variety of dances, including "The Galli-Curci Rag," "Trombone Jazz" and a double act, "The Shimmy Sisters" dancing the newest craze. Ironically, the times and national sentiment dictated the show's biggest and only hit song, the J. Will Calahan-Lee J. Roberts interpolation, "Smiles."

At the beginning of August, a "musical mess cooked up by the boys of Camp Upton with words and music by Sergeant Irving Berlin" found its way to Broadway. *Yip-Yip-Yaphank* was a necessarily intimate revue that clicked because of the know-how and genius of its creator. Richly satirical (it included a visit of the *Follies* to Camp Upton), it also had a ring of truth about its depictions of Army life in a basic training camp. Lightweight boxing champion Benny Leonard, a draftee like Berlin stationed at Camp Upton, gave a boxing demonstration, and the most realistic and lasting song from the score turned out to be the centerpiece of one of its simplest scenes: "Oh, How I Hate to Get Up in the Morning," sung plaintively, in his own high and distinctive voice, by the composer, sitting on a cot in an open tent, drew wild applause at every performance.

The demands of war ("We're Off to France" was the show's finale) forced the popular show to depart from the Century Theatre after a mere 32 performances, but Ziegfeld bought "Oh, How I Hate to Get Up in the Morning" for the *Follies*, and installed it immediately into the 1918 edition, where it became its only hit song.

It would be the end of December, after the Armistice, before another revue opened on Broadway, and it, too, was a soldier revue, this time imported from the Aberdeen Proving Grounds in Maryland. Frank Tinney, who had served at Aberdeen as a captain, headed a group of soldiers in *Atta Boy*, which followed the format of *Yip-Yip-Yaphank*. It was sincere and authentic, but the war was over, and *Atta Boy*, whose soldiers were no longer waiting to be shipped to France, left the Lexington Theatre after 24 performances for monetary, not military, reasons.

With wartime restrictions at an end, the Shuberts decided to celebrate with an extravaganza. It was a throwback, a whisp of a book as an excuse for a succession of desiccated vaudeville turns. *Monte Cristo, Jr.*, with music by Sigmund Romberg and Jean Schwartz, and a book and lyrics by Harold Atteridge, boasted familiar vaudeville faces such as Charles Purcell, Adelaide and Hughes, the Watson Sisters, Esther Walker and, as its star, Chic Sale. Audiences, evidently ready for bloated bushwa, kept the Winter Garden active for 254 performances.

150 ⇜ *Scandals and Follies*

In direct contrast, and promulgating the emergence of the pocket revue, *Toot Sweet*, the latest example of the species, produced by and starring Will Morrissey, opened on May 5. Its heart and its venue were right: Morrissey chose the Princess Theatre, whose 299-seat capacity had necessitated the beginnings of true modern American musical comedy in 1915. The problem with *Toot Sweet* wasn't in its form, but in its subject matter. The public had apparently had its fill of war, at least for the time being, and this pleasant enough concoction of doughboy-oriented and represented sketches and musical numbers, supported by Richard Whiting's first major score and some wartime but okay lyrics by Raymond B. Egan didn't catch on. The combination of forward-looking ideas and backward-looking subject matter made it history after 45 performances.

Still, the Broadway revue, after struggling for a decade for respectability and an identity, had, by the spring of 1919, established both. Ziegfeld was its regent; Dillingham its prime minister; the Shuberts its pretenders. The time was right for yet another showbusiness war, and in May of that year, the first, tentative shot was fired.

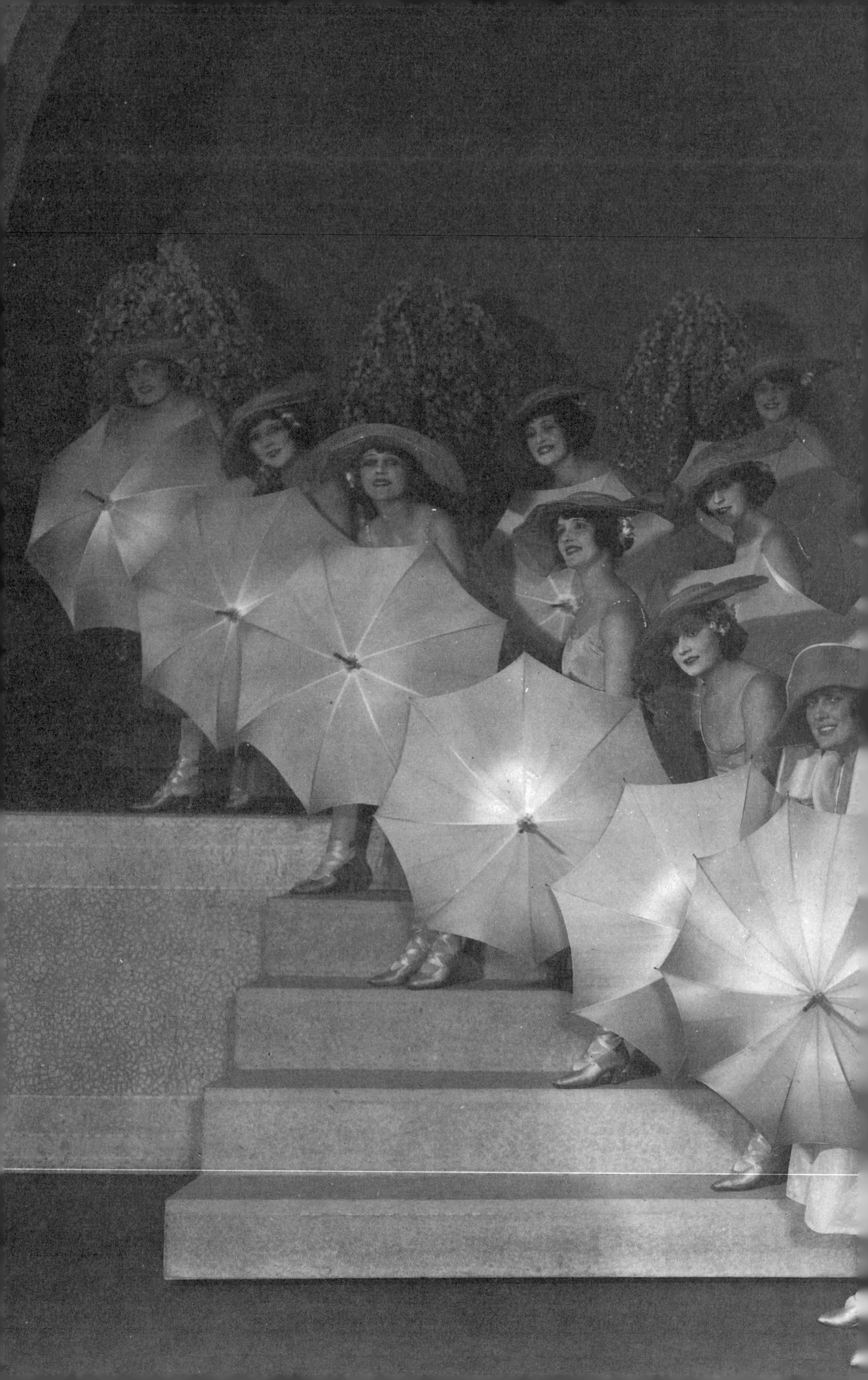

7

The Great Challenger

The Great Challenger

❦

If Ziegfeld was the Great Glorifier, George White was the Great Challenger. Or, if you were Ziegfeld, the Great Betrayer.

Born George Weitz, White learned show business in much the same way that Izzie Baline did on his way to becoming Irving Berlin. He battled his way through a childhood on the streets of New York, started hoofing in Piggy Donovan's dance hall in Five Points, formed a double act with another hoofer and comedian named Bennie Ryan, entered burlesque, quarreled with Ryan, and got a job dancing in the ensemble of Dillingham's short-lived and little loved *The Echo*, whose sole claim to historical fame was the fact that its mediocre score was Deems Taylor's only one for Broadway.

From there, he moved into the *Follies of 1911*, built a gradual reputation as a dancer/singer/actor in three successive Shubert shows, *The Whirl of Society* (1912), *The Pleasure Seekers* (1913) and *The Midnight Girl* (1914). By the time the 1915 edition of the *Follies* came around, he was a headliner, and Gene Buck hired him. Julian Mitchell paired him with Ann Pennington for that *Follies*, as did Ned Wayburn for *Miss 1917*.

But headlining wasn't enough for White. He watched while he played; he saw the flaws in the Winter Garden shows, noted the pluses and rewards of the Ziegfeld touch. He was going to do it, too, only better, and differently.

He was younger than Ziegfeld, and brasher. His shows would be jazzy, dancing revues, giving audiences what they'd missed in the *Follies*.

And so, George White convinced Ann Pennington, his partner from the *Follies*, to join him in his first *Scandals*. The not-so-magic persuasion was star billing, which she received in this and subsequent editions.

It was merely *Scandals of 1919* on June 2, when it opened at the Liberty on 42nd Street. And it was no world shaker. But it was what White promised: dancing was the subject matter, and dancing was the dominant entertainment. White was all over the place, producing, directing and writing, with Arthur Jackson, the truly mediocre sketches that were, nevertheless, up-to-date, poking good natured fun at Broadway's tastes for courtroom melodramas and bedroom farces, the woes of hotel living and the approaching specter of Prohibition. The score, by the highly active Richard Whiting and the lyrics by Jackson were entirely forgettable, but the charm of Ann Pennington, the energy, and the pretty girls kept the first *Scandals* alive for a healthy 128 performances.

The story goes that shortly after its opening, Ziegfeld wired White, offering Ann Pennington and him $2,000 a week to come back to the *Follies*. White supposedly replied that he would pay Ziegfeld and Billie Burke $3,000 to appear in his *Scandals*.[1]

Ziegfeld would never regard White as more than an annoyance, even at the peak of the younger man's success, which wouldn't arrive for another four years. The Great Glorifier was too busy maintaining his place at the top of the revue world. And if ever a *Follies* justified his title, it was the 1919 edition. Considered by some to be the pinnacle of the series, it will be remembered forever as the *Follies* that introduced Irving Berlin's "A Pretty Girl Is Like a Melody" to the world. Certainly, the song never again received a more elegant and stunning setting, nor a more appropriate singer of it than John Steel, who would eternally be the archetypical tenor, ushering a bevy of

Ziegfeld beauties down the signature staircase. In this edition, taking their cue from the lyrics of the song, their headdresses depicted various song styles ("Barcarole," "Spring Song," "Humoresque," "Serenade," etc.).

The presence of Irving Berlin as this *Follies'* major composer finally added the dimension of a decent score to the mix. Eddie Cantor cavorted, wide-eyed, to Berlin's "You'd Be Surprised," Van and Schenck, in their first *Follies* appearance, harmonized on *Yip-Yip Yap-hank's* "Mandy," while the chorus, in a minstrel setting, tapped and Marilyn Miller (the second, affected "n" in her name excised by order of Ziegfeld) did a soft shoe. Looking with disfavor upon the relentless approach of January 1, 1920, when the Volstead Act would go into effect, Bert Williams warbled the woeful Berlin statement, "You Cannot Make Your Shimmy Shake on Tea."

Meanwhile, Eddie Dowling introduced a Ziegfeld beauty salad in which the Fairbanks Twins portrayed pepper and salt, and Eddie Cantor convulsed the audience with a sketch involving a terrified patient visiting an osteopath. There was a Dutch number set to Gene Buck and Dave Stamper's "Tulip Time," a romantic sequence built around Harry Tierney and Joseph McCarthy's "My Baby's Loving Arms," a Sweet Sixteen number and a circus ballet, with music by Victor Herbert, for Marilyn Miller. And there was even an opium den number in which the dance team of Maurice and Walton created an Oriental melodrama; in which a drug-tranced Walton danced nearly nude. Nearly. The real nudes were reserved for Ben Ali Haggin's two tableaux—one of Jessie Read as the New Folly accompanied by her 12 sisters and another of Lady Godiva on a horse, surrounded by various Medieval cliches.

The "Tulip Time" number so pleased the Prince of Wales, who showed up one night, that Ziegfeld moved the entire number upstairs to the *Midnight Frolics* for a special, late night royal repeat. Even this, the last *Frolic* before Prohibition inhibited it, was a memorable one, featuring Fanny Brice, W.C. Fields, Allyn King, Ted Lewis and

Frances White leading the cast and, supposedly, the stage hands and waiters in a giant shimmy finale, to Gene Buck and Dave Stamper's "The World Is Going Shimmie Mad." On both levels the shows were gigantic successes with critics and audiences alike and would have enjoyed long, building runs. But the Actors' Equity strike would shatter their momentum.

The crisis for Ziegfeld took place on August 12, 1919, five nights after most of the theatres went dark on Broadway. He, along with the Shuberts and George M. Cohan, had decided to fight Equity. Immediately after the Shuberts sued the performers' union for $500,000, Ziegfeld obtained temporary injunctions against every member of the *Follies* company and every officer in Equity. The injunctions were handed to cast members as they arrived for the August 11 performance.

The next night, five *Follies* principals—Eddie Cantor, Ray Dooley, Van and Schenck and John Steel—failed to show up at the theatre, and the show was closed down. It remained shuttered until September 10, after the strike was settled. It resumed and ran until December 6.

But deep damage to formerly warm relationships had been done. Stars that Ziegfeld believed were his own established their new and hard-won independence. Eddie Cantor went over to the Shuberts and wouldn't return to the *Follies* until 1923. The 1919 *Follies* was Bert Williams's last show for Ziegfeld, and Marilyn Miller, shaken first by the producer's removal of her new husband, Frank Carter, from the *1919 Follies* when she married without his permission, then devastated by Carter's untimely death in an automobile accident, finished the run of *The Follies* and departed from them forever, although not from Ziegfeld's care and attention. He would send her to Europe to recover, then star her in *Sally, Sunny,* and *Rosalie*.

It was a time of change and crossed borders for Ziegfeld. Anna Held had died at the end of 1918 of a rare bone tissue ailment called myeloma; Olive Thomas would die of a drug overdose in 1920. For all the regal order of his shows, Ziegfeld's private life was a disordered mess.

The Ziegfeld Follies of 1919 also signaled something positive: in that summer preceding the Equity strike, the floodgates opened, and the revue became the reigning rage on Broadway, finally challenging the book show for musical supremacy.

It had a rocky climb to the top, lit only intermittently by hits. The first tangible manifestation of the rush of revues occurred on July 15, with John Murray Anderson's *Greenwich Village Follies*. Anderson, who grew up in Newfoundland, was used to improvising with whatever presented itself. Gathering together a group of young and inexpensive performers, plus a few veterans to give his venture legitimacy, he raised $35,000 from neighborhood businessmen, called his company the Bohemians, Inc., borrowed Lucille, Lady Duff-Gordon, to do the costumes, and opened his first revue, first as *Greenwich Village Nights*, and then, brazenly stealing what Ziegfeld thought was his alone, as *The Greenwich Village Follies*. Its venue was the Greenwich Village Theatre, at Seventh Avenue and Fourth Street, very far off Broadway.

A pocket edition of the real *Follies*, it was done with simplicity and taste and a smattering of nudity. There was a Javanese production number, a satirical ballet, Bobby Edwards playing his home-made cigar box ukelele and singing "I Do Not Care for Women Who Wear Stays," a girlie number titled "I Want a Daddy Who Will Rock Me to Sleep," a free love number titled, daringly, "I'll Sell You a Girl" and the expected attack on Prohibition, "I'm the Hostess of a Bum Cabaret," sung by Bessie McCoy Davis.

The score, by A. Baldwin Sloane, was several notches below the Philip Bartholomae and John Murray Anderson sketches and lyrics. The lasting song from the show was Andrew Sterling, Ted Lewis and Bill Munro's "When My Baby Smiles at Me," performed by Ted Lewis then and for the rest of his career.

Its novelty, a good-looking production and a non-Equity cast combined to make *The Greenwich Village Follies* a 232 performance success. Six weeks after it opened, it moved uptown to the Nora Bayes Theatre, located over the Shuberts' 44th Street Theatre.

Now, the Shuberts attempted a quick, cheap substitute for their customary *Passing Show*. *The Shubert Gaieties of 1919* was a tacky little enterprise that appropriated "You'd Be Surprised" from the *Ziegfeld Follies* and offered Gilda Gray, who was to the Shimmy what Ann Pennington would become to the Black Bottom, to heat up the proceedings. Even with Henry Lewis, and later, George Jessel to head the bill, *The Shubert Gaieties* could only eke out 87 performances.

Back from the war, where he had served as a captain in an Army espionage outfit, Charles Dillingham attempted the impossible: to open *Happy Days*, a Hippodrome extravaganza in the middle of the Equity strike. "Perhaps it[s title] is Mr. Dillingham's little joke," commented the *New York Dramatic Mirror*. It was anything but. It debuted on August 23, two days after the strike took absolute effect upon the rest of Broadway and managed to do brisk business for five days.

Then, just before the evening performance on August 28th, 412 stagehands struck, and the cast quickly followed. The other producers fully expected Dillingham to stand tough; he'd expressed anger at the strike when it began.

But he didn't. He settled with Equity, thus legitimizing the union and forcing the other producers, with the sole, defiant exception of George M.Cohan, to settle, too. Dillingham's chorus girls got a raise from $25 a week to $35, production costs escalated and ticket prices, frozen since the Civil War at $1.50 to $2.00, leaped to $3.00.

And *Happy Days*, a family-oriented fantasy, despite such critical notices as that of Alexander Woollcott, who described it as a show "...to palm off on Aunt Hattie when she comes on from South Bend for a giddy week in New York," ran on and on, for 452 performances.

Not so lucky was Raymond Hitchcock, whose *Hitchy-Koo, 1919* barely made it through 56 performances. Starring Hitchock, Florence O'Denishawn doing modern dance, and Chief Eagle Horse and Princess White Deer doing Native American dances, it contained Cole Porter's second score. Ironically, such characteristic Porter songs as "I'm an Anesthetic Dancer" and "My Cozy Little Corner in the Ritz" died abrupt deaths, while "Old Fashioned Garden," a sentimental production number, soon decorated thousands of family pianos.

Such were the divided times between the war and the Twenties. Ziegfeld, painfully aware that the nation was plummeting toward Prohibition, opened his second *Midnight Frolics* on October 2. Once again, he and Urban made it a midnight to remember, populating it with the customary beauties, plus Frances White, Fanny Brice, Chic Sale, Ted Lewis, Allyn King and W. C. Fields.

The Shuberts, who had a hit tenant in *The Greenwich Village Follies* and were busily planning to challenge Keith and Albee by establishing their own vaudeville circuit, finally got around to *The Passing Show of 1919* on October 23. What Jake Shubert lacked in taste, he made up for in girls, and there were 75 of them in this edition, all in ever briefer costumes, all playing hockey and kicking high on the runway. It was a Tired Businessman's Paradise, but not much more.

The Barrymores were mocked in one sketch, and the Avon Comedy Four scored a hit with their doctor's office sketch—a steady moneymaker for two of them—Smith and Dale—for the remainder of their careers. The rest of the cast consisted of eager and talented newcomers, among them Olga Cook, Reginald Denny, James Barton, Charles Winninger and Mary Eaton, who would soon depart for Ziegfeld as a replacement for Marilyn Miller in subsequent *Follies*.

The Jean Schwartz score was forgettable, but an interpolation by Jean Kenbrovin and John W. Kellette, "I'm Forever Blowing Bubbles," stuck in the public's minds and vocal chords. For all its mediocrity, this *Passing Show* stayed at the Winter Garden for 280 performances, thus convincing J.J. Shubert that it wasn't quality, but semi-clothed girls that made a producer a profit.

The last of the wartime camp shows, a "bomb proof revue" titled *Elsie Janis and Her Gang*, opened at the Cohan on December 1. The petit bombshell, noted as "The Sweetheart of the AEF" to the doughboys, reunited her wartime traveling troupe and surrounded them with various women, chief among them Eva Le Gallienne, playing "The Parisienne." It would be Ms. Le Gallienne's one and only revue appearance before greater moments onstage. Audiences, preferring to forget rather than remember the war, only kept this harmless bauble in business for 55 performances.

Like Ziegfeld, Morris Gest, formerly 50 percent of the producing duo of Comstock and Gest at the Princess Theatre, capitalized on the thirst of a public plunging toward Prohibition by opening *Morris Gest's Midnight Whirl* on December 27, on the Century Roof. Staged by Julian Mitchell and featuring Bernard Granville, Helen Shipman and the ubiquitous Bessie McCoy Davis, it had the muted virtue of George Gershwin's second Broadway score. Irving Caesar and John Henry Mears's lyrics didn't help much. "Poppyland", "Let Cutie Cut Your Cuticle" and "The Doughnut Song" headed the roster of Gershwin's least revived songs.

Three days later, at the stroke of midnight, December 31, 1919, the Volstead Act kicked in, and liquor became illegal in the United States. Free vintage champagne flowed until the last minute at the Claridge Bar, a drunk entertained an openly weeping multitude at the Waldorf with a tear-stained rendition of "Auld Lang Syne," Ziegfeld shuttered his bar—forever, it turned out—at the *Frolics*, and the Roaring Twenties arrived.

Appropriately enough, the first revue of the Twenties was *Frivolities of 1920*, a rapidly disappearing frippery if there ever was one. Its score by William B. Friedlander, with additional songs by Harry Auracher and Tom Johnstone and sketches by William Anthony McGuire, and its appealing cast headed by Henry Lewis and Irene

Delroy, failed to attract audiences to the 44th Street Theatre for more than a red-ink consuming 61 performances.

Interestingly enough, even the opposite side of the coin failed to attract customers undergoing the twin onsets of Prohibition and an economic depression; a production of Tolstoy's *The Power of Darkness* opened a week later, down the street from *Frivolities of 1920*, and lasted only 40 performances.

So it went until January 27, when E. Ray Goetz imported a "fantastic revue" from Paris called *As You Were*. Actually a throwback to the days when revues needed skeleton books to justify their existence, it featured Sam Bernard (now that the war was over, a German comedian once again) tripping backward through time to survey the great beauties of the ages. It had the virtue of Irene Bordoni as his wife, most of the beauties, and Clifton Webb as their constant lover. The songs by E. Ray Goetz and Herman Darewski, with the collaboration of Cole Porter for "Washington Square," were bland and bloodless, but audiences didn't seem to notice. It ran for 143 performances.

It would be the end of February before the next honest revue—and definite flop—arrived. Herman Timberg, not one of the musical theatre's immortals, wrote, composed and produced a pocket revue for the Princess Theatre titled *Tick-Tack-Toe*. Up-to-date and jazzy it was, with such songs as "Chinese American Rag," "Hoppy Poppy Girl" and "Take Me Back to Philadelphia Pa." And trashy it was, too. It folded after 32 performances, after which Timberg took it out of town, to Far Rockaway, where it really sank.

Now deprived of the party atmosphere that permeated his pre-Prohibition *Midnight Frolics*, Ziegfeld attempted to make up for lost fun by increasing the size of the productions. He opened his last 9 O'Clock Frolic, titled *Ziegfeld Girls* on March 8, on the New Amsterdam roof, with an all-star cast that included Allyn King, Fanny Brice, W.C. Fields, Mary Hay and, from the past, Lillian Lorraine. A week later, on March 15, he added his *Midnight Frolics of 1920*, with the same cast plus Carl Randall and Joe Frisco. *9 O'Clock Frolic* did mediocre business; the *Midnight Frolics*, possibly because its audiences had discovered the use and stimulation of bootleg hootch in hip flasks, frolicked on.

The first big Broadway revue of the Twenties was a John Murray Anderson creation that introduced a major new talent to Broadway: Irish artist James Reynolds. His and Murray Anderson's tastes instantly merged into stunning, tasteful and imaginative creations that were the first real challenges to Joseph Urban's previously undisputed domination of scenic Broadway. Adding to Murray Anderson's fascination with and utilization of new stage machinery—treadmills, projected scenes, wind-billowed curtains and inner and outer Greek stages—Reynolds managed to make an insubstantial show look wonderful.

And insubstantial *What's in a Name?* was. Its score by Milton Ager was thoroughly undistinguished, save for "A Young Man's Fancy," used for a scene evocative of Watteau, which contained living Dresden figurines atop a giant music box before a yellow taffeta backdrop. That was the way the evening went: a parade of places and beauties à la Ziegfeld—Japan, the Far East, a sumptuous wedding—but without the leavening of humor that Gene Buck customarily battered Ziegfeld into including. The result was an 87 performance flop, but a classy one, which concerned Ziegfeld. Jake Shubert had no taste; George White was obsessed by dancing. But Murray Anderson had the kind of eye for beauty presented in tasteful surroundings that the Great Glorifier had previously claimed for his own. And he had Otto Kahn's money to back him, besides. Ziegfeld hated him.

On April 5, Ed Wynn, thumbing his nose at the producers who had not yet forgiven him for his leadership of the Equity strike, opened, in the tradition of the Cohan revues, *The Ed Wynn Carnival* at the New Amsterdam. The great clown was everywhere—producing, writing the sketches, writing the music and the lyrics and splitting the direction with B.C. Whitney, who received a program credit as "Business Director." He even dashed out into the lobby after each performance to shake hands and receive compliments. George Gershwin supplied one interpolated, forgettable melody, and Wynn surrounded himself with a cast mostly culled from vaudeville.

But it was the star that not only his old Equity buddies but audiences came to see, and he provided them with what they wanted, pratfalling, flicking cigar ashes into the orchestra pit, stepping on another actor's violin solo. This, the first of four Ed Wynn revues, was not, for all its energy, a success. It departed from the New Amsterdam after a mere 64 performances.

It would be the end of the 1919–1920 season before the first revue to justifiably be called a hit arrived. George White opened his *Scandals of 1920* at the Globe Theatre on June 7, and it was again, the liveliest and dancingest show in town, starring the producer and Ann Pennington and featuring Lou Holtz in the comedy department. It was the first *Scandals* to sport a score by George Gershwin, but the great composer hadn't hit his stride yet and was still saddled with lyricists—Arthur Jackson in this instance—who nullified some of his more daring efforts. "Tum on and Tiss Me" was an example from the *Scandals of 1920*. Possessing all the subtlety of a dinosaur charge, the show didn't even work satirically. Still, audiences of the age loved it all, and the show remained at the Globe for 318 performances, a solid hit.

The 1920–21 season began with the 14th edition of the *Ziegfeld Follies*, which opened at the New Amsterdam on June 22. It was more opulent than ever, presaging a decade of enormous activity and growth for all of Broadway. A total of 157 productions would open this season, more than ever before.

Once more, Irving Berlin was the creator of the major part of this *Follies'* score, but the remainder of the roster of lyricists and composers was as large as the show's concept. Victor Herbert, Joseph McCarthy and Harry Tierney, Gene Buck and Dave Stamper, Bert Kalmar and Harry Ruby, Ballard MacDonald and Harry Carroll,

Grant Clarke and Milton Ager—even King Zany and Van and Schenck contributed to the general melange of music and words.

A major addition to the creative staff occurred with the 1920 *Follies*. Edward (Teddy) Royce, the pilot of the George Edwardes revues at the Gaiety, Savoy and Daly's in London, joined Julian Mitchell and Ned Wayburn on the list of distinguished directors for Ziegfeld.

In this edition, Mary Eaton replaced Marilyn Miller in the ballets and the affections of *Follies* audiences. W.C. Fields scored heavily with an original sketch, "The Family Ford," in which Ray Dooley, as a screaming brat, joined him in an outing in a car that faced repeated assault by a variety of forces—a blind man smashing a headlight with his cane, a stranger striking a match on the fender to light a cigarette, Fields himself tearing off the steering wheel, etc.

Fanny Brice had three crazy moments: her singing of "I'm a Vamp from East Broadway," one of the few songs in Irving Berlin's long career that he wrote in collaboration—this time with Bert Kalmar and Harry Ruby—it framed a scene involving a man who chronicled her ruination of his life; "I Was a Florodora Baby," with music and lyrics by Ballard MacDonald and Harry Carroll told the tale of the only Florodora Girl who married for love and consequently stayed in the chorus; and in an elaborate sketch, Brice dragged W.C. Fields from his seat in the theatre after accusing him of flirting with another woman.

The production numbers featured more and more rapturously beautiful women, some in larger headdresses, some wearing fewer clothes. Irving Berlin's "The Leg of Nations" and "Girls of My Dreams," sung again by John Steel, involved the trademark Ziegfeld staircase and tons of Urban scenery; Victor Herbert's "The Love Boat," with lyrics by Dave Stamper, musicalized a Venetian tableau by Ben Ali Haggin; Van and Schenck and Charles Winninger added more comedy; Jack Donahue replaced George White as principal dancer, and Art Hickman's Orchestra, imported from far California, introduced a new aspect of the *Follies*, the name orchestra. It was a huge success and ran through October.

The Shuberts opened their summer revue a scant two days after the curtain rose on the *1920 Follies*. Eschewing another *Passing Show*, the brothers settled for a throwback, time-and-place-traveling revue titled *Cinderella on Broadway*. Its ponderous sketches by Harold Atteridge and insignificant music by Bert Grant and Al Goodman (Romberg was noticeably absent) accompanied the heroine chasing Prince Charming from the moon to Broadway. The girls on the runway wore less and less and pleased the tired businessmen more and more, and *Cinderella on Broadway* stayed at the Winter Garden for 126 performances, three more than the *Ziegfeld Follies of 1920*.

July brought *Buzzin' Around*, a revue directly out of and deeply immersed in vaudeville, to the Casino. This unruly concoction, slapped together by Will Morrissey and Edward Madden, featured Elizabeth Brice and included sendups of French theatre, opera, the Barrymores and *The Mikado*. It expired after 23 performances.

But that wasn't the only July revue. The Shuberts piggy-backed two of them, one in the Century, the other on the Century roof. At 8:40, there was *The Century Revue*, with a score by Jean Schwartz and Alfred Bryan and sketches by Howard E. Rogers; at midnight, the same cast, composer, lyricist and sketch writer moved upstairs for *Midnight Rounders of 1920*, a blatant copy of Ziegfeld's *Midnight Frolics*. The cast was headed by Walter Woolf, Mlle. Madelon La Verre, Vivian Oakland and Ted Lorraine, but the chief attraction was the bevy of girls, bottled downstairs, surrounded by flowers upstairs. The double feature worked; *The Century Revue* remained for 148 performances; the *Midnight Rounders* for 120.

Three nights after this double-dose revue premiered, and *Satins*, with music by Leon Rosebrook, lyrics by Louis Weslyn and sketches by Thomas Duggan, opened at the Cohan. It was a sorry affair, sending up Shakespeare with a song titled "Was Mrs. Macbeth Really Sleeping When She Took That Famous Walk?", transporting the audience to what was becoming the obligatory Oriental den to the strains of "Nanking Blues," and introducing a dance with "That Colored Jazzboray," an interpolated number by Arthur Freed and Oliver G. Wallace. It was a 53 performance failure.

It again remained for John Murray Anderson to restore the reputation of the revue with *The Greenwich Village Follies of 1920.* It could be intelligently argued that if John Murray Anderson hadn't had a worse ear for good music than Ziegfeld, he might have outdistanced the master. But, although James Reynolds once again challenged Joseph Urban with his opulent, subtly shaded sets, and Robert Locher equaled Lucille, Lady Duff-Gordon, in the costume department, none of the *Greenwich Village Follies* except the 1924 edition—for which Cole Porter would supply some interesting if not outstanding songs—could disguise their consistently mediocre music. This time, it was A. Baldwin Sloane who provided the tunes for Arthur Swanstrom and Murray Anderson's lyrics, all of them mercifully forgotten.

Blatantly conscious of its origins, this *Greenwich Village Follies* opened with an artist's studio scene titled "The Naked Truth," which satisfied a growing taste for nudity in revues. The parade of clothed and unclothed models, students and general bohemians eventually gave way to the slapstick humor of James Brennan and Bert Savoy. Savoy had assumed the crown of Julian Eltinge as Broadway's premiere female impersonator, a role he maintained throughout this and succeeding *Greenwich Village Follies*. There were numerous exotic locales—fourteenth century Russia, the French Empire, a birthday cake with girls for candles, the funnies for the Krazy Kat Ball, and an Oriental den for a perfume allegory titled, not very subtly, "Tsin." The singing chores were given to Frank Crumit, the dancing ones to Margaret Severn, and Phil Baker, with his comedy accompanied by an accordion, rested somewhere in between.

The Greenwich Village Follies of 1920 was an immediate hit, transferred by the Shuberts from the Greenwich Village Theatre to the Shubert a week after it opened. It remained there for 192 performances.

Raymond Hitchock was back again in October, opening yet another *Hitchy-Koo*, this time at the New Amsterdam. Despite Ned Wayburn's knowledgeable staging, the presence of Julia Sanderson and Florence O'Denishawn, and the music of Jerome Kern matched to the lyrics of Anne Caldwell and Glen MacDonagh, it was a hopelessly old fashioned melange, termed by Heywood Broun in his review "undeniably old and frayed." There was not one survivable Kern standard in the score, nor anything else memorable about *Hitchey-Koo, 1920*. It departed after 71 performances, and it would be the last of the series, and the last revue for which Kern would ever write a score.

Even with the acceleration in production of revues that began at the turn of the decade, they were still considered basically warm weather fare, and it would be nearly the end of the year before the next, *The Passing Show of 1921*, opened. It was a confusing year for the Shuberts. They had skipped the 1920 edition of their series, then opened the new one on December 29—a more or less certain sign of trouble in the ranks or at the top.

The problem was vaudeville. Not only were the Shuberts preparing to mount 30 new shows during the 1920-21 season; they were now ready to enter the vaudeville arena full time. Their circuit contained 22 theatres, and they were determined to better Keith by hiring—which in some cases meant raiding—stars of great magnitude and expense. Ziegfeld, for instance, paid Will Rogers $1,500 a week in the *Follies*. The Shuberts offered him $5,000 a week. He would have been a fool not to accept, so he did.

And so did Jack Benny, Nora Bayes, Eddie Cantor, Al Jolson, Eva Tanguay, Mae West, the Marx Brothers and Walter Huston, in a dramatic sketch as Old Kris Kringle.

With all of this going on, Jake Shubert settled for the safety of repetition. It was 1912 again onstage at the Winter Garden, with

Willie and Eugene Howard doing an opera burlesque and takeoffs on the current productions of *Not So Long Ago, The Charm School, Lightnin', The Bat, Mecca* and *Spanish Love*. Marie Dressler opened, but was replaced early in the run by May Boley. The Jean Schwartz score, to lyrics by Harold Atteridge, was easily forgettable, but customers came, lured by the runway and the girls, and *The Passing Show of 1921* remained at the Winter Garden for a comfortable 200 performances before leaving for a profitable road tour.

Following the usual custom of renewing their roof top shows after six months, the Shuberts and Ziegfeld obliged within three days of each other. On February 5, *The Midnight Rounders of 1921*, a dim imitation of the earlier edition, opened at the Century Promenade. Jean Schwartz again supplied the music to Lew Pollack's lyrics, with a number of interpolations by, among others, Cliff Friend, Kalmar and Ruby, and Eddie Cantor, Harry Tobias and James Blyler. But the bloom was off the cabaret rose without liquor, and attendance was poor.

Ziegfeld did little better with his *9 O'Clock Frolic*, which opened on February 8. Staged by Edward Royce, it featured Oscar Shaw, the Fairbanks Twins, Anna Wheaton and Princess White Deer. The music was by Harry Carroll with interpolations by Irving Berlin and Dave Stamper. Despite its tasteful opulence, it again suffered from lack of liquor and folded after 35 performances. Ziegfeld faced reality, and this edition became the last *9 O'Clock Frolic* ever.

And that would be it for the winter. It would be spring before another revue arrived on Broadway. It was a return volley of *Biff! Bing! Bang!* now on a cross-country tour. Audiences seemed to love the nostalgia, and it ran out the season.

On May 23, *Sunkist*, a California revue mounted by the dance team of Fanchon and Marco, poked fun at Hollywood in a series of satirical sketches, surrounded by music and lyrics by the dance team, including such immortal underpinnings for production numbers as "A Pretty Dance Is Like a Violin" and "The I Donno What." The critics loved it; the public stayed away; it was thus squeezed out of Broadway rapidly.

Now, spring truly arrived, and so did a rush of revues. On June 2, it was *Snapshots of 1921*, a revue that, like old-time burlesque, poked fun at current shows on Broadway and featured an all-star cast of veterans—Nora Bayes, Lew Fields, DeWolf Hopper, Lulu McConnell and Gilda Gray. It was a solid hit. Fields, who, with the Selwyns produced it, hired an army of creators; the list of composers looked (and sounded) like a Ziegfeld company. *Sally*, Ziegfeld's Marilyn Miller hit, came in for kidding with "Every Girlie Wants to Be a Sally" by Alex Gerber and Malvin Franklin; *Irene* was sent up in a sketch that featured an Irene Rosensteen who didn't "...wear blue gowns of Alice." George Gershwin and E. Ray Goetz contributed two songs, Con Conrad one and Morrie Ryskind and Lewis Gensler three.

Six days later, *The Broadway Whirl* opened at the Times Square. A harmless confection and a chance for Richard Carle, whose career was fading, to appear as star and co-lyricist with Joseph McCarthy, B. G. DeSylva and John Henry Mears, it contained one of Harry Tierney's more obscure scores. Nevertheless, an amiable cast, headed by Carle and featuring Blanche Ring, Charles Winninger, Winona Winter, Jay Gould and the Janet Sisters, hit all the bases: the New York scene, with "From the Plaza to Madison Square;" family, with "Stand Up and Sing for Your Father;" Prohibition, with "Wood Alcohol Blues"; the production number with girls, with "All Girls Are Like a Rainbow;" and a trip to an exotic locale, with "Carefree Cairo Town." Even "Let Cutie Cut Your Cuticle" put in a repeat appearance. The show remained at the Times Square for a major part of the summer.

And now it was the end of June and time for the *Ziegfeld Follies* to appear—except that the New Amsterdam was still filling up nightly with audiences for *Sally*, the longest running musical that Broadway had yet seen or supported. Ziegfeld was not about to close his Marilyn Miller-Jerome Kern-Guy Bolton-P.G. Wodehouse-Clifford Grey bonanza, and so, for the first time since 1913, he opened *The Ziegfeld*

Follies of 1921 elsewhere, this time at the Globe.

It would be the most expensive edition yet, a reported $270,000 production in a year in which the average musical was mounted for $50,000. Much of it went into the Joseph Urban sets, which achieved new heights and depths in exoticness, and the increasingly inventive and elegant costumes of James Reynolds. Once again, Edward Royce directed.

The Ziegfeld stock company of the Twenties was in place: Fanny Brice, W.C. Fields, Van and Schenck, Ray Dooley, Mary Eaton and John Steel were joined by Raymond Hitchcock, Florence O'Denishawn and the scandalous Parisian dance team of M. Tillio and Mlle. Mitti. Clad in a spider web that allowed most of Mlle. Mitti to be visible (*Variety* reported that she "wore more on her hair than on the rest of her"), she slithered and slid around M. Tillio in a dance that became Ziegfeld's furthest step toward nudity—beyond the Ben Ali Haggin tableaux—yet.

But it was spectacle that audiences came to see, and it was spectacle that they were given: the multi-hued Persian "The Legend of the Cyclamen Tree" in which Florence O'Denishawn, as the tree, performed the seemingly impossible task of dancing without moving her feet, and "The Birthday of the Dauphin" in which the court of Versailles was elegantly and opulently reborn.

Comedy was abundant and original in this edition. W.C. Fields created a sketch in which Brice, Fields, Raymond Hitchock and Ray Dooley turned climbing into a subway train on the way to a family picnic into 15 minutes of catastrophic hilarity. The Barrymores, every revue's favorite target, were once again skewered by Brice, Fields and Hitchcock. Charles O'Donnell, as a piano tuner, destroyed the piano and the room surrounding it. Fields and Hitchcock presided over a few moments of madness in which a minister invited a magician who can only change water to wine and vice versa to entertain his Sunday School class. When Prohibition agents arrived to arrest the magician, drunk on the wine he created, they found only water, to the thunderous delight of the audience. And, finally, there was a demented prizefight, in which Fanny Brice was the French boxer Charpentier and Dooley, in drag, was Jack Dempsey.

The music was a melange of second-shelf melodies by Victor Herbert, Rudolph Friml and Dave Stamper, uncomfortably underpinning the lyrics of Channing Pollock, Gene Buck, Willard Mack, Ralph Spence and Buddy DeSylva. The show's two hits were interpolations, both sung by Fanny Brice. "Second Hand Rose," by Grant Clarke and James F. Hanley, was an expected ethnic humorous ditty. But "My Man," Maurice Yvain's "Mon Homme" with English lyrics by Channing Pollock, was quite another experience—an astonishing moment, and the source of one of show business's most enduring stories.

"Mon Homme" was supposed to be a spot for the American appearance of the French music hall star Mistinguette. But Ziegfeld, after importing the chanteuse from Paris, decided, after one hearing, to send her back to France. Fanny Brice, now embroiled in a hopeless, destructive and public relationship with gangster Nicky Arnstein, needed a new dimension to help the public forget the headlines, and Ziegfeld seized the moment, instructing Pollock to write translation lyrics and ordering Fanny Brice to memorize them for a dress rehearsal.

She did, and appeared onstage looking like Fanny Brice imitating Ray Dooley, in a grotesque red wig and an elaborately fringed shawl. Ziegfeld let out a high-pitched yell, rushed onstage, ripped the wig from Fanny's head and flung it into the wings. He removed the shawl, then proceeded to rip the dress from neck to hem; knelt on the stage, smeared his hands with dust, then smeared the dust on her costume and her. Bewildered and distraught, Fanny began to cry. "*Now* sing it!" Ziegfeld shouted and left Fanny, sobbing and desolate, alone on the stage. She sang "My Man" with such heartbreak in her voice and demeanor then, and from then on, that audiences received a double shock—first, seeing their clown of yesteryear, ragged, dusty and forlorn, and second, having their hearts torn out by a voice whose other dimension they hadn't yet heard, expressing emotions they hadn't believed she possessed. It was one of the great moments not only in the *Follies* and in revues, but in theatre itself.[2]

It would be July 11 before *George White's Scandals* opened at the Liberty. The cocky, Runyonesque White had been given some fatherly advice by Abe Erlanger after his first *Scandals*. "Revues are through," said the little Napoleon. "They haven't made a dollar with the Follies in three or four years. Take my advice, Georgie, and do a book show."[3]

White was canny and streetwise enough to know that the producer was lying in every department. And in early 1921, Ziegfeld and Erlanger's skullduggerous maneuvers to finally edge Klaw out of the partnership forever further convinced him to never listen to a syllable of advice from this Rasputin of Broadway. "When I opened my second edition in Atlantic City, Erlanger found out," said White later, "and he wouldn't talk to me for two years."

The third edition, to which White had now attached his name, was no better than the first and slightly worse than the second. Ann Pennington was back, tossing her long hair and shaking her derriere, winning over tired businessmen with her dimpled knees, and being partnered by Lester Allen and White, himself, who also appeared in the box office selling tickets and in the lobby after the show. (Jolson swore that White stole this routine from him; White swore that Jolson was the thief.)

Lou Holtz was in charge of the comedy which poked fun at the Bible and Trotsky, among other subjects. The girls were beautiful, but George Gershwin's music, again tethered to the lyrics of Arthur Jackson, produced only one enduring number, "Drifting Along with the Tide." The *Scandals* departed for the road after three months, where, as usual, it recouped its investment and made a hefty profit.

The Shuberts, juggling many projects, managed to light the Century Promenade on August 15, with *The Mimic World*, an after-the-usual-theatre cabaret that, without the elevating power of liquor, fizzled quickly. Despite a cast that included Lou Edwards, Mae West and Cliff Edwards (three years before *Lady Be Good!* transformed him into Ukelele Ike), its humdrum music by Jean Schwartz, Lew Pollack, Owen Murphy and Harold Atteridge and lyrics by James Hussey and Owen Murphy sank the show after 27 performances.

The summer's final revue was, in contrast, a justifiable hit, further cementing John Murray Anderson's place in the upper echelon of revue producers. *The Greenwich Village Follies* didn't even bother to open in the Village in 1921; it went straight to the Shubert Theatre, and, in so doing, in the minds of some critics and theatregoers, began to lose its intimacy and its edge of bohemianism. Their evaluation had validity; this edition clearly borrowed from both Ziegfeld and White, but mostly from vaudeville. Irene Franklin, one of that medium's biggest stars, sang to the accompaniment of Ted Lewis's onstage jazz band. Another vaudeville team, Brown and Watts, cavorted through a series of slapstick turns, including "A Dying Duck in a Thunderstorm" and "Love's Awakening." The James Watts half of the team had little lasting power and soon left show business; the Joe E. Brown half, with his endearing ears and smile, grew bigger and bigger.

Murray Anderson continued to experiment with new theatrical effects. He utilized venetian blinds instead of travelers; he experimented with lighting changes by Nicholas V. Lipsky that transformed a ballroom into a moonlit garden in an instant; the erotic conceptions of Aubrey Beardsley were translated by Robert Locher into a black and silver landscape of shimmering and inviting decadence.

What was clearly missing was anything resembling a solid musical score. Carey Morgan's music to Murray Anderson and Arthur Swanstrom's lyrics was barely listenable, and the one number that outlasted the show and, indeed, seasons of Broadway shows, was the centerpiece of the tasteful, understated finale, built around an interpolated waltz brought back from London by Murray Anderson, where he had been working on a Cochran revue that incorporated past

Greenwich Village Follies numbers. "Three O'Clock in the Morning," by Dorothy Terris and Julian Robeldo, was first sung by Rosalind Fuller and Richard Bold against a solid blue set, then danced, in black and white, by Margaret Petit and Valodia Vestoff.

Still, the lack of a sustained and memorable score was becoming a rule and a noticeable weakness in the Broadway revue, which was now trading upon girls, spectacle and vaudeville comedy for its character and its audience. It was ready, although not necessarily waiting, for someone to have the acumen to add this vital dimension to a thriving theatrical expression. That person was already on Broadway. He knew whereof revues came, and what made them succeed and what made them flop. And he was building a theatre that would become a showcase for revues that, in contrast to the past, paid attention to their composers. It was time, he felt, for the revue to move either forward into this dimension, or die of repetition.

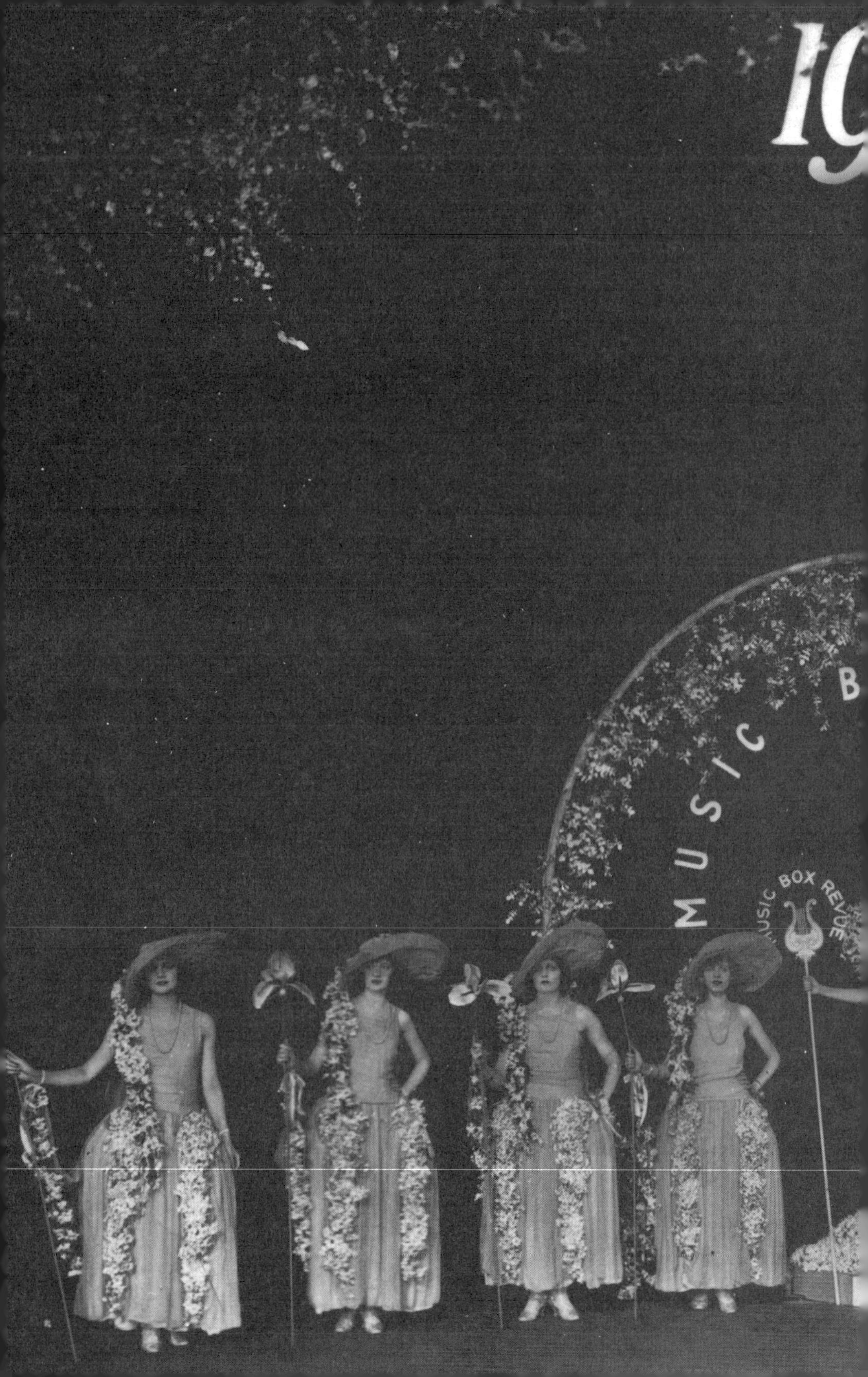
19
MUSIC B
MUSIC BOX REVUE

23

8
Say It With Music

Say It With Music

&

September, 1921, began with a taste of what was to come and eventually sweep the Broadway landscape clean of classic revues: utilized for movies all summer, the Hippodrome, under the imaginative but realistic eye of Charles Dillingham, opened its new spectacular *Get Together* with a "motion picture prelude." So far, it was a novelty. So far.

The rest of the evening was given over to customary expectations for an afternoon or evening at the Hippodrome: elephants, Jocko the amazing crow, some knockabout vaudeville comedy, an ice ballet by the famous but now a bit long-in the blade Charlotte, and one remarkable premiere: a serious ballet, "The Thunderbird," commissioned for and danced by Fokine and his wife Fokina.

It was, in other words, a mostly typical Charles Dillingham-R. H. Burnside creation for their 6,000-seat dirigible hanger, and audiences came for 397 profitable performances.

The end of September was reserved for a revolution. Its seeds had been sewn nearly a year before, when two men with the same idea mentioned that idea over lunch. Sam H. Harris, who had been George M. Cohan's partner for years, wanted his own theatre. Irving Berlin, who had been a tenant in nearly everyone else's house on Broadway, also wanted his own theatre. They discussed it casually. Then seriously. Harris proposed the title "Irving Berlin's Music Box."

"Too much Berlin," Berlin answered but agreed to everything else, and the site was purchased on 45th Street, west of Broadway. Work began immediately on what the two hoped would be a theatre with the most up-to-date stage machinery, plushest seats, deepest carpets and jazziest shows on Broadway.

Its cost skyrocketed; Berlin had to go to his friend Joe Schenck, not yet the boss of United Artists but successful enough to supply the difference between what they had and what they needed to finish their theatre.

Finally, at the end of the summer of 1921, the Music Box was ready for its first tenant, *The Music Box Revue,* the first of four namesake spectacles, with music and lyrics entirely by Irving Berlin. Sam Harris, ever the entrepreneur, invented purple prose to announce it: "The young man who has puckered the lips of a nation into a whistling position, stimulated the hurdy-gurdy industry and increased the dividends of the gramophone and pianola companies is going on the stage," the advance publicity announced, totally forgetting *Yip-Yip-Yaphank.*

The first *Music Box Revue* possessed the taste and theatrical savvy of Ziegfeld, provided by Berlin, the business head of Sam Harris and the directorial genius of a new name on the show business horizon: Hassard Short. And it had the crucially important element that had been largely and noticeably missing from revues until this moment: an integral, memorable Irving Berlin score.

The Music Box Revue opened on the night of September 22, 1921, to ecstatic reviews. "The Music Box was opened last evening before a palpitant audience and proved to be a treasure chest out of which the conjurers pulled all manner of gay tunes and brilliant trappings and funny clowns and nimble dancers," gurgled Alexander Woollcott, who then added, "Its contents confirmed the dark suspicion that Sam H. Harris and Irving Berlin have gone quite mad."[1]

Mad like a couple of Broadway foxes. The production budget was high—$187,613—but well-spent. The production numbers were opulently tasteful, ranging from a curtain of pearls portrayed by girls wearing them while Wilda Bennett sang "The Legend of the Pearls," "Dining Out," in which the girls became individual foods at a banquet, and "Eight Notes," in which eight beauties accompanied Irving Berlin, himself, seated at the piano, activating their movements.

There was minimal comedy, most of it lampooning theatrical styles. But the best moments of the evening centered on the dancing and singing numbers, the highlights of which were Rene Riano twisting herself into several pretzels in "I'm a Dumbbell," Ms. Riano and Sam Bernard sending up the new craze of marathon dancing in "They Call It Dancing," the Brox Sisters raising the roof and the dust from the stage floor with "Everybody Step," and, particularly and memorably, Wilda Bennett and Paul Frawley simply singing "Say It with Music."

The Music Box Revue kept the Music Box lit for the remainder of the season.

It would be November before another revue appeared on Broadway, and it would be another Ed Wynn vehicle. Titled *The Perfect Fool,* it again allowed Wynn to be star, director, composer, sketch writer and lyricist—everything but producer. This was left to Abe Erlanger, who brought the show into the Cohan on November 7, where it stayed for 256 performances.

November was also the month for the new edition of *Ziegfeld's Midnight Frolics.* This one starred Will Rogers, back from Shubertdom, Leon Errol, Carl Randall, Dorothy Clarke, Althea, and Kitty Kelly. Despite the dryness of the bars and the increasing presence of eagle-and gimlet-eyed revenue agents assigned to enforce the Volstead Act, it weathered the winter, but not the spring, as we shall soon see.

A postwar recession had settled gloomily over the country by the beginning of 1922, and when the soldiers of *Elsie Janis and Her Gang* sang feelingly of "The Bonus Blues," they struck a responsive chord in the audiences at the Gaiety. The pocket revue, a duplicate of the

1919 edition minus Eva Le Gallienne, but plus Ms. Janis singing "Mon Homme" in the original French, remained for 57 performances.

February brought two imported revues, the first of their genre, but by no means the last. The failure of *Pins and Needles*, despite some intriguing writing by Edgar Wallace (it could draw customers to the Shubert for only 46 performances), boded ill for imports. But the appearance, three nights later, of a beguiling oddity, *Chauve-Souris*, caused a more palpable ripple, which rapidly became a wave, then a tsunami.

Originally an in-house entertainment for their own diversion, devised by the players of Stanislavsky's Art Theatre and presented in the cellar of the Bat Theatre of Moscow, *Chauve-Souris* gradually developed a life of its own, traveling to London, then Paris, then New York. All of this occurred through the aegis of Ray Comstock and Morris Gest, who made a mint.

Chauve-Souris's charm was in its simplicity, and the introduction of a master of ceremonies—a device that, within a month, most American revues would now adopt as a necessary, sustained and sustaining feature. In the case of *Chauve-Souris*, the master of ceremonies, who stepped through the curtain before the house lights dimmed, was a charming destroyer of the English language named Nikita Balieff.

"It is my tuty of my manager, Mr. Morris Gest, who brought me to this country," he began, "to introduce myself. But he is so afret—he spiks bat Eenglish, therefore I introduce myself. I, too, spik bat Eenglish, but I gif you my wort, in ten or twenty or forty years, I will spik better Eenglish as you spik Russian."

Ethnic humor was in vogue, but this was the real thing, and audiences were convulsed, as they were entertained by what was essentially a Russian vaudeville, with references to Chekhov, Pushkin and Glinka, folk dances and British and American interpolations, the most notable of which, "The Parade of the Wooden Soldiers," by Ballard MacDonald and Leon Jessel, became the hit of the show and a standard.

Chauve-Souris was adopted by the fashion 400 and their fringe hangers-on, plus those who were in the know on Broadway, and it remained in New York for two years, first at the 49th Street Theatre, then the Century, where Ralph Burton painted an intermission curtain that captured the social world in attendance—yet another reason for that world's repeat appearances in choice orchestra and box seats.

Thus, in small ways, the theatre notches forward, and in February, *Frank Fay's Fables* opened at the Park. A revue of no distinction whatsoever, save for some of its cast members, notably Bernard Granville and Helen Groody, it was an ego trip for a man who lived on ego trips, and probably would have closed in a night had it not been for the dogged persistence and master of ceremonies air that Fay copied from *Chauve-Souris*. Even so, this show, devised by, about and for Frank Fay, collapsed after 32 performances.

1922, after all, was a strange, conflicted year. 1921's *Blossom Time*, Sigmund Romberg's telling of a fictitious biography of Franz Schubert, with Schubert's music set in three-quarter time whether it was written that way or not, was still the runaway musical hit on Broadway. But Eugene O'Neill was causing a sizable stir with *The Hairy Ape* at the Provincetown Playhouse, the Theatre Guild was producing George Bernard Shaw's metaphysical drama *Back to Methusulah* in "three divisions" at the Garrick, and *Abie's Irish Rose* was about to open its record-breaking run at the Fulton.

The revue, too, began, more and more to reflect the age as clearly as if it were a polished and ruthlessly focused mirror. Most of the time. While *Chauve-Souris* and *The Music Box Revue* chugged merrily on, breaking new ground, *Make It Snappy*, a Shubert creation, with sketches and lyrics by Harold Atteridge and music by Jean Schwartz, opened at the Winter Garden. Its sole saving grace was Eddie Cantor, who originated a sketch he would repeat, onstage and on film, for the rest of his career. Max the harassed tailor became as identified with Cantor as his trademark bouncing dance, rolling eyes and rising inflections. The rest of the show was pure vaudeville, including a troupe of tumblers. In 1923, it was good enough for a run into the summer.

Two days later, on April 15, *Some Party* opened at the Jolson. It was even more of a throwback, enough for Alexander Woollcott to comment that "the three leading comedians were in show business when Lillian Russell was a babe in arms." Not quite so, but almost. DeWolf Hopper, Jefferson de Angelis and Lew Dockstader came back to haunt the halls of revuedom with such relics of the turn of the century as an opera parody with a Mascagni heroine named Rustic Anna. R. H. Burnside staged this inexpensive, minimally decorated—almost in defiance of Ziegfeld—revue with yet more sounds from the past supplied by the music of Silvio Hein, Percy Wenrich and Gustave Kerker. This was overdoing nostalgia, and *Some Party* broke up after 17 performances.

In May, Ziegfeld returned from Palm Beach in a foul mood. Nothing seemed to please him anymore. In 1921, in mid-Atlantic, on the *Mauritania*, upon which Jack Pickford had been returning the body of Olive Thomas to America, Anna Daly, Olive's best friend, swallowed Veronal and died. Her suicide note read, "He doesn't love me anymore and I can't stand it and Olive is dead." The "he" was Ziegfeld, who had been keeping regular company with Anna Daly for several months. The press knew this, but this was 1921, and they reported merely that the man was "a New Yorker, now in Chicago."

Now, in 1922, Marilyn Miller was consistently and publicly humiliating Ziegfeld, his marriage to Billie Burke was about to be rattled by a divorce threat that would be only that and nothing more. And the presence of police in the audience at the *Midnight Frolics*, waiting to catch one of his patrons nipping from a pocket flask, sent the impresario into a final fit of fury.

He shut down the *Frolics* and sent one of his verbose telegrams to the New York Times:

THE CLOSING OF THE MIDNIGHT FROLICS ROOF IS SYMBOLIC OF THE FACT THAT THE MOST PRIZED POSSESSION OF AMERICAN LIBERTY IS DEAD. PATRIOTISM IS AT A LOW EBB WHEN AMERICANS RETURNING FROM ABROAD LOOK AT THE STATUE OF LIBERTY AND LAUGH OUT LOUD. I AM QUITTING FOR A PRICIPLE AND THAT PRINCIPLE IS MORE FAR REACHING THAN MOST PEOPLE KNOW.

The New Amsterdam roof would remain vacant for five years, until, five years before the end of Prohibition, Ziegfeld would stage one last, grand *Midnight Frolics*.

And now, in 1922, he engaged in another fight with Equity, this time over the firing of a chorus girl in Chicago, and threatened to move to London and give up the *Follies*. Within a week, he was conducting auditions for the 1922 New York edition.

By most accounts, *The Ziegfeld Follies of 1922* was the most opulent of them all; to most chroniclers, it was the last great edition. It was missing most of its greatest stars: Ann Pennington was with George White, Eddie Cantor with the Shuberts, Fanny Brice and W.C. Fields were in vaudeville, and Bert Williams had died suddenly, at the age of 49, in March. Only Will Rogers remained, and he was the centerpiece of the *1922 Follies*. Surrounding him were some of the most ravishing girls yet discovered by Gene Buck and Ziegfeld. In fact, it was with this *Follies* that Ziegfeld originated the achievable boast that would forever identify him: "Glorifying the American Girl."

This time, Ned Wayburn was back to direct, and this time, the staircase was golden, surmounted by—what else?—golden gates. The show opened with its most stunning and extravagant number: after the standard "Hello Hello Hello" (Louis A. Hirsch-Gene Buck), the girls left, the curtains parted and Mary Eaton, as a Dutch weaver, sang Victor Herbert's "Weaving My Dream." Gradually, dancers representing lace articles such as a handkerchief, stockings, a bridal gown, and the like, entered, and the number evolved into a ballet.

The costumes, however, were painted with radium paint, which cost $6,000 to apply and had to be reapplied periodically, and exposed to sunlight or heavy light for 15 minutes before each entrance of the dancers. As the number grew and grew, until 54 radium-clad dancers and eight soloists populated the staircase, the stage went to black, and the audience gasped at the first use of what would become black light on Broadway. Ziegfeld spent $31,000 on this number alone.

Other moments were only minimally less extravagant. James Reynolds pulled out all of his designer stops to frame two Fokine ballets (if Dillingham could do one Fokine ballet at the Hippodrome, Ziegfeld would do two at the New Amsterdam; that was the way it was in the mind of the Great Glorifier). One, "Farljandio," was set in a Sicilian gypsy camp in which Muriel Stryker danced the gypsy bride; the other, "Frolicking Gods," was set in a museum in which the classic statues came to life.

Harlem's presence on the Great White Way was the subject matter of yet another production number titled "It's Getting Awful Dark on Old Broadway" (music by Louis A. Hirsch, lyrics by Dave Stamper) in which more black light was utilized against a backdrop of glittering marquees.

This *Follies* had the virtue of the wildly and literately humorous presence of Ring Lardner, who fashioned a side-splitting baseball scene featuring Will Rogers, Andrew Tombes and Al Ochs. But the comedy team that audiences came to see again and again was Gallagher and Shean, singing their own creation, "Mr. Gallagher and Mr. Shean." It would outlast them, the Twenties and the *Follies*.

In fact, this edition of the *Ziegfeld Follies* never seemed to close, but segued into the next edition, which segued into the next, thus confusing the chroniclers. Which was number 17, number 18, number 19? Only Ziegfeld seemed to know.

In direct contrast, the 1921–22 season ended emphatically. Raymond Hitchcock, finally shedding his outdated *Hitchy-Koo* title, opened a "Kaleidoscopic Revel in Twenty Parts" titled *Raymond*

Hitchcock's Pinwheel at the Earl Carroll Theatre on June 15.

Borrowing the absence of scenery from *Elsie Janis and Her Gang* and *Some Party* and the pantomime necessities from *Chauvre Souris*, *Pinwheel* was devoted largely to classical dance, choreographed by Michio Itow and performed to the music of such composers as Brahms and Debussy. Frank Fay was on hand as master of ceremonies, and he and Hitchcock supplied what little humor there was. *Pinwheel* remained on view for only 33 performances, but it brought the total of revues in the 1921–22 season to 17—a trifle less than 50 percent of the 37 musicals that opened on Broadway that season.

On June 19, the first show of the 1922–1923 season arrived, a black revue, the first full-fledged one of its genre but certainly not the best. In an attempt to capitalize on the huge success of *Shuffle Along*, the 1921 hit with music and lyrics by Noble Sissle and Eubie Blake, the Minsky Brothers brought Henry Creamer and Turner Layton together on and offstage to provide the music and lyrics and some of the dialogue and singing for *Strut Miss Lizzie*, an otherwise largely dancing show. It remained at the Times Square for only 32 performances.

An almost equally dismal fate awaited *Spice of 1922*, which attempted to justify its title by pushing the limits of nudity a little bit further in two production numbers, one set in an artist's studio and the other in the Garden of Eden. Its cast included Georgie Price and Nan Halperin, and its score was ostensibly by James F. Hanley and Jack Lait, but its only popular numbers were interpolations. Benny Davis, Georgie Price and Abner Silver contributed "Angel Child," J. Fred Coots supplied "Back Numbers in My Little Red Book," and George Gershwin, Buddy DeSylva and Irving Caesar "Yankee Doodle Blues." But the added hit of the show was a tune that had been dropped from *Strut Miss Lizzie*. Henry Creamer and Turner Layton's "Way Down Yonder in New Orleans" became *Spice of 1922*'s sole legacy to the music literature of Broadway.

Yet another entry designed to fill an evening with struts, cakewalks, shuffles and soft shoes opened on July 17, at the 48th Street. *Plantation Revue* bettered *Strut Miss Lizzie* by three performances, then was swiftly forgotten.

It would be the end of August before a revue of substance and importance found its way to Broadway. *George White's Scandals of 1922* was, in many ways, a seminal revue for a number of reasons.

First, it established—or reflected—beyond a doubt, the beginning of the Roaring Twenties. The postwar recession was receding;speakeasies and private bootleggers had made Prohibition glamorous and dangerous. The popular music of the time was beginning to both echo and drive the energy of the generation that Gertrude Stein would term "Lost," whose participants Scott Fitzgerald would name Flaming Youth, and whose times he would name the Jazz Age.

And because, in the Twenties, Broadway was the major generator of popular music, the music of an age would be born there. And because revues were the closest of all forms on Broadway to contemporary happenings and tastes—both reflecting them and setting them, it was here that the sounds of the times were first heard. Just as Irving Berlin had brought ragtime to the public via the revues of the teens, George Gershwin would bring jazz undeniably into the public consciousness through the revues of the Twenties, particularly the *Scandals*. And the 1922 edition was the first show to finally give Gershwin the room and the reason to work his particular magic.

But more. This edition of the *Scandals*, the first to carry George White's name as part of the title, would give a renewed, now undeniable emphasis to the fact that the future of the revue, like that of book shows, would have to rely on a strong musical score as the real assurance of success. No longer could the score be ignored, as Irving Berlin had proved a year earlier and that Gershwin now underlined and capitalized.

The reverberations from the Gershwin score for *George White's Scandals of 1922* would echo far beyond its 11-week run, the shortest of any of the *Scandals*. While it didn't contain the catalogue of Gershwin hits that would come in two years, when his brother Ira joined him, it did contain two deathless compositions. One was "Stairway to Paradise" in which Buddy DeSylva's lyrics seamlessly fit the insistence of Gershwin's jazzy, bluesy melody. (Gershwin's father misinterpreted the sound for a march, and constantly pestered his son at parties. "Judge," he'd say in his 400-pound accent. "Play dot var song for me.")

Winnie Lightner delivered "Stairway to Paradise" before a staircase that was framed in Art Deco leather, then the jazz possibilities were explored by the pit orchestra conducted by Paul Whiteman, while Pearl Regay danced with abandon. It would have been Ann Pennington, but she'd gone back to Ziegfeld temporarily, while W.C. Fields, in an even swap, became a temporary tenant of the *Scandals*. Fields contributed a baseball sketch that didn't come close to Ring Lardner's in the *Follies*, but he had better luck with a sendup of radio, which was in its infancy and no great challenger to Broadway. Not yet.

The rest of the score and the show was tame and derivative: a toned down "Garden of Eden" number, and a bucolic reverie titled "I Found a Four Leaf Clover," introduced by Collette Ryan and Richard Bold.

What was most revolutionary and important in *George White's Scandals* was to be experienced only on opening night. Gershwin and DeSylva had written a 25 minute "jazz opera" titled *Blue Monday Blues*, which opened the second act. The sappily sentimental libretto and plodding lyrics of Buddy DeSylva were the major, uncredited culprits in convincing White that he should pull the work from the show immediately. But its music was exciting, varied and inventive, and if it didn't satisfy the producer and the first night audience, it did impress Paul Whiteman and cement his relationship with Gershwin. Re-orchestrated by Ferde Grofé, *Blue Monday Blues* became *135th Street* and, under Whiteman's baton and urging, was performed at

Carnegie Hall twice, with—weirdly—Benny Fields and Blossom Seeley singing major roles.

A quaint, imperfect oddity now in the meteoric career of a musical genius, *Blue Monday* was, nevertheless, important beyond the understanding of most of its first auditors, and a solid testament to the forceful contemporariness of the Broadway revue.

But, for all its accomplishments, 1922 was still a year of contrasts. If *George White's Scandals of 1922* looked forward, the Hippodrome's final extravaganza, ironically and accurately titled *Better Times*, was a glorious last hurrah. Heywood Broun pronounced "*Better Times*...quite the best show which the Hippodrome has seen," then went on with enthusiastic accuracy: "Indeed, *Better Times* is about the sort of show which Ziegfeld and Barnum might have been expected to put on if they had happened to be partners."[2]

The Barnum portion was provided by Powers' Elephants, the Three Bobs, the Berlo Sisters and Long Track Sam and Co. The Ziegfeld portion was in varied abundance, and included "The Land of Mystery," a light show that involved skeletons floating down from the upper reaches of the Hippodrome. Mixed in with the skeletons were marionettes, peirrots, pierettes, harlequins, witches, paper dolls, some as tall as the gigantic proscenium. Peach Blossom Time, with lots of two-legged peaches, appeared to the strains of "Down on the Farm," another tuneless air by Raymond Hubbell, set to inane lyrics by R. H. Burnside. "The Story of a Fan," in which hundreds of chorus girls became living panels in a gigantic fan, dropped in cascades of colored lights. And finally, "The Grand Opera Ball," in which characters from grand opera emerged from a gargantuan Victrola horn wowed spellbound aud ences.

But the *piece de resistance* was the finale, "The Harbor of Prosperity," a depiction of a golden, Oz-like city by the sea, from which gilded costumed girls moved forward, past the piers, and into the pool, down, down, and finally out of sight. It was another of the famous Hippodrome finales in which the casts of most of the 18 editions disappeared into water, never to be seen again—at least until the next performance.

Better Times stayed at the Hippodrome for a comfortable 409 performances, but Charles Dillingham, tired of the Hippodrome shows, had other ideas crowding into his creative supply closet. He was leaving the Hippodrome, and without him the Hippodrome would leave Broadway.

On the night of April 12, 1923, the eighteenth anniversary of its opening, a sentimental slide show chronicled its history. After the April 18 performance, R. H. Burnside gathered the staff and cast of one thousand and said goodbye. Some of the unfeatured performers had soared into the clouds and disappeared beneath the Hippodrome's sea for 15 years. It was as if a lifetime were ending.[3]

And, in many respects, it was. Rumors abounded that the Hippodrome was to be turned into the world's largest hotel, but they were false. Instead, Edward F. Albee bought it for the Keith-Albee vaudeville circuit, narrowed the proscenium, scrapped the 60-foot apron, drained the pool and ripped out the pumps, the lifts, the pistons, the hydraulics and the special effect cables. What Albee didn't know was that, in less time than he imagined, vaudeville would be as dead as the Hippodrome.

But not quite yet. On September 11, in the Greenwich Village Theatre, the former transit home of the *Greenwich Village Follies*, *A Fantastic Fricasee* opened. It was neither stewed nor fantastic, though it did manage to fill the small space in which it was produced with marionettes, a soldier ballet, and literate lyrics by Robert Edwards, who was listed as the headliner. Headliner he might have been, but a shapely redhead named Jeanette MacDonald, a singer who was making her Broadway debut, would last far longer than his lyrics or the show, which closed after a nearly respectable 112 performances.

On the next night, *The Greenwich Village Follies*, long liberated from its former wellspring and location, opened at the Shubert. It was as elaborate as a *Follies*, which was not so surprising considering that

James Reynolds supplied some of the more striking scenery for its most ambitious pageantry, notably "Sweetheart Lane" and "You Are My Rainbeau," a colorful mating ritual. Erté, the Parisian artist of slim, art deco models, added a series of Harper's Bazaar covers as frames for beautiful girls singing "Beautiful Girls," one of Kalmar and Ruby's lesser known numbers.

The most impressive decor was the Overture curtain, designed by Reginald Marsh. Its depiction of the Greenwich Village of 1922 contained portraits of denizens of the neighborhood, which lured audiences to the Shubert early, to play guessing games about who was who and where. Among the scores of Village characters and/or frequenters depicted on the curtain were Max Eastman, William Gropper, Maxwell Bodenheim, Burton Rascoe, John Peale Bishop, Gilbert Seldes, Edmund Wilson, Stephen Vincent Benét, John Dos Passos, Ben Hecht, F. Scott and Zelda Fitzgerald, Marcel Duchamp, Donald Ogden Stewart, John Sloan, Eugene O'Neill, Susan Glaspell, Helen Westley, Djuna Barnes, Edna St. Vincent Millay and, hovering like a benevolent Zeus over it all, Reginald Marsh, himself.

John Murray Anderson inserted the first of his "Ballet Ballads" into this edition of the *Greenwich Village Follies*. Oscar Wilde's poem "The Nightingale and the Rose" was introduced by a singer singing "Nightingale, Bring Me a Rose," then danced to a series of Chopin Nocturnes, arranged by Alfred Newman, long before he ascended to Oscar winning fame as a composer of film scores for Twentieth Century Fox.

Murray Anderson, who, like Ziegfeld, remained oblivious to the scores for his revues, commissioned yet another meaningless one by Louis A. Hirsch for this *Follies*. The only memorable music in the edition came from two interpolations, Yvonne George singing the hardy "Mon Homme" in its original French, and Ted Lewis and his band swinging through Ray Henderson and Buddy DeSylva's "Georgette." The comedy chores were handled by Jack Hazzard, who poked fun at the good old days by singing "Goodbye to Dear Old

Alaska," and by Savoy and Brennan in their knockabout, show-stopping, double and triple entendre arguments. Bert Savoy, who had inherited Julian Eltinge's mantle as Broadway's leading female impersonator and who had become wildly popular with 1922 audiences, was struck and killed by lightning at Long Beach, Long Island, two weeks after *The Greenwich Village Follies of 1922* closed. To musical comedy audiences it was as if Jolson had been suddenly removed from the world.

Meanwhile, Jake Shubert was slamming and growling his way into the Twenties with yet another *Passing Show*. The competition was growing. He hadn't been able to unseat Ziegfeld, and now here was George White with whom to contend. "So what's the tap-dancer going to do when he has his first flop?" he would snarl when White's name came up, then launch into a familiar tirade. "I remember George White when I fired him, which I will be glad to do again after he goes broke," he would add, chewing mightily on his cigar.[4]

The Passing Show of 1922 was neither much better nor much worse than the other revues surrounding it in the early Twenties. The runway was there, groaning under the combined weight of 65 showgirls and ponies, wearing very little for the visiting firemen and tired businessmen. Willie and Eugene Howard were bringing down the house nightly with their sendup of David Warfield and their turn as Tonsilitis and Abdullah, two street singers. But they had competition in the comedy department in the debut of a young, gravelly voiced standup comic whose future wife, Portland Hoffa, was in the chorus. Fred Allen's creation of "The Old Joke Cemetery" established him as a comic force with which to be reckoned. The blonde bombshell Ethel Shutta also delighted audiences with her slightly weird musical, satirical take on Eugene O'Neill's "The Hairy Ape."

The score, this time by Alfred Goodman, Harold Atteridge and Jack Stanley, was slightly more atrocious than usual, but there were some fortunate interpolations: Janet Adair sang "Pour J'En ai Marre," a Parisian ditty that Alice Delysia was simultaneously making famous

Three from *Three's a Crowd* (1930). *(Princeton University Library)*

Top: Dockwalker Libby Holman tantalizes sailor Fred MacMurray. *(Shubert Archives)*

Center: Fred Allen and Tamara Geva deal with reality. *(Princeton University Library)*

Bottom: Tamara Geva attempts to ruffle the crust of Clifton Webb. *(Princeton University Library)*

The Band Wagon (1931), one of the two greatest Broadway revues. Top: Hollis Shaw and the Albertina Rasch dancers *(Princeton University Library)*; center: one of the revolutionary, revolving turntables *(Princeton University Library)*; bottom: Fred and Adele Astaire, appearing for the last time together. *(Photofest)*

Right page: Top: The principals of *Flying Colors* (1932) multiplied by mask *(Princeton University Library)*. L to r: Charles Butterworth, Patsy Kelly, Clifton Webb, Tamara Geva.

Center: Webb operates operatically on Rags Ragland in *Flying Colors*. *(Shubert Archives)*

Bottom left: Ed Wynn in *Simple Simon* (1930). *(Courtesy of The Rodgers & Hammerstein Organization)*

Right: Libby Holman in *Ned Wayburn's Gambols* (1929). *(Photofest)*

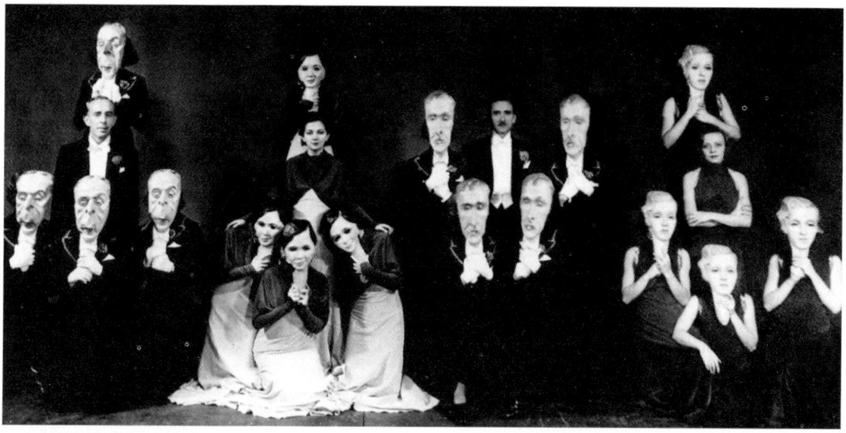
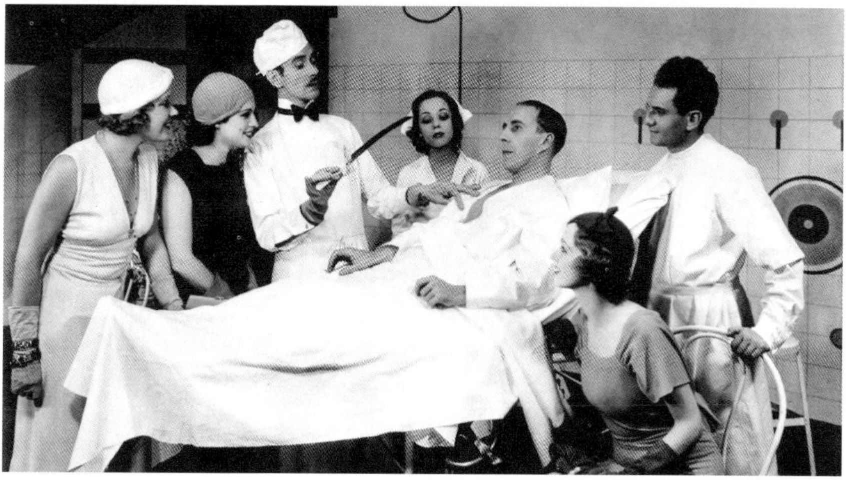
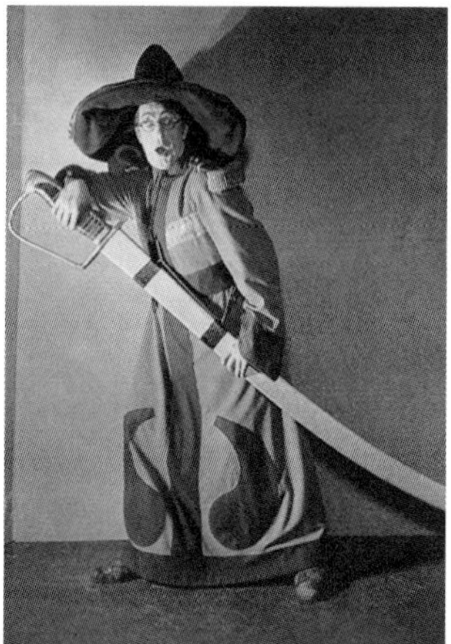
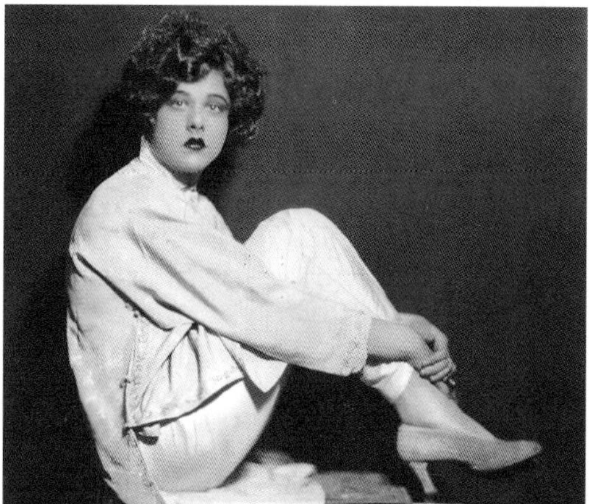

The Depression and remembered opulence figure in *Face the Music* (1932).

Top: "Let's Have Another Cup of Coffee" at the Automat.*(Courtesy of The Rodgers & Hammerstein Organization)*

Center: "Rhinestones of 1932," a revue within a book show. *(Courtesy of The Rodgers & Hammerstein Organization)*

Bottom: Beatrice Lillie and Reginald Gardner enjoy a shipboard encounter in *At Home Abroad* (1935). *(Photofest)*

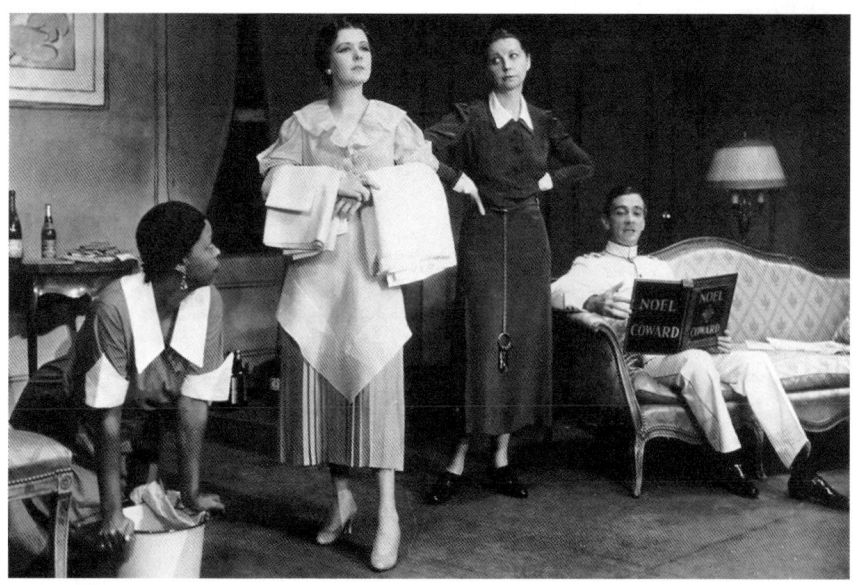

As Thousands Cheer (1933), the other of the two greatest Broadway revues.

Top: Contemporary headlines identify each episode of the show. *(Courtesy of The Rodgers & Hammerstein Organization)*

Center: Noel Coward has just vacated a hotel room, leaving the help—Ethel Waters, Marilyn Miller, Helen Broderick and Clifton Webb—speaking in clipped epigrams. *(Courtesy of The Rodgers & Hammerstein Organization)*

Bottom: Marilyn Miller and Clifton Webb, as Joan Crawford and Douglas Fairbanks, Jr., weather their divorce. *(Photofest)*

NEW YORK THEATRE REVIEW

WEEK OF OCTOBER 12th, 1934

"Life Begins at 8:40"
BERT LAHR
RAY BOLGER LUELLA GEAR
FRANCES WILLIAMS
NOW AT THE WINTER GARDEN

Left page: The Thirties revue personified, its curtain time advertised: 1934's *Life Begins at 8:40*. *(Shubert Archives)*

Top: The star lineup of *Life Begins at 8:40*: Ray Bolger, Luella Geer, Frances Williams, Bert Lahr. *(Shubert Archives)*

Center: playing against type, Bert Lahr (l) contemplates a sophisticated suicide as a French aristocrat, as Luella Geer and Ray Bolger egg him on. *(Shubert Archives)*

Bottom: The Weidman Dancers writhe through the Thirties staple, a South American production number. *(Shubert Archives)*

The Show Is On (1936), in true revue style, had something for everybody.

Top: Beatrice Lillie, as Mlle. Leonore, an acerbic grand-dame of the theatre. (*Shubert Archives*)

Center: Bert Lahr as a burlesque comedian kept at work by the WPA. (*Shubert Archives*)

Right: Ms. Lillie checking her face and furs before exiting on roller skates. (*Shubert Archives*)

Top left: Beatrice Lillie and Bert Lahr share a shadowy moment in *The Show Is On*.
(Shubert Archives)

Right: Fanny Brice and Bobby Clark in high society in the Shubert 1936 *Ziegfeld Follies*.
(Ziegfeld Club)

Bottom left: Abbott and Costello with Della Lind, in *Streets of Paris* (1939), their only Broadway foray *(Shubert Archives)*; Bert Lahr warbles "The Song of the Woodman" in *The Show Is On*. *(Shubert Archives)*

Top: Willie Howard, Rudy Vallee and Bert Lahr with three of the girls of *George White's Scandals of 1935-36*. *(Photofest)*

Center: The tapping queen, Eleanor Powell, in a more classic moment from *George White's Music Hall Varieties* (1932). *(Shubert Archives)*

Right: Billie Burke, who, in partnership with Ziegfeld's rivals, the Shuberts, prolonged the life of the Follies after her husband's death in 1932. *(Nils Hanson)*

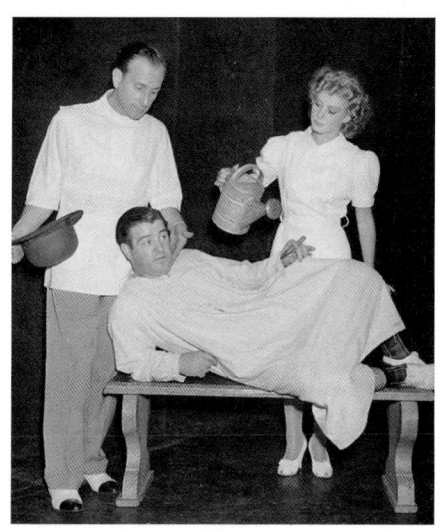

Audiences were served nostalgia and escape in *Streets of Paris* (1939).

Top: Willie and Eugene Howard and friends recreate their *Rigoletto* quartet. *(Photofest)*

Center l: Abbott and Costello bring back burlesque *(Photofest)*; r: Bobby Clark cavorts as "The Roué from Reading, Pa." *(Shubert Archives)*

Bottom: Bob Hope and Fanny Brice exchange quips in *The Ziegfeld Follies of 1936*. *(Ziegfeld Club)*

The chaos heard round the world: 1938's *Hellzapoppin*. *(Shubert Archives)*

Top: Ole Olsen and Chick Johnson even overwhelmed Jake Shubert with their theatrical hurricane, *Hellzapoppin*. (*Shubert Archives*)

Center: Audience participation unlimited: Johnson awards a toilet seat to Lyle Talbot's girlfriend during a performance. (*Shubert Archives*)

Bottom: The promotion for *Hellzapoppin* was as wild and profuse as the show itself. (*Shubert Archives*)

Top: Youth, in the person of Imogene Coca and Danny Kaye, reigns in *The Straw Hat Revue* (1939). *(Shubert Archives)*

Center: Ann Miller gets in the South American groove in *George White's Scandals of 1939*. *(Photofest)*

Bottom: Contemporary social awareness is rampant in 1939's *Pins and Needles*. L: Fritz Kuhn (Harry Clark) Senator Reynolds (Berni Gould) and Father Coughlin (Al Eban) discuss Un-American Activities *(Shubert Archives)*; r: Mussolini, Hitler and Chamberlain conduct a Munich roundelay. *(Shubert Archives)*

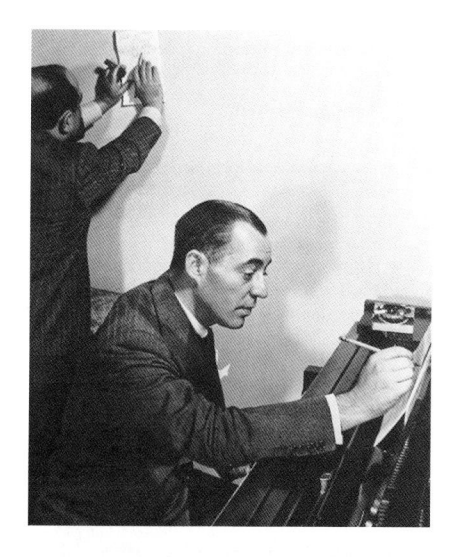

Change is the rule in the 1940s.

Top left: Richard Rodgers and Lorenz Hart dissolve a seemingly indissoluble partnership. *(Courtesy of The Rodgers & Hammerstein Organization)*

Right: Jimmy Durante is an unlikely Romeo, serenading Ilka Chase as a bewildered Juliet in the 1940 flop *Keep Off the Grass*. *(Shubert Archives)*

Bottom left: Carmen Miranda shakes it up in Olsen and Johnson's *Sons O' Fun* (1941). *(Shubert Archives)*

Right: A GI Lynn Fontanne holds forth in the "Stage Door Canteen" number from Irving Berlin's *This is the Army* (1942). *(Courtesy of The Rodgers & Hammerstein Organization)*

The Broadway revue's last hurrah.

Top left: Betty Garrett buries the Thirties with "South America, Take it Away," in *Call Me Mister* (1946). *(Photofest)*
Right: William Eythe and Carol Channing send up French films in *Lend an Ear* (1950). *(Photofest)*

Bottom left: Jack Haley and Beatrice Lillie recreate strange Americana in *Inside U.S.A.* (1949). *(Photofest)*
Right: Alice Ghostley endures the agonies of experiencing "The Boston Beguine" in *New Faces of 1952*. *(Photofest)*

in London, and the Howard Brothers were handed the melodious plum of Gus Kahn and Walter Donaldson's "Carolina in the Morning."

The Passing Show of 1922 opened on September 20 and barely kept the Winter Garden lit for 85 performances. The Shuberts, however, weren't easily discouraged. The success of *Chauve Souris* still resonated within their conclave, and, in concert with Bessie Marbury, who had once worked with Morris Gest, they imported the *Revue Russe*, in hopes of cashing in on a revolutionary phenomenon. This "Russian vaudeville" was just that, and not very good, either, and could eke out only 20 days in October at the Booth Theatre.

Far more to the public's taste was Irving Berlin's second *Music Box Revue*. Once again, Berlin and Sam Harris proved that a strong score enhanced spectacle. And in this, the *Music Box Revues* were constantly ahead of the other extravagant revues. This one was a knockout, employing every elevator, trap and winch on and off the Music Box's stage. Steam, shooting flames and disappearing celebrities were the focus of the "Pack Up Your Sins" production number, in which Charlotte Greenwood, as a long-limbed devil, consigned look-alikes of Gilda Gray, Ted Lewis, Bee Palmer, Joe Frisco and other worthy entertainers to a fiery, volcanic pit.

Hassard Short repeated himself as director, as did Grace LaRue in two marvels of costuming. One, titled "Diamond Horseshoe," involved Ms. LaRue as an opera prima donna ascending a staircase and trailing a train behind her which, as she ascended, gradually enveloped the entire stage. Later in the revue, she returned in "Crinoline Days," wearing a hoop skirt that, as she rose on an elevator, also consumed the stage.

There was jazzy dancing by the McCarthy Sisters and Charlotte Greenwood while singing "I Want a Daddy Long-Legs." And John Steel, who was still introducing the showgirls at the *Follies* as he did with "A Pretty Girl Is Like a Melody," sang the show's hit ballad "Lady of the Evening."

But for all of that, this *Music Box Revue* is most notable for its introduction to Broadway of two comedians who, having traveled the burlesque and vaudeville circuit, had to go to London to be discovered by Irving Berlin. Bobby Clark and Paul McCullough brought the house down nightly, and few respectable revues from then on could open without them. Once more a solid success, *The Music Box Revue of 1922* ran through the season and into the summer of 1923.

The final revue of 1922 was a grand experiment so far ahead of its time that the public chose to ignore it. As Burns Mantle put it, "The multitude sniffed and would have none of it." It would take a Depression, apparently, before this multitude would accept intellectual challenges and truly literate satire in its revues. And so *The 49ers*, a 1922 preview of the great revues of the Thirties, came and went from the tiny Punch and Judy Theatre after 16 performances.

The product of several long lunches at the Algonquin's notoriously famous Round Table, it boasted a roster of writers that read like a catalogue of the greatest wits of the time, led by George S. Kaufman and Marc Connelly, the only ones who had any Broadway experience. Lack of knowledge of the form did nothing to dampen the enthusiasm of Robert Benchley and Dorothy Parker, who sent up historical dramas in a sketch that muddled Richelieu, Queen Victoria and Robert E. Lee in one indigestible stew. Franklin P. Adams fashioned a musical comedy from a business routine; Heywood Broun turned Hans Christian Andersen's "The King's New Suit of Clothes" into a Pirandellian exercise; Ring Lardner contributed surreal sketches, and operetta was skewered in a piece called "The Love Call." But the public didn't buy it, and the Algonquin gang went back to lunch on 43rd Street more convinced than ever that the world was full of philistines.

It would be June, the end of the 1922–23 season, before another revue appeared, and it was yet another *Passing Show*, this an even paler shadow of its former opulent self than its September, 1922, version. The Howards were gone now, replaced by a bright young deliverer of monologues named George Jessel. And Walter Woolf did a sendup of a bloodthirsty revolutionary in a production number titled ponderously, "Beginning of the French Revolution 1789." But that was it for the specialty department, unless, of course, you counted a desperation oddity, golf champion Alex Morrison doing an exhibition of putts and mashie shots.

Sigmund Romberg and Jean Schwartz were back to try to make some musical sense of Harold Atteridge's lyrics. They didn't succeed, but the visiting firemen hardly noticed. It was girls they came to see, and it was girls they got, wearing considerably less than ever before. There were chandeliers with nudes glowing from them, fruit baskets with naked chorus girls adorned with strategically placed clusters of fruit (Nancy Carroll, who eventually donned her clothes and became a Paramount star, was a grape in this number); there were semi-feathered "Birds of Plumage" and semi-naked book covers sporting some of the titles of the day, such as "The Beautiful and the Damned" (Nancy Carroll was the Beautiful), "Blood and Sand," "Simon Called Peter" and just plain "Damned."

If Jake Shubert couldn't keep up with George White and Irving Berlin by adding music that mattered to his revues, he could remove the girl's clothes and still fill his theatre. And this he did, and, in so doing, set a standard that even Ziegfeld would grudgingly be obliged to follow in order to survive the coming Roaring Twenties.

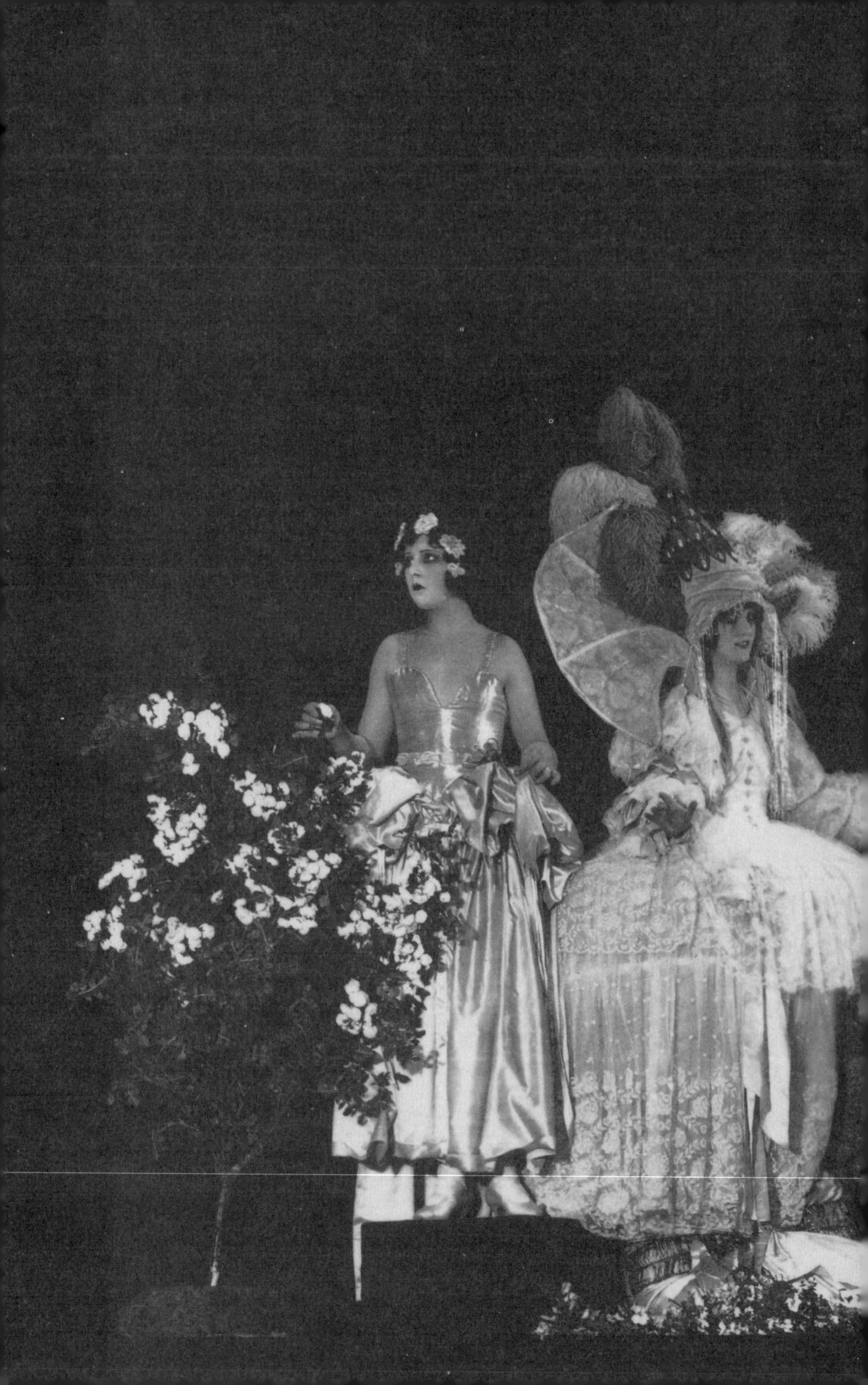

9

Less Is More

Less is More

❦

At first, George White resisted the nudity that was drawing male audiences, like iron filings to a magnet, into the revues that featured it. His stock-in-trade was the up-to-date jazziness of the Gershwin scores and the energetic brightness of his dancing girls. But Ann Pennington, the best of them, had left him, as had Paul Whiteman and his orchestra, Jack McGowan, W.C. Fields and Ed Wynn. Dancer Lester Allen was there for the early June opening of *George White's Scandals of 1923*, and so, fortunately, was singer/dancer Winnie Lightner, who had introduced Gershwin's "Stairway to Paradise" in 1922.

But, unfortunately, Gershwin, still shackled to a gaggle of conflicting lyricists—this time E. Ray Goetz, Buddy DeSylva and Ballard MacDonald—turned out not one hit song for this edition. In fact, the entire show fell considerably below the level White had first set for himself. But 1923 audiences, starting to ride the wave that would crest at the end of the decade, didn't seem to notice and kept the Globe Theatre full for 168 performances.

However, on September 5, the nudity quotient of the Broadway revue took a significant leap upward and outward with the debut of the tackiest take yet on the *Ziegfeld Follies*. Earl Carroll, an ambitious producer and songwriter, whose level of taste was located considerably below that of Ziegfeld and White and a bit beneath even Jake

Shubert's, would become hugely wealthy and a force on Broadway on the strength of an overheated potboiler set in the South Seas, *White Cargo*. Its fame would rest on a pronouncement by its leading native lady, who was no lady. "Me Tondeleyo," she would moan, at which point, on opening night, critic George Jean Nathan rose from his seat, said, "Me George Jean Nathan. Me go home." And did. The public, however, titillated by reports that the police were keeping a steady watch on the steamy goings on onstage, would flock to the play for 864 performances in New York, and God knows how many by the nine road companies that would fan out before the New York run finally ended.

That, however, would all come later in the 1923–24 season, in which Earl Carroll mounted his first *Vanities*.

Carroll's rise to fame had been anything but meteoric. He came to New York from Pittsburgh in 1912, as a composer whose first Broadway effort was, ironically "Isle D'Amour," sung by Jose Collins in *The Ziegfeld Follies of 1913*. After a stint in the Army Air Force during World War I, Carroll returned to Broadway as a producer of 14 plays that ranged from terrible flops to moderate successes.

His secret of longevity in the big time, which included having, at an early age, and without much to show for it, his own theatre, was the presence of Colonel William R. Edrington, a Texas oil millionaire who had endless faith in Carroll and an apparently equally endless appetite for beautiful girls.

Carroll's ambition was to produce a revue to challenge Ziegfeld. "Look at Flo Ziegfeld!" he was reported in a 1923 *Variety* as saying. "The tremendous success he's had in presenting beautiful girls bedecked in jewels and furs. Let Flo spend money dressing them. My plan is to *undress* them, and display them in more expensive settings than Ziegfeld ever imagined..."[1]

He made good on half his threat. There would be more nudes per square inch of stage space in his *Vanities* when it opened in July of 1923, than in any other revue on Broadway. His sets, on the other hand, would consist mostly of basic cubes, lit imaginatively and arranged creatively.

But he did have an eye for ravishing and, in some cases, notorious women. Ziegfeld's agents reportedly auditioned 14,000 girls a year; Carroll started small, but he was obviously out to better the master when he had the words THROUGH THESE PORTALS PASS THE MOST BEAUTIFUL GIRLS IN THE WORLD emblazoned on the front of his theatre.

Dorothy Knapp was his Lillian Lorraine. For his Marilyn Miller, he chose a former Ziegfeld beauty, Peggy Hopkins Joyce, who was currently coming off her third divorce, would soon be immortalized by Anita Loos as the model for the character of Lorelei Lee in *Gentlemen Prefer Blondes*, and who already had a reputation in the tabloids that would assure unstinting press coverage.

Peggy Hopkins Joyce was the apotheosis of the lately liberated flapper of the Twenties, and then some. Asked why she kept marrying and divorcing men, and becoming romantically involved with scores of others, she quipped, "I owe it to my pubic."

Not satisfied with merely dispensing quotes for the press, she began to keep a diary which would be anything but private. Of Dorothy Knapp's offstage behavior in the *Vanities of 1923*, she wrote, "They say she's sleeping with Mr. Carroll. I don't think it's right to have an affair with the producer you're working for, but if another actress wants to go places on her back, it's okay with me..."[2]

With that sort of advance publicity, and the promise of acres of unadorned young female flesh, the *Vanities of 1923* opened to great anticipation but no word-of-mouth from out of town. Carroll, who wrote the score, the lyrics, the sketches, and both directed and produced, opened the show cold in New York on July 5, 1923. It was the sort of brash behavior for which he would be known for the rest of his not-very-long life.

The first *Vanities* began, appropriately enough, with a parade of beauties representing other Broadway revues, past and present—the

Cohan Revue, Follies, Scandals, Passing Show, Greenwich Village Follies and, finally, a babe in the buff—Alice Weaver—representing the birth of a new revue, the *Vanities*. Bernard Granville sang Carroll's inane songs, most of them with "Girls" in the title. Joe Cook did his circus and vaudeville routines while the scenes and the girls changed. Living curtains of nudes, nudes posing before statuary and "virgins in cellophane," as Carroll's publicity described them, adorned other production numbers.

And the public and the critics loved it. Mostly. George Jean Nathan did opine that "...Had nature endowed Peggy Hopkins Joyce with even a little talent in addition to her beauty it would have been manifestly unfair to the rest of the female sex."[3] But the *American* captured the popular view: "Earl Carroll and his new opulently eye-filling *Vanities*...makes a strong bid for the distinction of the gaudiest, spiciest, and most lavish entertainment on view...The lovely, young and shapely Carroll beauties match anything in Paris, or for that matter, Flo Ziegfeld has to offer." The first *Vanities* ran for a healthy, profitable 204 performances.

Ziegfeld looked upon the *Vanities* with bemusement, then he offered Dorothy Knapp a larger salary to appear in his next *Follies*. She accepted with alacrity.

Two weeks after the *Vanities* premiered, Ted Snyder and Harry B. Smith, whose résumés were several miles long by now, tried to resurrect the old-fashioned, unspectacular revue/vaudeville that had hardly made it in the early days of the form. Their *Fashions of 1924*, directed and produced by Alexander Leftwich, came and went from the Lyceum after 13 performances.

August brought a novel revue to the Ambassador Theatre. Had its creator been a little less concentrated upon himself and a little more observant of talent, the show might have been progressive, at the very least. Will Morrisey, who had made his Broadway debut in *Toot Sweet*, the wartime revue-within-a-show, assembled a cast of unknowns, appointed himself master of ceremonies and guiding force, and presented an obviously inexpensive revue called, appropriately, *The Newcomers*. But these newcomers were not very talented, and the evening amounted to a not very distinguished vaudeville show. It departed after 21 performances, and the proper, final manifestation of the good idea that began with the *Garrick Gaieties* would have to wait for 11 years, and Leonard Sillman's first *New Faces*.

Meanwhile, Jake Shubert, ever enterprising, ever ambitious and ever imitative, was busily preparing a revue that would outnude the nudes in the *Vanities*. Several months before, he had announced that "A successful, high-type, sophisticated revue which was done by the Society of Illustrators is going to be expanded into a sparkling Broadway-type production by the Shuberts. We are calling it *Artists and Models*."

Actually, Jake's agents had caught the unassuming amateur show done by the Illustrators' Society in Greenwich Village, informed Jake that it had a certain smartness and some possibilities, and he had bought it sight unseen. When he walked into an early rehearsal of its Broadway transference, the story goes, he was apoplectic, as usual. He excoriated director J.C. Huffman before firing him. "When I say *Artists and Models* what the hell do you think of?" he fumed, then amplified his indignation. "You see a whole lot of men with hands on their hips, holding paintbrushes, making living tableaux with girls all full of clothes? Is that what you see?"

Jake went on to yell about Paris, where the girls were naked and the artists were real men; he then climbed onto the stage and began to rip the blouses of the chorus girls from neck to waist, until half the line was naked from the waist up.

"No broad who won't show her tits can work this show," he yelled, conclusively, "And that's final!"

Some of the girls left the stage, covering their breasts and their dignity. But most remained. They saw the writing on the dressing room wall. Nudity was in, and if they wanted to work, they would have to live with it.[4]

Now, under the tutelage of the one and only (thank heaven) J. J. Shubert (the directing credit would read "staged by Harry Wagstaff Gribble and Francis Weldon, under the supervision of J.J. Shubert"), *Artists and Models* leaped into being, and, as promised, it featured more undraped girls than anything Broadway had yet seen. With artists' studios and oversized palettes as excuses, they posed, danced and even delivered lines in the buff or the near buff. Ziegfeld kept his nudes still in Ben Ali Haggin's living tableaux; Carroll posed his. Jake Shubert had his strutting into and out of the feeble sketches and bantering with a leering Frank Fay as the master of ceremonies.

It got the attention of the visiting firemen and tired businessmen, all right. And the forces of censorship which began to organize themselves. *Variety* opined that "it contains the dirtiest jokes ever heard on the Broadway boards," and another critic called its raunchy sketch version of *Rain*, "the rawest, smuttiest, most shameless misdemeanor ever committed." It was sweet music to Jake Shubert. The demand for seats—particularly down front, single seats—was huge and unending. The first of the intermittently produced *Artists and Models* remained at the Shubert for 312 performances—longer than any other revue, except the Hippodrome shows, yet.

The return to sanity and some propriety fell to John Murray Anderson and Irving Berlin, who began the fall season of 1923-24 with their continuing series within two days of each other.

The Greenwich Village Follies opened at the Winter Garden on September 20. And although Murray Anderson bowed to the inevitable and used some nudes, he employed them tastefully and as decoration rather than the focus of the show. That focus was fairly evenly divided among the cracker-barrel comedy wisdom of Tom Howard, the female impersonation, in the style of Julian Eltinge, of Karyl Norman, the stunning scenic designs of Reginald Marsh, and the two Ballet Ballads, One, based upon Poe's "The Raven" was bad enough to be withdrawn; the other, "The Garden of Kama," an evocation of ancient India that featured Martha Graham, was good enough to remember.

Though Marsh's splashy set for the "Moonlight Kisses" production number that featured, yet again, ladies of history, and his evocation of Velázquez in a Spanish dance for Martha Graham, accompanied by Rita Hayworth's parents the Cansinos, received the most attention and applause, But his special curtain, which pictured a Greenwich Village of yesterday and included Anna Held among its recognizable paintings of famous dwellers there, was most revealing of the traditional place the once offbeat and daring *Greenwich Village Follies* now occupied on a changing Broadway. This edition, which, also traditionally possessed a forgettable musical score by Louis A. Hirsch, Con Conrad, Irving Caesar and John Murray Anderson, ran for a respectable 140 performances.

On September 22, the eagerly awaited *Music Box Revue of 1923-1924* arrived and it was in some respects the best and in other respects the worst of the series. Its major negative was its size. Evidently in an effort to underline the production effects that Ziegfeld always considered foremost and that some of the new revues—particularly *Artists and Models* were downplaying, Berlin replaced Hassard Short with John Murray Anderson and brought in James Reynolds to do his last revue designs.

Not only that. The cast read like a *Follies* cast. Onstage were Fanny Brice, Grace Moore, John Steel, Oscar Shaw, Clark and McCullough, Carl Randall, the Brox Sisters, Robert Benchley and Clair Luce, a young specialty dancer appearing on Broadway for the first time.

Benchley, in a letter to Alexander Woollcott, described the melee of rehearsal, the "...men with their hats on, each sitting on as much of an aisle seat as he can uncover from the big sheet which spreads out over all the orchestra chairs...crazy lights come up from the stage..." and then "a little man in a tight-fitting suit with his hands in his pockets walks on from the wings. He looks very white in the glare from the foots. You almost expect him to be thrown out, he seems so casual and like an observer. They don't throw him out, however, because he is Mr. Berlin."

And the ever observant Benchley notes one overriding contradiction: "Irving Berlin is so little. And The Fourth *Music Box Revue* is so big."[5]

And it was. But the 20 original songs, while serviceable, contained not one hit. At the last minute, Berlin interpolated his already established "What'll I Do?" into the show.

Still, there was something refreshingly new in this *Music Box Revue* and, as in the first, a presage of things to come. Probably because of his own presence at the lunchtime gatherings of the Algonquin Round Table, Berlin brought in two of its brightest creative talents. Robert Benchley delivered the now classic "Treasurer's Report" with its deliciously subtle humor ("I don't know if you know it, but most of the boys at the camp we support are between the ages of fourteen..."). And George S. Kaufman, who would be responsible for some of the most dazzling sketches of the revues of the Thirties, contributed yet another classic, "If Men Played Cards As Women Do."

The 1923–1924 edition of *The Music Box Revue*, while extravagant and beautiful—and profitable, with a run of 184 performances—was the last of the brief series. Berlin, like Gershwin and Kern, was being lured away from writing for revues and into the more satisfying creation of complete, interpolationless scores for book shows.

Three nights after the *Music Box Revue* opened, Charles Dillingham, himself a master of extravaganza, assembled an interesting cast of new and old faces for a challenge to the smut of Jake Shubert and Earl Carroll. Advertised, à la Ziegfeld, as a show dedicated to "glorifying clean American humor," *Nifties of 1923* was an understated, well-intended, but ultimately unsuccessful return to the revues of a decade earlier.

It certainly had all of the elements that should have made it a success; Van and Schenck did their old time routines to their own old time music; Sam Bernard and William Collier, their contemporary counterparts, supplied the material for the show's remaining sketches; Hazel Dawn sent up Jeanne Eagels in *Rain*; Frank Crummit lent his warm personality and singing voice; Helen Broderick and Ray Dooley spread sparkle through the sketches, and Dillingham imported, from London, the 12 Tiller Girls, a precision dance team that would be a continuing presence on Broadway for years to come.

What is more, Dillingham paid attention to the music, although nothing of note survived the 47 performance run of the show. George Gershwin, Buddy DeSylva and Arthur Jackson supplied five songs; Kalmar and Ruby one, Frank Crummit one, Van and Schenck, Benny Davis and Harry Akst three, while "Fabric of Dreams," a forgotten underpinning for a production number, had music by Raymond Hubbell and lyrics by Buddy DeSylva and Arthur Francis—the pseudonym behind which Ira Gershwin lurked in 1923.

The rush of revues continued unabated into October (ultimately 63%—12 of the 19 musicals that opened in the 1923–1924 season—would be revues). On October 4, Arthur Hammerstein imported a Harold Simpson and Morris Harvey revue from London, opened the Century roof and rechristened the show *Hammerstein's 9 O'Clock Revue*. It had been a big late night hit at the Little Theatre in the West End, but, perhaps because of the liquid loosener denied its audiences in New York, it failed to amuse Broadway and departed after 12 performances.

And now it was time for *The Ziegfeld Follies of 1923,* which was really a sort of segue from 1922. There is some, although not convincing, evidence that Ziegfeld was becoming distracted by a rising interest in staging plays and book shows as the 1920s unfolded. Prevented by Prohibition from demonstrating his energy and imagination in his formerly profitable roof top after-theatre revues, he seemed to lose concentration and spirit for his downstairs extravaganzas. The fall 1923 edition of the *Follies* and the attendant dissatisfaction of some of its greatest names seem to confirm this.

Fanny Brice was reportedly so unhappy with her material that she made this her last *Follies*. James Reynolds left after this edition too, although the defection of both had probably been telegraphed by their appearances in the *Music Box Revue*.

Still, although not listed in the original program, Ann Pennington returned to this edition to team with Brooke Johns, Ziegfeld's substitute for the departed (and now sadly dipsomaniacal) John Steel, for a Harry Tierney-Joseph McCarthy song "Take Oh Take Those Lips Away," then danced while Johns plucked away at a banjo. Eddie Cantor's feud with Ziegfeld dissolved in the producer's promised creation of *Kid Boots* later in the season, and the popeyed comedian, similarly uncredited in the opening night program, made an abbreviated appearance in the 1923 *Follies*.

Bert and Betty Wheeler (Bert Wheeler would soon become half of the comedy team of Wheeler and Woolsey) were a pleasant new duo (he brought down the house by singing an emotional "Mammy song" while eating a sandwich), and Paul Whiteman and his orchestra made the crossover from the *Scandals* and jazzed up the proceedings. Ziegfeld's answer to the nudity of the age was to have exotic dancer Muriel Stryker paint herself with gold paint and do her stuff in an opulent Reynolds production number titled "Maid of Gold." When Ms. Stryker's doctor aborted the idea after the first two weeks, warning her that she wouldn't survive if she kept poisoning herself with paint, Ziegfeld simply clothed her in body-clinging, gold designs by Erté and made sure the press was informed of every step of the transformation.

Dorothy Knapp was in radiant evidence, as was the usual staircase parade of Ziegfeld lovelies. Reynolds designed gorgeous production numbers—particularly a fiery revolution recreation titled "The Legend of the Drums." Dave Stamper not only composed the bulk of the score with Gene Buck as lyricist, but appeared with his wife, singing comedienne Edna Leedom. Victor Herbert contributed suitably nostalgic moments with three classically production-number-oriented songs, also with Gene Buck lyrics, "That Old Fashioned Garden of Mine," "I'd Love to Waltz Through Life with You" and "Lady of the Lantern." And Rudolph Friml presented the second of three versions of a hardy melody which began life as "Lady Fair," became, for this *Follies*, "Chansonette" and finally matured into "The Donkey Serenade."

Distracted Ziegfeld might have been, but this *Follies* ran for 333 performances, which made it the longest-lived edition so far.

Topics of 1923, the last revue of 1923, which opened shortly before Thanksgiving, was a Shubert try at capitalizing on the international reputation of Mlle. Alice Delysia, one of Charles B. Cochran's favorite attractions in London. Mlle. Delysia had already experienced an unsuccessful debut in New York in 1921, with *Afgar*. Jake Shubert now put to work on her behalf his *Passing Show* production team of Harold Atteridge and Harry Wagstaff Gribble, composers Jean Schwartz and Alfred Goodman, lyricist Harold Atteridge and director J. C. Huffman. In contradiction to his concentration on nudes (and in imitation of Ziegfeld), he clothed his star in fashions by Erté, Pascaud, Patou and Trais Banton. And although historic accounts call *Topics of 1923* a flop, attendance records show a 143-performance run—scarcely a failure in 1923.

There could be no disagreement, however, with the first revue of 1924. It was historic, dynamic proof that the concept of less being more could be applied to something other than undressing large numbers of chorus girls. The move toward bright intelligence, hinted at by *The 49ers* and improved upon in *The Music Box Revue of 1923*, burst into full-fledged maturity with the arrival of *Andre Charlot's Revue of 1924*.

Actually a compilation of the best material from a series of *Charlot's Revues* that had run in London for the previous few years, this milestone revue flew merrily in the face of almost everything the American revue had espoused since its inception.

It was small; it was intimate; it contained no big production numbers, no nudes and hardly any girls; it was intelligent to the point, at times, of being intellectually challenging; it paid attention to the music and lyrics of its army of composers and lyricists, among them, Philip Braham, Douglas Furber and Ivor Novello, Noble Sissle and Eubie Blake, and most lastingly, Noel Coward.

And it introduced three performers who would instantly ascend to the firmament of Broadway stardom in this production: the debonair singer/dancer Jack Buchanan, the charismatic actress/singer Gertrude Lawrence, and the raucous and inimitable comedienne Beatrice Lillie. Buchanan would come into his own later. But Gertrude Lawrence immediately won the hearts and applause of New York audiences with her heartrending delivery of two songs, Douglas Furber and Philip Braham's "Limehouse Blues" and Noel Coward's "Parisian Pierrot." And Beatrice Lillie took New York by storm, first with her depiction of an aging soubrette, and then with a hilarious stint as the leader of a marching unit (to music by Ivor Novello) which degenerated into chaos and a wildly disarranged costume. It became a classic part of her repertoire from that moment on.

Andre Charlot's Revue of 1923 immediately became the cause of the intelligentsia, a reason for the first string critics to toss their hats collectively into the air, and a big money maker for the Selwyns, who had imported it. It would run out the season and then some at the Times Square Theatre.

The winter passed, and at the end of March, *Vogues of 1924*, a Shubert creation with sketches by Fred Thompson, lyrics by Clifford Grey and music by Herbert Stothart, opened. Some of the intelligence of the Charlot revue seemed to rub off on this show, which featured Fred Allen in an algebra lesson ("Let X equal my father's signature") very much like Benchley's "Treasurer's Report" in *The Music Box Revue of 1923*. Come to think of it, *Vogues of 1924* borrowed— successfully—from the earlier *Nifties of 1923*, with Hazel Dawn's violin playing duplicated by Odette Myrtil, and Miss Dawn's sendup of

Rain from that revue expanded into a veritable Floradora production. Jimmy Savo and a gaggle of girls provided less cerebral entertainment, and *Vogues of 1924* played out the season.

Three successive nights in May of 1924 formed a particularly busy island of time for the Broadway revue. First, on May 19, a brother act of volcanic power and supreme zaniness tumbled out of vaudeville and onto Broadway in a revue pretending to be a musical comedy called *I'll Say She Is.* Intriguingly, although Carlotta Miles was listed in the program as Lotta Miles (and was the butt of Groucho Marx's jokes—for example: "You are charged with murder and if you are convicted you will be charged with electricity."), the brothers, for their debut, used their real names. The later Chico, Harpo, Groucho and Zeppo were listed, respectively, as Leonard, Adolph, Julius H. and Herbert. The excuse for many scenes of mayhem was the search by Miles, a hypnotized beauty, for the thrills that a trip through history and geography provided. The music—what there was of it—was by Tom Johnstone, the minimal book and lyrics were by Will B. Johnstone.

One day later, *Innocent Eyes* opened at the Winter Garden. The Shuberts attempted to follow up the popularity of *Charlot's Revue* and to capture some of the success of *Topics of 1923* by importing yet another star from abroad. Once again, the Winter Garden creative team, with Sigmund Romberg back in the fold, surrounded the star—in this case, the Parisian chanteuse Mistinguette—with an opulent production. They apparently neglected available history, for Ziegfeld had auditioned and rejected her, appropriating only her song "Mon Homme" for Fanny Brice in his 1921 *Follies. Innocent Eyes* proved Ziegfeld right. Despite the overall *Folies Bergere* look of the revue and the presence of a personable and talented supporting cast including Cecil Lean and Cleo Mayfield doing comic sketches, the singing of Edyth Baker and, in the chorus, a cherubic future comic named Jack Oakie, the show closed before the middle of the summer.

That same night, the tradition of *The 49ers* and *Charlot's Revue* was given a considerable boost with the opening of *The Grand Street Follies*. It and the revue that opened on the next night confirmed the importance of wit and bright intelligence, as well as a willingness to forgo spectacle for the small and economical. In fact, the pocket form that the revue would eventually assume reached a respectable and acceptable plateau in the 1923–1924 season.

The Grand Street Follies played for seven months Off-Broadway, giving Sunday shows in order to attract the performers in the Broadway houses. The product of the young people of The Neighborhood Playhouse, at 466 Grand Street on the Lower East Side, it was originally concocted, in the 1921–22 season, as in-house relief from the diet of heavy drama the Neighborhood Playhouse normally presented. Billed for its small subscription list as "A low brow show for high grade morons," it attracted enough attention to warrant a public showing in a new edition for 1923–24.

It was a rollicking roundup of satirical versions of contemporary plays and players—in other words, classic burlesque brought refreshingly and winningly up-to-date. The Russian Art Players were skewered with a hillbilly tragedy, *These Fine Pretty Depths*. The most revered stars of the day were parodied mercilessly: John Barrymore, Elsie Janis, Beatrice Lillie, Fanny Brice (as Ophelia!), Eva Le Galliene, Pola Negri, Valentino—all came in for a lashing. The leading roles of the past few seasons came in for their licks, too: Joan of Arc, Sadie Thompson and Tondelayo were treated irreverently by a young cast that included Martin Wolfson, Dorothy Sands and Aline MacMahon. The music was undistinguished, and the sets, distinctive and minimal, were by Aline Bernstein, who would later acquire lasting literary fame as Thomas Wolfe's matronly mistress.

The Grand Street Follies was a runaway hit and attracted audiences off Broadway until the middle of December.

One night after it opened, still another appeal to the intellect and the taste of audiences for the pocket philosophy of revue making, titled *Round the Town,* was unveiled on the Century Roof. Produced by Herman Manckiewiez and S. Jay Kaufman, who wrote for the *New York Telegram*, it was a series of satirical sketches penned mostly by journalists. Perhaps that was its problem. It needed more theatre-savvy creators, like the authors of the revue's best ten minutes, George S. Kaufman and Marc Connelly. Their sendup of their own *Beggar on Horseback* was the evening's brightest exercise, but not enough to save the show. It closed after 13 performances.

And finally, a night after the opening of *Round the Town*, the last revue—and next to last musical—of the season premiered at the Morosco. An unbalanced concoction, *Keep Kool*, which derived its title from "Keep It Cool With Coolidge," the current political slogan of the man who wanted to be president, did have some engaging satire, but its incongruous mixture of youth and declining stars didn't allow it to continue through the summer.

And so, a season of upheaval came to a close. Less is more was the rule in two ways: nudity proliferated to the point that no big Broadway revue could be expected to open without a healthy quotient of it. And smallness, encapsulated in one critic's observation that the Marx Brothers' debut piece, *I'll Say She Is*, "is presented with what seems to be twenty four dollars worth of scenery"[6] was more reality than criticism when *The Grand Street Follies* debuted.

Of course, new ideas take time to take root. That summer brought the new edition, in its accustomed opening slot, of *The Ziegfeld Follies*, and its scenery cost the Great Glorifier considerably more than 24 dollars.

Once again, Julian Mitchell staged the expected cascade of beautiful girls and beautiful scenery, punctuated by the comedy of Will Rogers, making his final *Follies* appearance. Later in the long run of this edition, W.C. Fields joined the cast after the out of town closing of *The Comic Supplement*, a vehicle Ziegfeld created for the comedian but one that audiences failed to accept. Two sketches from the show were salvaged and brought, along with Fields, into *The Ziegfeld Follies of 1924*.

Vivienne Segal made her first appearance in this *Follies*, and Ann Pennington her last. And it was Victor Herbert's final work for the *Follies* and on Broadway. He had died the previous May, and his last composition, "The Beauty Contest," formed the musical underpinning for the *Follies* debut of the Tiller Girls, skipping glowing jump ropes on a darkened stage. Ray Dooley reentered the *Follies* with W.C. Fields; George Olson and his band added the requisite jazz, which was battling with operettas that season for the affections of Broadway audiences. But the band and the show's singers had little with which to work. The score by Harry Tierney was, as usual for the *Follies*, humdrum, as were the interpolations by Dave Stamper, Raymond Hubbell and James F. Hanley, all to lyrics by Gene Buck and Joseph McCarthy.

With feather finales and nudes in the Ben Ali Haggin tableaux, this edition, while damned with faint praise by the critics, became the longest-lived so far, filling the New Amsterdam for a record 401 performances.

Six days later, *George White's Scandals of 1924* opened at the Apollo. It would be George Gershwin's last score for White; the producer's refusal to raise Gershwin's salary from $125 a week was a perfectly good excuse for Gershwin to quit White and lyricist Buddy DeSylva for considerably greener pastures with Alex Aarons, Vinton Freedley, and his brother Ira—and a long string of successful book shows, beginning with that season's *Lady Be Good!*

Gershwin did add to his legacy by leaving one hit song behind. Winnie Lightner, surrounded by a hokey production number involving a wild array of lovers that included Romeo, Mark Antony, Harold Loyd and William S. Hart, sang, for the first time, the immortal "Somebody Loves Me." Otherwise, the score was forgettable.

This edition of the *Scandals* was, however, rich—or heavy, depending upon your taste—in comedy, involving Lester Allen and Winnie Lightner sending up *Abie's Irish Rose*, Will Mahoney spoofing Jolson's "Mammy" delivery, and Ann Pennington's dimpled knees, which became the butt of a Lester Allen and Patricola sketch. It was a middling *Scandals* that ran, nevertheless, for a comfortable 192 performances.

September brought the final *Passing Show* to Broadway. It was a sorry ending for what had once been a noble tradition. But the tastelessness of Jake Shubert, his overuse of his one claim to revue fame, the Winter Garden runway, and a continuing lack of inspiration among the creative staff made this last edition particularly dismal. Once again, J.C. Huffman, with much kibitzing and shouting and ripping of costumes by Jake Shubert, staged it; the music was by Sigmund Romberg and Jean Schwartz and the lyrics by Harold Atteridge. The taste level of the show was reflected in some of the song titles: "When Knighthood Was in Flower," "Society Blues," "Gold, Silver and Green" and "Nothing Naughtie in a Nightie."

James Barton, not yet the beloved Broadway character actor he would eventually become, was saddled with the comedy and some of the songs; flappers, Coolidge, Prohibition and mah-jongg were the focus of the sketches; Bee Palmer, the current shimmy queen, opened the show but left shortly afterward, along with a number of other cast members.

One unknown chorus dancer, however, with an almost unpronounceable last name of LaSueur—which she would change to Crawford when Hollywood called her—stayed for the entire 93 performance run, appearing as a beaded bag in a living curtain sequence and as Labor Day in yet another "Girls of the Seasons" pageant. Later, Lee Shubert would boast about her presence: "Maybe now people will learn that Ziegfeld isn't the only producer who discovers beautiful women," he told Claude Greneker, the Shubert press representative, then added, in a sentence worthy of Sam Goldwyn, "I found Nancy Carroll, and my brother found Joan Crawford before she was Lucille LaSueur."[7]

And that was that. *The Passing Show* now belonged to the past, if not the ages.

Audiences hardly noticed. Earl Carroll was, after all, opening his new edition of the archetypical girlie revue, now with his name attached. *Earl Carroll's Vanities* appeared a week after *The Passing Show* debuted, and it rode in on a wave of chorus girl stories, some true, some manufactured, and all good for business.

Lee Shubert's notorious summoning of chorus girls to his office for circumscribed matinees and Jake's dalliances with both chorus girls and boys was show business gossip which stayed within the business. And Ziegfeld, who insisted that his girls maintain a public image of carefully groomed decency, maintained a thin curtain of propriety around his shows, although, again, his own dalliances were well known to the circle of Broadway insiders.

Still, in 1924, even Marilyn Miller's previous attempts to embarrass him in public paled before a multiplicity of scandals surrounding that year's *Follies*. A cooperative press simply couldn't ignore them. Lillian Lorraine, by now a hopeless alcoholic, hearing, accurately, that Ziegfeld's latest paramour was showgirl Peggy Fears, showed up in Peggy Fears's dressing room one night bearing two bottles of liquor, which she tried to force upon the frightened girl. She passed out before she succeeded.

And then there was the sordid story of comedian Frank Tinney and *Follies* showgirl Imogene Wilson. Tinney began an affair with the young girl and neglected to tell her that he was married. When she found out, his reaction, reported in the tabloids of the time was succinct and devastating: "I have a mortgage and an appendix as well as a wife. Why bring these things up and spoil a pleasant time?"

Imogene Wilson thought otherwise and tried to drink poison, but, foreseeing that possibility, Tinney had substituted something harmless for the poison. She called the police anyway, and they brought along a reporter, whose presence so infuriated Tinney that he assaulted the girl, badly enough that Ziegfeld's *Follies* physician, Dr. Jerome Wagner, testified later that she looked as though she had been "struck by an automobile."

The publicity embarrassed Ziegfeld, but since it sold tickets, he retained Imogene Wilson in the *Follies*, until she followed Tinney as he boarded the S.S. Bremen to get away from the scandal, launched into a furious argument with him in front of reporters and was bounced from the ship. Finally, Ziegfeld bounced her from the *Follies* as well.[8]

So much for impresarios who maintained some decorum.

If Zeigfeld cared about public scandal sullying his reputation, Earl Carroll seemed to revel in it. He knew the value of a good, juicy scandal in selling tickets. And there was a varied menu of sensations in and around his *Vanities*. There was, first, the fixing of a beauty contest in Atlantic City to publicize the replacement of Dorothy Knapp in this edition of the *Vanities* by Kathryn Ray, a former chorus girl from Texas Guinan's nightclub. Then, there was the odious incident of Florence Allen, who supposedly was replaced after having won a spot in the *Vanities*. The following day, *The New York Times* carried the headline story:

CHORUS GIRL TRIES TO DIE
DRINKS LYSOL IN TAXI
WAS TRYING TO GET HER JOB BACK

> Miss Florence Allen, 22 years old, rehearsing to regain her place as chorus girl in Earl Carroll's *Vanities* of attempted suicide early yesterday by drinking Lysol in a taxicab at Seventh Avenue and 55th Street. She was reported improved last night at Roosevelt Hospital.[9]

Carroll, of course, hired her back as soon as she was discharged, and advance ticket sales soared. Meanwhile, onstage, Carroll decided to push the limits of nudity further than he already had. This time, he told his staff, he would bring on 108 girls, whose only clothing would be one huge peacock fan for each. When the girls waved their fans, the audience would see that they were all totally nude.

Reminded by his staff and some of the more modest girls that total frontal nudity was now permissible on a New York stage only if the subject didn't move, he fashioned a series of three flesh colored pasties, two for each chorus girl's nipples, and one for her pubic area, and put the number into rehearsal, while his publicity department leaked stories of the coming, scandalous "Pastie Parade."

On opening night, the overflow audience contained two plain-clothesmen who reported the goings on onstage to the New York district attorney's office. On the second night, patrolman Tom O'Leary, of the vice squad, was stationed in the wings with orders to see that any moving, full frontal nudity was immediately ceased and desisted.

O'Leary apparently took his job too seriously. When Kathryn Ray appeared, minus pasties but swinging on a pendulum (and therefore not moving), he ran out onto the stage and attempted to cover her with a blanket. She screamed and ran off. Thereupon, it all turned into a tumbling Keystone Kops scene, followed by a curtain speech by Carroll decrying censorship. Carroll ended up in the Tombs for three days and nights but was acquitted of indecency at a magistrate's trial.[10]

The decision turned into a joyful license for Carroll and Jake Shubert. John S. Sumner, the head of the Society for the Suppression of Vice, announced publicly that "...the Theater is a sewer!" and, in the next three years, more than a dozen straight plays would be either closed or told to modify their subject matter, language or nudity. But the *Vanities* and *Artists and Models* revues rolled merrily on, apparently immune to further raids and thus able to continue their bare and bawdy ways.

Still, the *Vanities of 1924*, for all its attendant furor, remained on view for no more than 133 performances—the shortest run of any edition before or after. Six days after the hullabaloo of the second *Vanities* debut, the more solidly based, tasteful and clothed *Greenwich Village Follies of 1924* opened at the Shubert. It was firmly in the tradition of the *Ziegfeld Follies*, with James Reynolds tinting and constructing huge, opulent production numbers that climbed to the moon, depicting "Destiny" in all four seasons, and giving multiple views of showgirls—and the Dolly Sisters, who starred—in a Hall of Mirrors. His most dazzling effect occurred in the Ballet Ballad, this time an Oscar Wilde fable, *The Happy Prince*, in which Reynolds employed yards of various colored and textured drapes, cascading from the top of a depiction of the Orangerie at Sans Souci.

John Murray Anderson directed with skill and strength, but the show was plagued with problems. The Dolly Sisters were out of their element and overshadowed by the comedy team of Moran & Mack, and, later, the droll, intellectual monologues of Fred Allen.

Cole Porter was hired to write the score, but, except for one ballad that later became a standard, "I'm in Love Again," his efforts were considered weak and esoteric. Owen Murphy and Jay Gorney, whose previous work had been more commercial, were called in to flesh out the score. Their contributions were more accessible but less likable, and so, again, in contrast to the *Scandals* and *Music Box Revues*, the show's music and lyrics became a hindrance. This edition of the *Greenwich Village Follies* enjoyed only 127 performances, despite the constant tinkering during its run by Murray Anderson.

The very next night, September 17, 1924, Hassard Short, who hadn't been seen or heard from for a while, opened *Hassard Short's Ritz Revue* at the tiny Ritz Theatre. Short, of the old school of extravagant revues, managed to fill the minuscule stage of the Ritz with stunning production numbers. And he intelligently packed his cast with some of the best comic talent of the age. Charlotte Greenwood, Raymond Hitchcock, Hal Forde, and Chester Hale all performed the sketches with elastic alacrity and wise timing.

But, maintaining the tradition of pre-1920s revues, Short too gave the score short shrift. Composed by an army of songwriters, including Anne Caldwell, Owen Murphy, Frank Harling, Harry Raskin, Jay Gorney and Graham John, it had no identifiable character or cohesion and grounded the show every time it threatened to soar. Consequently, *The Ritz Revue* remained for only 103 performances.

October brought Ed Wynn back to Broadway, with his own particular kind of lunacy, in *The Grab Bag*. He wore more absurd costumes, with wild props attached, and promised songs with titles such as "He Eats French Dressing Every Night So He Can Wake Up Oily in the Morning" or "She Might Have Been a School Teacher, But She Hadn't Any Class." It was basically a one-man enterprise—Wynn directed, wrote the sketches, composed the music and lyrics of such real songs as "What Did Annie Laurie Promise?" and took credit for others. It did, however, sport a heady roster of talent that included Jay and Janet Velie, Janet Adair and Marian Fairbanks of the popular Fairbanks twins. Audiences loved *The Grab Bag*, for 184 performances.

By the middle of the month, it was time for more nudes, and, at the Astor, Jake Shubert provided them in abundance in *Artists and Models of 1924*, the second of his intermittent series. The song titles from the innocuous Sigmund Romberg-J. Fred Coots-Sam Coslow-Clifford Grey score indicated the emphasis of the evening: "What a Village Girl Should Know," "What a Beautiful Face Will Do," "Pull Your Strings," "Model Doddle" and "Behind My Lady's Fan."

A simple-minded story line put a young girl from the sticks into the dens and among the denizens of Greenwich Village, which in turn transformed itself into Oriental splendor, etc. There were Charlestons, to allow the girls to kick high, and a mysterious dance number titled "I Love to Dance When I Hear a March." All of which, plus plenty of nudes, kept this edition alive for a healthy and profitable 261 performances—nearly eight months.

On October 29, Lew Leslie's *Dixie* to *Broadway*, a black revue that kidded white performers, settled in for a comfortable run at the Broadhurst. Eva Tanguay, Gallagher and Shean, George M. Cohan, even the wooden soldiers of *Chauve Souris* came in for skewering, and the dancing, the music—particularly, the heartbreaking delivery of the songs of George Meyers and Arthur Johnston by Florence Mills—and a general, pervasive sense of merriment kept the show alive for 77 performances.

True class returned to the Broadway revue in December with the last *Music Box Revue*. Sensing, as his fellow composers George Gershwin, Cole Porter and Jerome Kern had, that the future of the musical lay in the book show, Irving Berlin determined that he would henceforth fill his theatre with something besides his own revues.

John Murray Anderson and James Reynolds joined Berlin for this final edition, assuring opulence. Reynolds designed a miniature "Little Old New York," Tokyo with its geishas and the Brox Sisters (who had, at the last moment, replaced the Duncan Sisters) singing "Tokio Blues", a billowing weeping willow tree full of showgirls, and once again, the Tenniel illustrations for "Alice in Wonderland" brought to extravagant, larger-than-life.

Fanny Brice begged the audience "Don't Send Me Back to Petrograd"—she'd even wash the sheets for the Ku Klux Klan if they let her stay—and teamed up with Bobby Clark for another sendup of classical ballet.

Irving Berlin, in fact, seemed to concentrate on filling the *Music Box Revue* with so much decor and so many comic stars, he neglected the score, which had been the strong and distinctive underpinning of the earlier editions. Finally, at the last moment, he interpolated "All Alone," which he had written years before when he was courting Ellin MacKay, and gave it to Grace Moore and Oscar Shaw, who sang it on opposite sides of the stage into lighted telephones. It was the hit of the show and a memory of the original intent of the *The Music Box Revues*—to underpin the production and the comedy with a strong, coherent score. It would take time for this to become the rule rather than the exception, and when that time arrived, Irving Berlin would be at the creative center of it.

In January of 1925, the touring *Chauve Souris* returned for a 61 performance run at the Forty-Ninth Street Theatre. And the first new revue of 1925 was a return, in February, of what was advertised as Elsie Janis and Her Gang in a brand new creation, titled, enigmatically, *Puzzles of 1925*. The intimate and warmhearted show, no puzzle at all, was much like her previous productions. She was the singing master of ceremonies, introducing a series of sketches and performances by a cozy cast that included Walter Pidgeon and Helen Broderick. At the conclusion of the evening, Ms. Janis did what she did best and what audiences demanded for 104 performances: she sang a medley of the World War I songs she had sung for the troops in France and did her impressions of Lenore Ulric, Beatrice Lillie and John Barrymore.

Although there was no dearth of operettas and musical comedies for the remainder for the 1924–1925 season, it would be June 8, before the next revue opened. And it would be a revolutionary arrival, the apotheosis of the non-nudity phase of the "less is more" philosophy that was beginning to insinuate itself into the world of the Broadway revue. It would be so successful and striking that from then on no producer of revues could remain unaware of this form.

Admittedly, the pocket sized *Garrick Gaieties* had plenty of precedents, stretching back to the World War I camp shows, *Charlot's Revue* and, most directly, the *Grand Street Follies*. In fact, Lorenz Hart, the young and nimble-knowledged lyricist for the *Gaieties*, paid homage to the Neighborhood Playhouse in the opening chorus by referring to those who "shine below the Macy-Gimbel line."

And, like the performers and creators of the Neighborhood Playhouse's *Follies*, the *Gaities'* cast and production staff were all youngsters, the so-called "junior members" of the Theatre Guild, which had just built its new theatre/home, the Garrick, on West 52nd Street. Money had run out before the auditorium tapestries had been purchased; the kids were pressed into service to write a fund-raiser that would be cheap and bring in some revenue.

When it opened for a projected two performance run on May 17, 1925, one critic noted that it had "about $3 worth of scenery." Actually, it was a little more; the production cost $5,000 for everything—a small enough price for a milestone in theatre history.

The cast was composed of a group of eager kids: among them, Sterling Holloway, Romney Brent, June Cochran, Philip Loeb (who also staged it), Sanford Meisner, Alvah Bessie and in the chorus, Betty Starbuck and Elizabeth Holman, who within a year would change her name to Libby Holman.

The dance coach was Herbert Fields, the son of Lew Fields, and the composer-lyricist team consisted of two young veterans of the Columbia University Varsity Shows, who had only one Broadway musical comedy in their background, 1920's *Poor Little Rich Girl*.

Richard Rodgers and Lorenz Hart sparked the show with their music and lyrics, the like of which had heretofore only rarely appeared on Broadway, and never with such consistency. "Manhattan," sung in a simple setting (everything was in a simple setting) by Sterling Holloway and June Cochran became an immediate hit and standard; the opening chorus, "Gilding the Guild," delighted the cognoscenti and the not-so-knowledgeable alike; "Sentimental Me" was a second delight by Holloway and Cochran, dropped in when the composer/lyricist team's jazz opera *The Joy Spreader* was pulled at the last minute (shades of Gershwin and *Blue Monday*), and "Do You Love Me?" was a lighthearted ditty that remained in the mind and on the tongue.

The sketches, most of which were written by Morrie Ryskind and Howard Green, were of an equally high caliber, both in wit and execution. The Guild's own *They Knew What They Wanted* was spoofed as "They Didn't Know What They Were Getting," Ziegfeld and Friml's *The Three Musketeers* came in for a rococo drubbing, the Coolidges appeared silently in another sketch; in yet another, the Scopes Monkey Trial was played before a jury of monkeys.

Not since *Charlot's Revue* had there been such a perfect match of sketch material, inventive staging, engaging music and literate lyrics. The original two showing schedule became a 211 performance run, and the Broadway revue moved upward a considerable notch. As its founders were greying, youth was doing what the revue had set out to do at its very inception: comment upon, deflate and, most importantly, reflect and sound like the times in which it appeared.

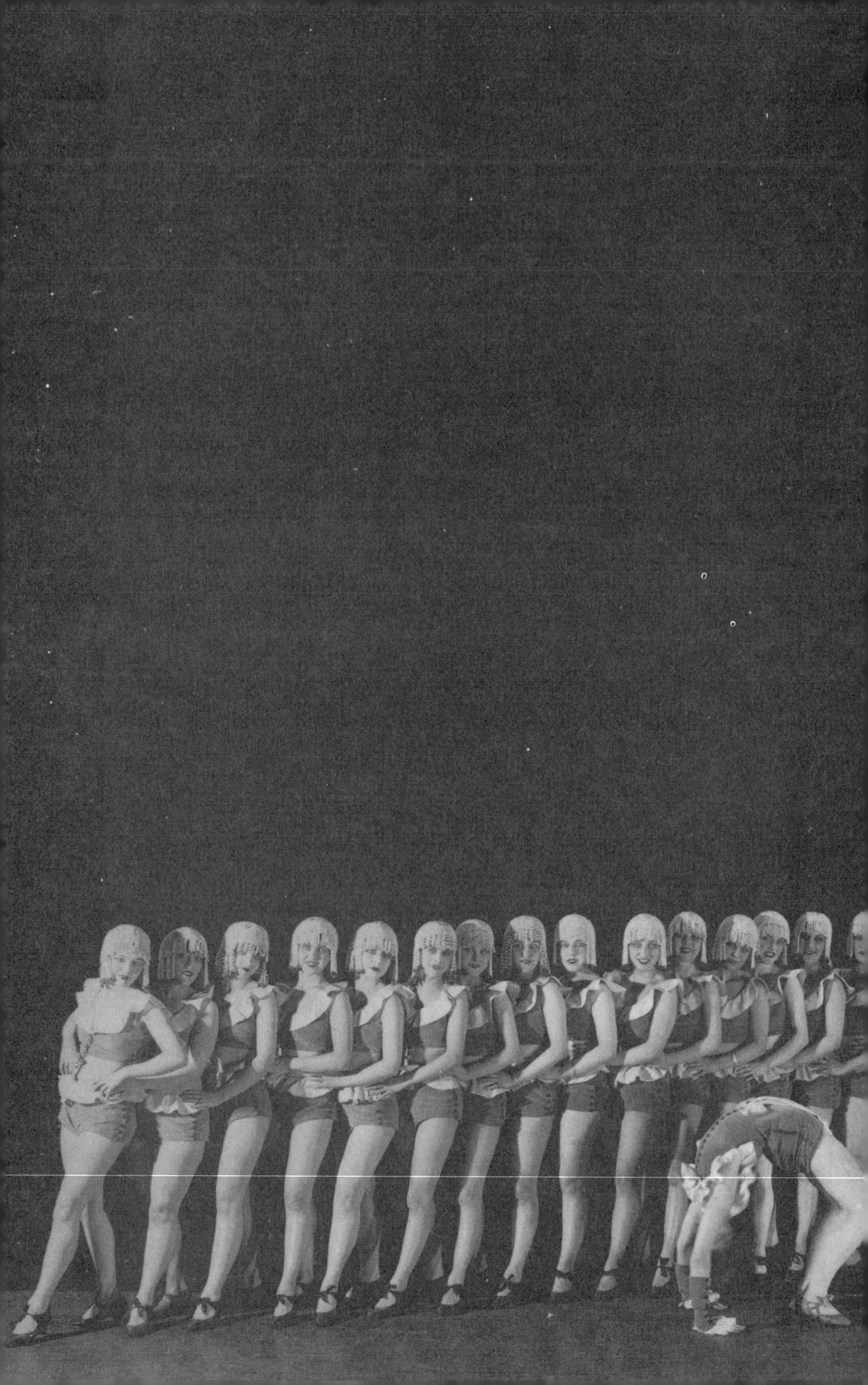

10
HIGH
TIMES

High Times

～⁂～

Broadway was booming now, as was the rest of America. Radio, a potential enemy, had arrived, but radio was, after all, a disembodied voice. The movies, another possible adversary, had become established, but the movies didn't talk, or sing. While Prohibition had come and swept away the *Midnight Frolics* and after-theater *souper* clubs, in their place were speakeasies which possessed an extra added aura of illegality. They also attracted the young and introduced the new speakeasy invention, the cocktail, which was designed to mask the taste of rotten liquor. The result: a whole new generation of alcoholics catered to in places that were also providing jobs for chorus girls and entertainers.

In this carefree boomtime, hundreds of theatres in New York were giving homes to hundreds of plays per season, and audiences, out for a good time, invariably included a play, a musical comedy, an operetta or a revue in that good time. And there were plenty from which to choose. During the 1925–1926 season, 254 shows opened on Broadway, and bigger seasons were to come. Of the 254, 42 were musicals (slightly fewer than in the preceding season), and of the musicals, 14, or one-third of them, were revues. If that was less than the preceding season, it was no indication of a lessening of interest in the revue. Everything was getting better, tighter, more intelligent, more focused. It was a good time to be working in the theatre, and many were.

Intriguingly and provocatively, the first revue—in fact, the first show—of the new season was the second edition of *The Grand Street Follies*. It was, like the first edition, squarely in the burlesque tradition (and the unwitting ancestor of the present *Forbidden Broadways*), sending up the hit shows of the season with gusto and delight. *They Knew What They Wanted* and *Desire Under the Elms* were combined into "*They Knew What They Wanted Under the Elms*," *Abie's Irish Rose* was turned into an Italian opera, and *What Price Glory?*, which was having trouble with the censors because of its language, was presented in a pristine, puritanical translation. The novelty of a score by two women—Agnes Morgan and Lily Hyland—was offset by its mediocrity. Nevertheless, this edition provided hot weather entertainment 148 times.

Five days later, on June 22, 1925, the new edition of *George White's Scandals* opened at the Apollo. With George Gershwin gone, White, one of the first producers to pay attention to the scores of his revues, cast about for a substitution and found it in Buddy DeSylva, Lew Brown and Ray Henderson. The team of DeSylva, Brown and Henderson hadn't hit its stride yet, although the three showed glimmers of bright originality, enough for White to hire them for the next edition.

There wasn't much to sing in this one, and, thus, the melancholy beauty of Helen Morgan's voice, making its debut on Broadway, was forced to wait for speakeasy gigs to find its truest exposure and widest audience.

Still, it was dancing that White knew best and featured most, and to combat the popularity of the Tiller Girls at the New Amsterdam, he presented the Albertina Rasch Girls in ballet turns, production numbers and a rousing demonstration of the latest authentic dance craze. First introduced in 1923's black musical comedy *Runnin' Wild*, Cecil Mack and Jimmy Johnson's "Charleston" had captivated the public for two years, and now, in 1925, it became the perfect expression of the double-jointed, devil-may-care, wild abandon of Flaming Youth and the Roaring Twenties. For the rest of the decade, no revue would be complete without a Charleston number, and White discovered its power when it contributed mightily to the 171 performance run of his 1925 *Scandals*.

If Jake Shubert could have had his chorus girls doing the Charleston naked in his new edition of *Artists and Models*, he probably would have, but the legal prohibition against moving nudes was still in force. It was just as well. Sigmund Romberg wasn't exactly a composer of Charleston-type music, and once again the score of a Shubert revue was its least important feature, although J. Fred Coots did provide a Charleston for an obligatory flapper scene that grew out of, of all things, a hula sequence.

The comedy chores fell to Phil Baker's monologues, which were accompanied by an accordion and razzed by Sid Silvers, an accomplice in a stage box. Jake's dancing line was called The Gertrude Hoffman Girls, and they took care of the movement while the visiting firemen concentrated on the nudes.

Two weeks later, on June 6, Earl Carroll opened his new edition of the *Vanities*, and the visible flesh quotient on Broadway increased perceptibly. Taking a cue from the runway of the now defunct *Passing Shows*, Carroll extended the apron around the orchestra pit and set tables on the extension to emphasize the cabaret atmosphere he had chosen for this edition.

The show was a marathon, playing into the early hours of the next morning, but audiences seemed to enjoy Ted Healy's comedy, the bird ballet, the color ballet, the nudes and—what else—the stage-rattling Charleston number. This *Vanities* established a record by remaining in the Earl Carroll Theatre for 390 performances.

Jake Shubert was back in harness on August 18 with *Gay Paree*, a deceptively named revue that completely ignored its title, offering not one note of music or one line of dialogue that even suggested Paris. In its place, the American South came in for extensive attention, with

"Glory of Sunshine," "Bamboo Babies" and "Florida Mammy," which told of an "old-fashioned Mammy [who] owns half of Miami."

The comedy was in the hands of Chic Sale and Billy B. Van; the quotient of vaudeville acts was high; the solo singing and dancing was given over to Winnie Lightner and the young and untried Jack Haley, although, as usual in a Shubert show, they were offered few songs worth singing. The music by Alfred Goodman, Maurie Rubens and the busiest composer of the season on Broadway, J. Fred Coots, contained nothing memorable or even noticeable. Still, the girls were beautiful, the pace peppy, and *Gay Paree* ran for a robust 190 performances.

It would be November before another revue graced Broadway, and the nip in the air was warmed considerably with the arrival of *Charlot's Revue of 1926*. Once again, Beatrice Lillie, Gertrude Lawrence and Jack Buchanan headed a cast that included, in its chorus, Constance Carpenter and Jessie Matthews, both of whom would go on to star in hit book shows with Rodgers and Hart scores—*A Connecticut Yankee* in New York for Miss Carpenter and *Ever Green* in London for Miss Matthews. The missing element in this edition was Noel Coward, but there was an abundance of cleverness, nevertheless, in an eclectic score by an army of composers and lyricists, including Irving Caesar, Franz Lehar, Philip Braham, Ronald Jeans and Ivor Novello. The hit song of the show, and a lasting standard for Gertrude Lawence was, however, one composed on this side of the Atlantic: "A Cup of Coffee, a Sandwich and You" by Billy Rose, Al Dubin and Joseph Meyer. *Charlot's Revue of 1926* remained at the Selwyn for 138 performances.

On Christmas Eve, *The Greenwich Village Follies*, now a mere glittering shadow of its original bohemian, downtown self except in its clear-eyed, good-humored spoofing of current serious Broadway fare—opened at the 46th Street Theatre. John Murray Anderson was gone, as was James Reynolds. Hassard Short—who had been responsible for some of the nicest parts of the *Music Box Revues* and who had yet to hit his stride as a director of the best of the 1930s revues, acquitted himself well enough directing material that was not up to previous editions' originality and daring.

The *Greenwich Village Follies* never did concentrate much on its music, and this edition was no exception. The music by Harold Levey and the lyrics by Owen Murphy and Irving Caesar lived and died with the show. One interpolation, Cole Porter's "I'm in Love Again," which had been introduced to Broadway in *The Greenwich Village Follies of 1924*, outlasted the revue and the decade. Otherwise, this was a formula production whose most memorable feature was a "Lady of the Snow" number in which Della Vanna, surrounded by Jack Frost and girls as snow balls and snow flakes, eventually melted.

Formula, however, worked in 1925. *The Greenwich Village Follies* stayed alive for 180 performances, one of the longest runs of the series.

Three nights before the end of 1925, another British revue, *By the Way*, arrived through the courtesy of Abe Erlanger. Both Erlanger and the public expected another *Charlot's Revue*, and although this collection of songs and sketches didn't quite reach that height, it was witty and intelligent, and the Vivian Ellis songs to Graham John lyrics, plus a clutch of interpolations by others were pleasant and bright. Jack Hulburt and Cicely Courtneidge made their American debuts, along with Harold French, who would later turn to producing. *By The Way* remained on these shores for a comfortable 176 performances.

With the coming of 1926, Jake Shubert pursued his usual creative course, and imitated himself. Because *Gay Paree* was a hit, he repeated the formula with lesser known and therefore cheaper performers in *A Night in Paris*. The revue used the *Passing Show* gang of Harold Atteridge (dialogue) and J.C. Huffman (director) with forgettable music by J. Fred Coots and Maurice Rubens to equally forgettable lyrics by Clifford Grey and McElbert Moore.

Jack Pearl, establishing his character of Baron Munchausen, did heavy dialect comedy, Norma Terris sang sweetly, and the Gertrude

Hoffman girls danced, in and out of all manner of costumes and headdresses. The public loved it and filled the Casino de Paris for 196 performances.

Then again, life was certainly good for the purveyors of any sort of theatre in 1926. There was something on Broadway for just about every taste, and the audiences came in ever increasing numbers. John Mason Brown summed up the state of the theatre of the time precisely in the *New York Post*. "Its aims were high, its costs were low," he wrote, "and happily its offerings were not condemned to being flops just because they were not hits."

The contrast with the Broadway of today is beyond dramatic, and in no case was this more thoroughly exemplified than in the arrival, on February 16, way uptown at the Hecksher Theatre, of an unprepossessing revue by the young actor Gene Lockhart. Recklessly and accurately titled *Bunk of 1926*, it was peopled by likable young performers, headed and directed by Lockhart and featuring singer/actress Carol Joyce. It was formula stuff; it satirized British drawing room comedy; it had a couple of songs by Lockhart, one of them, "Cuddle Up," with music by Robert Armbruster.

But it caught on, and, despite some reviews that dubbed it "feeble-minded," it succeeded enough to move downtown to the Broadhurst in April and continued there for a 104 performance run.

This is not to say that it was impossible for a bad show to flop that year, as *Bad Habits of 1926* amply proved. A revue at the Greenwich Village Theatre, with music by Manning Sherwin and lyrics by Arthur Herzog, which included in its small cast the young Robert Montgomery and featured a sendup of operetta titled "The Student Robin Hood of Pilsen." The target of scathing notices, it expired after 19 performances.

But then, despite the meteoric rise in quality of book shows with music by the Gershwins, Rodgers and Hart, Jerome Kern, Vincent Youmans, Sigmund Romberg and Rudolph Friml, the Broadway revue reinstated itself quickly with five hits in a row.

On May 10, The Garrick Gaieties of 1926, with its operetta parody "Rose of Arizona," featuring a classic Mexican bandit named Caramba, set up shop at the Garrick. Most of the original cast was back. Philip Loeb, Romney Brent, Sterling Holloway and Betty Starbuck all danced and sang and clowned to more Rodgers and Hart melodies and lyrics, notable among them, the bucolic version of "Manhattan," "Mountain Greenery," with its wicked interior rhyming, to wit: "Beans could get no keener reception/In a beanery/Than our Mountain Greenery home!" Sterling Holloway sang it to Bobbie Perkins, since June Cochran was in the current Rodgers and Hart hit *The Girl Friend*. The Garrick Gaieties of 1926 was greeted with the same enthusiasm as its predecessor and ran into the next season.

Jake Shubert climbed aboard the success wagon with a typical Winter Garden revue, this time titled *Great Temptations*. The temptations were, of course, the minimally clothed (to say the least) show girls and the dancing Foster Girls, but there was plenty of comedy to go around, too.

Jay C. Flippen, Miller and Lyles and Paul Maul did their vaudeville routines, and Jack Benny convulsed audiences with his understated monologues ("I drove from Atlantic City to New York in four hours and five subpoenas"). Hazel Dawn was featured in a spoof of one of the season's biggest hits, *The Shanghai Gesture*, and sang the show's only memorable song, mercifully interpolated into a score largely by Winter Garden regulars Maurice Rubens and Clifford Grey. José Padilla's exotic "Valencia" soared several cuts above everything else musical, but the weakness of the rest of the score didn't seem to bother audiences a bit. They came for 197 profitable performances.

Slightly less than one month later, on June 6, the indefatigable Jake Shubert directed and brought in yet another revue. The Merry World was an English import as far as most of the cast and some of the sketch material were concerned. Everything else was homegrown, including yet another typically low-grade Shubert score by Maurice

Rubens, J. Fred Coots, Herman Hupfeld and Sam Timber to lyrics once again by Clifford Grey. It had the right ingredients to produce yet another profitable run for the Shuberts of 176 performances.

The high point in Twenties Broadway revues, however, was reached with the *1926 George White's Scandals.* No edition of these dance-oriented, high-energy revues surpassed this one in its popularity, class, inventiveness and, most important, musical score. Brown, DeSylva and Henderson quashed their critics handily, thoroughly transcending the pedestrian score they had ground out for the previous edition. For years after it ended its record 424 performance run, the 1926 *George White's Scandals* would be remembered fondly as everything a revue should be but seldom was.

White assembled his best cast of the series, entrusting the comedy to Eugene and Willie Howard, and writing the sketches himself, in concert with Wiliam K. Wells. *The Shanghai Gesture* came in for a drubbing once more, as did David Belasco, Lenore Ulric, J. P. Morgan, Otto Kahn and the recent marriage of Irving Berlin and Ellin Mackay, sung to the strains of "Western Union."

William K. Wells penned a brilliant sketch, built around one word, "my." The scene, as in many revue sketches, was a boudoir, The wife (Frances Williams) holds a pair of trousers in her hand. A Friend (Harry Richman) enters.

>   Wife: My goodness!
>   Friend: My sweet!
>   Wife: My love!
>   Friend: (Pointing to trousers) My word!
>   Wife: My husband's.
>   Friend: My friend.
>   Wife: My fool!
>   Friend: My kiss?
>   Wife: My weakness. (They kiss.)
>   Friend: My queen!

Wife: My king.
(Offstage, a door slams.)
Friend: My lands!
Wife: My husband! (Points under bed)
Friend: My move! (Crawls under bed)
The Husband (Jim Carty) enters.
Husband: My wife!
Wife: My dear—
Husband: My eye! (He grabs her by the neck.)
Wife: My neck!
Husband: (Pulls Friend from under the bed) My rival.
Friend: My finish!
Husband: My friend!
Friend: My error!
Husband: My home! My gun! (Takes gun from his pocket)
Wife: My heavens!
Friend: My funeral!
Wife: My fault!
Husband: My foot! (Points gun at friend)
Friend: My life!
Husband: My price! (He shoots Friend, who falls.)
   My end! (He shoots himself and falls.)
Wife: My God!
(The shifforobe opens, and the other man steps out.)
Other fellow: My pants! (He picks up pants and exits.)
BLACKOUT

Ann Pennington was very much in evidence, and it was in *Scandals* that she introduced "The Black Bottom," the only dance of the Twenties to challenge the Charleston in popularity. Nobody, however, ever danced it with quite such abandon and panache as La Pennington.

Harry Richman and Frances Williams had two hit songs to sing together, one the romantic and moody "The Girl Is You and The Boy Is Me," and the other, the bouncy "Lucky Day," which turned up over and over, as a solo, as an ensemble, and as the punch line sung by an undiscovered lover in yet another sketch about marital infidelity.

But the megahit of the revue was "The Birth of the Blues," sung by Richman as the centerpiece of a staircase production number, in which the conflict between the modern (danced, somewhat, by the McCarthy Sisters) and the classical (posed, as Schubert and Schumann, by the Fairbanks Twins) spun on and on and on around him. The 1926 *Scandals* packed enough punch to give Ziegfeld pause. Until this time, he had regarded White as an annoyance. Now, he had to concede that he might be a formidable opponent.

One night after the *Scandals* opened, the new edition of *The Grand Street Follies* appeared at the Neighborhood Playhouse. Once again, intelligence and wit persevered. Albert Carroll and Dorothy Sands headed a cast that included the velvet voice of Jessica Dragonette. Agnes Morgan, responsible for the sketches and lyrics, let her imagination range from the obvious (still another sendup of *The Shanghai Gesture*) to the esoteric, in which *Uncle Tom's Cabin* received a new life a la the Theatre Guild's use of "sympathetic elastic theatre," as an Otis elevator took Tom, Little Eva, and others to heaven, to the strains of "Uncle Tom's Cabin." The lyrics were by Ms. Morgan and the music was by Arthur Schwartz, making his Broadway, or rather, Off-Broadway debut.

Much of the show was set in the far and frigid north, possibly as an antidote to the lack of air conditioning in 1920s theatres. A veritable blizzard of songs had to be written to sustain this: "A Little Igloo for Two" and "The Polar Bear Strut" (Agnes Morgan and Arthur Schwartz), "Aurory Bory Alice" (Agnes Morgan and Lily Hyland), "The Eskimo Blues" (Robert Simon and Walter Haenschen), a Skating Ballet and a Reindeer Dance by Lily Hyland, and in the one and only stint of Randall Thompson as a Broadway composer, "The Booster's Song of the Far North" and "My Icy Floe" both written with

Agnes Morgan, and an ice mazurka. The two also provided the music for a Dorothy Sands impersonation, "A Beatrice Lillie Ballad."

The pleasant, youthful revue lasted through the summer.

And so, the 1925–1926 season melted into the 1926-1927 season, the biggest yet on Broadway, with 48 new musicals of which 12 were revues, a drop once again. But then, this was the season of *Oh, Kay!*, *The Desert Song*, *The Ramblers* and *Countess Maritza*. Book musicals were beginning to make more and more sense, while revues, for this season, at least, continued on in their happy go lucky ways, breaking no new ground, presenting a little bit of the past, a little bit of the present, and a lot of flesh.

Ziegfeld's 20th *Follies* was the first musical in town, except that it wasn't titled the *Follies*. It began life in the winter of 1926 in Palm Beach, where Ziegfeld and Billie Burke had settled comfortably after an ocean voyage and a European sojourn that successfully patched together a fraying marriage and momentarily inhibited the 61-year old impresario's fixation with young showgirls. Enlisting the help of millionaires Paris Singer and A.J. Drexel Biddle, plus a few other silent partners, Ziegfeld, with Joseph Urban's necessary taste and know-how, transformed the dilapidated Palm Beach Supper Club into the Club de Montmartre, a blue-domed wonderland which would house his Florida *Follies*—titled, first, *Palm Beach Night*, then *The Palm Beach Girl*.

He brought in his New York production team, headed by Julian Mitchell, Joseph Urban, Ned Wayburn and Gene Buck. Rudolph Friml, already living in Palm Beach and enjoying its Jazz Age capital status, was hired to provide the score to the lyrics of Gene Buck, J.P. McEvoy and Irving Caesar.

Opening night seats sold for $200; thereafter, they went for $12, and, as is usually the case in resorts, everyone loved everything, regardless of its quality. But Ziegfeld, as usual, gave his Palm Beach audiences an abundance of good things. Joseph Urban designed an enormous crystal ball into which Mitchell fit Claire Luce who, when the ball split in two, danced into a bevy of beauties outfitted with exorbitantly expensive but fabulously impressive feathers by Ziegfeld's new, young costume designer, John Harkrider. Harkrider had been introduced to the impresario by Louise Brooks, the former chorus girl and eventual Hollywood legend. One more nascent legend appeared in the chorus of *The Palm Beach Girl*: Paulette Goddard. When Ziegfeld renamed the show *No Foolin'* and brought it into the Globe in New York, Goddard (then a blonde), was used as a spokesperson in a publicity stunt in which the blond chorus girls in the show went on a one-day strike after Ziegfeld made a public remark about gentlemen not preferring blondes. When *No Foolin'* opened, it kept most of its girls, including Peggy Fears and Louise Brown, and acquired the comic talents of James Barton and female impersonator Ray Dooley, plus Bugs Baer and director Edward Teddy Royce. During rehearsals for the New York transfer, Julian Mitchell had suffered a heart attack and died, much to Ziegfeld's and Broadway's distress. Royce stepped in and presented the usual smoothly running, tasteful and predictable Ziegfeld revue.

The song titles, as in any revue, were clues to its direction ("We're Cleaning Up Broadway"), emphasis ("Gentlemen Prefer Blondes," "When the Shaker Plays a Cocktail Tune"), and attempt at newness ("Don't Do the Charleston"). Fokine added ballets for Greta Nissen, set to classical music, and the entire evening added up to an exercise in class and beauty.

By July, however, attendance began to falter, and Ziegfeld, also with an eye toward numbering his various *Follies*, changed the title to *The Ziegfeld American Revue of 1926*. When it closed after a disappointing run of 108 performances, it toured as *The Ziegfeld Follies of 1926*.

The second revue of the season, which ran only one performance less than Ziegfeld's opulent entry, was accurately called *Bare Facts of 1926*. A midnight opening at the Triangle gave its rampant nudity an even more sinful tinge; its sketches by Stuart Hamill sent up contemporary straight plays, among them O'Neill's *The Great God Brown*. The score by Charles M. Schwab and Henry Myers was squarely in the forgettable category. Still, bared breasts brought customers, and the show made money.

It would be up to *Americana*, which opened a week later, to assure critics and some audience members that intelligence still occupied a room in the edifice of the Broadway revue.

Americana opened at the minuscule Belmont Theatre, which made it the antithesis of a Ziegfeld spectacle. And it paid close attention to its score, which also made it the antithesis of just about every Twenties revue except the *Scandals* and the *Garrick Gaieties*. Richard Herndon assembled Con Conrad, Henry Souvaine (credited with the main score), George Gershwin, Phil Charig, Ira Gershwin (long since emergent from his pseudonyms) and Morrie Ryskind, who also contributed to the sketches, which were mostly by J.P. McEvoy. George and Ira Gershwin delivered "That Lost Barber Shop Chord," and Ira Gershwin and Phil Charig supplied "Blowing the Blues Away" and the enduring "Sunny Disposish"—a lyrical licensing of the trademark speech of the Jim Marvin character in the first Bolton and Wodehouse and Kern Princess show *Oh, Boy!* ("Why do you always abbreviate your words?" asks a girl of Jim. "Oh, just a hab," he answers.) And, tellingly, Morrie Ryskind and Henry Souvaine gave Helen Morgan the opportunity to climb upon a piano and thus achieve immortality through the plaintive "Nobody Wants Me." Legend has it that the wistful and vulnerable Miss Morgan, who had begun her Broadway life in the chorus of *Sally* and then did a featured but unnoticed turn in the *The George White Scandals of 1925* first captured Jerome Kern's attention when she sat on a piano on an empty stage in *Americana*, after which he hired her for *Show Boat*.

Other young talent carried off the comic chores with grace and delight. Charles Butterworth did a "Treasurer's Report" style address to a Rotary meeting, and Betty Compton, Mayor Jimmy Walker's girlfriend (which was the major reason she was given so many speaking parts in so many musicals of the time), charmed her way through other sketches.

Americana remained in place for a more than healthy 224 performances.

Not so *Nic Nax of 1926*, which occupied the Cort Theatre for only 13 performances. The problems that plagued the show in rehearsal spilled over on opening night in the form of missed dialogue cues, songs listed in the program but not performed and scrambled light and scenery cues. The only composing feat of Gitz Rice and Werner Janssen, the revue couldn't be saved, even by the spectacular hoofing of Nat Nazzaro, and it left almost before it was noticed.

August was the time for the intermittent appearance of Earl Carroll's girlie extravaganzas, and the new edition of the *Vanities*, another marathon whose first act ran until nearly 11 o'clock and whose opening night ticket prices reached $100 a seat, was dazzling in its effect and its minimally attired beauties.

This time, Carroll turned over the score and sketches to other talent, contenting himself with merely directing and producing. Consequently, there was a slight elevation in both departments. The Morris Hamilton-Grace Henry score was passable; the comic delivery of the Stanley Rauh and William A. Grey sketches was given over to Will Morrissey, Smith and Dale, Julius Tannen, Harry Delf and Joe Smith. Spanish and Russian numbers abounded; Dorothy Knapp was back as a stunning centerpiece; and it was all enough to keep the old Earl Carroll Theatre occupied for 303 performances.

That, combined with the help of Carroll's constant, bottomless-pocketed benefactor William R. Edrington, allowed Carroll to begin tearing down the old structure in order to replace it with a new, chrome-and-velvet, art deco interiored Earl Carroll Theatre. His reason? Ziegfeld and Urban were already building Ziegfeld's new, opulent and elegant namesake theatre uptown at Sixth Avenue and 54th Street. And although Ziegfeld was still regarded as king of the revues, for Carroll kings were there to be dethroned. It was as easy and illogical as that.

Ever the non-innovator, Jake Shubert, tried again to repeat his initial success with *Gay Paree* by bringing in an "all-new 1926 edition" in November. The Winter Garden staff was in place; a new composer and lyricist team, Alberta Nichols and Mann Holiner (from whom nothing was heard after this), replaced the long list of contributors to the original edition; some of the original cast was back, including Chick Sale, Jack Haley and Winnie Lightner; and some of the original sketches were repeated, as were some of the most beautiful girls. The combination once again worked, although not as spectacularly as the first time around. *Gay Paree* number two was the last of the "series" despite a respectable 175 performance run.

And now 1927 arrived, without a new revue to herald it. This didn't mean that Broadway was idle. Far from it. There was a new kind of turmoil besetting its producers, a conflict that would give rise to an all-out war between Florenz Ziegfeld and Earl Carroll. It began at a distance from musical Broadway, with a police raid.

On the frigid night of February 9, 1927, paddy wagons loaded with uniformed officers from the West 47th Street precinct swooped down on three Broadway theatres, those housing, *Sex,* Mae West's play about her favorite subject, *The Captive,* Eduard Bourdet's play about lesbianism, and *The Virgin Man*, a William Francis Dugan confection about three Broadway babes and their unsuccessful attempt to purloin the virginity of an upright and upstanding Yale man.

Forty-one actors were hustled into the wagons, including Mae West, Helen Mencken and Basil Rathbone. It was a triumph for the advocates of censorship and the politicians who stood to benefit from that advocacy. Ever since *Desire Under the Elms, White Cargo* and *Craig's Wife*, not to mention the earlier *What Price Glory?* with its authentic, salty dialogue from the trenches, and the later *Stolen Fruit* and *The Fall of Eve*, the censors had been accumulating evidence of the theatre's public debauchery. In the 1926–1927 season, there had so far been plays with titles like *The Blonde Sinner, Naughty Riquette*,

Henry's Harem, Kept, Treat 'Em Rough, Saturday Night, Where's Your Husband?, Lady Alone, The Love Thief, Sinner and *Trial Marriage*. The guardians of public decency ignored the potboilers and went after the most successful plays. However—and this was the interestingdimension to the raids—as usual, the police also ignored the nudity in every revue. No summons appeared for Earl Carroll or George White or Jake Shubert or the producers of *Bare Facts*.³

It was selective enforcement, and Ziegfeld was furious. Carroll, particularly, had a year ago contributed to the general Jazz Age sense of abandon by throwing a birthday party for his benefactor, Colonel Edrington, which turned into a monument to bad taste.

Orgies, of course, had taken place among the wealthy and well-known since the Age of Caesar. But those revels had been treated to the secrecy of silence from the journalists who were invited to them. This one, held onstage and in the orchestra of the old Earl Carroll Theatre, included a cross-section of New York and international society, dancing wildly to the strains of Nick LaRocca's orchestra, aided and abetted by a bevy of Earl Carroll beauties, wearing scanties, who obligingly drank and danced with the men in the party—among them Irvin S. Cobb, Frank Tinney, Walter Winchell, Ed Sullivan and, escorting Peggy Joyce, Philip Payne, managing editor of the *Daily Mirror*.

Even Harry K. Thaw, fresh out of the insane asylum to which he had been sentenced after he killed Stanford White, appeared, as Earl Carroll shouted, "Here's Harry Thaw! Three long cheers for Harry!"

As dawn broke outside the theatre, the party descended to its climax. Carroll escorted a very drunk young chorus girl named Joyce Hawley to center stage and signaled for a bathtub to be brought on. It was filled with champagne. Ms. Hawley was helped up onto a chair, where, hidden by a sable coat provided by Peggy Joyce, she disrobed entirely and settled into the champagne-filled bathtub. Picking up a slipper handed to her by Carroll, Ms. Hawley ladled out a slipperful of champagne and handed it to the guest of honor, Colonel Edrington.

After this, it was every man for himself, as a goodly number of the male guests lined up and dipped glasses into the champagne, thereby gradually revealing more and more of Ms. Hawley, until, the story goes, she stretched back languorously in the tub, spread her legs apart and murmured, with a look of infinite relief on her face, "Guess what I'm doing?"

Philip Payne didn't have to guess, and, anxious to please his boss, William Randolph Hearst, who had vowed to put the *Daily News* out of business, he went home and wrote the story of the orgy.[2]

Earl Carroll wound up with a year's sentence to a federal penitentiary for breaking the Prohibition law. And this peek behind the curtain of contemporary show business morals convinced the guardians of public morals that if, in 1924—as Sumner put it then—the theatre was a sewer, in 1927 it was a sewer, a swamp and a sump.

Ziegfeld wholeheartedly (and opportunistically) endorsed Sumner and his crusade and dashed off telegram after telegram to New York District Attorney Benton, encouraging him to close more shows, particularly those in competition with him. A typical one read:

"ACCEPT MY CONGRATULATIONS ON THE STAND YOU ARE TAKING. I HOPE YOU WILL INVESTIGATE THE REVUES NOW PLAYING IN NEW YORK. NOT ONE OF THEM WOULD BE TOLERATED IN BOSTON AND PHILADELPHIA. THE BARING OF THE BREASTS OF THE YOUTH OF AMERICA TO DRAW A FEW EXTRA DOLLARS AND ABSOLUTE NUDE FIGURES DANCING AROUND THE STAGE SHOULD BE STOPPED BOTH IN THE REVIEW [sic] AND THE NIGHTCLUBS..."[3]

Some nightclubs were raided. But no revues. They spun merrily on, and so did Ziegfeld with the Ben Ali Haggin tableaux that had introduced musical nudes on Broadway in the first place.

1927 would be nearly four months old before a revue opened. This time it was *The New Yorkers*, a title that had been used in 1901 to moderate success and would be used to far greater success in 1930. The 1927 incarnation was a sorry, disjointed venture with sketches and lyrics by Jo Swerling and music by Edgar Fairchild, Charles M. Schwab and Arthur Schwartz, who had yet to find his proper identity. Bereft of much comedy, many songs, or real stars, it remained on view at the Edyth Totten Theatre for an uncertain 52 nights and matinees.

Rufus LeMaire's Affairs was a considerably better show that ran only a bit longer than *The New Yorkers*. Boasting an impressive roster of performers, including Ted Lewis, Sunny Dale, Charlotte Greenwood, Peggy Fears, Bobbe Arnst and the Albertina Rasch dancers, it had a singable score by Martin Broones with lyrics by Ballard MacDonald, who also wrote the sketches. Charlotte Greenwood was featured in a spoof of *Gentlemen Prefer Blondes*; Lewis led his band through "Land of Broken Dreams" and the Albertina Rasch girls danced imaginatively. But the revue, which opened the new Majestic Theatre, was bereft of nudes, and departed after 56 performances.

The Shuberts once again tried to make a good thing last forever by building upon the success of *A Night in Paris* to bring in, on May 3, *A Night in Spain*. Shubert regulars Harold Atteridge (sketches) and Jean Schwartz (music) were in evidence; the lyrics were provided by the fleeting Al Byram.

Their judgement was sound; a surge of Spanish faddism in 1927 insured that numbers like "International Vamp," "Promenade the Esplanade," "My Rose of Spain," "A Spanish Shawl" and "Columbus and Isabella" were met with friendly applause. And, as extra insurance, the Shuberts brought in Phil Baker and his stooge-in-a-box Sid Silvers to brighten matters up with their stage-to-audience exchanges, Ted and Betty Healy to offer more orthodox comic turns, and a very young Helen Kane, in her pre-boop-oop-a-doop stage, to deliver such numbers as "Hot, Hot Honey" in her own, distinctively squeaky way. It was all enough to keep *A Night in Spain* alive for 50 performances.

At the end of the month, Merry-Go-Round, a delectable mix of old and new, settled into the Klaw Theatre for a 136 performance run. The old was represented by Marie Cahill and William Collier; the new by Philip Loeb, Leonard Sillman and the fast-rising Libby Holman.

What was most interesting and forward looking, however, took place in the creative wing. The music, which included its hit "Hogan's Alley" sung to a fare-thee-well by Libby Holman, was provided by Jay Gorney and Henry Souvaine, and the sketches and lyrics by Morrie Ryskind and Howard Dietz, both of whom would largely write the history of the revue—and some of the musical theatre itself—in the next decade.

Their sharp-edged and sometimes surreal looks at New York life—among them a withering examination of an ambulance chasing law firm named Gogeloch, Babblekroit and Svonk, and the redesigning of new double-decker Fifth Avenue buses with yet another floor, complete with such amenities as fresh towels to wipe away the grime of the city—were fresh and funny. The revue lasted into the summer.

And now the most populated season in the history of the American Theatre dawned. No fewer than 270 plays, including forty revivals, opened on or near Broadway during the 1927–1928 season. Obviously, not all of them were hits. In fact, Burns Mantle commented acidly, "You can count [the season's] outstanding successes on the fingers of two hands. It would require the seeds of a watermelon to tally its failures."

Nonetheless, any season able to support the opening of 270 productions—including a record 51 musicals, of which 15 were revues—can't be discounted. Nor can Christmas week of 1927 pass unnoticed. A forever unbroken record of 18 shows opened in a mere 6 days, 11 on Monday night, December 26, alone—which meant that eleventh-string critics were reviewing a few of the them—a lucky situation for some, no doubt, and an unlucky one for others. But those are the breaks. On December 27, the first-string critics all went to see Philip Barry's *Paris Bound*, leaving *Show Boat*, the only other show opening that night, to the second stringers. Instant word-of-mouth eventually brought the first chair reviewers in for a follow-up look.

In the time since the February, 1926 raids on supposedly smutty plays, the New York State legislature had passed the Wales Padlock law, which gave authorities the power to not only arrest and bring to trial the producers and performers of a raided production, but also, upon conviction, to padlock for an entire year the theatre in which the play was given. Falling victim to the new law, a trifle called *Maya*, starring Lenore Ulric wearing not very much, was raided and closed, while Eugene O'Neill's *Strange Interlude* and a revival of *Volpone* were investigated by the district attorney's office, though not padlocked.

Meanwhile, the nudes in revues continued to cavort at will, which they did in the first revue of the season, the 1927 edition of *Bare Facts*. Once again at the Triangle Theatre, it contained nothing more interesting than naked chorus girls and lasted the summer.

More ambitious, and still following the dictum that no nudes is bad news, the Shuberts on July 5 tested their pull with the authorities to the utmost and brought in the pointedly titled *Padlocks of 1927*. Just in case the nudes weren't enough, the Shuberts hired Texas Guinan to be the headliner, riding a horse onstage, singing and ad-libbing with the customers. "She made the horse nervous, but audiences soon got used to her," Burns Mantle observed.

The music was by a trio of itinerant composers, Henry Tobias, Lee David and Jesse Greer, to whose notes Billy Rose appended some lyrics and a song title that summed up the score succinctly, "That Stupid Melody." The sketches were by Paul Gerard Smith and Ballard MacDonald, and a sprightly young cast featured Lillian Roth, Jay C. Flippen and a beady-eyed, glossy-haired hoofer named George Raft. It ran out the summer, whereupon Texas Guinan went back to her nightclub.

The week after *Padlocks of 1927* premiered, two black revues opened within a night of each other. On July 11, *Africana* debuted at the Daly. It was primarily a dance show, i.e., African dance amalgamated with shuffles, Charlestons, cakewalks and other dances associated, in the white Broadway mind, with blacks. It contained music and lyrics by Donald Heywood. Both were of no consequence, except to underpin the dancing debut of a young and vibrant Ethel Waters. Called by one critic, a "dusky Charlotte Greenwood," she had yet to find her voice and her immortality in the American musical theatre. *Africana* remained at the Daly for 72 performances.

Rang Tang, which opened at the Royale one night later, carried the same burden of a disposable score, this time by Kaj Gynt and Jo Trent, but it did have spirited dances, which prompted the *Times* to comment that "First rate dancing is a concomitant of all negro shows," F.E. Miller and A. Lyles, veterans of *Shuffle Along*, added the comic dimension. The notices and the stars energized audiences, and *Rang Tang* outlasted *Africana*, remaining at the Royale for 119 performances.

Earl Carroll, opting for more class than flesh, snared both J. P. McEvoy, the creator of *Americana*, and its star Charlie Butterworth, plus the veteran and furiously popular Victor Moore for *Allez-Oop*, the summertime tenant of his new namesake theatre. The revue took its title from the popular comic strip caveman character of the time. Its music was by Phil Charig and Richard Myers with lyrics by Leo Robin. The sketches were slightly derivative, including one of the last possible sendups of silent films and a recognizable variation on Butterworth's show-stopping Rotary speech from *Americana*.

The girls weren't ignored. Madeline, half of the Fairbanks twins, was on hand, and yet another one-shot dance hoping to become a craze, "Doin' the Gorilla," was introduced by "50 Dancing, Dashing Alley-Oopers." Audiences were delighted enough to keep *Allez-Oop* swinging for 120 performances.

One day later, on August 3, *The Manhatters*, a brave attempt at

Broadway by a bunch of youngsters from Greenwich Village, opened at the Selwyn. The problem was that, although it was intimate and youthful, it wasn't very good. George Oppenheimer, who would eventually become a prominent Broadway playwright, joined with Aline Erlanger to provide the sketches and the lyrics. The music was by the equally unknown Alfred Nathan. *The Manhatters* struggled through 68 performances, then left, making way for professionalism, which arrived in splendid form at the New Amsterdam on August 16, with *The Ziegfeld Follies of 1927.*

$239,000 worth of opulence maintained Ziegfeld and Urban's untarnished images of taste and extravagance. And Irving Berlin, the show's only compass, was back to provide, if not exactly a top-notch score, one that was considerably above the level of any of the revues so far this season—or last season, for that matter.

Two songs became hits: Irene Delroy and Franklyn Bauer in a uniquely simple setting sang "It All Belongs to Me," and on a plantation set Ruth Etting, backed by an army of dancers (the Jazzbow Girls), female musicians (the Banjo Ingenues) and the Albertina Rasch Dancers, set title to motion with "Shakin' the Blues Away."

Obeisance to the Ziegfeld past was paid in the opening number, set in a staggering recreation of Ziegfeld's office, in which girls eager to be glorified met Andrew Tombes, as Ziegfeld, and actresses representing Ann Pennington, Marilyn Miller and Fanny Brice.

The show's most lavish number was a multi-level creation called "Melody Land," in which the Ingenues were discovered strumming the scene's title song with the duo piano team of Fairchild and Rainger. The scene gave way to an enormous staircase and the source of what would later become one of Busby Berkeley's most memorable film sequences: 12 women playing 12 white pianos, which were soon buried under a parade of military dancing girls as well as the Albertina Rasch troupe.

The oddest act in the show was the obligatory-for-the-season jungle number, set to a tune Berlin probably wished to forget, "Jungle

Jingle." It was introduced by the Brox Sisters, who rapidly got out of the way of Clair Luce, dressed in ostrich feathers and riding a live ostrich. One night, the ostrich, having developed a yen to return to its stable, dashed across the stage and through the stage door, with Ms. Luce aboard. After this edition of the *Follies* closed, the ostrich, according to the busy Ziegfeld publicity machine, was sold to a zoo for $911.11.[6]

Ukelele Ike, fresh from his triumph in *Lady, Be Good!*, did his specialty, but the only performer with star billing in this *Ziegfeld Follies* was Eddie Cantor, who collaborated with Harold Atteridge on the sketches. He gave himself a memorable one about a severely battered and abused Hollywood stand-in who is called upon to receive every kind of indignity imaginable while the leading man retires to his dressing room.

This was only one among many, many appearances by the comedian in the production, and at one point Cantor asked for more money. Ziegfeld refused, whereupon Cantor announced that he was too fatigued to continue in the show, which closed after 167 performances. It could have run a good hundred more, and Ziegfeld brought Cantor up before Equity. The producer won the dispute, but the damage had been done.

Too bad, because there wasn't much competition at this point in the season. *A la Carte* was a promising little revue with music and lyrics by Herman Hupfeld (whose fame awaited him when he wrote "As Time Goes By" for the 1931 revue *Everybody's Welcome*), Louis Alter, Norma Gregg, Paul Lanin and Creamer and Johnson. Its sketches and direction were by the gifted Pulitzer Prize winning playwright George Kelly (Grace's uncle), but its many disparate parts never truly came together, and it departed after 45 performances.

That would be it for revues until October 10, when Comstock and Gest, almost as tenacious as Jake Shubert in milking a good idea to death, brought in yet another edition of *Chauve Souris* from the Bat Theatre of Moscow. Bereft of novelty and its original master of ceremonies, the harmless little revue lasted for 80 performances.

A subtle change in the Broadway air had occurred the same week that *Chauve Souris* returned, and the juxtaposition is instructive. On October 6, 1927, the first feature length musical film opened at the Warners Theatre. Its history, considering its later impact upon the musical theatre, is heavily ironic. It was based upon a Broadway show and featured one of the Broadway musical's biggest stars. *The Jazz Singer*, in its original stage form, had first faced an audience in early 1925 and had been a comfortable, homey hit, which influenced Jack Warner's decision to buy it and make it into a silent film.

But that had been before 1926 and the advent of Vitaphone and the coming of talking pictures. George Jessel had originally been hired to play the part of Jakie Rabinowitz, a role modeled upon the persona of Al Jolson. After Jessel withdrew in an argument over money for the first talking feature Warner turned to the obvious choice as star and hired Jolson.

The rest is well-documented history, and represents the beginning of the end for what had become the formula Broadway musical. With the advent of sound in motion pictures, the next step would obviously be the introduction of singing and dancing. And so the old formula of bringing on 100 girls and 50 costumes in foolish routines underscored by forgettable music might no longer suffice in attracting enough paying audiences to keep a show alive and well on Broadway.

While the Stock Market Crash that would stun the country was still two years away, it would soon be panic time in the musical theatre. As in some panics, its beginning, monumental in hindsight, was subtle enough in actuality not to be noticed. Not at first, anyway. For the rest of the 1927–28 season, it was as if films weren't yet talking or singing.

On November 15, the Shuberts brought in another *Artists and Models*. This time, the Winter Garden stage was populated by a reported 100-Girls-100, a large percentage (and proportion) of them unclothed. A living bracelet of nudes was a particularly popular moment in a production that, although full of predictability in the flesh and spectacle department and bereft of good songs in the score by Harry Akst and Maurie Rubens, was surprisingly strong in its comedy moments.

Jack Pearl, with his sidekick Charlie, created insane memories of being a deck-hand on a submarine and of playing hookey from a correspondence school. The brand new dance duo of Veloz and Yolanda, who like most of the current dance teams were clones of the Castles, delighted audiences, as did Ted Lewis, his battered top hat and his band. This edition ran for 151 performances, not enough to keep Jake Shubert happy.

Less than two weeks later, Harry Delmar brought *Delmar's Revels*, his "revue in twenty-four exhibits," to the Shubert. He assembled a strong cast. Winnie Lightner was on hand to sing, although she was given nothing of value by composers Jimmy Monaco, Jesse Greer and Lester Lee, and lyricists Billy Rose and Ballard MacDonald. Billy K. Wells, on the other hand, supplied a spate of imaginative sketches that sent up the established revue targets of the Provincetown Players and the Theatre Guild. And with Frank Fay as its dashing master of ceremonies, an underwater ballet that became the talk of the season, and the Chester Hale Girls stepping high, there was enough to keep *Delmar's Revels* alive for a healthy 112 performances.

It would be the last revue of 1927, and the last before the earth-shaking appearance of *Show Boat*.

For musicals, 1928 didn't begin very auspiciously. On January 30, the night that Eugene O'Neill's *Strange Interlude* opened at the Golden, *The Optimists* premiered at the Casino de Paris. Its title was hopeful but, ultimately, baseless. The almost one-man effort of ragtime pianist Melville Gideon, who produced it, starred in it and wrote the music, it failed to reflect either its title or its successful five-month shakedown run in London. Nor could it sustain the delightful presence of a young and hitherto unknown tap dancer named Eleanor

Powell. *The Optimists* crashed after 24 performances.

It would be April before another revue opened, and it would be a reminder of the past—some of its glories and more of its problems. With the Shuberts in charge, *The Greenwich Village Follies* minus John Murray Anderson was like *The Ziegfeld Follies* without Ziegfeld. The price of opening at the Winter Garden was the use of the predictable staging of J.C. Huffman, the uneven sketches of Harold Atteridge, and the forgettable music of the Winter Garden stable of composers. This time out, it was Ray Perkins and Maurie Rubens, with lyrics by Max and Nathaniel Lief. Not a single song survived, nor deserved to.

The material by Atteridge was largely subordinated to tested and, therefore, familiar vaudeville routines by the likes of Blossom Seeley and Benny Fields, Dr. Rockwell and Bobby Watson, and Grace LaRue, while Ben Dova indulged in his acrobatic antics. One critic, in fact, observed that it "resembled a weekly bill at the Palace."[7]

To fill in the production numbers there were the Chester Hale Girls and the Ralph Reader Girls, minimally costumed and mediumly talented. The only truly original spark of contemporary life (besides the obligatory sendups of contemporary plays) came from the appearance of Martha Graham and her group dancing a complex calypso number.

This pale shadow of a bright past remained for 158 performances, enough to turn a profit and run out the summer. But if ever there was a clear indication that something new had to be done, that the lessons of the past three years had to be learned in the name of survival, this final parting shot proved it.

And the very next revue proved that the lessons could be learned, and then some. It was the last of the season and the first of the mature revues that would raise this Broadway form to its highest, proudest level.

Promises are made, but the number kept are few indeed. The initial promise came in 1921 with Sissle and Blake's *Shuffle Along*, the

252 ～ Scandals and Follies

first truly important and successful black show on Broadway, which ran for an astonishing—for the times—504 performances. Imitations, most of them revues, followed. Some of them were blatant mirror images, some were sincere tries undermined by inferior material and talent. It would be seven years before the initial promise was kept. But kept it was by *Lew Leslie's Blackbirds of 1928*.

Leslie had been one of the imitators; his *Plantation Revue* in 1922 and *Dixie to Broadway* in 1924 had left scarcely a ripple on the pond of theatre history. By 1928, he had already experimented with the *Blackbirds* concept in London with *Blackbirds* in 1926 and *Whitebirds* in 1927. They had been pleasant enough successes, but nothing approaching what was to happen at the Liberty Theatre on May 9, 1928.

It was logical for Leslie to search out black talent at Harlem's Cotton Club for his Broadway incarnation of *Blackbirds*. What he didn't expect was to encounter the white composer-lyricist team of Jimmy McHugh and Dorothy Fields. Fields, the daughter of Lew Fields, was a mere 22-years old when she met McHugh. She instantly impressed the already established composer, who tried her out on the 1927 Cotton Club revue which featured Duke Ellington and his orchestra.

Lew Leslie went uptown, saw the revue, was impressed and hired the composer and lyricist for *Blackbirds of 1928*. He had already hired tap dancer Bill Robinson, singers Adelaide Hall and Elizabeth Welch and a cast of bright and enthusiastic singers, dancers and actors.

The combination proved to be magical. McHugh and Fields turned out a remarkable score, one of the three or four best revue scores so far and palpably one of the ten or so best revue scores of all time.

Adelaide Hall led yet another jungle number, but this time it had the jungle jingle of all time, "Digga Digga Doo." Her other large scale solo resided at the other end of the musical spectrum. "I Must Have

That Man" was a plaintive plea, and she wailed it out with the same sort of dedication and to the same sort of audience response that Fanny Brice's first rendition of "My Man" had had over a decade before.

The most enduring song, with the most recorded history, was "I Can't Give You Anything But Love, Baby" (originally "I Can't Give You Anything But Love, Lindy"). Legend has it that late in rehearsals of *Blackbirds* there was still a spot that needed filling musically. McHugh and Fields were at an empty impasse until, strolling down Fifth Avenue in search of ideas, they passed a young couple gazing longingly at the display in Tiffany's window. As they passed, the young guy was confiding, sadly, to his girlfriend, "Gee, honey, I'd like to get you a sparkler like dat, but right now, I can't give you nothin' but love!" Voila.[8]

The song's first appearance was as a solo for Aida Ward, which rapidly became a trio for Ms. Ward, Adelaide Hall and Lois Deppe. In the second act, it was rendered, opera-style, by the entire cast.

The remainder of the score was functional, underpinning a serious tribute to Dubose Heyward's current Broadway triumph, *Porgy*, another Bill Robinson specialty, "Shuffle Your Feet and Roll Along," and a clutch of plantation numbers that would be regarded as racist today. But in 1928, the show's total effect was electrifying and edifying. The combination that would save the revue—and in fact, the Broadway musical—from the invasion of talking motion pictures and the coming Stock Market Crash would be a combination of fine performers, intelligent writing, and solid scores, an essential partnership that only a handful of producers of the time recognized, despite *Blackbird's* record 518 performance run.

But progress and common sense come slowly, and as the 1927–1928 season ended, with the country still on a high roll and Ziegfeld's economic advisors scolding him for not investing the fortune he was amassing from the twin successes of *Rio Rita* and *Show Boat* in the stock market, the new edition of *The Grand Street Follies* opened at the Booth with its usual combination of economy, cleverness, competent talent and a score to be forgotten. Agnes Morgan did the sketches and lyrics; the music was by Max Ewing, Lily Hyland and Serge Walter.

Once again, the high moments of the revue were its spoofs of current Broadway fare and its fairest. Ethel Barrymore and Mrs. Fiske received their lumps again, as did Mae West (imagine her doing Juliet on the steps of the New York Public Library). Regulars Albert Carroll, Dorothy Sands and Marc Loebell had a high time with O'Neill's current *Strange Interlude,* substituting Herbert Lehman, Al Smith and Calvin Coolidge for the men in Nina Leeds's life.

The production numbers were incidental, but its chorus contained a young hoofer with a bright destiny by the name of James Cagney. *The Grand Street Follies* ran out the summer, and then some, 155 times.

And now, the last truly busy season of Broadway's high times arrived. The critics were unanimous in pronouncing it a sorry season for quality, and they had a point. For quantity, however, 224 shows opened on Broadway in the 1928–1929 season, a mere 74 of them musicals (can you imagine 74 new musicals opening on Broadway in one of today's seasons?).

But there were dark forces, already defined, that were impinging upon the theatre. It wasn't as easy to succeed as it once had been. It was getting increasingly difficult to make money with a bad play or a revue with nude showgirls as its primary attraction. The public now had bad movie musicals to occupy its time and empty its pockets—pockets which would, in many cases, soon be emptied by factors other than the products of show business. The revue, always more reflective of and sensitive to its times than the book musical, began to feel mounting pressure.

George White brought his 1928 *Scandals* into the Apollo in July with a cast of proven standbys: Willie and Eugene Howard, Ann Pennington, Frances Williams and Harry Richman. Once more, DeSylva,

Brown and Henderson were hired to provide the score, but the team, unfortunately, sustained its now established reputation for unevenness. One of their song titles said it all: "Not As Good As Last Year."

It was, however, the dancing that audiences came to see at a Scandals, and they weren't disappointed. The new step of the year according to George White was "Pickin' Cotton," a sort of plantation shuffle/shag that Ann Pennington wiggled through. It never made it to the dance halls.

The girls were gorgeous, and the comedy was first rate. Billy K. Wells was again in top form, going after *Strange Interlude*, sending up Prohibition and its gangster profiteers, and prefiguring Comden and Green's *Singin' in the Rain* with a fearless takeoff on talking pictures: actors shouted their lines out from behind a screen—and, of course, fell behind the action so that the heroine and hero's voices became intermingled.

But the most popular sketch was "The Ambulance Chaser," in which Eugene Howard, as a lawyer, badgered a hospital patient, played by Willie Howard, into suing for an accident:

Patient: I saw the automobile coming—
Lawyer: You didn't see anything.
Patient: The chauffeur blew his horn—
Lawyer: He didn't! Without a warning he knocked you down.
Patient: When I was knocked down I jumped up—
Lawyer: You couldn't move.
Patient: I hollered for help—
Lawyer: You was unconscious. Now regarding your wife when she heard of your accident—
Patient: She took charge of my store.
Lawyer: She went to bed with a nervous breakdown.
Patient: She didn't!
Lawyer: I'll arrange it.

256 ❧ Scandals and Follies

The *Scandals* ran out the summer, and then some. Its 230-performance run was one of the best of the series, although nothing compared to its previous edition which, with a great score, remained for 424 performances—an object lesson, again, for tin-eared producers, who of course ignored it.

One of them was Earl Carroll, who had other attractions besides music to fill his theatre. The 1928 edition of the *Earl Carroll Vanities* opened on August 6, at the Earl Carroll with a bulging stable of composers and lyricists, none of them major. Poor Lillian Roth, appealing as always, was given nothing of quality to sing, not even "Oh, How He Can Love!", a song she and Herb Magidson wrote.

But then again, it was the flashing of flesh that attracted the customers who filled the down-front, single seats and kept the *Vanities* going. There was plenty of this, and for those with other interests, Carroll beefed up the comic portions of the 1928 edition. Joe Frisco, Ray Dooley and W.C. Fields performed the comic chores in sketches that Fields, himself, wrote—some of which became classics. As Dr. Pain, the Dentist, his assault upon an unwary female patient was eventually made into a sound movie short; "School Days" was imitated to death, and "Stolen Bonds," his trip to the country, with its famous "It ain't a fit night for man or beast and it's been stormin' for a fortnit," later became "The Fatal Glass of Beer," which Mack Sennett filmed.

Comedy and nudes worked all right, and the *Earl Carroll Vanities* stayed on for 203 performances.

On October 30, J.P. McEvoy, who had written the sketches for the original *Americana* in 1926, attempted to recapture the runaway success of that landmark revue by now doing it all himself. He wrote, produced and directed the 1928 *Americana* and it was a case of runaway impossibility. The sketches, although clever, picked targets that were already tattered from the volleys aimed at them by other revues. Talking pictures, Prohibition and *Strange Interlude*—this time played on roller skates in order to shorten its running time—all reappeared.

There was a duplication of *Show Boat's* matching white and black choruses, energetic dancing by Georgie Tapps and the Harlem Dancers, and the first and only Broadway appearance of George and Ira Gershwin's sister Frankie, freshly back from her triumph in Paris. The songs she was given to sing—music by Roger Wolfe Kahn, lyrics by McEvoy and Irving Caesar—were not the same sort of gift with which her brothers had presented her for her Paris debut. She and the show remained for only 12 performances.

It would be an import that would once again restore the faith of those who longed for a revue that was simultaneously intelligent, witty and musically valid. Arch Selwyn brought Charles B. Cochran, Noel Coward and Beatrice Lillie to New York to restage Coward's London hit, *This Year of Grace*. Finances, Actors' Equity and the fact that the show was still packing in audiences in London caused them to leave behind Jessie Matthews, Sonnie Hale, Maisie Gay, Douglas Byng and Tilly Losch. It scarcely showed. Coward and Lillie made up for an army of entertainers.

And, as in the *Charlot Revue* that introduced the two to American audiences, everything was of a high order, from the Cochran Girls, who were much prettier than the Tiller Girls, and whose illustrious alumnae would include Constance Carpenter, Anna Neagle, Binnie Hale and Sheila Graham, to the sketches, the performances and the music.

There was a drawing room murder featuring Sir James Barrie and Frederick Lonsdale; there was Beatrice Lillie as a channel swimmer determined to prove that "Britannia Rules the Waves," and there were razor sharp attacks on community theatre companies and the obligatory new dance craze with Coward and Lillie doing a mazurka to his "Teach Me to Dance Like Grandma."

The songs cascaded over each other, each one better than the next: "World Weary," which Lillie sang while eating an apple, "Dance Little Lady," in which Coward and Florence Desmond twitted the youngsters of the age, and "A Room with a View," with which Coward and Madeline Gibson charmed everybody but Alexander Woollcott.

Costumed grandly by four London designers—Oliver Messel, Gladys Calthrop, Doris Zinkeisen and Norman Hartnell—*This Year of Grace* was another standard by which astute producers would have to measure future revues, particularly after the times worsened. It remained in New York for 157 performances before returning to London where it continued to run.

And now 1929, the pivotal year, dawned, and its first revue was both a throwback and an experiment. Perhaps that was what sank it, not, as some contemporary observers concluded, the failure of local critics to allow a black musical to be anything but "meaningless whirling and fizzing with 'pep.'" Depending upon your point of view, *Deep Harlem* was distinguished or enfeebled by a thin story line that traced its characters from Africa, through plantation slavery, to contemporary Harlem. But it was clumsily mounted; its music by Joe Jordan failed to catch on, and its performers were unknown. It lasted a mere 8 performances.

Eight days after *Deep Harlem* opened, *Ned Wayburn's Gambols* appeared at the Knickerbocker. It had much to recommend it. Morrie Ryskind supplied the lyrics, and Walter G. Samuels his one and only Broadway score. Arthur Schwartz wrote the music for two interpolations to Ryskind's words: "The Sun Will Shine" and "Gypsy Days"—both used for production numbers that utilized, in the fashion of the time, either elaborate costumes or no costumes ("Two nearly nude gentlemen tossed a nearly nude lady back and forth in the air for several minutes," observed one critic).[9]

There was a personable cast which included Charles Irwin, Lew Hearn and Fuzzy Knight. And Libby Holman was finally given an opportunity to transfix audiences, which she did with two numbers, "Salt of My Tears" and "Mothers o' Men."

But ultimately it didn't come together; and, much as he had not succeeded on his own in 1915 with his 68 performance *Ned Wayburn's Town Topics*, the now elderly Wayburn closed his *Gambols* after a mere 31 showings.

Refusing to give up the ghost, Morris Gest once again imported yet another *Chauve Souris* on January 22. But its time had definitely passed, and the show itself passed into history after 47 performances.

February brought another Shubert concoction with words by Harold Atteridge. *Pleasure Bound* began its out-of-town life as a book musical, but gradually the book went, and the result was something that looked as if it were the residue of another idea. But the Shubert nudes were there, and some very pretty chorus girls, kicking high to choreography by Busby Berkeley.

The music by Muriel Pollock was, as usual for a Shubert show, incidental. But there was comedy aplenty in the hands of Phil Baker (with a new stooge, John Muldowney, arguing with him from a stage box). Jack Pearl woke the echoes of Weber and Fields with his hyper-German accent, and the whole concoction remained for 136 performances, enough to make production costs and a bit more.

April brought yet another try at breaking *Blackbird's* phenomenal record. *Messin' Around* made the same mistakes as the earlier *Deep Harlem*. It layered a thin story line over a set of vaudeville turns and suspended it over mediocre music by Jimmy Johnson and wandering lyrics by Perry Bradford. It lasted for 33 performances.

It was all a discouraging beginning to what would eventually become one of America's most cataclysmic years. But the season would end strongly, with another of Broadway's landmark revues. Developed over time in a series of Sunday night concerts staged by James B. Pond and Tom Weatherly at the Selwyn Theatre, *The Little Show* was that in size but not in either content or intent.

The first musical produced by Dwight Deere Wiman (in association with William Brady) and staged by Wiman, who had, since 1925, associated himself exclusively with straight plays, it was a convergence of talent and taste that hadn't been equaled in America since the first *Music Box Revue*. Appropriately enough, it opened at the

Music Box on April 30, 1929.

Wiman culled the best of the Pond-Weatherly concerts and added more. He concentrated wisely upon maintaining the intimacy of the Sunday night events, while emphasizing taste and creativity. The young Jo Mielziner designed smashing, stylish sets, and the equally young Danny Dare devised refreshingly original dances. For the sketches, Wiman hired Howard Dietz, who had contributed sketches and lyrics for the 1927 *Merry-Go-Round*, and, for the stability of experience, the increasingly famous George S. Kaufman.

Arthur Schwartz, finally freed from inferior lyricists and given a main score to compose, was paired with Howard Dietz, and the match was magic from the very beginning. *The Little Show* would be the first of many revues to whose success the team of Schwartz and Dietz would make mighty and crucial contributions.

As for the fresh and abundant talent, Wiman made his choices with extraordinary care and insight. Fred Allen and his wife Portland Hoffa, Romney Brent, Harold Moffat, Bettina Hall, Libby Holman and Clifton Webb headed the small but fiercely gifted cast.

Dietz delivered some smart sketches, but Kaufman's "The Still Alarm" triumphed and entered the annals of revue's finest moments. Its premise was based upon wild juxtaposition: a couple of businessmen carry on a drawing-room-polite exchange between themselves and with a bellboy and two firemen as the hotel in which they reside incinerates around them.

"Going to burn down, huh?" Bob, played by Clifton Webb, says to the bellboy.

"Yes sir," he answers. "If you'll step to the window you'll see."

He does. "Yes, that's pretty bad. Hm..."

"Yes sir, the lower part of the hotel is about gone, sir."

"Still all right up above, though. Have they notified the Fire Department?"

"I wouldn't know sir. I'm only the bellboy."

Eventually, Bob and the bellboy are joined by two firemen, who enter into the small talk and small conclusions. At the end of the sketch, one of the firemen lights a cigar from the flames outside the window, while the other plays "Keep the Home Fires Burning" on a violin.

Webb, who had heretofore been considered only a dancer, came into his own in *The Little Show* as a singer and an actor. Schwartz and Dietz provided him with the jaunty "I Guess I'll Have to Change My Plan." Dietz and Ralph Rainger, who, with Adam Carroll, provided two piano jauntiness a la the Gershwin shows, wrote *The Little Show's* runaway hit, "Moanin' Low," which Libby Holman was to make her own for the rest of her career, Here, she first sang it in low-down torch style and then joinied Webb in a sexy dance, bringing down the house every night.

The interpolated "Can't We Be Friends?" by Kay Swift and Paul James, the nom-de-lyricist of her banker husband James Warburg, provided yet another melodic moment for the heart.

Stylish and stunning, *The Little Show* bewitched its audiences, who kept coming for 331 performances, despite gathering national reverses. The Depression began during its run.

Two nights after *The Little Show* opened, the latest edition of *The Grand Street Follies* arrived at the Booth, right across the street from the Music Box. *The Grand Street Follies* had been the first intimate revue on Broadway, but now, like all too many annuals, it became a victim of the very formula that had made it seem so fresh in 1924.

Albert Carroll and Dorothy Sands were there to take on the comic chores; James Cagney was still hoofing, one step up from the chorus. Agnes Morgan supplied the sketches and lyrics, and Arthur Schwartz supplied some music, but he was lost in a crowd of composers that also included William Irwin and Serge Walter, none of whom contributed anything memorable to the show.

Nor were the impressions of Harpo Marx, Bea Lillie, Constance Carpenter, Lenore Ulric and Irene Bordoni enough to save the *Grand*

Street Follies. And although it was a clever idea—to create a salad of history and Broadway, allowing the reporters of *The Front Page* to bang out the story of Paul Revere's ride, landing the Marx Brothers on Plymouth Rock and turning Belasco loose on the siege of Troy—the idea was never given a form and wings, and its translation to the stage more often than not remained resolutely earthbound. Consequently, this edition of *The Grand Street Follies* accelerated the series' downward spiral into oblivion. A 93-performance run wasn't a flop at that time, but it was far from a success.

At least *The Grand Street Follies* tried to link tradition with the present. The Shuberts dealt with tradition by tossing vaudeville, spectacle, nudes and bad music together and calling it *A Night in Venice*. It was the last of the *A Night In...series*, with a truly terrible score by Maurice Rubens and Lee David and lyrics by J. Keirn Brennan and Moe Jaffe. Vincent Youmans interpolated "The One Girl" from *Rainbow*. It failed there; it failed here.

Ted Healy led a large cast that included the Chester Hale Girls and the Allen Foster Girls clomping through Busby Berkeley's choreography. Into the midst of this Jake Shubert dropped an act he had seen at the *Folies Bergere* in Paris. The Dodge Sisters, naked to the waist, had done a dance in Paris in which one was the hunter and the other a bird. Jake made them pull up their blouses for New York, but it didn't satisfy critic Percy Hammond. "One thing I do regret," he wrote. "The Miss Dodge who was the hunter should have been given a gun."

Jake Shubert immediately barred Hammond from the theatre.

Still, the public liked it all well enough to sustain *A Night in Venice* for a profitable 175 performances.[10]

June and the beginning of the 1929–1930 season was a time for anticipation and delusion. Times, after all, were good and getting progressively better. Large movie houses were beginning to open on Broadway itself, while the legitimate theatres were relegated to the side streets. But that wasn't a threat; that was progress. At the turn of the century, George M. Cohan had looked through the window of his new office with Sam H. Harris and remarked to his partner, "I don't recognize Broadway anymore, Jed. Everything keeps changing." How right and prescient he was.

The first musical of the season was an auspicious entry. Contrary to the second-rate black revues that had intervened since *Blackbirds* with their inferior scores and desultory performances, *Hot Chocolates*, which had begun life as a night club revue in Harlem, emjoyed the extraordinary advantage of a score by Thomas "Fats" Waller and Harry Brooks, with lyrics by Andy Razaf.

Waller had composed the score and with Jimmy Johnson had appeared as a duo-pianist in 1928's *Keep Shufflin'*, a moderately successful book show. But *Hot Chocolates* would be his Broadway high point, a score that included "Ain't Misbehavin'." The show was fast-paced and up-to-date. It included a spate of specialty dances and featured the stage solo debut of a young trumpet player named Louis Armstrong. All of this kept it open for a healthy 219 performances.

A sorry mess inaccurately titled *Keep It Clean* opened four days later at the Hudson. Its score was by no fewer than nine composers, and there wasn't a hit in the show. The creation of comedian Will Morrissey, staged by Morrisey and Russell Markert (who would later achieve fame of a far better sort by inventing the Radio City Music Hall Rockettes), it was a melange of impersonations, contemporary references in song and sketch and generally second rate performances. It lasted for 16 showings.

The Little Show notwithstanding, audiences were still comforted by the old fashioned spectacle revue, provided the spectacle was beautiful and lightly clothed. On July 1, Earl Carroll obliged with *Earl Carroll's Sketchbook*, a fancy title for another *Vanities*. Still warring with Ziegfeld, Carroll, after starring Leon Errol and Fanny Brice in his one operetta, *Fioretta*, blatantly advertised that Eddie Cantor had left the Great Glorifier and was appearing in the *Sketchbook*. Cantor did, but only on film.

It was typical Carroll flim-flam, but audiences had come to accept it, along with the truly beautiful nudes, some comedy and some listenable if not distinguished music. The comedy was provided by Will Mahoney, William Demarest and Patsy Kelly; most of the music was by Jay Gorney and most of the lyrics by E.Y. Harburg, although neither their songs nor those of a battalion of interpolators survived the 400 performance run of *Sketchbook* which—if number of performances is the standard—turned out to be the musical hit of the season.

Broadway Nights was a poor successor to the *Sketchbook*, although it contained some truly funny monologues by Dr. Rockwell and some clever, outlandish choreography by Busby Berkeley, who also co-directed with Stanley Logan. Two sets of chorines, The Chester Hale Girls and the Foster Girls, filled the stage and threw articles at the audience to the forgettable melodies of Maurice Rubens, Lee David and Sam Timberg. Two of the titles may give a hint at the goings on: "The Lobster Crawl" and "Come Hit Your Baby."

Broadway Nights ended after 40 performances.

So much for the producers who ignored the lessons of *The Little Show*. Ziegfeld was busy with book shows, and Earl Carroll had the advantage of hype and nudes. But, as the country and Broadway began the not-so-long plunge toward the ruin that was waiting in October, salvation took the form of intelligence, wit and solid musical scores. The book shows, now the realm of Gershwin, Kern, Porter, Romberg, Youmans and other first-rate composers, had learned this. It remained for the revue producers to catch up.

John Murray Anderson attempted to put his instincts into practice but, mysteriously, didn't succeed with *Murray Anderson's Almanac*. As it had been when he staged the first *Greenwich Village Follies*, his judgment was sure and tasteful. What might have weakened his effort was a long memory and a reliance upon what had succeeded in the past. For example, he insisted upon throwing in yet another Ballet Ballad, this one based upon Oscar Wilde's "The Young King." It crashed and burned as did some of the more nostalgic moments offered by Trixie Friganza, as the show flicked through the pages of a magazine that surveyed the recent past.

The score was pleasant and bright. Although its main songs by Milton Ager and Jack Yellen haven't survived, the standard, an interpolation by Henry Sullivan and Harry Ruskin, "I May be Wrong (But I Think You're Wonderful)" did.

The young Jimmy Savo was the audience's favorite, and he was given much to do in sketches provided by Noel Coward, Rube Goldberg, Ronald Jeans, Paul Gerard Smith, Harry Ruskin, Jack McGowan, Peter Arno and Ed Wynn. Mixing artists (Reginald Marsh among them, providing the show curtain) and writers in the creation of the sketches must have resulted in an annoying unevenness. Only Jack McGowan's "The Age in Which We Live,"—a sketch about a married woman and a doctor having an affair who revert to their traditional roles when her husband surprises them and "I May Be Wrong" have outlasted the 69-performance run of the *Almanac.*

The Cape Cod Follies, which had created a stir on its home turf in the summer of 1929, moved, with its young and pleasant cast, into the Bijou in the middle of September. But what seemed hilarious in July proved to be leaden in September, and the marginally professional revue departed after 30 performances.

It would be Billy K. Wells and George White who would make show business history with the most interesting and prophetic few moments of 1929 in a *Scandals* that was, although competent and lively and characteristic, otherwise undistinguished. White, the man who, along with Irving Berlin, had made much of his reputation and part of his fortune by bringing worthwhile scores to revues, tripped badly this time, hiring Lew Brown's pal, Cliff Friend, to provide the music to White and Irving Caesar's lyrics. Brown and Henderson did supply one song, "Eighteen Days Ago," but the score created no stir.

However, White still knew comedy and dancing, and he himself appeared onstage, still dancing, still lively, still charming an audience. Like Murray Anderson, White offered nostalgia of his own devising, opening the show with an Ann Pennington-less but nevertheless rousing "Black Bottom." There was a Ziegfeld-like "Parade of All Nations," and a Cafe Lido de Paris scene for a bevy of bare showgirls and a finale in which memories of the old Hippodrome were awakened as the cast disappeared into a tank of water.

Willie and Eugene Howard were again on hand to do the comic chores, and it was to them, Harry Morrisey, Frances Williams and Frank Mitchell that Billy K. Wells gave some prophetic laughs which, by the end of October, would turn uncomfortable.

The sketch was titled "Stocks," and its comic device was simple and hilarious. It began with two amplified announcers (the Scott Sisters) noting that "For the benefit of those who play the stock market, we will now give you today's closing prices without interrupting the show."

The curtains part on a living room in which a broker is seated, reading the *Financial Times*. A butler enters.

> Butler: Yes, Mr. Kennicott 58 3/8!
> Broker: Turn off that Columbia Gramaphone 64 7/8 and
>   bring me a bottle of Canada Dry 108 1/2.
> Butler: Sorry, sir. All that Reeves Brothers 14 3/4
>   delivered was Coca Cola 168 1/2.
> Broker: Then American Telephone 155 3/8 to Park and Tilford
>   45 1/2 for some at once.

Later, a messenger boy arrives with a telegram (Western Union 226 3/4!) and the broker tells the butler to give the boy a tip. "Buy Sinclair Oil 36 1/8!" shouts the butler.

Now, the broker's girl friend enters, and we discover that she and the broker have broken the law and plan to flee. But before the can, two detectives (the Howard brothers) enter.

> Broker: Who are you?

First and Second Detectives: Abraham and Strauss 129 7/8!

Detectives for the Irving Trust 76 1/4, Chase National 208 1/2 and Chelsea 99 3/4!

First Detective: When people of the United States Steel 202 3/8, we always get 'em!

Second Detective: Come! This means twenty years for you in the American Can 164 7/8!

If ever comedy had the potential of coming true, it was this, and if ever the revue lived up to its contemporary focus, this was also it. *George White's Scandals of 1929* remained through the crash for 161 performances. It was a bridge to a new dimension, with new demands, for the nation and for the Broadway revue.

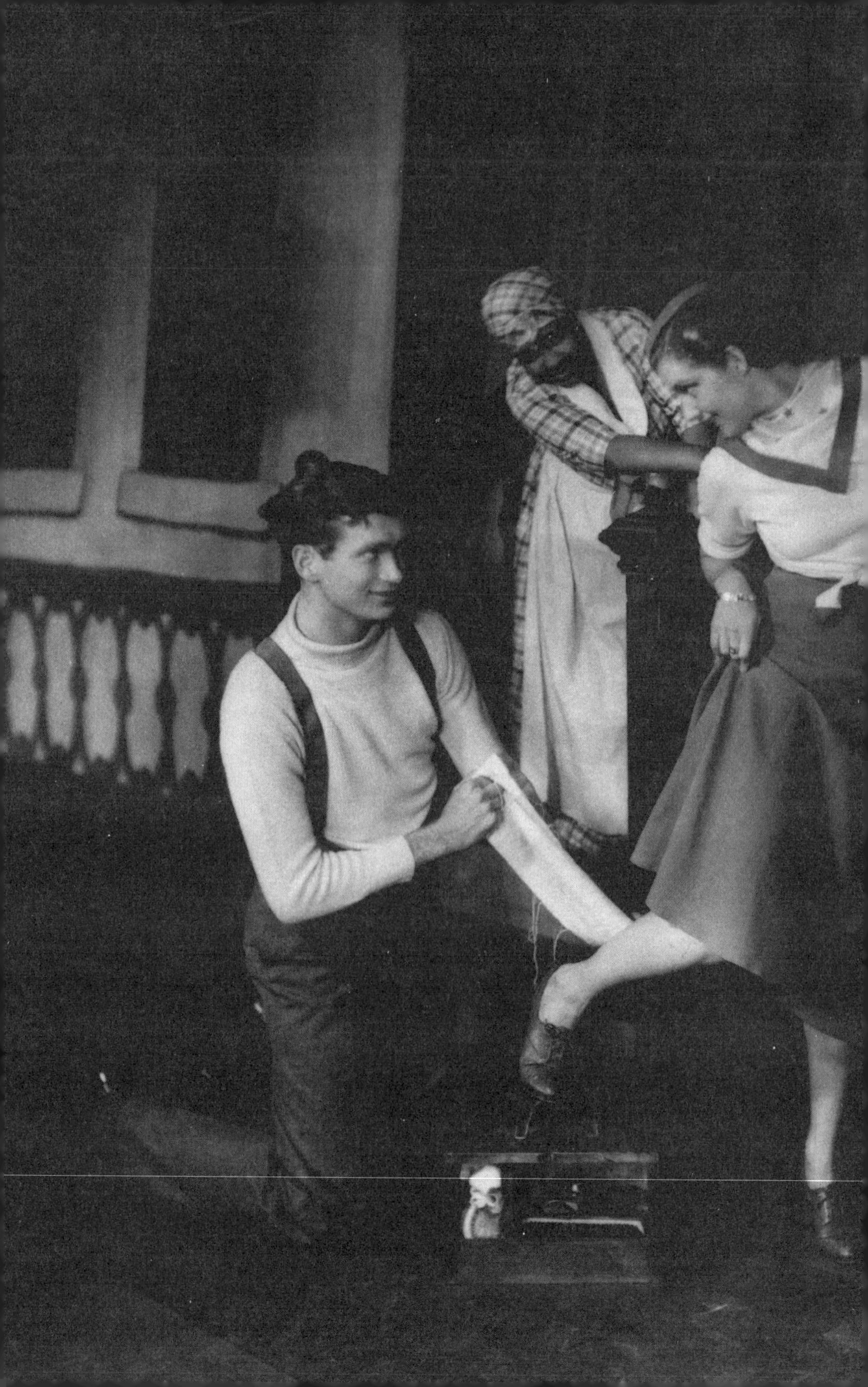

11

We're Out of the Money

We're Out of the Money

❦

In an instant, it seemed, in less time than it took to comprehend it, disposable income was disposed of. Millions and millions of dollars of it. And not just by deep-pocketed investors who kept ticker tapes in their offices and brokers on a retainer. Nearly everyone, from bankers to beauticians, from captains of industry to the "factory worker and his girl" to whom George M. Cohan said he directed his shows, had invested in the stock market. It had been like a giant game of roulette with the casino the entire United States. The winners won big and even the losers didn't lose much. Not, that is, until the Black Tuesday of October 29, 1929, when the floor of the New York Stock Exchange opened up and swallowed investments, investors and thousands of acres of dreams.

At that instant, the party of the 1920s ended for all except the very rich, whom no man-made disaster since the invention of money has ever touched. And, as the lights went out, one by one, reality crept in, even on Broadway. Ziegfeld, who had heeded the expert advice of his lawyer and invested $2,000,000 in the stock market, with $50,000 on margin, was wiped out, as were a dozen other producers, including Charles Dillingham who quipped sadly of his and Ziegfeld's mutual misfortune, "At least now, we're even."[1]

Ziegfeld would recover. But what of the audiences? All that money to spend, all those hours that had been devoted to fun. Both had disappeared as swiftly as if the backwash of a tidal wave had swept across Broadway. Radio, which had heretofore been a small annoyance, now became a major competitor. It cost nothing to stay home and listen to the radio, and an increasing number of Broadway stars, realizing radio's rising power and attracted by its huge salaries, moved rapidly from stage to studio.

Then, too, there were the motion picture companies and the gigantic amounts of money they were throwing around, and their voracious, sudden appetite for actors and actresses who could talk or sing. Or both. Suddenly, the trains heading west became packed with Broadway stars, writers, composers and chorus girls.

Another sort of migration had taken place in the 1920s that would, in an almost poetic way, shape the future form of the musical theatre and, particularly since it was most sensitive to the times in which it occurred, the revue. With the advent of Prohibition, an entire generation of temporary expatriates and vacationers, eager to penetrate the three mile limit, had left their native shores for the first time and discovered Europe.

Once there, they found that not only could you drink what you wanted when you wanted, and as much as you wanted, but that it was gloriously easy to live well on very little money. And when their delight in an extended binge faded, this enormous group of transatlantic travelers began to settle in and absorb the culture of Europe and England. They became used to creative intelligence as a way of life.

It may well be that without Prohibition Noel Coward would not have reached the remarkable heights of popularity he enjoyed in America from the mid-Twenties on. Perhaps one of the major reasons for Cole Porter's success and the adoration he achieved starting in the Thirties was the new level of sophistication that these travelers, escaping Prohibition and embracing European cultural values, brought home with them.

The revue's best decade, rising out of one of America's worst, was about to begin. It would be distinguished by the appearance of a new and authentic worldliness and a maturity that would, for the moment at least, outdistance that of the book musical, whose libretti, with the exception of Oscar Hammerstein II's for *Show Boat* and George S. Kaufman's for *Strike Up the Band*, continued to occupy themselves with either Cinderella stories or tales of hidden royal identities. None of this had much to with the world as it was.

That world had long been explored by playwrights and, in a satirical way, by some sketch writers. With the cataclysmic explosion of the '29 Crash and consequent Great Depression, an entirely new and urgent set of contemporary issues rushed to the surface of the public consciousness, and it would soon became apparent to a growing number of sketch writers and revue producers that it was possible to insinuate some of this material into their shows. In a year or two, such thinking would begin to enrich the subject matter of Thirties revues.

Intelligent sophistication, the consequence of increased world travel for more than the very rich, had arrived earlier on Broadway. And for it, much as they had in the past, American producers either turned to Europe for their models or imported European successes. Either way, these producers were forced to fashion a dimension of authenticity, since the rush of American travelers to Europe in the Twenties had brought back distinct memories from their transatlantic voyages.

There was no more successful producer of worldly-wise revues than Charles B. Cochran, whose *Wake Up* and *Dream* opened on December 30, 1929, at the Selwyn.

In terms of noteriety, Cochran, by 1929, was to London what Ziegfeld was to New York. His taste was impeccable but his preferences ran to intimate rather than spectacular productions. And, although he would be forever associated with the sophisticated revues that his chief rival in England, Andre Charlot, first brought to America, his own career actually and ironically began in America, where he spent his apprenticeship in American theatre, touring with Joseph Jefferson in *Rip Van Winkle*. He then returned to Europe and like Ziegfeld, experimented with all manner of impresario-ventures. He promoted fights; introduced roller skating to France, Belgium and Germany; managed zoos; and staged rodeos. He even began a brief stint as a manager of singers with Harlem's Florence Mills, the featured attraction in his early London production *Dover Street to Dixie*.

But it was to the revue that Cochran was drawn most thoroughly. He produced over 30 of them in a long life on the London and New York stages, and his distinctive touch could be discerned in whatever he mounted.

Wake Up and Dream, whose title couldn't have been more appropriate for the season in which it appeared, had been a smash hit in London, and Cochran wisely brought with him as many of his headliners as Equity would allow. Jack Buchanan was the direct antithesis of Ted Lewis as a master of ceremonies. Debonair and charming, he could deliver lines, sing and dance with the best, and was considerably handsomer than Sonnie Hale, whose London role he took over for New York. Jessie Matthews, who was also Mrs. Sonnie Hale, did come to Broadway, and her remarkable beauty, figure and dancing captivated audiences as surely as Buchanan's charm did. Tillie Losch was largely responsible for the dances of Matthews and Buchanan and a chorus of Cochran beauties who moved from the Barbary Coast to a Dream World to a lush art deco nightclub. Their words and music came from Cole Porter, who, in *Wake Up and Dream* cemented his place on Broadway with the suitably sardonic "I'm a Gigolo."

Porter, who had been merely apprenticing in his earlier shows on Broadway, truly came into his own in 1929. His *Twenty Million Frenchmen* (book by Herbert Fields), with its phenomenally rich score and reminders of the Paris that the Prohibition-beaters of the Twenties knew and loved so well, opened at the end of November and was running when *Wake Up and Dream* arrived. Now, with "Looking at You" and "What Is This Thing Called Love?" in *Wake Up and Dream*, there was no doubt that he was the expatriates' spokesman.

Strangely, while the show stopper of the London production *Wake Up and Dream* had been the Sonnie Hale-Jessie Matthews duet of "Let's Do It," the number was off-limits for the New York edition. It seems that Porter had already given it to Irene Bordoni a year earlier, to sing in a Broadway show called *Paris*. Still, even without that Porter classic, *Wake Up and Dream* delighted a new and more demanding revue audience for 136 profitable performances.

And demanding must have been the operative word, for how else to explain the mysterious, one-week stay of what in retrospect seems to have been a first rate revue? Perhaps the early 1930 *9:15 Revue* suffered from an embarrassment of riches. Its sketches were the work of Ring Lardner, Paul Gerard Smith, Eddie Cantor, Anita Loos, John Emerson, Geoffrey Kerr, H.W. Hanemann, Robert Ruskin, A. Dorian Otvos and Ruth Wilcox. The lyrics were by Paul James, Ira Gershwin, Edward Eliscu, Ted Koehler and Philip Broughton, and the music by Kay Swift, George Gershwin, Manning Sherwin, Rudolph Friml, Ned Lehac, Ralph Rainger, Roger Wolfe Kahn, Vincent Youmans, Harold Arlen, Victor Herbert and Will Johnstone.

In addition to this imposing lineup, the talented cast featured Ruth Etting, Paul Kelly, Frances Shelley, the popular dance team of Gracella and Theodore, and Oscar Ragland, who would soon trade his first name of Oscar for Rags and Hollywood stardom.

Nan Blackstone was charming in her rendition of George and Ira Gershwin's "Toddlin' Along;" Ruth Etting was transfixing in her two songs that long outlasted the show: "Up Among the Chimney Pots," by Kay Swift and her husband Paul James, and "Get Happy" by newcomers Harold Arlen and Ted Koehler.

The sketches were clever, particularly Anita Loos's modern take on *East Lynn*. Still, one can only imagine that rehearsals must have been either parties or nightmares. In any event, Alexander Leftwich,

Busby Berkeley and Leon Leonidoff couldn't pull it all together, and the *9:15 Revue* beat a hasty retreat.

A mere two weeks later, Busby Berkeley's dances for Lew Leslie's *International Revue* were greeted more enthusiastically by audiences, if not the critics, who lambasted the show. The "international" aspect of the revue was somewhat suspect. Gertrude Lawrence certainly qualified, as did British ballet dancer Anton Dolin and at first the highly touted Spanish dancer Argentinita. But Senorita Argentinita was so bad, that, along with Florence Moore, she was dropped from the show after the first week. That left Lawrence, Monsieur Dolin, Jack Pearl doing his overwrought German accent, and a "Russianized" apache dance set in Paris to supply its supposedly international flavor.

The show was simply Lew Leslie and his *Blackbirds* producers and creative team trying for another hit. Dorothy Fields and Jimmy McHugh certainly delivered, with "Cinderella Brown" for Gertrude Lawrence and "Exactly Like You" as a duet for her and the suave Harry Richman. Richman by himself was given the show's biggest hit, "On the Sunny Side of the Street."

The scathing reviews, however, thwarted a natural inclination to see any show that starred Gertrude Lawrence, Harry Richman and Jack Pearl, and *The International Revue*, despite its strong points, departed after 95 performances. This wasn't exactly a failure in 1930, when straight plays that might have stayed open for respectable runs two years earlier were closing in less than a week. The steadily deepening Depression, the competition from radio and talking pictures, and the European exposure of an aging generation had combined to raise the taste and demands of the theatre-going public. Nudes and nonsense, the trivia of a good and harmless time, just weren't enough anymore.

Youth and cleverness, however, made for a combination that did work in 1930, and the third and last edition of the *Garrick Gaieties*, which opened on June 4 at the Guild, provided an abundance of both. Philip Loeb and Sterling Holloway, of the original *Gaieties* cast, were on hand to provide continuity, and, although Richard Rodgers and Lorenz Hart were busy and famous elsewhere, a veritable corporation of talented youngsters mingled with a few oldsters to provide some good and some bad music and lyrics.

Among the group were Vernon Duke and E.Y. Harburg, who united for "Too, Too Divine," and "Shavian Shivers," and, with Ira Gershwin, "I Am Only Human After All," an ensemble statement sung by James Norris, Valma Vavra, Philip Loeb, Nan Blackstone, Sterling Holloway and a gamin named Imogene Coca.

Harburg wrote the lyrics to the music of Richard Myers in a musical spoof of the Walter Winchell style, titled "Ankle Up the Altar with Me". Marc Blitzstein supplied a takeoff on operetta. Johnny Mercer was the lyricist for Everett Miller's music in a duet for Sterling Holloway and Cynthia Rogers titled "Out of Breath and Scared to Death of You." And Paul James and Kay Swift provided the musical foundation for an uproarious sendup of police commissioner Grover Whalen, returned—as all merchandise is—to Wanamaker's. The song and the sketch, performed by Donald Stewart, James Norris, Ray Heatherton and Ted Fetter, involved all manner of outrageous improvisations by Whelan, including installing traffic lights in the aisles at Wanamaker's.

It was a fitting and successful finale for the last *Garrick Gaieties* which remained at the Guild for 158 performances, and then, with a revised cast and some new material, returned for 12 performances in October prior to going on the road. The additions included the satire to end all satires of *Strange Interlude*, with James Norris as an intruding Ferenc Molnar, Sterling Holloway as an equally intruding George Bernard Shaw, Roger Stearns as O'Neill and—as Nina—the former leading lady of Boston's Copley Theatre, here making her Broadway debut, Rosalind Russell.

Blitzstein's operetta sendup was replaced by Rodgers and Hart's "The Three Musketeers" from the 1925 edition, and "Rose of

Arizona" from the 1926 *Garrick Gaieties*.

In a cascade of contrast, the next to last *Artists and Models* ("Paris-Riviera Edition") arrived six days after the opening of *The Garrick Gaieties*. It had come to the Majestic Theatre by a long, circuitous route: a year before, it had begun life as *Dear Love*, a book show, in London. Somehow, during the pre-Broadway tryout, the original title, book and author/lyricist credits were dropped, and *Artists and Models* revealed itself as just another Jake Shubert display of nudity and questionable taste.

It was the past run rampant: minimally-clothed girls paraded as beauties of history and mythology in see-through evening gowns, and eventually wore nothing at all while posing in an artist's studio. To provide flash to go with the flesh, Phil Baker delivered monologues, once again being heckled from a stage box, only this time in a stormy exchange of very blue references.

What had tickled and titillated audiences in the Twenties bored them in 1930, and this *Artists and Models*, the last for 13 years, departed after 55 performances.

Maybe, for once, Jake Shubert had been too timid. Earl Carroll, hoping desperately not to fall into the bankruptcy and oblivion that Charles Dillingham and Arthur Hammerstein had lately suffered, pulled out the stops and pulled off the clothes of his stunning and obedient girls, and on July 1, brought in his 1930 edition of *Earl Carroll's Vanities*.

It established a record for anatomical humor and anatomical abundance in a series whose reputation rested mostly upon both. Carroll didn't stint in the music department; most of the score was the work of Jay Gorney, Harold Arlen and E.Y. Harburg, with an added "Tonight Or Never" by Harold Adamson and Burton Lane, and most particularly and successfully, "Goodnight Sweetheart" by James Campbell, Reg Connelly and Ray Noble. Only the last tune lasted.

Carroll employed a battery of comedians headed by Jimmy Savo, Jack Benny and Patsy Kelly. But for Carroll, hype and girls were his interest, probably in that order. And he managed to attract more police raids for this *Scandals* than any others so far.

First came Faith Bacon's fan dance, to the Ted Koehler-Harold Arlen "One Love." This time, Carroll omitted the pasties, and the police obligingly raided the show. Then, there was the swimming scene, in which a man chased a bevy of nudes around a tank and caught one at the instant of the blackout. The police arrived and made Carroll remove first the climax, then the man. Finally, reflecting the general burly-que level of the sketches, Jimmy Savo as a window dresser enthusiastically removed the clothing of several very live mannequins. The police raided that, too.

But the combination of stunning nudes, bathroom humor and multiple police raids kept interest high, and audiences kept coming to the *Vanities* for a profitable 215 performances. Ironically, this, the tackiest takeoff on the *Ziegfeld Follies* yet, played the *Follies* former, longtime home, the New Amsterdam.[3]

July also brought a well-intended failure by a group of out-of-work actors and writers who gathered at the Lamb's Club. Calling themselves the Satirists, they assembled a small revue, called it *Who Cares?* and brought it into the 46th Street Theatre. The answer to the title question was "not too many," and the revue closed after 32 performances.

Hot Rhythm, which tried to combine the popularity of black revues with the reputation of *The Little Show*, calling itself first "A Sepia-Tinted Little Show," then "The Little Black Show," was a dismal failure. Nothing worked in this show, not the sketches, not the jungle scenes, not even a last-minute interpolation of "Loving You the Way I Do" by Jack Scholl, Eddie DeLange and Eubie Blake. It was the last legitimate production to play the Times Square Theatre, which converted to films immediately after *Hot Rhythm*'s 68-performance run.

The real *Little Show*, in its second edition, was no improvement. In one of the most harebrained mistakes in the history of revues,

Dwight Deere Wiman, William Brady and Tom Weatherly decided that it was the material, not the stars, that had made the first *Little Show* such a hit. Therefore, they saved money by hiring lesser known performers, while retaining Howard Dietz and Arthur Schwartz to write the words and music, Monty Woolley to co-direct, Jo Mielziner to again supply the scenery and Herman Hupfeld to interpolate the show's only memorable song, "Sing Something Simple."

Despite the game cast headed by Jay C. Flippen, Al Trahan and Ruth Tester, and notwithstanding a classic sketch by Marc Connelly about a guest in a modern hotel whose push buttons become hopelessly and hilariously scrambled, *The Second Little Show* was missing an essential ingredient—stars—and so lasted only 63 performances at the Royale.

Little more than a month later, producer Max Gordon, exhibiting considerably better judgment, reunited the original stars and creative team of *The First Little Show*, added Hassard Short as director, Albertina Rasch as choreographer, and a blockbuster torch song by Edward Heyman, Robert Sour and Johnny Green titled "Body and Soul."

Three's a Crowd also had the virtue of a main score by Arthur Schwartz and Howard Dietz that included "Something to Remember You By," sung by Libby Holman to a 23-year old saxophonist formerly with the California Collegians named Fred MacMurray, and "Yaller," a wailer for Ms. Holman with the immortal couplet "Oh Lord, you can make a sinner a saint/Why did you start me and then run out of paint?"

Other revues satirized straight plays and book musicals; *Three's a Crowd* dared to send up other revues. In the very first sketch, a husband bids his wife goodbye, leaves, and her lover appears. The husband returns, the lover hides under the bed, and Fred Allen stops the proceedings. "Sorry folks," he says, "In this show there ain't gonna be no beds." Stage hands remove the bed as a chorus comes on to sing "Oh lordy, what will we do for blackouts?"

Allen created a hit as a lecturing Rear Admiral Allen (read: Byrd), who solves America's unemployment problem by bringing back enough snow to keep every unemployed man busy for thirty-one and a half years.

But the showstopper of the evening was a sketch written by William Miles and Donald Blackwell. Titled "In Marbled Halls", it involved "He—a fairly decent young man" (played by Clifton Webb) and "She—a nice enough young woman" (played by Tamara Geva). He is discovered in a bathtub, merrily taking a bath. The door opens, and She enters, realizes she's in the wrong room, and tries to exit. But the doorknob falls off.

They conduct embarrassed small talk as two strangers in this situation might do, and she advises him to make some more lather. "If you were a gentleman, you'd make a lot of lather," she says.

>He: Lather! No one will ever say I'm not a gentleman! (He starts to make lather industriously. Suddenly) My God!
>She: Now what?
>He: Oh My God!
>She: What's the matter?
>He: It's terrible!...
>She: What is it?
>He: The plug!
>She: The plug?
>He: I've lost it!
>She: Oh my God!
>He: Get me something! All the water's running out of the tub! And the lather is going down too!
>She: Here! Use this!
>(She comes toward the tub with the doorknob retrieved from the door.)
>He: Too late! Don't look!
>(She has involuntarily looked over the edge of the tub.)

She: Well if it isn't Harry Smith! Fancy meeting you here!
BLACKOUT

Three's a Crowd received glowing notices and attracted enthusiastic audiences. Robert Benchley, not known to parcel out praise too readily, enthused, "England (meaning Noel Coward) might produce a revue with as clever skits and as pretty songs as *Three's a Crowd*, but it is doubtful if any English producer would unbelt to the extent that Mr. Max Gordon has in the matter of costumes, scenery, and all the other little Cartier knickknacks which director Hassard Short, because he likes nice things, is accustomed to work with..."

It ran a comfortable 271 performances at the Selwyn.

And now, Lew Leslie joined the crowded ranks of producers hopeful of duplicating a fortune-making phenomenon. All of the pieces seemed to be in place for *Lew Leslie's Blackbirds of 1930* to mirror its illustrious predecessor; although Jimmy McHugh and Dorothy Fields were absent, their places had been taken by the equally, if differently talented Eubie Blake and lyricists Flourney Miller and Andy Razaf. The cast was headed by Ethel Waters in her second Broadway appearance, bolstered by Flourney Miller, formerly of the duo of Miller and Lyles, and in bouncy evidence, the astounding dance team of Buck and Bubbles.

There were clever sketches, one spoofing the current *Green Pastures* and one giving Aunt Jemima a batter of marital troubles. But there were also sketches about honeymoons and infidelity and yet another jungle number, this one titled "Mozambique."

The score, rich in melody and diversity, included "You're Lucky to Me," sung by Neeka Shaw and reprised by Ethel Waters, the lowdown "My Handy Man Ain't Handy No More" ("He's so shiftless, all he does is sit around and let my stove grow cold"), and the show's hit, "Memories of You," sung in a plantation setting by Minto Cato.

But Leslie succumbed to too much glamour and glitz, too much deliberate image making: he subtitled this edition "Glorifying the

American Negro," which it certainly didn't do. By now, it should have been apparent to even the most closed-minded producer that Depression audiences were more demanding than those who had first welcomed Ziegfeld. This *Blackbirds* lasted for only 57 performances. Jimmy McHugh and Dorothy Fields, meanwhile, were busy with her venerated father, Lew Fields, assembling his *Vanderbilt Revue*. Once again, everything seemed to be in place for a huge hit. E.Y. Harburg joined Dorothy Fields in the lyric department; Cole Porter provided an interpolation, "What's My Man Gonna Be Like?", for Evelyn Hoey, who was given the lioness's share of the show's songs. The husky voiced comedienne Lulu McConnell ran the gamut from addled tourist to desperate dowager. A young comedian named Joe Penner first asked his immortal question, "Wanna buy a duck?"

But, sadly, the team of McHugh, Fields and Harburg didn't come up with a single hit song, the comedy fell flat and Lew Fields, discouraged and bewildered by the changing taste of the public, closed the show after two weeks and announced his retirement from show business. The great but now embittered legend never performed again.

The November entry in the 1930 revue sweepstakes was a peripatetic creation of the not-very-retiring Billy Rose. It had begun life in Philadelphia under the title *Corned Beef and Roses* (get it?) with the subtitle "A Helluva High Toned Revue." Fanny Brice, currently married to Rose, starred, along with Hal Skelly and George Jessel. But the show was bombarded mercilessly by the Philadelphia critics and withdrawn for revisions.

When it reopened in New York on November 17, at the 46th Street Theatre, it bore the less self-referential title *Sweet and Low*. Jessel and Brice were still in the cast; Hal Skelly had been replaced by James Barton. Borrah Minevitch (who would later be joined by his Harmonica Rascals), Moss and Fontana, Arthur Treacher and Hannah Williams rounded out the principals.

Its score was by a melange of composers and lyricists including, for music, Harry Warren, Will Irwin, Vivian Ellis, Duke Ellington, Louis Alter, Phil Charig and Joseph Meyer, and for lyrics, Edward Eliscu, Mort Dixon, Ira Gershwin, Ballard MacDonald, Charlotte Kent and—pervasively—Billy Rose. (In Philadelphia, it also had contributions by George M. Cohan and Rodgers and Hart.) It was a combination of terrific tunes and terrible travesties such as "Ten Minutes in Bed" and "When a Pansy Was a Flower."

But it also had some gems: "Sweet So and So," with lyrics by Ira Gershwin and music by Phil Charig and Joseph Meyer, sung by Hannah Williams and Jerry Norris; "East St. Louis Toodle-oo," with music by Duke Ellington, sung by Roger Pryor Dodge, with onstage jazz licks by cornetist Bubber Miley; the popular and lasting "Cheerful Little Earful," with lyrics by Ira Gershwin and Billy Rose and music by Harry Warren, sung by Hannah Williams and Jerry Norris; "(M-m-m-m,) Would You Like to Take a Walk?" with lyrics by Mort Dixon and Billy Rose and music by Harry Warren, sung by Hannah Williams and Hal Thompson, and the steamy "Overnight," with lyrics by Charlotte Kent and Billy Rose and music by Louis Alter, sung by Fanny Brice.

Sweet and Low had clever sketches, one sending up the current Preston Sturges hit, *Strictly Dishonorable*, here "Strictly Unbearable." It was energetically staged and choreographed by Alexander Leftwich, Danny Dare and Busby Berkeley. And although it received lukewarm reviews, enthusiastic audiences kept it alive for 184 performances—enough to make a profit, but not good enough to prevent Billy Rose from working on it—hiring and firing and fixing—until yet another version with another name would resurface in 1931. More of that later.

It would be spring before another revue opened on Broadway, a sorry effort by Lew Leslie to recoup some of the losses from his last *Blackbirds*. Subtitled "A Symphony of Blue Notes and Black Rhythm," *Rhapsody in Black* opened at the Sam H. Harris Theatre on

May 4, 1931.

Ethel Waters starred with Valaida, the Berry Brothers and the Cecil Mack Choir. It was a revue without sketches, a situation that confused the critics into calling it, variously, "A Negro oratorio," "A Negro *Chauve Souris*," and "A Negro vaudeville." The last was closest to the truth. Solos alternated with choir numbers on a fundamentally bare stage.

The musical program was a mixture of forgettable new songs by Mann Holiner and Alberta Nichols, "You Can't Stop Me From Loving You" from *Corned Beef and Roses*, and such wildly differing numbers as the Hebrew chant "Eli Eli," Gershwin's "Rhapsody in Blue," Handy's "St. Louis Blues" and Victor Herbert's "March of the Toys." Its novelty and Ethel Waters kept it alive for 80 performances.

On May 19, *Corned Beef and Roses/Sweet and Low* was back, this time as *Billy Rose's Crazy Quilt* (apparently, the pint-size producer with the zeppelin-size ego couldn't resist restoring his name to the marquee). George Jessel had been replaced by Phil Baker and Ted Healy by James Barton. Baker brought updated, contemporary quips about bank failures ("The bank is going to reopen its doors Monday—to let in four more bank examiners") and putdowns of the orchestra ("Play 'Ol' Man River' and throw yourselves in it"), And Fanny Brice was given two new numbers, Rodgers and Hart's "Rest Room Rose" and Mort Dixon, Billy Rose and Harry Warren's "I Found a Million Dollar Baby (in a Five and Ten Cent Store)" sung by her in top hat and tails. *Billy Rose's Crazy Quilt* played out the season and some of the summer at the 44th Street Theatre for a run of 79 performances.

The false starts of most of this season were, however, obliterated by the success of its last two revues. The first was the third edition of *The Little Show*, which, although it enjoyed a run of 136 performances—quite respectable in 1931—its creators decided to call it a night with this edition. It was a pity, for *The Third Little Show* was a mine of riches. Its sketches were by Noel Coward, S. J. Perelman, Harry Wall, Peter Spencer, Edward Eliscu and Marc Connelly; the lyrics were by Max and Nat Lief, Harold Adamson, Earle Crooker, Edward Eliscu, Grace Henry, Noel Coward and Herman Hupfeld; the music was by Michael Cleary, Burton Lane, Noel Coward, Henry Sullivan, Ned Lehac, Morris Hamilton, Herman Hupfeld and William Lewis; Dwight Deere Wiman again produced (this time with Tom Weatherly), Alexander Leftwich again directed and Jo Mielziner once more designed the sets. The cast was headed by Beatrice Lillie and Ernest Truex and featured Constance Carpenter, Carl Randall and Edward Arnold.

Obviously then, all of the right elements were in place. Perhaps too many of them, for out of this cornucopia of material and talent, the only sketch patrons really remembered and history recalls was Beatrice Lillie's appearance on a bare stage, announcing, as she began an impression of the revered monologist Ruth Draper, "In this little sketch, I want you to imagine far too much."

It was, in fact, Ms. Lillie's evening, although Dorothy Fitzgibbon and Jerry Norris sang the lovely "Say the Word" by Harold Adamson and Burton Lane, Constance Carpenter and Carl Randall evoked fond memories with Edward Eliscu and Ned Lehac's "You Forgot Your Gloves," and Walter O'Keefe romped through Herman Hupfeld's "When Yuba Played the Tuba Down in Cuba."

But it was Beatrice Lillie, poised in a rickshaw, who sang the classic that Noel Coward created while motoring in Indo-China from Hanoi to Saigon, "Mad Dogs and Englishmen." Also, for the first time, she romped with the "Fairies at the Bottom of My Garden," an inspired creation by Rose Fyleman and Liza Lehmann that was to identify Bea Lillie for the rest of her career.

Perhaps the real reason for the merely moderate success of *The Third Little Show* was the appearance, two nights later, of one of the two greatest revues of the American musical theatre. All else in revuedom until that time would be eclipsed by the appearance, on June 3, 1931, at the New Amsterdam of *The Band Wagon*. The advance word from the cognoscenti who had journeyed down to far

Philadelphia to catch it was ecstatic (and further damaging to *The Third Little Show*). Legend has it that producer Max Gordon approached Howard Dietz and Arthur Schwartz about a new revue shortly after their hit of the previous October, *Three's a Crowd*. The songwriting team laid down some strict conditions: they demanded that they write the entire score with no interpolators allowed, that the sketches be written by George S. Kaufman and Howard Dietz and no one else; and finally that Fred and Adele Astaire star. And, oh yes. The New Amsterdam, with its *Follies* tradition, was the only possible venue for this show.

Gordon, no Jake Shubert he, acquiesced and proceeded to fill out the cast with Frank Morgan, Helen Broderick and Tilly Losch as the principals, supported by Philip Loeb, John Barker and Roberta Robinson. To assure continuity with *Three's a Crowd*, he hired Albertina Rasch to choreograph, Hassard Short to direct, and Albert Johnson to design.

The very economy of the creative team gave the show the focus other revues with armies of creators failed to achieve. Ironically, it would be Noel Coward who would set to paper the parameters of writing successful revue sketches. Calling it a "difficult, delicate art," he wrote, "A sketch for a revue must be quick, sharp, funny (or sentimental) and to the point, with a good, really good black-out line. Whether the performers are naked or wearing crinolines is quite beside the point; the same rule applies."[2]

And so the key to success was codified. With *The Band Wagon* it would gain the force of use. There wasn't a weak or unimaginative or unrealized sketch in the entire revue. Every one was original and clever and hilarious. In "The Great Warburton Mystery," Frank Morgan played a police inspector investigating the death of the host of a posh dinner party, with Adele Astaire as a wisecracking guest. Morgan decides that the decisive clue is the impression the killer made on a chair cushion, which leads him to measure the posteriors of each guest. "Now do you want to make a bust of it?" queries Adele. The killer almost outwits the inspector by stuffing a cushion in his pants, but the clue of a glass with a false bottom gives the eagle-eyed inspector his culprit.

The most popular sketch of a superior bunch was "The Pride of the Claghornes," in which Colonel Jefferson Claghorne (Frank Morgan), who is about to marry off his daughter Breeze (Adele Astaire) to her fiance Simpson Carter (Fred Astaire), is staggered by sudden, horrifying news. She's a virgin! And so, the wedding's off, and so is Breeze, although she pleads with her father: "But if I could have another chance, Pappy! Can't I have another chance?"

> Colonel: From this day forth, I have no daughter.
> Sarah (his wife, played by Helen Broderick): Jefferson! You mean she's got to—
> Colonel: She's got—to go.
> Breeze: All right, I'll go. But someday gals like me will be able to stand up before the world unashamed. Goodbye, Pappy.
> Colonel: Goodbye, Daughter-that-was. It ain't for me to censure you, but what has to be has to be.
> Breeze: Goodbye, Mammy.
> Sarah: My poor little girl! Go forth, my daughter. Go forth and wander upon the face of the earth.
> Breeze: Goodbye, Pappy and Mammy!
> Sarah: Goodbye, Daughter. You've made a great mistake, and you've got to go out into the world and rectify it.
> Breeze: I'll make good, Mammy. You watch! I'll make good! (She goes.)
> Sarah: Well, Jefferson, she's a-gone.
> Colonel: Yes, Sarah. Yes, she's a-gone.
> Sarah: She'll come back to us, Jefferson—I know she will. She'll come back when she's seen the error of her ways.
> Colonel: Our little Breeze. Who'd ever have thought it, Sarah? Who'd ever have thought it?

Sarah: She was always a peculiar child, Jefferson. Right from the start.
Colonel: No, Sarah, no. It's the younger generation, that's what it is. The younger generation. They ain't got no use for old-fashioned ways.
BLACKOUT

The brilliance of *The Band Wagon* didn't stop at the sketches. The score by Dietz and Schwartz was varied, gorgeous and imaginative, and Hassard Short's staging took advantaage of Albert Johnson's innovations—among them, two turntables and the abandonment of footlights—and translated them into unforgettable theatrical effects.

The revue began with the curtain up and the cast entering, to sit in theatre seats, the mirror image of the audience. "It better be good/It better be good and funny/It better be good/It better be worth the money..." the cast sang.

Fred Astaire, as a beggar begging on the steps of the Vienna State Opera House, encountered Tilly Losch as a ballerina, then the turntable spun until the dream of the interior materialized, and he danced with her to "The Beggar's Waltz." Memories of *Lady, Be Good!* were aroused by the Astaires as they kept the wolf from the door by singing "Sweet Music." Helen Broderick dashed from window to window wondering "Where Can He Be?" Fred Astaire preened, in white tie and tails, while singing "New Sun in the Sky," and he and Adele ignited the stage to "White Heat." John Barker, the epitome of sophistication and elegance, sang "Dancing in the Dark" at the base of a raked stage made of multi-lighted mirrors, while Tilly Losch and the Albertina Rasch dancers whirled behind him.

Critics and patrons were equally enraptured. Brooks Atkinson summed it up eloquently and precisely: "Mr. Schwartz's lively melodies," he wrote, "the gay dancing of the Astaires, and the colorful merriment of the background and staging begin a new era in the artistry of the American revue. When revue writers discover light humors of that sort in the phantasmagoria of American life, the stock market will start to rise spontaneously, the racketeers will all be retired or dead, and the perfect state will be here."[3]

It was not so much a new era as the culmination of a long development. Hints of it had been strewn along the path of the revue for a decade. It took the creators and the performers of *The Band Wagon* to show what could be done, when the best elements of the revue came together in one indelible experience. And so it happened, and would happen at least once again in the 1930s. As Atkinson prophesied, after *The Band Wagon,* revues would have to meet a new and higher standard. Perhaps this kind of perfection couldn't have occurred in the Twenties, when fun was uppermost, audiences were plentiful and money was everywhere. The ills of the Depression, which allowed the satire of *Of Thee I Sing* to thrive, may have been necessary for such a landmark event.

The irony and sadness was that *The Band Wagon*, a show greeted with unbridled acclaim that would have run for over 400 performances in the Twenties, could only notch 260 in the Thirties—enough for a profit of $90,000 in Depression dollars, but certainly not indicative of the revue's quality.

That was its slightest sadness. A greater one was the last appearance of Adele Astaire on Broadway. The closing of *The Band Wagon* marked her retirement from show business, as she married Lord Charles Cavendish and moved to Scotland.

It was probably only fitting, and suitably ironic, that the next revue to open on Broadway was the 22nd edition of *The Ziegfeld Follies*. It would be the last to be produced by the Great Glorifier, who, in direct contrast to *The Band Wagon's* minimal creative staff, expanded his to elephantine proportions. The sketches were by Gene Buck, Mark Hellinger and J.P. Murray; the lyrics by a mob that included Gene Buck, Joseph McCarthy, Mack Gordon, E. Y. Harburg, Jack Norwith and Noel Coward; the music by a throng of equal size that contained Harry Revel, Dave Stamper, Noel Coward,

James Monaco, Walter Donaldson and Albertina Rasch's husband, Dmitri Tiomkin.

Once again, Joseph Urban designed sumptuous sets; once again Gene Buck directed.

The cast was stellar and varied: Harry Richman, Helen Morgan, Ruth Etting, Jack Pearl, Buck and Bubbles, the new dance team of Hal LeRoy and Mitzi Mayfair, and Ziegfeld's last showgirl in the tradition of Lillian Lorraine and Olive Thomas, Gladys Glad.

For a while, and for publicity, Ziegfeld also hired a Polynesian woman named Reri, from a Robert Flaherty documentary, to lead the dancing in yet another jungle number. Ziegfeld hired her in typical fashion by firing off a series of his famous cables to a contact in Papeete: SEND ME THE TABU GIRL WITH THE BIG BREASTS was the first.

WHICH ONE? was the reply.

THE STAR YOU FOOL, Ziegfeld cabled back.

The scarcely revolutionary jungle number was included in order to feature gigantic Urban elephants which, by now, had turned in Ziegfeld's mind from a superstition to an obsession. A week into the run, it became obvious to the non-obsessed that the authentic Polynesian lady couldn't dance. She was fired, and rumored to be hiding out in Brooklyn.

The remainder of the revue was a tasteful throwback. There was a "Broadway Reverie" sequence in which the nineteenth century restaurant of the moment, Rector's, came alive, with Lillian Russell and Diamond Jim Brady in evidence, applauding Ruth Etting as Nora Bayes, singing the *Follies'* first song hit, "Shine on, Harvest Moon," Harry Richman as Al Jolson singing "You Made Me Love You," and Jack Pearl as Sam Bernard doing not one of Bernard's numbers but another Jolson song, "Who Paid the Rent for Mrs. Rip Van Winkle When Rip Van Winkle Was Away?"

A quick change, and a sleazy speakeasy, the modern day replacement for Rector's, became the scene for Ruth Etting to sing

"Cigarettes, Cigars," a bad imitation of Rodgers and Hart's "Ten Cents a Dance," by Mack Gordon and Harry Revel.

Helen Morgan was wasted. Given only Noel Coward's "Half-Caste Woman" and a duet with Richman, she was barely in evidence. But Hal LeRoy and Mitzi Mayfair scored big, as did Buck and Bubbles, and the impressive spectacles included a tribute to the recently built Empire State Building and a jazzy, Harry Richman-led "Doing the New York," in which copious quantities of balloons and confetti were tossed at the audience.

It was all uneven and old, if beautiful, a reminder of a glory that had once ruled Broadway, and was also reflected in the Urban-created elegance of Ziegfeld's namesake theatre, in which *The Follies* remained for 165 performances.

Not so glorious, except in its intent, was *Shoot the Works*, a cooperative revue assembled by newspaperman Heywood Broun. His sole, stated aim was to provide work for slightly more than a hundred unemployed actors, technicians and writers. Nobody who invested in the show (it cost a mere $6,000 to mount) expected to be paid back, and only the performers and technicians were salaried.

Unfortunately, although it was a noble enterprise during the first years of the deepening Depression, it neglected, to a large degree, entertainment. To Percy Hammond, it was "as full of fun as a Socialist picnic." The sheer number of creators, as in the revues before and after *The Band Wagon*, left it unfocused, despite the credentials of all the composers, lyricists and sketch writers: Peter Arno, Phil Charig, Jay Gorney, Dorothy Fields, Ira Gershwin, Robert Stolz, Dorothy Parker, Nunnally Johnson, E.B. White, Jack Hazzard, Irving Berlin, E.Y. Harburg, Jimmy McHugh and Vernon Duke. The cast included Jack Hazzard, Imogene Coca and a young hoofer/singer named George Murphy. Broun, himself, was a not-very-professional master of ceremonies, and the whole party broke up after 87 performances at the George M. Cohan Theatre.

At the end of August, it was time again for Earl Carroll to fill his new theatre at the southeast corner of 7th Avenue and 50th Street with his latest *Vanities*. It would be the premiere production to appear in the $4,500,000 art deco edifice, which playgoers were eager to see, particularly at a Depression era top of $3.30 a seat—the lowest price since before World War I.

Although Carroll tried to individualize his score, giving it to Harold Adamson and Burton Lane, he insisted upon the age-old device of dragging in interpolations, including Ravel's "Bolero" and yet again "Goodnight Sweetheart." The Bolero, performed with unfailingly execrable taste, offended Robert Benchley enough to send him into paroxysms in print. "[A] monstrosity of bad taste and bad coloring..." he fulminated, "three stages...with rising platforms disgorging dozens...at every beat of the drums, and a strange, unaccountable set piece of some sort, studded with naked ladies who do not fit into any picture except that of a carte postale..."[4]

Benchley had a point. The entire show was a tasteless, toothless confection, in which Will Mahoney, William Demarest and Lillian Roth, nearly ignored, were given bad songs to sing. Benchley concluded his diatribe with a truthful if somewhat inflated warning: "Mr. Carroll is offering a frightening example of how to spend money at a time when any money at all is hard enough to get. Revolutions have been started with less provocation."[5]

Revolutionary the Vanities were not, only Earl Carroll milking a formula. It worked, apparently, perhaps as an escape from reality, perhaps out of curiosity regarding the new theatre, perhaps because of its affordability. In any case, it remained on view for 278 performances, not enough to pay back the investors. During the run, financial difficulties caused Carroll to lose his new namesake theatre; its next tenant would be none other than Florenz Ziegfeld who would rename it the Casino and bring in a revival of *Show Boat*. It wouldn't succeed, despite its enormously positive reviews, particularly for Paul Robeson, whom Jerome Kern had wanted all along for the role of Joe.

Ziegfeld had experienced terrible losses ever since the crash. His production of *Smiles* was a disaster; his film, *Glorifying the American Girl*, was a mess, his production of *Hot-Cha* with Lupe Velez and Bert Lahr was a catastrophe. Increasingly eccentric and short of temper, he began to distance himself from even his closest friends. He hosted a radio show for Chrysler for a while; then, ill with pleurisy, he traveled to Hollywood, where Billie Burke had become an established motion picture star.

There, at 10:31 p.m. on July 22, 1932, he died.

In death as in life, publicity superseded events. Nobody that he knew was at his side when he expired; Billie Burke was on her way to the hospital. By the time she arrived, the press had already been informed. It seemed that the nurse on duty, also on the payroll of a local newspaper, had broken the news before even his family was told.

It was a sad ending for an era and the man who had shaped it. Others associated with that now lost age had passed away at the beginning of the Thirties: Abe Erlanger on March 7, 1930, David Belasco on May 15, 1931. Joe Schenck, Jack Donahue, Flo Irwin, Bessie McCoy, Tyrone Power Sr., Edgar Wallace, Mrs. Fiske, John Philip Sousa, Chauncey Olcott, Lady Gregory, Anna Pavlova, Nellie Melba—all died within a year of each other.

It would remain for George White to keep the annual revues alive, and on September 14, he brought his 1931 *Scandals* into the Apollo Theatre, one of the last surviving legitimate houses on 42nd Street. It was perhaps appropriate and possibly poetic that Joseph Urban, Ziegfeld's faithful designer, did the sets for this, the first production after Ziegfeld's death by Ziegfeld's only real rival.

Urban's presence assured its opulence; as spectacle it was the greatest of all the *Scandals*. It sounded fine, too, with a cast that included Ethel Merman, Everett Marshall, Ray Bolger and Willie and Eugene Howard. Two newcomers, one to Broadway, the other to revues, made their debuts: Rudy Vallee and Ethel Barrymore Colt.

Hidden in the chorus were Alice Faye (who would become Mrs. Rudy Vallee) and, in a quick dance specialty, Eleanor Powell.

Borrowing from *The Band Wagon* and his own best successes, White confined the musical chores to two-thirds of the team that had made his 1926 *Scandals* the best of the series—indeed one of the best revues in history. Buddy DeSylva had become a Hollywood executive, but Lew Brown and Ray Henderson, still writing and still available, turned out a first-rate score with no fewer than five hits.

Ethel Merman sang the fatalistic anthem of the Depression, "Life Is Just a Bowl of Cherries," and explained "Ladies and Gentlemen, That's Love." Rudy Vallee warbled the clever "This is the Missus" to Peggy Moseley and Everett Marshall was given the gorgeous "The Thrill Is Gone," backed up by Rudy Vallee, Ross McLean and the dancing Dixons.

The Howard brothers tore up the proceedings with their famous "Pay the Two Dollars!" sketch, in which a hapless Willie Howard, who has committed a minor spitting offense, nearly gets the chair through his lawyer's stubborn machinations. Close behind in popularity was their big game hunting trip to Africa, in which Willie explained his taking of a lion: "I bagged him and I bagged him—but he vouldn't go avay!"

Urban designed his second Empire State celebration scene, this time for Ray Bolger to dance on and around, and to impersonate Governor Al Smith. The girls were, of course, gorgeous, and the show was a solid success, running for 202 performances.

Not so the very next revue, which opened the night after the *Scandals* premiered. Forbes Randolph, who headed a black choir, attempted a black revue modeled on too many that had gone before. Harry Revel provided the music to Mack Gordon's lyrics, but no durable songs came from them, nor did the show last out the week.

In October, the stubborn, now sadly outdated Morris Gest tried again with a *New Chauve-Souris*, this time divided into three parts: a ballet, a Pushkin drama and a "buffonade," to music by Offenbach and Lecocq. Its residence at the Ambassador was for a mere 29 performances.

It would take the timeless master clown Ed Wynn to rally audiences to the revue. And "rally" is the operative word for *The Laugh Parade*, which was in dire trouble throughout its tryout and its first week of performances, when Wynn was forced to paper the house with willing friends.

But once it caught on, aided by the power of the burgeoning electronic monster, radio (Wynn shuttered the show on Tuesdays, in order to do his Texaco Fire Chief radio hour), it became a happy home for the outlandish antics of the man who could confidently advertise, "ED WYNN presents HIMSELF in THE LAUGH PARADE."

Produced and directed by Wynn, its emphasis was, as touted and usual, on laughs, practically all of them given to Wynn, who also wrote the sketches. Utilizing the Empire State Building yet again, he told the tale of a man who lived on the 99th floor, but kept a place on the fourth floor when he didn't want to go home nights. His parrot's pedigree was explained as being "One of the Parrots of Wimpole Street," and he advised the orchestra to underscore his juggling act by playing "something in a jugular vein."

He rode a two-man camel, pedaled and played a piano on wheels, modeled a derby with a detachable brim that allowed a gentlemen to tip his hat in winter and not catch cold, and became wildly entangled in an acrobatic act.

Between the nutty cavortings, there were satisfying dances choreographed by Albertina Rasch, who replaced Sammy Lee during the show's tryout, and pleasant songs by Harry Warren, Mort Dixon and Joe Young. Two of them became hits: "Ooh! That Kiss," given a French treatment and accent by Jeanne Aubert and Lawrence Gray, and "You're My Everything," sung by the same duo. *The Laugh Parade* remained at the Imperial for 231 performances.

Not so lucky was *Blackberries of 1932*, yet another blatant attempt to exploit the *Blackbirds* phenomenon. Its lyrics and music by Donald Haywood and Tom Peluso, and its sketches, by Lee Posner and Eddie Green, were less than memorable or clever or lively. It departed from the Liberty after 24 performances.

June arrived, the time when, in the past, a crop of lavish revues would spring up to brighten the summer months and bridge the gap between seasons when the big theatres were traditionally empty. But in 1932 only one show arrived: on June 6, a pleasant enough, promising enough enterprise titled *Hey Nonny Nonny* opened at the Shubert. Its credentials were solid: the sketches were by Frank Sullivan, Florence Calkins, E.B. White, Ogden Nash, Richy Craig Jr. and Harry Ruskin. Most of its music was by Michael Cleary, most of the lyrics by Max and Nathaniel Lief. Alexander Leftwich directed, and Jo Mielziner had a hand in the scenic design. It starred the sure-fire Frank Morgan, supported by Dorothy McNulty (who would later change her name to Penny Singleton and become the movies' Blondie) and Jack McCauley. It even had raciness with a song, sung by Dorothy McNulty and Jack McCauley and illustrated by a comely chorus, titled "On My Nude Ranch with You."

But it didn't click with audiences, who had apparently come to expect more than adequacy. It left the Shubert after 32 performances.

And except for a ten performance vaudeville titled *Chamberlain Brown's Scrap Book*, which momentarily lit the Ambassador Theatre in August, that was it for the summer.

The time since the crash had been a terrible tragedy for some producers, a learning experience for others. The old, road-strangling Trust was no more. The empires of the Shuberts and Erlanger lay in shambles. Ziegfeld, who had invented the grand, spectacular revue, was dead; Earl Carroll was temporarily bankrupt and theatreless; George White was struggling.

And yet 190 productions opened on Broadway in the 1930-31 season and 195 in the 1931-32 season. An overwhelming number of them were straight plays, more dramas than comedies, and, as always, far more flops than hits. Audiences, it seemed, had become even more selective and discerning. And although the old combines may have been shattered, the Theatre Guild survived, and young upstart companies like the Group Theatre were born. Audiences made *Mourning Becomes Electra*, *Of Thee I Sing*, and *The Band Wagon* successes. All shared a sense of integrity and sophisticated awareness.

It was no longer possible, it seemed, for producers of revues to merely dazzle the eye (it had become too expensive in the 1931-32 season to do that, anyway), to remove the chorus girls' costumes (the abandoned 42nd Street theatres brought back burlesque, an entertainment form that had left New York 30 years before), or to wow audiences with mediocre music and tired sketches. The shadows and the lights, the rare successes and the frequent failures, and the grinding struggle that now marked the Broadway revue reflected, as always, the climate of the country.

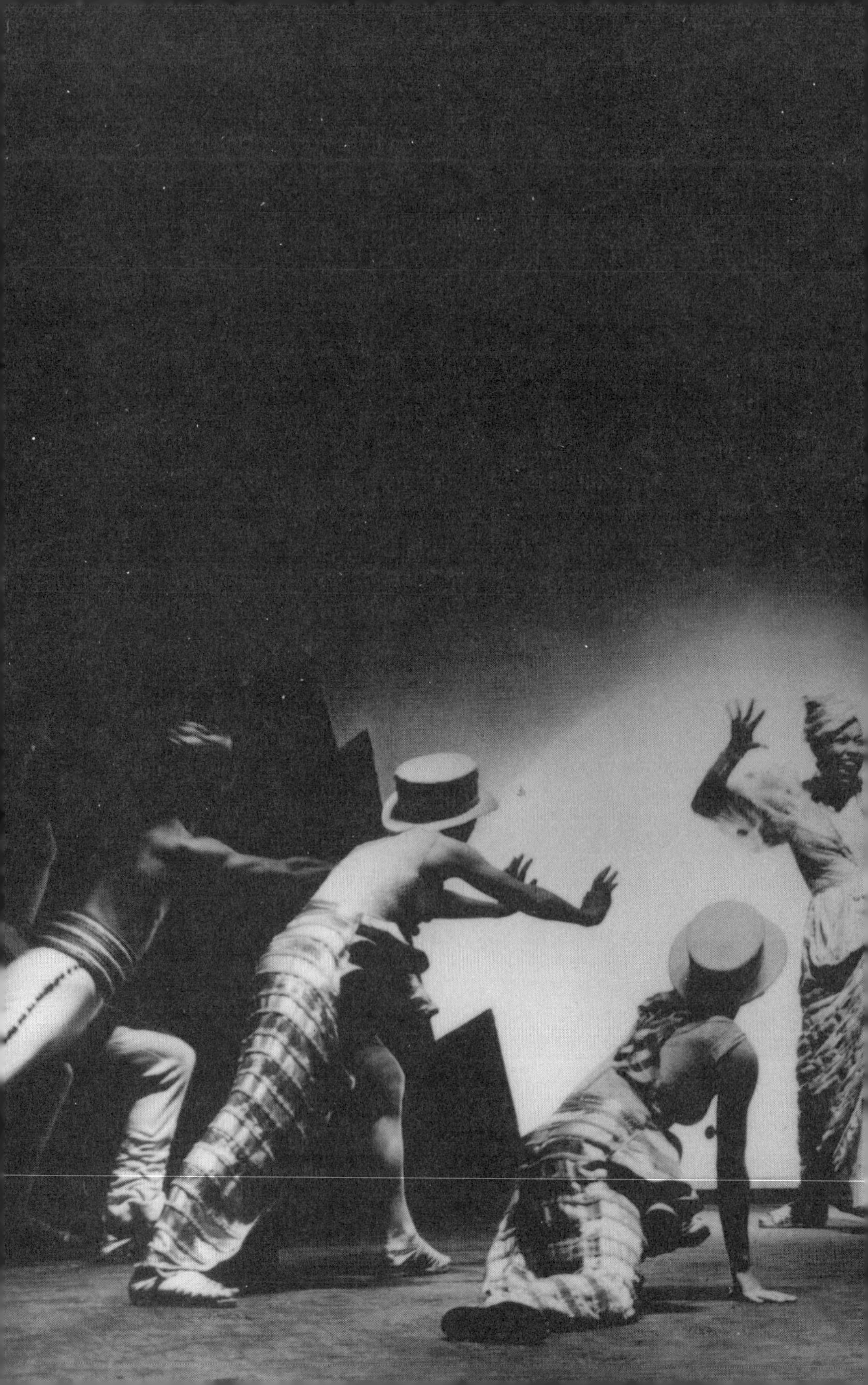

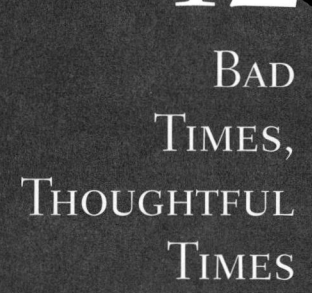

12
Bad Times, Thoughtful Times

Bad Times, Thoughtful Times

~

I f ever there was a moment of demarcation, it was the September night in 1932 during which former Mayor James J. Walker, joined by his family and separated from his girlfriend, Broadway's Betty Compton, boarded a ship for France. Forced by the revelations of the Seabury Commission to resign from his position as mayor—the jauntiest New York had ever had—he was going back to Paris, the party town, the city that had nurtured the Jazz Age and the Lost Generation.

In America, the Twenties had ended, and a forced seriousness—poisonous to the spirit that had powered Jimmy Walker and the Twenties—was gathering more and more force. Half the theatres were closed. Slightly less than half the actors in New York were out of work. And, as Burns Mantle would phrase it, "virtually all bankrolls were in hiding."[1]

Revivals were rampant—50 in a season in which 180 productions appeared. They were, after all, cheaper to mount than new plays or musicals. Producers could therefore charge less and ticket prices plummeted. Most seats for most revivals went for $1 apiece. "The day of the $3, $4, $5 and $6 theatre is about over," concluded Mantle.[2]

Of the 180 plays, 70 were musicals, not a bad proportion. Of the 70 musicals, 13 were revues, not a good proportion. But something valuable had been learned, and something important was about to happen. At the beginning of the new season, the pinnacle of the history of the revue was about to be reached, and the troubles and tragedy of the times, asserted undeniably in the 1932-33 season, would contribute mightily to it.

The season's first revue and second musical opened on September 6 at the 44th Street Theatre. *Ballyhoo of 1932* was patterned, in title and intent, upon the most popular satirical magazine of the age which, on the surface, seemed to make it a sure bet for success.

Its producer was the magazine's editor, Norman Anthony, and it boasted an abundance of humor, much of it enduring. Willie and Eugene Howard introduced two routines that they would repeat for the rest of their lives: First, the famous "Comes the Revolution!" sketch in which Willie harangued an imaginary audience from a soapbox at Columbus Circle, entreating them to "Rewolt! Rewolt!" Eugene, as a heckler, drives him to exasperation. "Comes the revolution, we'll all be eating strawberries and cream!" shouts Willie. "But I don't LIKE strawberries and cream!" bellows Eugene. "Comes the revolution, you muzzler, you'll EAT strawberries and cream!" concludes Willie just before the blackout.

The other sketch was their deathless *Rigoletto* quartet, in which they spent as much time concentrating on the heaving bosoms of the two women they flanked as they did on the notes.

Bob Hope made his debut as a suave master of ceremonies, and thus delivered the first of decades of standup routines. Jeanne Aubert was on hand to impersonate Greta Garbo (or Margreta Garbitch) and to sing the popular "Thrill Me," by Lewis Gensler and E.Y. Harburg. But audiences responded most positively to "Falling Off the Wagon," which suggested that love was the best antidote for drinking bad hooch in speakeasies. Paul and Grace Hartman premiered their patented comedy/ballroom dance routines, thus spawning a long line of comic club dancers. *Ballyhoo of 1932* made it through the rest of the year, chalking up 95 performances.

A considerably better and more enduring revue, *Flying Colors*, opened a week later at the Imperial. Once more, Max Gordon was responsible, and once more, the forces that had made *The Band Wagon* and *Three's a Crowd* what they were, were in place. Clifton Webb and Tamara Geva were joined by Charles Butterworth, Patsy Kelly, Philip Loeb, Vilma and Buddy Ebsen and harmonica virtuoso Larry Adler. The sketches were by Howard Dietz, with a great deal of assistance from George S. Kaufman and some help from Charles Sherman and Corey Ford. The music and lyrics were entirely by Arthur Schwartz and Howard Dietz, and although some critics noted the similarity to at least three sequences in *The Band Wagon*, the songs have endured nicely. "A Shine on Your Shoes," a Depression cheering-up song, was sung and danced by the Ebsens and Monette Moore, while Larry Adler provided a jaunty harmonica counterpoint. "Louisiana Hayride" was a stirring first-act finale, and "Alone Together" became a moody dance duet for Clifton Webb and Tamara Geva, choreographed sinuously by Albertina Rasch—who replaced Agnes DeMille during tryouts—and placed upon a disappearing stage designed by Norman Bel Geddes.

The sketches were firmly of the times. Charles Butterworth was given a hilariously confused—a la "The Treasurer's Report"—oration for delivery at Columbus Circle. Howard Dietz and Charles Sherman placed Butterworth in the middle of a crowd in midtown, asking for directions and receiving all sorts of wild responses, from handouts by men to promises by women. And Howard Dietz gave Clifton Webb ten minutes as a surgeon making his debut, with guests and a three-piece orchestra to accompany the surgery.

But the most popular sketch was one by Kaufman and Dietz titled "On the American Plan." It involved a hotel that rented rooms particularly for those who want to commit suicide after losing all in the stock market crash. "It's the best suite in the hotel," chatters the room clerk to a customer on the telephone. "Southern exposure. Wide windows and perfect landing space....Oh yes, we keep the street clear. Cars not allowed to park." The blackout involves the entrance of a man who identifies himself as a theatrical producer. "Say no more!" says the clerk and hands him a gun.

Flying Colors ran for a comfortable 188 performances, after dropping its $4.40 top to $2.20.

A week later, *Belmont Varieties*, a nearly formless vaudeville, opened at the Belmont Theatre. The creation of an army of unknowns, and featuring equally untested performers, it survived for only 8 performances. But the creators, undaunted, reshaped it, first as *Cosmo Vanities*, then *Manhattan Vanities*. Nothing would save a hasty, bad idea, and it disappeared rapidly.

Almost simultaneously, Earl Carroll returned with his tenth *Earl Carroll Vanities*. It was in the traditional mold of the previous nine *Vanities*, with all of its sketches by Jack McGowan and most of its songs by Harold Arlen and Ted Koehler.

Helen Broderick was on hand for veteran comedy chores, but two young, untried men made impressive debuts in this edition. Milton Berle, with his slambang antics, was an audience favorite, and 19 year old Vincente Minnelli devised delightful and imaginative sets and costumes, particularly a sequence in which some minimally attired young ladies paraded with glass tubes which, when exposed to an electromagnetic field, lit up in a variety of colors and designs.

McGowan's sketches were well-crafted, particularly one titled "Mourning Becomes Impossible," all about the circus surrounding the 1926 Rudolph Valentino funeral. Harold Arlen's haunting "I Got a Right to Sing the Blues" went virtually unnoticed by the critics, who preferred to concentrate, as Carroll hoped, on the girls. As Percy Hammond rhapsodized, "There are many shapely females—white, slim, rounded, dimpled and unashamed."[3]

But nudes were not enough in 1932. The male, single seat holders could get the same thrill for half the price at Minsky's on 42nd Street, and *Earl Carroll's Vanities* closed after 87 performances. Deprived of his theatre (this production was at the Broadway) and now his formula, Carroll discontinued his *Vanities* with this edition, although he would be back the following season with a book show version, titled *Murder at the Vanities*, which would be a moderate success.

The fifth revue in a row opened on October 5. Produced by Lee Shubert at the Shubert, *New Americana*, the third of the J. P. McEvoy *Americana* series, was imaginative and original. Perhaps too original, for its emphasis on modern dance, while certainly and refreshingly pioneering, wasn't popular. Not yet. Still, any show that would expose the public to the work of Charles Weidman and his company, which included Jose Limon and the Doris Humphrey group, recreating in dance a stylized prizefight and a barn-raising Shaker meeting, couldn't be all bad. Nor could a show that employed Richard Myers, Harold Arlen, Burton Lane, Jay Gorney, Vernon Duke and Henry Souvaine for its music and E.Y. Harburg and Johnny Mercer for its lyrics. From this perhaps unfocussed crowd of creators came what would be the acknowledged anthem of the Depression, E.Y. Harburg and Jay Gorney's "Brother, Can You Spare a Dime?" Sung by Rex Weber, who stepped out of a breadline to recount his history of loss and despair, it said it all for the millions who would hear and sing it from then until the Depression's end.

Although Phil Baker was recruited in November to beef up the box office, *New Americana* remained at the Shubert for only 77 performances.

George White returned at the end of November, but as a shadow of his former self. *George White's Music Hall Varieties*, which he brought into the cavernous Casino at a $2.20 top, was a very stripped-down *Scandals*, with sketches by Billy K. Wells and White, choreography by Russell Markert, music by Carmen Lombardo, Sammy Stept, Harold Arlen and Herman Hupfeld, and lyrics by Irving Caesar, Herb Magidson, Hupfeld and Ted Koehler.

The cast was a dynamic one: Harry Richman, Lily Damita, Bert Lahr and Eleanor Powell headed it, supported by Betty Kean and the

Loomis Sisters. Willie and Eugene Howard joined their old boss in January, with their, by now, vintage lawyer sketch, "Pay the Two Dollars!." Lahr did a marvelous sendup of Clifton Webb, Eleanor Powell did a spirited tap, Harry Richman raised the roof with Ted Koehler and Harold Arlen's "I Love a Parade" and, with Lili Damita and Bert Lahr, delivered what would become a tender ballad, Herman Hupfeld's "Let's Put Out the Lights and Go to Sleep."

But the show was not a success, remaining at the Casino for only 72 performances. It was enough to send a producer to Hollywood, and George White went.

A somewhat better fate awaited Courtney Burr's production *Walk a Little Faster*, which moved into the St. James—the new name for the old Erlanger Theatre—on December 7, 1932. It represented all that the 1930s revues had come to be: intelligence in the sketches by S. J. Perelman and Robert McGunigle, a fine score by one composer (Vernon Duke) and one lyricist (E. Y. Harburg), a bright cast headed by Beatrice Lillie and Clark and McCullough, and featuring Evelyn Hoey, Jerry Norris, Dorothy McNulty (still not Penny Singleton) and Sue Hicks, knowledgeable direction by Monty Woolley, imaginative dances by Albertina Rasch, and arresting sets by the young Boris Aronson.

Beatrice Lillie and Bobby Clark did a hilarious takeoff of the "Alone Together" dance of Clifton Webb and Tamara Geva in *Flying Colors*, and Ms. Lillie first performed what became a trademark exit, in which she wore an elegant evening gown, then raised her skirts and roller-skated offstage. Perelman gave the duo two sketches that Lillie and Clark tore into with glee: one, a college romp in which Ms. Lillie was Penelope Goldfarb, the 1906 scamp of the campus, and the other in which Clark portrayed an overbearing Joseph Stalin.

Vernon Duke and E.Y. Harburg's superior score included the immortal "April in Paris" (suggested by an offhand remark of Monty Woolley). But first night critics passed this musical masterpiece by, possibly because Evelyn Hoey, who sang it, had laryngitis that night. *Walk a Little Faster* remained at the St. James for a middling 119 performances.

Although no other revues appeared on Broadway during the remaining weeks of 1932, a show that recklessly defied the Depression made its debut not far from the Street. Radio City Music Hall opened in the spanking new Rockefeller Center, and its first program bulged with revue stars. Mixed in with the choruses, European divas, ballet dancers and dog acts, were Ray Bolger, Doc Rockwell, Martha Graham, Weber and Fields, DeWolf Hopper, Jimmy McHugh and Dorothy Fields, and, making their debut, the Radio City Music Hall Roxyettes (later Rockettes), choreographed by Russell Markert.

It would, in fact, be March 4, 1933, before another revue lit Broadway. That was the night of the inauguration of Franklin D. Roosevelt as President, a fact that was not lost on the creators and cast of *Strike Me Pink*. They rang up the curtain with the melody of Of *Thee I Sing*'s "Wintergreen for President" making only a contemporary name change.

True, the times were terrible. But a man who could—and would—guide the country out of the Depression was now in charge. A month of bank failures ended two days after *Strike Me Pink*'s opening with a bank holiday. And within days, the agencies and plans of the New Deal began to take shape, enunciated at the first of FDR's more than a thousand news conferences.

The excitement found its way onstage at the Majestic. A show that had been in trouble out of town, *Strike Me Pink* was saved by Waxey Gordon, one of a number of gangsters who were muscling in on Broadway in the Thirties. It was he who lured Jimmy Durante away from MGM and brought along Lupe Velez, who Ziegfeld had first brought East in *Hot-Cha*. (Another import from *Hot-Cha* was "It's Great to Be Alive", sung by Gracie Barrie, and written by the composer-lyricist team of Lew Brown and Ray Henderson, among many others.)

The two produced a notable score, although "Home to Harlem," a statement of social comment worthy of its *Show Boat* ancestry, and sung by George Dewey Washington as a former black chain gang prisoner returning to Harlem, was praised by critics for its honesty and power:

"I need music I need lights
Tired of slaving for these whites;
They feels bigger
I'm plain nigger
But up in Harlem
I's got rights..."

Durante, entering through the audience, wreaked his usual hilarious havoc, and Lupe Velez kept the decibel and energy level high. Hal LeRoy again charmed with his tap-dancing, and Eddie Garr scored with an impression of Ed Wynn. It was enough to keep the show running for 105 performances.

On June 1, trying to maintain his reputation as a master of ceremonies with whom to be reckoned, Frank Fay brought to the Broadhurst Theatre a revue he had first assembled in Hollywood, and whose California cast had included Betty Grable.

Tattle Tales had a checkered existence: sometimes Fay was joined by his wife Barbara Stanwyck, sometimes not. She was there when it arrived in New York, doing two scenes from her current motion pictures, *The Miracle Woman* and *Ladies of Leisure*. The rest of the evening was devoted to Fay and an army of composers, lyricists and sketch writers. But even with a movie star onstage (occasionally), the enterprise couldn't rise above its thrown-together nature and it departed after 28 performances.

It had been a middling season which had proved that throwback revues tended to die quickly. Bad times apparently were also thoughtful times. And if ever proof were needed of that, the first revue of the 1933-1934 season would provide it, underline it and italicize it.

As Thousands Cheer arrived in the midst of what critics were touting as a theatre revival. Although the Depression was deep and searring, there was a fairly universal feeling that, at least, something was being done about it at the top. Half the theatres on Broadway remained dark; a mere 125 productions—13 of them musicals and of those only four revues—would open this season, and few would achieve the magic number of 100 performances, which, for decades, had been the demarcation line between profit and loss. And yet, in the opening months of the 1933-1934 season, a rush of plays, including Sidney Kingsley's *Men in White* and Eugene O'Neill's *Ah, Wilderness!*, were heading for runs in the multiple hundreds.

But none, except the end-of-season long-run champion *Tobacco Road* would achieve the 400-performance peak of *As Thousands Cheer*, the inspired creation of Moss Hart and Irving Berlin. Drawing their material from the headlines of the day, and, in fact, utilizing, through Albert Johnson's sets, headlines as visual frameworks, they presented a living newspaper that was so clever, so tuneful, so witty and wise that its title immediately translated into a capsule reflection of the reactions of critics and audiences.

It utilized the production team of Berlin and Hart's earlier *Face the Music*, a book show that contained within it a revue titled "Rhinestones of 1932." Combining a keen awareness of what interested the public then and now with experienced, show business savvy, Hart, Berlin, and Berlin's partner Sam H. Harris brought to the friendly quarters of the Music Box Theatre a gem—to many, the finest product the revue form has ever produced.

Clifton Webb, Helen Broderick and Marilyn Miller, in her last stage appearance before her early, untimely death, headed a cast that also included Ethel Waters, Hal Forde and Jose Limon.

The Moss Hart sketches, each with a headline title, were priceless, each one on target, each one uproarious. FRANKLIN D. ROOSEVELT INAUGURATED TOMORROW flashed the first scene, and Herbert Hoover (Leslie Adams) and his wife Lou (Helen Broderick) are discovered packing. Lou is bitter over the whole idea of leaving and tries to pack as many valuables as she can—silverware, towels, linen, even a portrait of George Washington. Her reasoning, over the protests of her husband: "The White House is lousy with portraits of George Washington." She finally prods Hoover into calling up members of the cabinet and razzing them, which leads man and wife into higher and higher energy until:

Mrs. Hoover: Herbie!
Mr. Hoover: Yes, Lou?
Mrs. Hoover: The Roosevelts?
(They both dash for the phone at the blackout.)

There was a sendup of Joan Crawford's divorce from Douglas Fairbanks Jr., which is topped at the last minute by news that Mary Pickford and Douglas Fairbanks Sr. have just announced divorce.

There was a mad birthday party, in which John D. Rockefeller's children attempted to give him Radio City as a present. Rockefeller (Clifton Webb) resists, particularly after John D. Jr. (Leslie Adams) and Mrs. John D. Jr. (Helen Broderick) break down the details—Radio City Music Hall, the Center Theatre, the office building—

John D.: How many tenants in that eighty-story building?
John D Jr.: Well, there's just ourselves and the ushers
and a man named Arthur Vogel for the time being—
John D.: Those theaters making money?
Mrs. John D. Jr.: Well, you see, Father, it's kind of an
out of the way place—Fiftieth Street and Sixth Avenue. And we've just had the Jewish holidays, too.
John D.: Junior—that's no birthday present! That's a dirty trick!

There was a performance of *Rigoletto* at the Met nearly drowned out by the broadcast radio commercials, an agreement between Mahatma Gandhi and Aimee Semple McPherson to form a team to sell religion, and a scene in a New York hotel which Noel Coward had lately inhabited, leaving all of the help spouting clipped Coward-like epigrams, and Marilyn Miller, as a chambermaid, transformed into Lynn Fontanne.

Irving Berlin's music and lyrics were of a matching, elevated quality and were derived from similar headlines. The elegant "How's Chances?" grew out of a sketch for Clifton Webb and Marilyn Miller that dealt with the wedding of Barbara Hutton and Georgian Prince Alexis Mdivani. Ethel Waters was given three contrasting scenes and songs: "Heat Wave," evolved from a weather report; "Harlem on My Mind," was located in a scene headlined JOSEPHINE BAKER STILL THE RAGE OF PARIS; and "Supper Time" was a song and a scene that Berlin fought to retain in the show when some thought it too depressing. It was the lament of a black woman whose husband has been lynched by a white mob and will never come home again. "Easter Parade," the reincarnation of a 1917 trunk song of Berlin's originally titled "Smile and Show Your Dimple," was sung by Clifton Webb and Marilyn Miller in a tinted rotogravure scene. And the finale, the jaunty "Not for All the Rice in China" grew out of a scene in which the Supreme Court forbade reprises in finales.

Hart and Berlin had managed, then, not only to realize everything that a revue should be, but also to incorporate the integration that Jerome Kern and the Gershwins had first insinuated, then demanded in book musicals. It was a monumental accomplishment, one which critic John Mason Brown summed up eloquently: "Its satire is as daring as it is convulsing, and proves conclusively in its own gay way that in spite of the many jibes and much evidence to the contrary, America is still the land of the free, at least as far as entertainment is concerned, and that the *Music Box* continues to be the home of the brave."[4]

The amazing universality of the satire and its timeless qualities were demonstrated with telling effect in a 1998 revival of a trimmed-down *As Thousands Cheer* by the Off-Broadway company, the Drama Dept. If its stellar cast hadn't had full-salary commitments elsewhere, its run might well have equalled the 400 performances of the original.

The two revues that soon followed *As Thousands Cheer* were, alas, throwbacks, one a disaster, one a reasonable success. Lew Leslie, with backing from various sources joined under the title "Sepia Guild Players Inc.," tried the *Blackbirds* formula once more, this time with Bill Robinson as the headliner, lyrics by Alberta Nichols, Ned Washington and Joe Young, and music by Nichols and Victor Young. But not even the magical Mr. Robinson could keep *Blackbirds of 1933* flying for more than 25 performances.

The second revue offering of the season was the product of one of the more bizarre partnerships in theatre history, proof positive that bad times make strange bedfellows, even from the grave. No two producers could have been more diametrically opposite in taste, personality, approach or results than Jake Shubert and Florenz Ziegfeld, who had feuded for most of their professional lives.

But now, the empires that both had built were in shambles and bankruptcy. The Shakespearean epitaph that Billie Burke had chosen for Ziegfeld was apt:

For him being dead, with him is
    Beauty slain;
And Beauty dead, black chaos
    Comes again.

Now, Billie Burke was in deep trouble; her husband's namesake theatre had been turned into a movie palace; creditors were nipping at her; selling off properties still left her half-a-million dollars in debt. She did what she felt she had to do. She went to Ziegfeld's archenemies, the Shuberts, with the suggestion that they jointly revive the *Follies*.

It was a chance. Even broke, the Shuberts were no choir boys. A Fred Allen story still circulating around Broadway had Allen crossing Shubert Alley and encountering an irate producer storming out of the Shubert building.

"What's the matter?" asked Allen. "You look upset."

"Oh, what a miserable son of a bitch," groaned the producer.

"So's his brother," observed Fred Allen.[5]

Still, in a comparison of sons of bitches, Lee Shubert was a bit better than Jake, who received the news of Billie Burke's offer gleefully. Now he'd show them. He'd out-Ziegfeld Ziegfeld, out-Urban Urban—

But his brother, who was in control of the business, left strict orders before departing for Europe on a short holiday. Jake Shubert was to have nothing to do with the *Ziegfeld Follies of 1934*.

It was one of Lee Shubert's wiser decisions. Still, preparations for the show were suitably Shubertian. Bobby Connolly, who had been hired as director, was obviously in over his head, so badly that John Murray Anderson had to be called in at the 11th hour. Vernon Duke, who had been wisely hired to supply the music, recalled, "After weeks of quarrels, tantrums, firings, hirings, Connolly's disappearances, Lee Shubert's dreaded entrances, money and tears flowing, stagehands fleeing, we got off to an unpromising start in Boston."[6]

The unpromising start had turned into a pleasant and nostalgic evening by the time the show arrived at the Winter Garden on January 4, 1934. Besides Vernon Duke, in true *Follies* style and in defiance of the success of the best revues of the 1930s, a mob of other composers, including Samuel Pokrass, Joseph Meyer and Peter DeRose, was dragged in. The lyrics were by another army that included E. Y. Harburg, Ballard Macdonald, Billy Rose, Billy Hall and Edward Heyman. The sketches were by H.I. Phillips, Fred Allen, Harry Turgend and David Freedman.

The cast was all-star: Fanny Brice, Willie and Eugene Howard, Everett Marshall, Jane Froman, Vilma and Buddy Ebsen, Patricia Bowman, Don Ross, Eve Arden, Cherry and June Preisser, and two rising youngsters, Brice Hutchins, who would change his name to Robert Cummings, and Ina Ray who, restoring her real name of Hutton, would become one of the most popular big band singers of the 1940s.

Fanny Brice was still a show stopper. In one scene, she sent up Aimee Semple McPherson (fast becoming a favorite revue target) with "I'm Soul-Saving Sadie from Avenue A/Vending salvation and making it pay." In "Countess Dubinsky," a sendup of the influx into America of White Russians, she was a fan dancer, "without her kolinsky, who right down to her skinsky is working for Minsky." As Baby Snooks, the sole personification of Fanny Brice that radio listeners would know for years to come, she demolished the legend of George Washington and the cherry tree. She joined forces with Willie Howard as Stonewall Annie and Dynamite Moe in a wild parody of the season's current hit, *Sailor Beware*, and she evoked some echoes by reprising "Rose of Washington Square" from the 1917 *Follies*.

Howard, on his own, convulsed audiences as both an outgoing and incoming Cuban dictator, setting in place his Raw Deal and wearing a target on his back as the most secure protection against being shot by his countrymen.

Interestingly enough, the mass of composers and lyricists turned out a surprisingly good and durable score. Two cowboy melodies by Billy Hill and Peter DeRose, "Wagon Wheels" and "The Last Roundup" (the last reprised by Willie Howard in a Yiddish accent) were the contemporary hits, but Vernon Duke and E.Y. Harburg's "I Like the Likes of You," and "What Is There to Say?," and "You Oughta Be in Pictures," written by Dana Suesse and Edward Heyman and added during the run for Jane Froman, became standards.

With the requisite girls singing "Only God can make a knee— that's where we come in" and with the requisite Depression social comment number, the 1934 *Ziegfeld Follies* added up a successful 182-performance run.

And the largesse kept flowing. Finally, 11 years after the tentativeness of *The Newcomers* and nine years after the promise of *The Garrick Gaeities*, the concept of a revue peopled by young unknowns reached maturity and longevity.

In May, 1933, Leonard Sillman, the son of a successful jeweler, had assembled a cast of knowns and unknowns at the Pasadena Playhouse for an original revue titled *Low and Behold*. Former opera star (and former wife of Guy Bolton) Marguerite Namara was its star, along with Teddy Hart, Kay Thompson, Charles Walters, Tyrone Power and Eunice Quedens, shortly before she changed her name to Eve Arden. Sillman and his sister June were also in the cast. Lee Shubert caught their act, liked it and proposed a transfer to Broadway.

As the wait between the proposal and the wedding lengthened, Sillman turned for help to Elsie Janis, who in turn asked the ailing and destitute Charles Dillingham to lend his name to the enterprise for a small stipend. He agreed, and with that, the $15,000 needed to mount *New Faces*, as it was now called, was raised, although not easily. It would take 137 backers' auditions to finally hit the magic, modest investment goal.

Only the Sillmans and Charles Walters made the trip from Pasadena. The rest of the cast—with the exception of Imogene Coca, who had already paid her revue dues on Broadway—consisted of former chorus members, understudies or bit players. Nancy Hamilton, who had understudied Katharine Hepburn in the 1932 *The Warrior's Husband*, was hired to act and write sketches, and James Shelton to sing and write sketches. Two friends who looked a great deal alike were tied for a spot in the show; the producers flipped a coin and hired Henry Fonda. His pal Jimmy Stewart lost out.

An extended roll call of composers, lyricists and sketch writers produced some fresh and funny material for the game youngsters onstage. Nancy Hamilton gave herself a Katherine Hepburn sendup and the show a memorable Walt Disney rip-apart, with the three little pigs doing their versions of *Ah, Wilderness!*, *The Green Bay Tree* and *Tobacco Road*, with its immortal Hamilton line, "I ain't et anything, pappy, since we et mammy last week."

Imogene Coca was at her droll best as she strolled across the stage wearing Charles Walters' polo coat buttoned up to her chin and carrying a single, scrawny ostrich feather. "Fan Dance" she announced to the audience in her cracked delivery.

The songs were generally serviceable, and James Shelton's "Lamplight," sung by him, and Haven Johnson's "My Last Affair," sung by Billie Haywood, lived on to become cabaret standards.

New Faces charmed critics and audiences and remained at the Fulton Theatre for 149 performances.

Charles Dillingham died before the end of the run, and one more giant of the Broadway musical was lost. Others who departed during the 1933-34 season: Marie Cahill, Texas Guinan, Ring Lardner, Otto Kahn (who backed so many musicals), Hal Skelly and Joseph Urban.

Summer, 1934, the traditional season for new revues, was noticeably bereft of them until August, when all was forgiven, and then some.

True, first night critics had to endure August 23, when a less-than-mediocre revue titled *Keep Moving* arrived for a 20-performance stay at the Forrest Theatre. It consisted of a loosely textured melange of vaudeville routines, featuring the Singer Midgets and Tom Howard, who warned audiences not to make too much noise lest they wake the critics. No such luck. The critics woke, and *Keep Moving* kept moving.

Fortunately, four nights later, on August 27, *Life Begins at 8:40* opened at the Winter Garden. Another Jake-less Shubert revue, it profited from his absence as well as from the presence of John Murray Anderson and Philip Loeb, who directed, and Albert Johnson, who provided some intriguing sets positioned on nesting turntables that could revolve in opposite directions.

The sketches were mostly by David Freedman; the music was by Harold Arlen and the lyrics by Ira Gershwin and E.Y. Harburg. This, then, was a revue in *The Band Wagon* and *As Thousands Cheer* mode—smart, witty and supplied with superior music and lyrics.

The cast was headed by Bert Lahr, Ray Bolger, Luella Gear and Frances Williams, with Brian Donlevy as a straight man of great variety to Lahr in the sketches, and Dixie Dunbar as an effervescent dancing partner for Ray Bolger.

Lahr was at the top of his form, as a French aristocrat contemplating suicide, a befuddled and ruined Wall Street investor and a concert diva at a garden party. Ray Bolger was equally energetic and loose limbed in sketches and dances.

And then there were the Arlen-Harburg-Gershwin songs, in prolific profusion: the buoyant dance-fest "You're a Builder Upper" (a breaker downer, a holder outer..."); the exquisitely masochistic "Fun to Be Fooled," sung by Frances Williams; the paean to procrastination, "Let's Take a Walk Around the Block," sung and danced by Earl Oxford and Dixie Dunbar; the quizzical "What Can You Say in a Love Song?", mulled over by Josephine Huston and Bartlett Simmons, and, finally, the cavalcade of special material, including "Quartet Erotica," in which Balzac (Lahr), Boccaccio (Bolger), de Maupassant (Donlevy) and Rabelais (James MacColl) mourned, "We thought that our erotica was very very hotica/[but]... A volume like Ulysses makes us look like four big sissies."

A grand finale that involved Mayor LaGuardia (Lahr), Mr. and Mrs. Jimmy Walker (Bolger and Frances Williams), four Grover Whalens and Eleanor Roosevelt (Luella Gear) was another indicator of the timely, suitably on target nature of the evening. *Life Begins at 8:40* ran for a comfortable and profitable 237 performances.

On October 3, Arch Selwyn and Harold B. Franklin imported a disjointed European vaudeville, titled it *Continental Varieties*, and installed it in the Little Theatre. Its featured performer was the French diseuse Lucienne Boyer, who sang ten character songs, among them her famous "Parlez-moi d'Amour." Escudero, Carmita and a band of Sacre Monte Gypsies pounded out some flamenco, and a Magician named simply De Roze made wine and a few other assorted liquids appear from a pitcher of water. Audiences came for 77 performances, 22 more times than they allowed Noel Coward's brilliant *Conversation Piece* later that same October.

It would be December before another revue appeared. And disappeared. *Calling All Stars* was a well-meant venture that had the distinction of occupying a movie house turned back into a legitimate theatre. A first. But this solo venture of Lew Brown (formerly of DeSylva, Brown and Henderson) was weak in lyrics, music and sketches, although not in performers. Lou Holtz, Phil Baker, Everett Marshall, Mitzi Mayfair, Jack Whiting, Patricia Bowman and in minor capacities, Judy Canova, Martha Raye and Ella Logan, all struggled against the material.

Phil Baker and Lou Holtz's turns were decried by some critics as smutty and by others as old—certainly accurate on both counts. Holtz climbed into a stage box and heckled Baker with some of the same lines previous stooges had shouted decades ago.

The music and lyrics were largely forgettable, except for an imaginative, socially conscious first act finale, which took cognizance of the five million families on relief in the country. "Hey There, High Hat," Everett Marshall sang in Harry Akst and Lew Brown's best musical contribution, "You're a high and dry hat/Won't you do a little something/For the straw hat in the rain?"

An even shorter run was accorded Leonard Sillman's next effort, *Fools Rush In*, which rushed into the Playhouse on Christmas night and departed a mere two weeks later. Imogene Coca was back, heading a large cast that featured Richard Whorf, Betzi Beaton and Billy Milton. The dance director was Chet O'Brien, Marilyn Miller's husband, which made Ms. Miller an unbilled producer. She lost money.

A mere two nights later, the revue form was redeemed by Eddie Dowling, who brought *Thumbs Up!* to the St. James. It was a lavish revue in the old mold, but directed with taste by John Murray Anderson and designed elaborately by James Reynolds.

The comedy chores were given to Clark and McCullough and Ray Dooley, Eddie Dowling's wife. She climbed a pyramid of Arabs in "My Arab Complex" and did an eccentric Sonya in a sendup of *The Merry Widow*. Clark scored as a microphone-hogging judge in a broadcast trial. The Pickens Sisters sang sweetly, and Paul Draper and Hal LeRoy danced brilliantly.

A host of sketch writers, lyricists and composers were hired, but the two hits from the show were the work of two individual composer/lyricists. James F. Hanley, whose "Zing Went the Strings of My Heart!" was sung and danced by Eunice Healey and Hal LeRoy, and Vernon Duke, who wrote the exquisite and deathless "Autumn in New York," sung by J. Harold Murray before photo blowups of Manhattan.

Thumbs Up ran a respectable but not earthshaking 156 performances.

It would be five months later, the end of May, before another revue appeared. In that year of 1935, at the very depth of the Depression, a mere ten musicals would open on Broadway, but six of them would be revues.

The first, *Parade*, was advertised as "A Social Revue," but Socialist would probably be more accurate. Just as the Right Wing would find Communists under every bed and behind every desk in the 1950s, the Left Wing found Fascists in the same venues in 1935. Paul Peters and George Sklar first assembled their revue under the increasingly respectable auspices of the Theatre Union, then the Group Theatre, and finally, the Theatre Guild.

From its very first moments, the message of the show was clear. In the opening scene, New York cops sit around joking and playing tic-tac-toe while mayhem erupts around them, but then are galvanized into breaking heads after they receive news of a march by the poor.

A trio composed of Huey Long, Father Coughlin and General Hugh Johnson did a soft shoe. A domestic sang of her contempt for her rich employers, and Eve Arden sang a song about calling out the militia. Jimmy Savo, the primary comedian and attraction, became hopelessly entangled in machinery as a boss who thought he could run his factory without his striking workers.

Directed with spirit by Philip Loeb, the cast, which also included Earl Oxford, Charles Walters and a young Ezra Stone, performed with unified purpose to the music of Jerome Moross and particularly the lyrics of Paul Peters, George Sklar and Kyle Crichton:

Life could be so beautiful
Life could be so grand for all
If just a few didn't own everything
And most of us nothing at all

Parade, you'll excuse the expression, marched off after 40 performances.

In stark contrast, Earl Carroll returned to Broadway with yet another girlycue show, the *Earl Carroll Sketch Book,* subtitled a "Hysterical Historical Revue." The hysteria was presumably supplied by the cigar-chomping comedian Ken Murray; the history was from the point of view of a chorus girl who took audiences from 1776 to the present, with interruptions for an animal act and Mlle. Niska and her Butterfly Dance. Some fun. John Murray Anderson recalled it in his memoirs: "The girls stand behind curtains and then come out in front of them; or vice versa. They wear feathers and they don't wear feathers. They put on costumes and take them off, sit on the edge of the stage, and throw their garters at the audience. The girls can sit, stand, dance, lie down, and move their arms and legs. And they can do it all with or without mirrors. They probably can say 'mama' and 'papa'."[7]

But again, it was the girls the audiences came to see—notable among them Beryl Wallace, Carroll's latest Lillian Lorraine—and his companion when, a little more than a decade later, he would die in a plane crash. *The Earl Carroll Sketch Book* resided at the Winter Garden for 207 performances.

A quickly forgotten pocket revue titled *Smile at Me* opened at the end of August at the Fulton. A string of lampoons of current

Broadway fare (*Tobacco Road* became "Tobacco Juice") and South Sea island and Broadway anthems ("There's a Broadway Up in Heaven," for example), it had sketches and lyrics by Edward J. Lambert and music by Gerald Dolin. All failed to either satisfy or to sustain the show, which collapsed after 27 performances.

Then, just as it seemed as if the lessons learned by revue makers were being forgotten again, proof to the contrary arrived, at the hands of, of all people, the Shuberts. Say what you might about the brothers, they had theatre savvy, and that savvy now told them the future of the revue resided in wit, music and point of view. Real, not manufactured, sophistication didn't hurt, either.

All of this was in place in *At Home Abroad*, Vincente Minnelli's first directorial as well as designing assignment. To find the show's talents, the Shuberts went to the top. Arthur Schwartz and Howard Dietz were hired as composer and lyricist, satirists Dietz and Marc Connelly as the primary sketch writers. And the cast was headed by Beatrice Lillie, Ethel Waters, Herb Williams, Eleanor Powell, Eddie Foy, Jr., Vera Allen, Paul Haakon and, making his Broadway debut, Reginald Gardiner.

At Home Abroad was made topical by an act of exclusion. Billed as "A Musical Holiday," and essentially a world tour made by a Middle American couple, it assiduously avoided Germany, where Hitler was beginning his program of devastation and conquest. But elsewhere, the skies were sunny and tuneful. Bea Lillie was everywhere—in England as Mrs. Blogden-Blagg, ordering a dozen double damask dinner napkins; in Monte Carlo as a Russian ballerina who has trouble "facing the mujik"; halfway up a drop, in a Parisian poster, singing strangely of "Paree"; in the Swiss Alps yodeling "O Leo"; in Vienna warbling that "I'm the toast of Vienna and most of Vienna/ Can boast they've been host of the toast of Vienna"; and in Tokyo, in full geisha rig, noting that "It's better with your shoes off."

Eleanor Powell hoofed madly in a cricket game, tapped out code as an international spy, and sang delightfully of "Cricket and a

Wonderful World." Ethel Waters as a Hottentot Potentate in Africa sang wistfully and torchily of the "Thief in the Night" who stole her love, and sadly as a ship left Panama in "Loadin' Time." Paul Haakon stopped the show nightly as a dancing Spanish matador.

Schwartz and Dietz's music and lyrics were so integrated into the scenes that none stood alone as hits, except possibly the exquisite "Love is a Dancing Thing," sung by Woods Miller and danced by Haakon and Nina Whitney. Many of the rest endured in the repertoires of Beatrice Lillie and Ethel Waters.

At Home Abroad, which opened on September 19, 1935, remained docked at the Winter Garden for 198 performances.

It would be November before New York would have another revue (in between, the world would be treated to *Porgy and Bess* and *Jubilee*) and it opened at the Provincetown Playhouse in Greenwich Village. The *Provincetown Follies* was a pocket revue with a British flavor and a dedication to the immediate present. Although *Porgy and Bess* had opened less than a month before, "Poor Porgy," with lyrics by Frederick Herendeen and music by Sylvan Green, was rushed into service. Barry Oliver was a continental master of ceremonies, Cyril Smith a pleasant comedian, while Beatrice Kay sang torch songs by Dave Stamper and Herendeen that were of no consequence. The only lasting song from the score was an interpolation, "Red Sails in the Sunset" by James Kennedy and Hugh Williams. *The Provincetown Follies* lasted for 63 performances.

As the season reached midpoint, it seemed as if the past were revisiting. The Hippodrome was lit again, with Billy Rose and Rodgers and Hart's *Jumbo*, Sigmund Romberg had yet another hit operetta, *May Wine*, and now *George White's Scandals* reappeared, to be followed by another *Ziegfeld Follies* in January. So much for progress.

White gathered his old crew around him: Billy K. Wells and Howard Shiebler joined him in writing the sketches; Ray Henderson was back as composer, with a new lyricist, Jack Yellen, and Russell

Markert staged the dances. The cast read like a *Scandals* who's who: Rudy Vallee, Willie and Eugene Howard, Bert Lahr, Cliff Edwards, Gracie Barrie.

Out of the trunk came the Howard's *Rigoletto* quartet and the French Lesson, taught by Willie as Professor Pierre Ginsberg; Not to be outdone, Bert Lahr appeared as Professor Von Kluck of Vienna, mixing a soup that contained his toupee. Rudy Vallee had precious little to croon, although his black-face "Pied Piper of Harlem" brought bright applause, as did Gracie Barrie's "I've Got to Get Hot," in which she complained that she had to abandon Puccini and Verdi in order to make a living singing.

The showstopper turned out to be the one number in the show that boasted a contemporary reference—to Mussolini's invasion of Ethiopia. The dance team of Sam, Ted and Ray did a routine as Haile Selassie and two of his generals, while Willie Howard sang as Mussolini. *George White's Scandals of 1936*, which opened on Christmas night of 1935, remained at the New Amsterdam for 110 performances.

At the end of January, *The Illustrators' Show*, a new edition of the melange of sketches and songs about members of the Society of Illustrators appeared. Some of the material in the original was off-color enough to draw the attention of the police. No such luck for this version, which enjoyed a lightning engagement at the 48th Street Theatre. Notable for the debut of Frank Loesser as lyricist to Irving Actman's music, and for Otto Soglow's outrageous and offensive take on his own "Little King" cartoon character, the show, directed and produced by Tom Weatherly, with Carl Randall's dances and featuring Earl Oxford, departed after five performances.

A week later, the 1936 edition of *The Ziegfeld Follies*, again produced by Billie Burke with Lee Shubert as a silent but controlling partner, opened at the Winter Garden. Once again, hewing to a successful 1930s formula and ignoring Ziegfeld's methods, the Shuberts hired one sketch writer, David Freedman; one lyricist, Ira Gershwin;

and one composer, Vernon Duke. John Murray Anderson directed and Vincente Minnelli only designed the sets and costumes. The important addition to the creative staff was choreographer George Balanchine, who would, in his very next assignment, *On Your Toes*, revolutionize the use of dance in musicals, changing it from a force outside of the action to an integral device for plot and character development. In the *Ziegfeld Follies of 1936*, his insertion of a storytelling, modern ballet in the "Five A.M." sequence was a tantalizing glimpse of things to come.

The assembled cast was stellar. Fanny Brice was back, as were Cherry and June Preisser and Eve Arden. But now, with them were Bob Hope, Gertrude Niesen, Harriet Hoctor, Judy Canova, Hugh O'Connell, the Nicholas Brothers and, just back from Paris, Josephine Baker.

Freedman provided some hilarious moments in his sketches. In one, Fanny Brice wins the Irish Sweepstakes but can't figure out why her husband Monty (Hugh O'Connell) isn't hysterically happy about it.

Monty: A terrible thing has happened.
Norma: What could be terrible when we won the sweepstakes?
Monty: I met the landlord in the hall and had to pay the rent—$45.
Norma: What's that? We'll buy the house.
Monty: You don't understand. All I had was $42.50, so I made up the other $2.50 by giving the landlord the sweepstakes ticket.
Norma: So what? (Freezes) What did you say?
Monty: I gave the landlord the sweepstakes ticket.
Norma: Monty, dear, you should drop dead.
Monty: I'd like to throw myself out of the window.
Norma: Who stops you?

Norma spends the rest of the sketch trying to seduce the landlord into giving up the ticket.

In another, Brice, as Baby Snooks, tears up Hollywood, and in a third, Bob Hope is a fumbling and not very comforting elevator operator in an elevator stalled between the 19th and 20th floors. "It looks pretty bad," he tells the passengers. "Thirteen people in the elevator, but it's lucky it's Friday. It's a funny thing. I could have told you this was going to happen. A year ago today my brother was killed in a falling elevator. It got stuck just like this one and after a couple of quivers it fell right to the bottom. (The elevator jolts.) That's the quiver."

Fanny Brice kidded her own delivery of "My Man" by singing "He Hasn't a Thing Except Me," while even the streetlamp deserted her.

Gertrude Niesen sang "Island in the West Indies" sexily while Josephine Baker danced—unimpressively, if the critics are to be believed. The sophistication level of the *Follies* was raised immeasurably as Hope sang to Eve Arden of his travels and accomplishments in the Duke-Gershwin classic "I Can't Get Started," then, when she succumbed to him, walked jauntily away. And the first act finale, a riotous take-off on movie musicals, starred Fanny Brice as Ruby Blondell, Bob Hope as Bing Powell and Gertrude Niesen as Dolores Del Morgan in "The Broadway Melody Gold Diggers of 42nd Street."

The *Follies* ran successfully for 115 performances, then closed because of Fanny Brice's illness. When it reopened in September, Bobby Clark took over the Bob Hope role, Cass Daley assumed Judy Canova's chores, and Gypsy Rose Lee brought from burlesque both her comedic and ecdysiastic talents to expand upon the Eve Arden role. The show continued for another 112 performances, making it one of the most successful *Follies*.

Sadly, just before Brice's illness forced the *Follies* to close the first time, Marilyn Miller died at the age of 37. The previous August, Will Rogers had been killed while on a plane trip to Alaska with Wiley Post. The original *Follies* crew was shrinking, too fast.

As the Depression stubbornly continued, federal government pr grams designed to help the growing army of the unemployed increased in various ways. The Works Progress Administration (WPA) came into being, and with it the Federal Theatre Project. Out of that grew a musicless revue. Borrowing openly from *As Thousands Cheer*, minus the satire, and called *The Living Newspaper*, it gave work to 100 actors and 70 journalists, all of whom turned the news of the day into sketches held together by William Randolph, Jr.'s narration. The show premiered at the Biltmore Theatre on March 14, 1936, with 20 scenes from the present and proceeded, at intervals, for the rest of the Depression.

Gus Edwards brought vaudeville to Broadway in April with *Broadway Sho-Window*. It survived for one performance, its opening one. But on May 19, Leonard Sillman brought in his second *New Faces*, with some of the old faces (Mindret Lord, June Sillman) in the creative ranks and the indestructible Imogene Coca featured.

There were plenty of new faces in evidence, including Marsha Norman, Ralph Blane and Van Johnson. The latter two appeared with Helen Craig in a sendup of the literary lions of the age. Ms. Craig, as "Lottie of the Literati," crooned "No matter who said it/Dorothy Parker gets the credit," while Van Johnson chimed in as Sinclair Lewis and Ralph Blane became George Jean Nathan. Ms. Coca still sported Charles Walters' polo coat, this time as a Cinderella who realizes her dreams and becomes a stripper.

But the sketch that received the most attention—and the least attention from the Hearst press—was Elizabeth Wilde's impersonation of Hearst columnist Louella Parsons, ceaselessly gushing over William Randolph Hearst's mistress, Marion Davies.

One standard survived from the score, "You Better Go Now," by Bickley Reichner and Irvin Graham. And this *New Faces* also survived nicely, despite a strange device to boost attendance conceived by Martin Jones, its chief backer and owner of the Vanderbilt Theatre, in which it was housed. In the fall of 1936, he hired and gave star billing to the then superannuated Duncan Sisters, who proceeded to recreate sequences from their *Topsy and Eva*. The show, nevertheless, ran for 193 performances.

The 1936-1937 season was a rich one for straight plays and book musicals. Maxwell Anderson and Elmer Rice were the kings of drama, George Abbott and the team of George S. Kaufman and Moss Hart the royalty of comedy. Robert Stolz's old fashioned spectacle, *White Horse Inn*, graced Rockefeller Center's Center Theatre, Noel Coward brought in his daring *Tonight at 8:30*, a nine-play cycle with some music. *Red Hot and Blue*, with Durante, Merman and Hope (who left Broadway forever after the show closed) and a Cole Porter score and a book by Howard Lindsay and Russel Crouse, triumphed early in the season. But the biggest Broadway Christmas present of all was *The Show Is On*.

Once again, Lee Shubert collected the current cream of the revue crop. Vincente Minnelli was back to direct; the sketches were by David Freeman and Moss Hart. And while Arthur Schwartz and Howard Dietz resurfaced to provide music and lyrics, they were surrounded by a host of others, including Rodgers and Hart, George and Ira Gershwin, E.Y. Harburg and Harold Arlen, Ted Fetter and Vernon Duke, Will Irwin, Stanley Adams, Hoagy Carmichael and Herman Hupfeld. The principals of *At Home Abroad*—Beatrice Lillie, Reginald Gardiner, Paul Haakon, Gracie Barrie, Charles Walters and Vera Allen—all returned, and were joined by Bert Lahr and, in place of Eleanor Powell who had left Broadway for Hollywood, Mitzi Mayfair.

Show Business was the thread that tied the revue together, and most of its forms came in for merciless kidding. Beatrice Lillie was at her peak, singing, with wild abandon and a huge orchid corsage Rodgers and Hart's "Rhythm," which interpolated all sorts of songs, including "The Star Spangled Banner;" hanging from a half moon as a music-hall temptress; or assaying the role of Mlle. Leonore, a French grand dame of the theatre. In this spoof by David Freedman, a company, anxiously reading plays for her critique, finishes one convoluted tragedy and asks her for her evaluation. "I did not understand a goddamn word," she answers. The producer begins to introduce the next play. "The play," he says, "is about a man and a woman." "Too much plot!" Ms. Lillie interrupts.

Bert Lahr had his lunatic times, too, as Hollywood actor Ronald Traylor, and as another Hollywood actor locked in mortal combat with an IRS officer, played officiously by Reginald Gardiner. In his mile-wide vibrato, Lahr sang Harold Arlen and E.Y. Harburg's "Song of the Woodman." He also did a cakewalk and a burlesque routine with Lillie, and tore up a takeoff of the current hit *Tovarich*, in which a Republican couple is forced to work as servants in a household of Democrats, where they secretly worship a portrait of Herbert Hoover that's concealed behind one of Thomas Jefferson.

The highlight sketch was, however, Moss Hart's spoof of the current John Gielgud-Leslie Howard "Dueling Interpretation of Shakespeare Feud." Ms. Lillie, as a loud-mouth chatterer arrives late at a Gielgud (Mr. Gardiner) performance, hissing "Communist!" at anyone who tries to shush her. Gielgud is forced to shout to rise above her chatter. Finally, exasperated, he offers her a ticket to Leslie Howard's performance. "Oh, I couldn't take it," she answers. "Mr. Howard gave me the ticket to come here."

The outstanding score included two standards, Hoagy Carmichael and Stanley Adams' "Little Old Lady" and the Gershwins' last song together for a Broadway show, "By Strauss." During the run, George Gershwin died, with tragic abruptness, at the age of 38.

The Show Is On was greeted with cheers and ran for 237 performances. The Shuberts unwisely tried to return it in September of 1937, installing a new cast headed by Willie and Eugene Howard. But deprived of its originals, it fled after 17 performances.

And that was that for the 1936-1937 season. One revue. From the highest recorded percentage in one season to one seminal show in the next. And so, with suitable drama, the decline of the Broadway revue was foretold, just as it was reaching a new level of maturity and identity.

But this was a strange, conflicted decade on Broadway. The overall number of productions continued to shrink, dipping in 1937 for the first time below 100, while the number of musicals rose slightly to 15. The job of reflecting the present, its people and its issues, heretofore mostly the province of the revue, was now being shared by the book musical. Rodgers and Hart's *I'd Rather Be Right* spoofed a sitting president, Harold Arlen and E.Y. Harburg's *Hooray for What!* dealt with war in Europe, and Marc Blitzstein's searing musical for the Federal Theatre Project *The Cradle Will Rock*, dealt with labor unrest.

A mere two revues opened in the 1937-1938 season, but one established a long run record. It was, like its somewhat distant ancestor *The Garrick Gaieties*, a little revue that began with few hopes and matured into a phenomenon.

Two years before *Pins and Needles* opened, Louis Schaefer, in charge of theatre activities for the International Ladies Garment Workers Union, approached 27-year old Harold Rome, who had never had a show on Broadway but had written music at a summer resort called Green Mansions. Schaefer asked Rome to write some songs and act as rehearsal pianist for a projected in-house labor union revue.

Rome accepted, but the show developed slowly. According to Rome, "With Charles Friedman directing, we rehearsed *Pins and Needles* for a year-and-a-half, three nights a week...these were untrained kids for the most part and it was pretty slow going."[8]

Finally, with an orchestra that consisted of two pianos, one played by Rome, the other by Baldwin Bergersen, and a cast of ILGWU workers, *Pins and Needles* opened on November 27, 1937 at the old Princess Theatre, where Bolton, Wodehouse and Kern had invented modern American musical comedy. It was now called the Labor Theatre and the show, scheduled to be performed only on Fridays and Saturdays (so that the cast could work their regular jobs elsewhere) didn't invite the theatre critics. But word of mouth began to spread.

And before long, the show's schedule expanded to full time, the cast earned their Equity cards, and *Pins and Needles* was on its way to a 1,108 performance run, the longest of any musical to that point in history.

The most pervasive feature of *Pins and Needles* was its good humor. It very well could have been an angry show; its subject matter often deserved anger. But it always kept its equilibrium. As Heywood Broun, writing in *Pic*, eventually noted, "Although the raillery is sharp and pointed, the wounds inflicted are not painful since the weapons are anesthetized with humor."

Rome's lyrics and music were largely responsible for the character of the show. It opened with "Sing Me a Song with Social Significance" in which a young woman advised, "Sing me of wars and sing me of breadlines/Tell me of front page news." No gauzy thinking, lyrics, music or production numbers, in other words.

The jazzy and jaunty "Doing the Reactionary" skewered the Right while inventing a new dance step. When love appeared, it was in labor terms: "One Big Union for Two" advised that "No court's injunctions can make us stop/Until your love is all closed shop/...We'll have no lockouts to make us frown/No scabbing when I'm out of town." But there was also a moment for dreaming of time off, in the tuneful "Sunday in the Park," whose couples strolled until a rainstorm scattered them.

Some of the sketches did have an edge of anger, particularly one by Marc Blitzstein about government censorship, and another featuring Mr. Warmonger who makes a speech while the statue of a general comes to life behind him and whips a crowd into a frenzy.

These sketches and others of a more benign nature were constantly being revised, while new ones were added and old ones dropped, as the run of the show continued and historic developments in the country and the world tumbled over each other. Chamberlain appeared and disappeared; when the Daughters of the American Revolution barred Marian Anderson from singing at Constitution

Hall in Washington, a version of *The Mikado* appeared in *Pins and Needles* in which the Three Little Maids, transformed, sang, "Three little DAR's are we/Full to the brim with bigotry;" Fascist dictators came and stayed; the Far Right was a constant target, with anti-Semitic and anti-New Deal Father Charles Coughlin, Virginia Senator Robert Reynolds and Nazi bund leader Fritz Kuhn billed as "The Harmony Boys from Demagogue Lane."

Of the moment and in the moment, but always with a heart for the downtrodden, *Pins and Needles* became *Pins and Needles 1939*, *Pins and Needles 1940* and finally, *New Pins and Needles*. As the war deepened, the revue summed itself up in its finale, "We Sing America":

> We sing to a man's dignity and his place
> With no thought of creed or race
> We sing a land that is too free and great
> To sow the seeds of hate.

The only other revue of the season opened on March 1, 1938, at the Hudson Theatre. By rights it should have been called *New Faces of 1938*. But Leonard Sillman, short of money as usual, accepted the proffered largesse of Elsa Maxwell, who promised him the moon, and then some, provided he would call it *Who's Who* and favor her friends, who lived on the other side of the political world from the heroes of *Pins and Needles*.

This he did, but Elsa Maxwell failed to come through with the backing she promised, and ended up merely donating $1,000, food for the cast, and a load of trouble. Sillman and Everett Marcy wrote a series of sketches that satirized Mrs. Roosevelt, went in for blackface in a "Dusky Debutantes" number and, in a routine titled "Forgive Us Odets," satirized playwright Clifford Odets describing the upper classes plotting a revolt against labor.

The indestructible Imogene Coca, with her polo coat, returned, as did Sillman's sister June, who was maturing as a writer of sophisticated and original music and lyrics. Other cast members who, under other circumstances, might have scored, were Rags Ragland, Mildred Todd and Bowen Charleton Tufts III, who later, fortunately, shortened his first name to Sonny.

Opening night was chaos. 375 comped friends of Elsa Maxwell arrived late, then talked and giggled among themselves through most of the performance, then, in Sillman's recollections, "...a third of the audience left in the middle of the second act to sail for Europe."[9]

The reviews were scathing, and the show closed after 23 performances.

"A demented vaudeville brawl without the Marx Brothers..." is the way the Times' Brooks Atkinson described *Hellzapoppin*, the next revue to arrive—no, tumble onto—Broadway. It had been in preparation for nearly three decades; in fact, Ole Olsen, half of the vaudeville team of Olsen and Johnson, admitted that it was "the same old hooey we've been doing for twenty-five years."

It was in Philadelphia, the story goes, that nightclub impresario Nils T. Granlund (known usually as NTG) caught the show in a one hour version, then convinced Lee Shubert to come down and have a look.

Shubert realized the potential of Olsen and Johnson's murderous mayhem, a combination of burlesque, music hall, audience participation and Grand Guignol. "Stretch it to two hours, and I'll book it into one of my theatres," Lee told Olsen and Johnson, and they did, and he did. On September 22, 1938, *Hellzapoppin* stormed into the 46th Street Theatre, with its repeated pistol shots and audience plants who, among other shenanigans, got up and ran out screaming at various moments, remembered they'd left their baby in the automat, wandered up and down the aisle looking for Oscar, or carried a plant for Mrs. Jones that increased in size with each trip down the aisle. Spiders were lowered from the ceiling onto patrons, who were also battered with beans, bananas and eggs; unicyclists rode furiously around the stage; a gorilla dragged a girl offstage, and all of this while Olsen and Johnson wandered serenely through the blizzard of insanity. There were songs by Sammy Fain and Charles Tobias, but hardly anyone noticed.

With mixed reviews but a constant drumbeat of wild support from Walter Winchell on radio and in the *Daily Mirror*, *Hellzapoppin* turned into yet another phenomenon. In November, the Shuberts moved it into the larger Winter Garden, where the show remained for 1,404 performances—300 more than *Pins and Needles*, which made it the longest-running musical in Broadway history, a record it retained until the advent of *Oklahoma!*

A far more intelligent, Broadway-smart and Depression-era-oriented revue, titled, contemporarily, *Sing Out the News*, opened at the Music Box two nights after *Hellzapoppin's* appearance. Max Gordon produced, Charles Friedman directed and took credit for the sketches (actually the work of George S. Kaufman and Moss Hart), and Harold Rome wrote the music and lyrics. Philip Loeb, Hiram Sherman, Mary Jane Walsh, and Will Geer headed the cast which included, in its chorus, Hazel Scott, June Allyson and Richard Huey.

The point of view, like that of *Pins and Needles*, was distinctly li beral, sending up—literally—the GOP with a take on Rodgers and Hart's *I Married an Angel*, "I Married a Republican." When the Republican angel, played by Hiram Sherman, disavows the New Deal and decides to oppose Roosevelt in the coming election, he loses his wings. In a Hollywood sketch, Louis B. Mayer cancels production on the film *Marie Antoinette* when he's told it's about a revolution.

The most acclaimed moment in the show included its best known song. In it, a Harlem gathering, led by Rex Ingram, celebrated the birth of "Franklin D. Roosevelt Jones." For all its credentials and cleverness, however, *Sing Out the News* remained on Broadway for only a disappointing 105 performances.

A number of forces worked against its longevity: similarity to the still-running *Pins and Needles*, the opening of the 1939-1940 World's

Fair and the approach of yet another consuming, demarcating World War. The rumblings in Europe were about to turn into a conflagration. Chamberlain's bumblings would soon be swallowed up in Hitler's invasion of Poland.

But on Broadway, it was still the Depression. In 1939, as before, fewer shows opened, but the percentage of musicals increased, and revues again accounted for slightly more than half of them.

In January, Noel Coward brought in what seemed, at least to British expatriates in New York, a scrapbook of songs from other shows interspersed with new and not very inspired sketches, some of them reworked, too. Beatrice Lillie was the star of *Set to Music*. No doubt about that—the lion's share of the music went to her. Four of the songs, "Mad About the Boy," "Children of the Ritz," "Three White Feathers" and "The Party's Over Now," had originally graced the 1932 London production, *Words and Music*; another, "The Stately Homes of England," was from Coward's more recent *Operette*. But the best number of all was brand new. The idea for it came to Coward after he and Lillie had attended an Elsa Maxwell soiree in the South of France, where they were expected to perform gratis. "I've Been to a Marvelous Party" was cruel and accurate and inspired, and it subsequently entered the night club repertoires of both Lillie and Coward. *Set to Music* fared moderately well, remaining at the Music Box for 129 performances.

At the beginning of February, 1939, Park Avenue's answer to *Pins and Needles*, a show, in the words of Stanley Green, "...tailored for the International Ladies Garment Wearers," opened at the Booth Theatre. *One for the Money* was the accurate title of a revue conceived and written by Nancy Hamilton and directed by John Murray Anderson. "We think that right is right and wrong is left," sang a well-heeled family in the opening number, and the show went on to poke fun at parlor games, Wagnerian operas, Mrs. Roosevelt and, in the most successful routine, Orson Welles, who "knew Shakespeare backward at the age of two, forward at three, and personally at four."

334 ◆ *Scandals and Follies*

Ms. Hamilton, who had been associated with Leonard Sillman, gave her talented cast no music and lyrics of consequence but populated the show with fresh new faces, among them, Grace McDonald, Alfred Drake, Gene Kelly and Keenan Wynn. Described by John Anderson of the *American* as "...an intimate revue that is smartly, prettily and disastrously empty," it nevertheless racked up a comfortable 132 performances.

A week after *One for the Money* premiered, a nearly broke Lew Leslie tried one last time to revive *Blackbirds*, his original gold mine, at the Hudson. Borrowing money from his wife, Belle Baker, he loaded the composing and lyric staff with Johnny Mercer, Mitchell Parish, Dorothy Sachs, Irving Taylor, Sammy Fain, Louis Haaber, Vic Mizzy and Rube Bloom, injected Gershwin's "Rhapsody in Blue" into the mix and introduced a young, torchy, mesmerizing singer named Lena Horne.

But, as with every black revue of the 1930s, *Blackbirds of 1939* crashed and burned, after nine performances.

At the end of April, the Federal Theatre Project presented a revue that sounded its own death knell. *Sing for Your Supper* had been in preparation for a year-and-a-half, and had grown beyond the conbined ability of its creators and stagers to blend it into a cohesive evening. It had its moments, however. Paula Laurence and Sonny Tufts shone in the cast. And notably, *Sing for Your Supper* was the only musical of the year to deal in any way with the growing menace of the Nazis. Anna Sokolow fashioned a dance treatment of "The Blue Danube" in which Adolph Hitler joins in and turns it into a military *anschluss*. Harold Rome, using the alias Hector Troy, wrote a couple of interesting lyrics, but it was the finale of the revue that had the greatest impact and longest staying power. "The Ballad of Uncle Sam," with words by John LaTouche and music by Earl Robinson, celebrated the diversity and determination of the country's people; later, as the war deepened and consumed America, too, its title was changed to "Ballad for Americans," and it became one of the era's most eloquent and often played morale-boosters.

Congress, however, regarded *Sing for Your Supper* as too leftist and, citing its 60 performance run as a failure, withdrew all funds for the Federal Theatre Project, thus killing it.

It would once again be the Shuberts who tapped into popular taste and brought in the longest running revue of 1939. With their eyes firmly planted on the tourists in town for the World's Fair, they teamed up with Olsen and Johnson to produce *The Streets of Paris*. The only authentically French moments in the entire evening were provided by Jean Sablon, singing Al Dubin and Jimmy McHugh's "Rendezvous Time in Paree."

The rest was pure Broadway romp. Luella Gear and a sizeable, toothy chorus provided the pulchritude. Bobby Clark supplied much of the comedy, particularly in a sketch in which he played four characters—a very old father, a faithful butler, an escaped convict and a warden. As the pace of the sketch quickened, so did the costume-changing demands, turning Clark into a frantic madman.

More bedlam arrived in the personae of burlesque comics Abbott and Costello, making their one and only—and block-busting—Broadway appearance. They crammed every burlesque schtick and slapstick sight gag in their repertory into odd settings—A French rest home, a French hospital, etc.

The dancing team of Gower Champion and Jeanne Tyler shone in a dance sendup of Chamberlain in Munich, called "Doin' the Chamberlain." But the biggest hit of the evening was the explosive debut onstage and on these shores of Carmen Miranda, singing and swiveling to "The South American Way."

The Streets of Paris accomplished exactly what it had set out to do. It ran for 274 performances at the Broadhurst, then transferred to the World's Fair (with Bobby Clark gone, Carmen Miranda off to Hollywood, and Gypsy Rose Lee new to the cast), where it played out the run of the Fair.

Not to be outdone in the tourist-attraction business, George

White brought his *George White's Scandals of 1939-1940* into the Alvin in August. White utilized his old know-how, confining the score to Sammy Fain (music) and Jack Yellen (lyrics). They turned out a superior score that contained the theme song of the year, "Are You Having Any Fun?," sung with a delightful Scottish burr by Ella Logan. The lyrics were printed on the chorus girls' hats, so that the audience could sing along.

Willie and Eugene Howard were back, but, cognizant of the demand for mayhem humor that Olsen and Johnson had brought to Broadway, White also hired The Three Stooges and Ben Blue to perform in a retinue of sketches that sometimes tipped over into Minksy-style blueness. Ray Middleton was a fine singer of ballads, a la John Steel, and the equivalent of Carmen Miranda's *Streets of Paris* spot was filled by Ann Miller, making her debut and tapping joyously through "The Mexiconga."

But for all its talent and professionalism, this *Scandals* only managed a 120-performance run, and thus became the last of the series. It was fitting that an example of the Broadway revue at its extravagant best should be the last to appear before its final, decisive decline began.

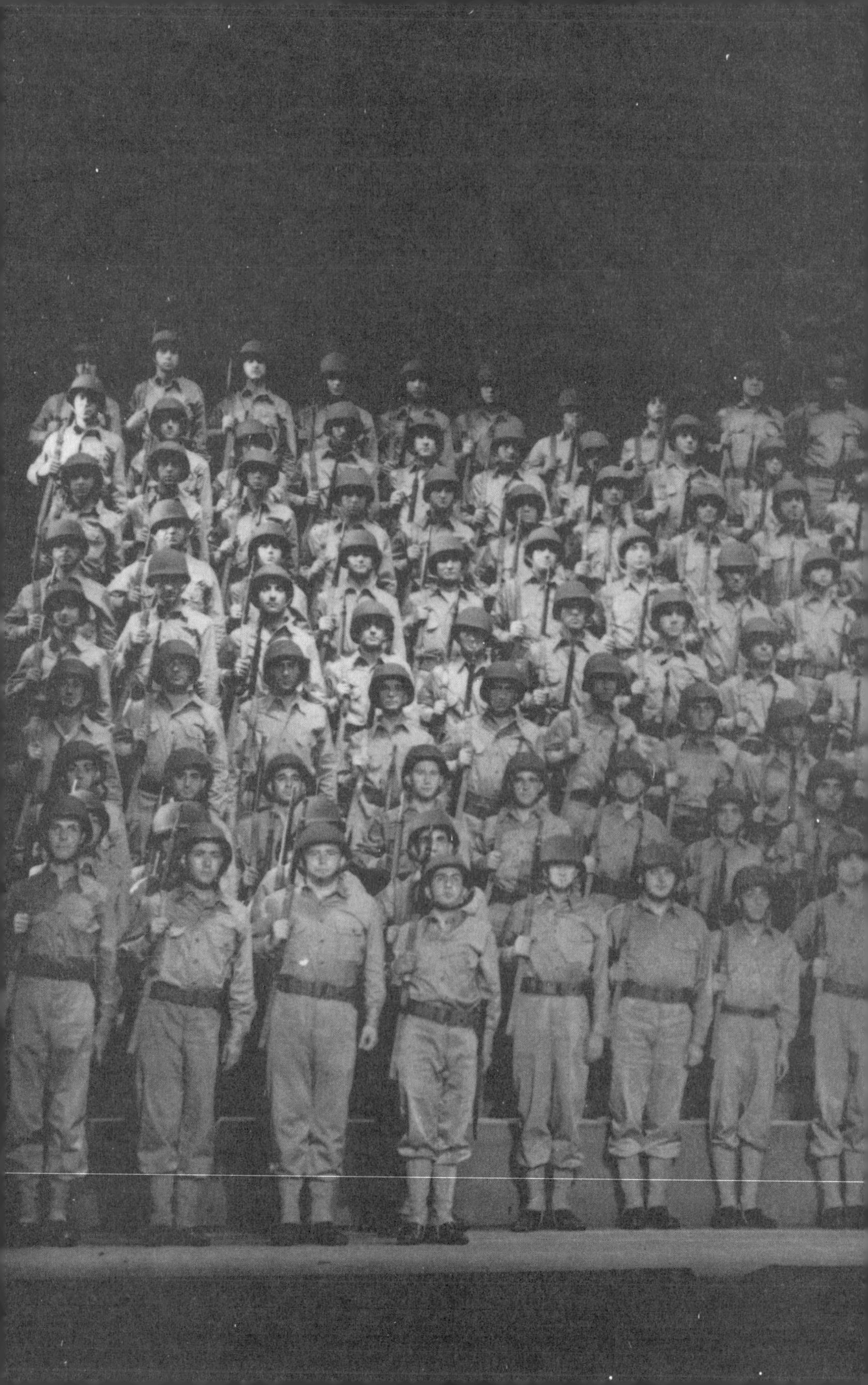

13

The War Effort

The War Effort

❦

Hitler invaded Poland on September 1, 1939, and World War II officially began. On September 29, 1939, *The Straw Hat Revue* opened at the Ambassador Theatre, and within its creative team and onstage personnel were two major talents who would eventually become generals in an army that would fight and defeat the Broadway revue. Rarely, if ever, has such a small show contained such huge potential.

Nor did *The Straw Hat Revue* come to Broadway in the customary way. In the summer of 1939, Harry Kaufman, a garment district graduate and former ticket agency owner, who had gone to work for Lee Shubert in 1931, caught a resort show at Camp Taminent, in Bushkill, Pennsylvania. He saw potential in the producing, directing and writing skills of Max Liebman, the comic talents of young Danny Kaye, and the songwriting skill of Sylvia Fine, who had done Kaye's material while James Shelton wrote the rest of the original score.

The Shuberts added Imogene Coca, Alfred Drake, dancers Mata and Hari and another young dancer named Jerome Robbins to the mix, and brought the Taminent show to Broadway. Danny Kaye scored in the brilliantly written "Anatole of Paris," fashioned for his talents by the eventual Mrs. Kaye. And Imogene Coca convulsed audiences in the Liebman-penned sketches in which she sent up Carmen Miranda in "Soused American Way" and joined with Kaye in an operetta lampoon.

The Straw Hat Revue lasted no more than 75 performances on Broadway. But Max Liebman and Imogene Coca, with Sid Caesar (another comedian schooled on the training ground of the Broadway revue), would, a short decade hence, effectively transfer the revue from Broadway to the television screen with "Your Show of Shows", thus eliminating the pure form forever from live theatre.

But that was the future. Now, the war and the World's Fair were governing the tastes of producers and audiences on Broadway. On Christmas night of 1939, Clifford C. Fischer, apparently energized by the success of *Streets of Paris*, brought in a French vaudeville, titled it, inaccurately, *Folies Bergere*, and played it two-a-day at the Broadway Theatre for a profitable 121 performances.

On January 13, 1940, Earl Carroll returned for one last, brief foray on the New York stage. Having done well in Hollywood with his dinner theatre, he dared to bring this show, fairly intact, to the St. James. It was a blast from the past that audiences no longer favored, and that the LaGuardia administration had severely muffled. Wholesale nudity was no longer allowed in New York, and clothed beauties weren't exactly Earl Carroll's forte.

In between the parades of gorgeous, minimally-clothed girls, Jerry Lester did his burlesque bits, and Professor Lamberti his comic xylophone routine. The show lasted a mere 25 performances, after which Earl Carroll packed his bags for good, leaving behind one benign legacy—that of stages full of girls whose talent was only in looking ravishing, and one horrendous, damaging legacy—the 1940 *Earl Carroll Vanities* was the first Broadway show to employ microphones. Enough said.

The following month, Nancy Hamilton was back with a less right wing sequel to *One for the Money*. *Two for the Show* was more debonair than anti-Democratic; it retained Alfred Drake, Keenan Wynn and Brenda Forbes from *One for the Money*, and added Eve Arden, Richard Haydn and a volatile young talent named Betty

Hutton, who brought down the house with an energetic jitterbug routine—for the 1940s equivalent of the latest dance craze. John Murray Anderson directed, and the score introduced one deathless standard, Morgan Lewis and Nancy Hamilton's "How High the Moon," sung by Alfred Drake in a wartime setting of a moody, blacked-out London. *Two for the Show* ran for a profitable 124 performances.

In June of 1939, a group of European refugees had presented *From Vienna*, a vaudeville that showcased their varied talents. On February 23, 1940, the same group, slightly expanded, arrived back at the Little Theatre with much of the same material. Retitled *Reunion in New York*, it provided nostalgia for the growing refugee population of the city, as well as for some others, and it remained for 89 performances, enough, because of its size and expectations, to make a profit.

In fact, everything that began the season was on a small scale. It would be up to the Shuberts to pump up some show biz excitement and bring in what looked like a sure winner. *Keep Off the Grass* had music by Jimmy McHugh and lyrics by Al Dubin, and sketches by another army. It starred Jimmy Durante, Ray Bolger, Jose Limon, Larry Adler, Jane Froman and Ilka Chase, with George Balanchine promising a serious ballet for Bolger.

But word from out of town was terrible. Howard Dietz was called in to doctor. Already on tender terms with Lee Shubert over past dealings with his wife, costume designer Lucinda Ballard, Dietz wrote three lyrics, and hated one of them.

The result was chaotic and, what was worse, unfunny. The stars struggled with material that had received no laughs in its first read-through. Fred De Cordova did what he could with the direction, but it was hopeless. *Keep Off the Grass* should have been kept off Broadway. It departed after 44 humiliating performances.

The 1940-1941 season was described by Burns Mantle as part of the "years of transition in the theatre." Years of shrinkage would be more like it. Twelve years before, over 250 shows had opened on

Broadway. During this season, less than a hundred did, and only 11 of them were musicals—including *Pal Joey* and *Lady in the Dark*, and of these, five were revues. It was a fairly constant percentage, even if one of the revues took place mostly on ice, and only one of the others really succeeded.

The first revue of the season was its high point. The irrepressible Ed Wynn, absent from Broadway for three years, returned with just the sort of entertainment audiences expected of him. *Boys and Girls Together* was strictly a no-brainer, a wild romp produced, directed, written by and starring Wynn. Wisely enough, he employed Sammy Fain and Jack Yellen to provide the music and lyrics, Jane Pickens to sing them and Albertina Rasch to stage the dances.

But fundamentally, as in any Ed Wynn enterprise, it was 99 percent Wynn, who couldn't lose. Arriving onstage in a theatre trunk and shaking mothballs off his costume, he proclaimed that his cast had been recruited entirely from river boats. "I bred my cast upon the waters," he chuckled. He played a traffic policeman whose territory is bounded by 284th Street on one side and the Catskills on the other; he rowed into a woodland scene wearing a Chinese mandarin outfit; he did a marksmanship routine using a rifle with a curved barrel; he piloted his piano on a tricycle, he got involved in Ms. Pickens' solos and the acts of acrobats and jugglers. Audiences loved it and kept the show at the Broadhurst for 191 performances.

Over in Rockefeller Center, the management was having trouble filling the cavernous space of the Center Theatre. From *White Horse Inn*, they had gone to Kaufman and Hart's patriotic pageant *The American Way*. But no other tenants presented themselves. So, over the summer of 1940, they closed down and covered the acres of stage space with ice. On October 10, *It Happens on Ice*, produced by Sonja Henie (who didn't appear) and Arthur Wirtz, and directed by Radio City Music Hall producer Leon Leonidoff, opened. An attempt to cross a revue with an ice spectacle, it had a score mostly by Vernon Duke and Fred Ahlert, with one Peter DeRose song, sung mostly by a chorus on dry land. Joe Cook filled in the gaps that comedy sketches once occupied between Ziegfeld parades or Hippodrome hyperbole. The audience loved it, came for 386 performances, and cemented—or rather, froze—the character of the Center Theatre for the next decade.

On dry Broadway, a small revue called *'Tis of Thee* opened and closed in one night at the Maxine Elliott. Another summer camp show transferred to Broadway, this time by Nat Lichtman, it had neither the material nor the talent that its model, *The Straw Hat Revue*, had enjoyed.

But a second transfer, this one from Hollywood, fared better. *Meet the People*, which cost a mere $3600 when it opened on Christmas day of 1939, had been a success in Los Angeles and San Francisco, but it came to New York slowly, via Chicago, rewriting and gathering new composers, lyricists and sketch writers along the way. When it opened at the Mansfield on Christmas Day, 1940, exactly one year after its original premiere, it sported a creative staff that included Jay Gorney (most of the music) Henry Myers and Edward Eliscu (most of the lyrics and most of the sketches) Danny Dare, Sid Kuller, Ray Golden and Milt Gross.

Its cast included Jack Gilford, Doodles Weaver, Eddie Johnson and a young singer named Nanette Farbares, who would later change her last name to Fabray. Jack Gilford had a winning monologue, all about being a movie fan at a triple feature plus shorts and previews. In tune with the current South American craze begun by Carmen Miranda, there was wild Danny Dare choreography (he also directed) to "In Chi Chi Castenango."

Meet the People joined good company in Broadway legend. Just as *Show Boat* had opened on the same night as *Paris Bound*, *Meet the People* shared its first night with *Pal Joey*. As a result, no first-string critics attended. The producers gave thought to closing the show when, on the second night, the first-stringers came and pronounced it a hit. It remained one for 160 performances.

Crazy with the Heat, the last revue of the season, which opened on January 14, 1941, at the 44th Street Theatre, underwent a similar 24 hours of despair, with a slightly different ending. Scanning its cast list suggested a beautiful future: Willie Howard, Richard Kollmar, Carl Randall, Luella Gear, Betty Kean, among others. Its sketch writers included Max Liebman, although its music and lyrics were by relative unknowns. In any caste, the show received devastating reviews and was about to close when, just as Walter Winchell decided to champion *Hellzapoppin*, Ed Sullivan took *Crazy with the Heat* under his journalistic wing. But Sullivan went even further, hiring Lew Brown to invigorate Kurt Krazner's original staging, and adding the dance teams of Raye and Naldi and Tip Tap and Toe and, for 1941. the requisite South American number. Sullivan's service was enough to cancel the closing notice and keep the show open for a total of 99 performances.

Concern about the war's toll was clearly deepening as the next season opened. It proved to be a good one for comedies, a confusing and dispiriting one for musicals. Fourteen opened, and aside from the first two and the last book shows—*Best Foot Forward, Let's Face It* and *By Jupiter,* none were of high quality. And of the six revues, only one was a true hit.

And that one was an obvious spinoff. *Hellzapoppin* was winding down; the movie had been made; it was time for the Shuberts to revisit their Olsen and Johnson gold mine. They opened *Sons o' Fun* on December 1, 1941, six days before the bombing of Pearl Harbor would bring America formally into World War II.

It was the same old mayhem; patrons had to climb rope ladders to get to their box seats; ushers purposely scrambled other seating assignments. Onstage, Ella Logan sang the songs of Sammy Fain, Will Irwin, Jack Yellen and Irving Kahal, including the delightful "Happy in Love," and Carmen Miranda again tore up the boards, South American style. Reflecting the spirit of the times, the patriotic affirmation "It's a Mighty Fine Country We Have Here" interrupted the bedlam. In all, it kept wartime audiences coming, and the Winter Garden box office jingling for a highly profitable 742 performances.

The draft had arrived before Pearl Harbor; after it, the ranks of young entertainers thinned drastically. In consequence, the pocket revues that had been only now-and-then diversions began to proliferate.

On February 11, 1942, a group of semi-professional youngsters under the guiding hand of Alexander Cohen brought to the tiny Concert Theatre an entertainment that, as *V for Victory*, they had presented at the Malin Studio Theatre five months earlier. Now titled *Of V We Sing*, it was a fast-paced, jitterbugging showcase for some strong, struggling young talent, among them, Betty Garrett, Phil Leeds and Curt Conway. The public liked what it saw enough to keep the Concert lit for 76 performances.

Another wartime modification of the revue followed on March 12, with *Priorities of '42*. Clifford Fischer, who had brought the ersatz *Folies Bergere* to Broadway in 1939, reasoned that with the city full of servicemen who had never seen a Broadway show, vaudeville resurrected and appropriately disguised might once again be a moneymaker. The result was a sketchless variety show, headed by Willie Howard, Lou Holtz, Phil Baker, Paul Draper and Hazel Scott. Because it was so cheap to produce, tickets could be priced at $1 for matinees and $2 for evening performances. It became one of the most popular shows on Broadway, eventually racking up a hearty 353 performance run.

Priorities of '42 was so successful, in fact, that Fischer proceeded to open another variety show, with the same format and ticket scale, a block south at the 44th Street Theatre. Fischer hired Arthur Pierson and Eddie Davis to bang out some simple sketches, assembled William Gaxton, Victor Moore, Hildegarde, Paul and Grace Hartman, the Jack Cole Dancers and a young Cafe Society almunus, Zero Mostel, for his cast and called the new show *Keep 'Em Laughing*, although *Keep 'Em Coming* would have been more honest. It did for a while, but after 77 performances, began to falter.

Undiscouraged, and clinging to the age-old fiction of producers—repeating a success meant making a fortune—Fischer revised *Keep 'Em Laughing*. He kept Mostel and the Hartmans and brought in Argentinita (who was enjoying a vogue, thanks to Carmen Miranda), Carlos Montoya and Gracie Fields, retitled it the *Top-Notchers*, and hoped for the best, which didn't arrive. *Top-Notchers* expired after 48 performances.

Everybody got into the act in wartime. Ed Sullivan, encouraged by his first Broadway fling, teamed up with Noble Sissle and Flournoy Miller to bring in a black revue, modeled upon the Fischer variety format. *Harlem Cavalcade* didn't make it, however, and left after 49 performances.

Even the great Ed Wynn succumbed to the siren promise of avoiding the agony of creating a real revue by slapping together a name-headed variety show. On June 22, he brought *Laugh, Town, Laugh* to the Alvin, with a vaudeville bill that included Hector's Dogs and the Volga Sisters. Smith and Dale appeared, doing ages-old routines; Jane Froman sang popular songs of the day not written for the show, and Wynn just wandered around. This sorry excuse for entertainment left after 65 performances, sadly marking Ed Wynn's final appearance on a New York stage.

But soon, as in 1917, wartime became boomtime on Broadway. Although the overall number of plays in the 1942-1943 season shrank to 80, 24 of them were musicals, a big leap upward for escapism. And sometimes quality did prevail, as in straight plays like Noel Coward's *Blithe Spirit* and Thornton Wilder's *The Skin of Our Teeth*. And in *Oklahoma!*, which would arrive in March of 1943.

But except for one production by an old master, which would be the other blockbuster musical of the season, most of the revues that came in, while popular, were united in their crass commercial origins.

Take, for instance, *Star and Garter*, the brainchild of the decade's most flamboyant and successful producer, Mike Todd. If ever there were to be a rightful heir to the Ziegfeld legend, it might have been Todd. Like Ziegfeld, he started in show business at a fair—in his case, the 1933 Chicago World's Fair. It took him six years to get to Broadway, with the 1939 Bill Robinson phenomenon, *The Hot Mikado*. In 1943, he returned with two simultaneous hits: *Something for the Boys*, in which Ethel Merman belted out a Cole Porter score, and *Star and Garter*, a semi-sophisticated burlesque show starring Gypsy Rose Lee and Bobby Clark and featuring Pat Harrington and Professor Lamberti.

Fiorello LaGuardia had closed down all of the burlesque houses on 42nd Street, but Todd, shrewd showman that he was, assumed that the GIs in town, accustomed to going to Minsky's outlets in other cities, would certainly be attracted to the name Gypsy Rose Lee on a marquee. He was right. *Star and Garter* was an immediate smash hit that filled the formerly elegant Music Box for 609 performances.

Almost everything about the show was borrowed, including its title, from the short-lived 1900 Marie Cahill revue of the same name. The score, although credited to Irving Berlin, Harold Rome, Harold Arlen and others, actually contained only old tunes of theirs, supplemented by a pack of forgettable melodies by some secondary composers and lyricists.

Gypsy Rose Lee had been doing her intellectual strip for years; Bobby Clark's material was mostly culled from burlesque, from his own and Abbott and Costello's routines in *The Streets of Paris*, and from *Thumbs Up!* His new material, written by Clark, himself, consisted of the Malamute Saloon scene in which Clark asks the bartender the way to the powder room, the bartender points to a door, Clark opens it and gets hit by a faceful of snow. He slams the door shut and announces, "It's too cold outside. I'll wait till Spring."

Fortunately, patrons of real revues didn't have to wait that long for the season's only true Broadway revue. And, as in 1921, with the first *Music Box Revue*, it would be Irving Berlin who reminded producers and audiences alike that it was the score that mattered in a musical, and that a revue without strong music was an airplane flying with only one wing and no rudder.

Early in 1942, at the age of 55, Berlin had been asked by the U.S. Army to stage *Yip-Yip-Yaphank* again for the benefit of the Army Emergency Relief Fund. Berlin accepted with alacrity and moved back to Camp Upton, where he had written his World War I revue. There, he arranged to have slightly over 300 men—some professionals, most not—assigned to him, as he began to fashion, not a revival, but a brand new revue, *This Is the Army*.

It included sketches by James McColl but they were insignificant. What mattered was the music, a flood of varied melody, with all but two of the songs written specifically for the show and providing a kaleidoscopic reflection of the times. In a lights-out barracks scene, Pvt. Stuart Churchill sang the poignant "I'm Getting Tired So I Can Sleep" ("I want to sleep so I can dream/I want to dream so I can be with you...") and Cpl. Earl Oxford sang the show's hit ballad, "I Left My Heart at the Stage Door Canteen." The score included stirring tributes to the Army Air Corps ("American Eagles") and to the Navy ("How About a Cheer for the Navy?"), the mocking title song ("This Is the Army, Mr. Jones") and a tears-to-the-eyes, patriotic finale ("This Time Must Be the Last Time").

The two holdover numbers. both from 1918, were "Mandy," again part of a minstrel show scene, and the nightly show-stopper, "Oh, How I Hate to Get Up in the Morning," sung by Berlin himself, in his World War I uniform, standing before a pup tent, and, in the last chorus, accompanied by six other veterans of *Yip-Yip-Yaphank*.

There was, as there was in the World War I show, a scene in which Broadway stars were impersonated by soldiers. In 1918, the subjects had been *Ziegfeld Follies* luminaries, including Lillian Lorraine, W.C. Fields, Will Rogers and Marilyn Miller. In 1942, it was Jane Cowl, Joe Cook (done by his son, Pfc. Joe Cook Jr.), Noel Coward, Vera Zorina, Gypsy Rose Lee, Lynn Fontanne and Alfred

Lunt. *This Is the Army* packed the Broadway Theatre, with full standing room, for 113 performances, and closed, not because it had failed, but because the Army had other duties in mind for its cast and creator. It toured the U.S. and overseas, with varying casts that eventually included Staff Sgt. Ezra Stone (who also directed), Pvt. Gary Merrill, Pvt. Richard Reeves and Pvt. Burl Ives. At the end of its two-year tour and with the release of the Warner Brothers movie, the Army Emergency Relief Fund was wealthier by $9,561,501.[1]

The remainder of the revue season was overshadowed by the quality and intent of *This Is the Army*. A week before the Berlin revue opened, on July 4, 1942, a new ice revue, *Stars on Ice* debuted at the Center Theatre. The formula held, and the show ran for 860 performances and added a big hit to the war effort: Paul McGrane and Paul VanLoane's "Juke Box Saturday Night."

Clifford Fischer was back on Broadway in September with his vaudeville/variety format, this time titled *New Priorities of 1943*. His stars were Harry Richman, Bert Wheeler, Henny Youngman, Carol Bruce and the Radio Aces. But, apparently, audiences were tiring of the cut-rate approach to show business, and *New Priorities of 1943* folded after 54 performances.

On the other hand, and for some unexplainable reason, *Show Time*, an almost identical vaudeville show that had originated in California and was shepherded by Fred Finklehoffe, the co-author of *Brother Rat*, succeeded wildly well. Doing their old vaudeville turns and singing old tunes were George Jessel, Jack Haley, the DeMarcos, Ella Logan, Lucille Norman and the Berry Brothers. The show remained at the Broadhurst for 342 performances.

And then there was *Wine, Women and Song*, the Shuberts' attempt to cash in on the city's burlesque drought. Although the brothers hired Max Liebman to direct, it was Jake Shubert whose taste permeated the stage of the Ambassador. Jimmy Savo and Margie Hart tried to better Bobby Clark and Gypsy Rose Lee down the street by being considerably dirtier and barer. The censors were on them almost immediately, and adjustments were made, then unmade. Altogether, *Wine, Women and Song* chalked up a 150-performance total before the police finally shut it down for good, and padlocked the Ambassador for a year. The show's performance record was, incidentally achieved in half the usual time because it was giving 16 performances a week.[2]

A revue of considerably more merit and purpose was the Youth Theatre production of *Let Freedom Sing*, briefly at the Longacre in October. Its main score was by Harold Rome, but it had a large number of interpolations, including "Fraught," by Marc Blitzstein, which was sung by the show's star, Mitzi Green, and "The House I Live In" by Earl Robinson and Lewis Allan, a song that nightly moved the show's few audiences and that was eventually recorded and made immensely popular by Frank Sinatra. Betty Garrett was back again, stopping the show with her takeoff on the South American craze,"Give Us a Viva." But it was all for naught. Bombarded by the critics, the show closed after a week.

Shortly before Christmas, Leonard Sillman brought in his fourth *New Faces*, the only revue series still, if intermittently, running. The creative staff, Sillman and his sister, who, now married, had become June Carroll, continued in place, now supported by John Lund, who both wrote and acted in some of the sketches. One of them yet again targeted Orson Welles. Another employed Professor Irwin Corey causing Hamlet to, in the words of Gerald Bordman, "suffer the slings and arrows of outrageous recapitulation." Newcomer Alice Pearce was the other comedian to cause a stir. Tony Farrar made an impression doing Fanny Brice doing Paul Draper in a bullfight dance. But neither the material nor the actors seemed to excite audiences. Perhaps the novelty of new performers was no longer a novelty. *New Faces of 1943* faded after 94 performances.

Yet another variation on the revue format came along in February, further diluting matters. *For Your Pleasure* was a mixture of dance and vaudeville, featuring Veloz and Yolanda, accordionist

Jerry Shelton and the Golden Gate Quartette. It lasted a mere 11 performances.

And now, one night after *Oklahoma!* burst upon the Broadway scene, the past arrived with a vengeance, in the form and shape of *The Ziegfeld Follies of 1943*. Again, the ubiquitous Shuberts were involved, and this time, they brought in Alfred Bloomingdale and Lou Walters, the owners of the Copacabana, one of New York's largest and most successful night clubs.

Nightclubs and *The Follies* certainly had a kinship, and possibly, if Lou Walters had had a stronger hand, this *Follies* wouldn't have been described by Burton Rascoe in the *Telegram* as "More Shubert than Ziegfeld," with music as "raucous and unrhythmical [and] largely scored for percussion instruments" and scenery "look[ing] as though it came from Cain's storehouse without much retouching."

And yet, astonishingly enough, the crowds came, and came, for 553 performances—the longest run by far of any *Ziegfeld Follies*. It certainly wasn't for the music, mostly by Ray Henderson but abetted by a mob of others. It might have been for John Murray Anderson's knowledgeable direction and his selection of gorgeous girls. It could have been for the Jack Cole dance routines that incorporated the requisite bumps and grinds for a burlesque-obsessed wartime Broadway. And it most probably was for the *Hellzapoppin* approach the Shuberts now felt they had patented. Milton Berle tore up the proceedings like a young Ed Wynn on speed. Arthur Treacher let down his British reserve and careened into slapstick. And Ilona Massey, imported from Hollywood, just looked stunning. It was enough.

Still, *Oklahoma!*'s impact upon musical Broadway couldn't be discounted. The American musical was about to enter a period of confusion and reorientation. The thoroughly unexpected success of the Rodgers and Hammerstein masterstroke clearly rattled other producers, and while the nonmusical stage continued with a logical balance of wartime comedies and wartime dramas, the musical theatre degenerated into disarray. One musical—*One Touch of*

Venus—saw the writing on the choreographer's wall. But others, and particularly the creators of the once proud and dominant Broadway revue, seemed to have lost their way and their origins.

Morris Gest, stubborn and past-bound to the end, misread the boomtimes of war as a fertile planting ground for yet another imitation of his 1922 hit import, *Chauve Souris*. It was an emphatic misjudgment; the 1943 version, a mirror image of the 1922 version, fled after 12 performances.

In September, Fred Finklehoffe, likewise, tried to duplicate a more recent success, his vaudeville with class, *Show Time*. But despite a cast headed by Ethel Waters, Bert Wheeler, Buck and Bubbles and Frank Fay, *Laugh Time*, as the new version was feebly called, failed to fully ignite. There was still an audience for slapped-together vaudeville but it was waning. *Laugh Time* eked out a 126 performance run.

Later in September, Alexander Cohen reached back into early revue history to attach a thread of a plot to a revue with music by Jerry Livingstone and Mack David. The conceit: two waiters from Sardi's, played by Smith and Dale, decide to put on a show, auditioning such talents as James Barton and Frances Williams. Titled *Bright Lights of 1944*, it was a sorry mess that closed after four performances, long before 1944.

Impresario Sol Hurok fared better in *A Tropical Revue*, which was a unified showcase for Katherine Dunham and her dancers, and an indication of one of the places toward which the revue would now tend. It remained at the Martin Beck for two months.

In November, Lou Walters, still convinced that the Broadway revue was nothing more than a one-a-day nightclub show, resurrected the old Shubert title *Artists and Models*. His reasoning: it titillated once; it could titillate again. Walters brought in 15 of his Copacabana girls, dressed them up in outlandish outfits and paraded them around the stage. He brought in Phil Charig and Milton Pascal to do the music and lyrics, starred Jane Froman to sing the uninteresting songs (with the possible exception of "Swing Low Sweet Harriet," a jazzy centerpiece for an embarrassing minstrel show sequence), brought on the Radio Aces and featured a rising young comedian named Jackie Gleason. The public rejected it after 29 performances.

And so it was a sorry season for revues, and it ended on a sorry note, with yet another cobbled-together vaudeville, *Take a Bow*. Trapped in this Benny Davis-Ted Murray exercise were veterans Pat Rooney, Jay C. Flippen, Gene Sheldon and Chico Marx. It lasted for all of four performances.

What was happening? Something, obviously. Straight plays were thriving, with first plays by playwrights whose last names were Williams and Miller; musicals, taking their cue from *Oklahoma!* were rife with literate books and dream ballets. And the revue had almost lost its identity. Almost.

Hats Off to Ice, the latest ice extravaganza at the Center Theatre, continued, unabated. So if the spectacular aspect of the revue had indeed departed from Broadway, it had found itself, at least, with no joke intended, on ice.

The impulse to revert to vaudeville, an itch that undoubtedly contributed to the public's fading regard for the revue, was resurrected yet again in September of 1944, ushering in the new season with *Star Time*. The plenitude of the past was again mined for the DeMarcos, Benny Fields and Lou Holtz. It remained at the Majestic for 120 performances.

And then, Billy Rose, of all people, decided to revive the sound and sight and scope of the Great Bygone Broadway Revue. Assembling an enormous cast that looked like a personnel sheet for a Depression play, he reopened the Ziegfeld Theatre, which he had bought, with *The Seven Lively Arts*, the sort of revue he remembered and loved.

To do this, he put together a team that could only spell success in major, neon letters. He hired Hassard Short to direct, Norman Bel

Geddes to design, Cole Porter to write the music and Igor Stravinsky to compose a serious ballet, to be danced by Alicia Markova and Anton Dolin, with choreography by Dolin. He brought in Moss Hart to write the sketches, and he brought back Bert Lahr, absent from the New York stage for five years, and Beatrice Lillie, absent for five-and-a-half. And if that weren't enough, he threw in Benny Goodman with his immortal sidemen Teddy Wilson and Red Norvo. As the Gershwins would put it, Who Could Ask For Anything More?

The original plan was to have seven young hopefuls, played by then unknowns Dolores Gray, William Tabbert, Billie Worth, Nan Wynn, Jere McMahon, Paula Bane and Mary Roche, arrive in New York, each with a separate hope for a career in one of the seven arts. But by the time the show arrived on Broadway, the youngsters had been absorbed into the ensemble, and Doc Rockwell had been recruited to introduce each of the arts in a narrative written by Ben Hecht.

Opening night was a gay and glittering affair. At a $24 top, first performance patrons were also treated to a champagne reception in a lobby decorated with specially commissioned Salvadore Dali panels. Beatrice Lillie, who had spent the war entertaining British and American troops, and whose son had just been reported missing in action, received a five-minute ovation when she made her first entrance.

And then the show began. And it wasn't really all that bad. In the Thirties and certainly in the Twenties, it would have been an unqualified hit. Lillie's Moss Hart-written material was not inspired but it was solid. She cooed through a takeoff on *Angel Street*; in "There'll Always Be an England," she portrayed a British dowager trying to speak American slang; in "Ticket for the Ballet," a variation on Hart's earlier *Home Abroad* sketch "Mr. Gielgud Passes By," she had trouble recalling the name of the ballet she was attending but thought it might be called "Shurok;" and Cole Porter gave her a superior comic piece titled "Dancin' to a Jungle Drum" and subtitled "Let's End the

Beguine."

Lahr's material was less hardy, although, again, thanks to Porter, he had a marvelous sendup of Gilbert and Sullivan and Romberg operettas. As a plastered Lord Nelson, Lahr sang "Drink" ("Drink to Nelson Eddy before you faint/And here's to J.J. Shubert, our patron saint.")

True, Porter was in the creative slump out of which he would emerge four years later with *Kiss Me, Kate*. But he did give the two leads workable material, and the show a lovely ballad, "Ev'ry Time We Say Goodbye (I die a little)." True, the Stravinsky ballet was considered pretentious by the masses and inferior by the aficionados. But *The Seven Lively Arts* really deserved a longer run than the fortune-losing 183 performances it achieved.

It certainly stood stories higher than the other revues of the last season of World War II. In December, 1944, the Shuberts attempted to strike back with *Laffing Room Only*, yet more Olsen and Johnson anarchy. This time they set Burton Lane and Al Dubin to work writing music and lyrics. The two produced only one hit song, a hillbilly satire, "Feudin' and Fightin'," which the Shuberts refused to release to radio until 1947. Lane finally wrested it from their grip and gave it to Dorothy Shay, cabaret's popular "Park Avenue Hillbilly," who immortalized it.

Betty Garrett, Mata and Hari and Fred Waring's Glee Club were all involved in *Laffing Room Only*, but while the formula was beginning to wear thin, the show lasted for a respectable 233 performances, but no longer.

Later in December, a folksong history of America, *Sing Out Sweet Land*, opened, and like the earlier *A Tropical Review* suggested the thematic direction in which some future revues would move. Burl Ives and Alfred Drake led the enterprise, which had been conceived by Walter Kerr and was staged by Leon Leonidoff. It remained at the International for 102 performances.

Buried in a flurry of blockbuster book musicals was *Blue Holiday*, a try by Irvin Shapiro and Doris Cole to present a quality black vaudeville with music by Duke Ellington and Earl Robinson and lyrics by E.Y. Harburg—added at the last minute to cover the original, inferior Al Moritz score. The onstage presence of Ethel Waters, the Hall Johnson Choir and the Katherine Dunham Dancers failed to save the show, which departed after a week.

The last of the slapped-together vaudevilles premiered on June 1, 1945. Trying to recoup some of his losses from *Seven Lively Arts*, Billy Rose constructed an evening he called *Concert Varieties*, and let it loose on the cavernous stage of the Ziegfeld. Its cast and credits were impressive: Imogene Coca and Zero Mostel were rising in comic recognition, Deems Taylor was pressed into service as master of ceremonies, the Katherine Dunham Dancers were on hand, and Jerome Robbins, fresh from his remarkable success in ballet with *Fancy Free* and on Broadway with *On the Town*, provided "Interplay," a fascinating ballet to music by Morton Gould. But there was no longer a place for this kind of vaudeville on Broadway. Its home was now in the interstices between film times in the major movie palaces, like the Roxy, the Capital, and Radio City Music Hall. *Concert Varieties* departed after 36 performances.

And so, as all of the pieces in the book musical now fell comfortably into place, as the war ended and quality began to matter in the musical, an uncomfortable question presented itself: had the time passed for the Broadway revue? The encouraging answer was "No." The disquieting modifier was "Not quite."

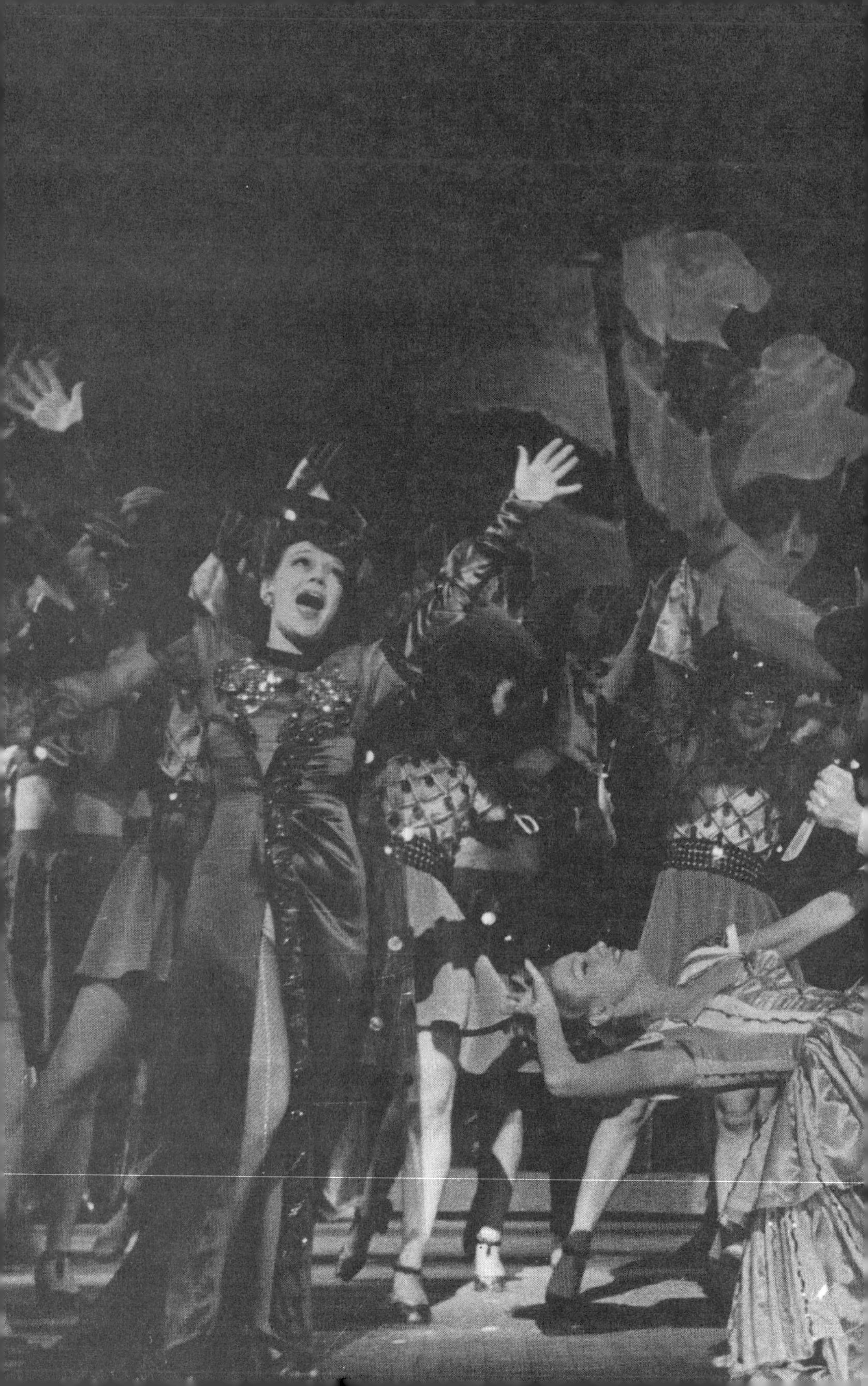

14

Death by Electronics

Death by Electronics

In the musical theatre, yesterday had dimmed. Rodgers and Hammerstein and Agnes DeMille had put the last, balletic piece of the musical puzzle in place, and Jerome Kern's lifelong campaign for verisimilitude in the musical was becoming the rule. Nevertheless, the 1945-1946 season still had room for revivals of operettas—City Center brought back *The Desert Song*, *The Gypsy Baron*, and a remounting of Victor Herbert's *Red Mill* ran for 531 performances—while the previous season's venerably rooted *Song of Norway* and *Up in Central Park* were doing brisk businesses.

But revues? It would be nearly the end of the season before the first one appeared. And that revue would be not an entirely new creation but the next to last link in a series that Nancy Hamilton had begun in 1939 with *One for the Money*. *Three to Make Ready* was its title, and its acceptance boded well for the genre's hardiness.

With John Murray Anderson directing, it was like old times. The music by Morgan Lewis and the lyrics by Ms. Hamilton were disposable. Ms. Hamilton's sketches were a delight. The cast consisted of a group of bright young things named Bibi Osterwald, Meg Mundy, Gordon MacRae, Harold Lang and Carleton Carpenter. Its absolute but no longer very young star was Ray Bolger.

He was everywhere, dancing a soft shoe, heading up a sketch that poked fun at Rodgers and Hammerstein (what if they had set Dreiser's

An American Tragedy to music, and renamed it *Kenosha Canoe?*). The revue caught on and filled the Adelphi for 327 performances.

That would have been proof enough of the revue's continuing durability. But on April 18, 1946, close on the heels of *Three to Make Ready*, *Call Me Mister* arrived at the National, and its 700-performance run eclipsed every other revue in wartime and afterward.

It was clearly the right moment for a mustering-out musical. The broad identification with the bouncy title song, the memories of the Red Ball Express that had taken the war veterans to battle and the "Goin' Home Train" that had brought them back, the once-in-demand canteen hostesses who had become obsolete ("Little Surplus Me," complained one of the many superior songs by Harold Rome)—all smartly reflected the mood of the times. Certainly Americans would respond to a dignified tribute to the passing of Franklin D. Roosevelt ("The Face on the Dime"), and, for one last time, they might well have wanted to hear a ballad of wartime longing ("You've Always Been Along With Me").

Of course, all these elements rested on the exceptional quality of the creative work. Besides Rome's first rate music and lyrics, there were the Arnold Auerbach and Arnold B. Horwitt sketches that poked delighted fun at Army red tape, saw traces of Noel Coward in the behavior of army pilots, and suffered through the molasses words and thinking of Southern senators.

And then, there was the talent—Jules Munshin, Lawrence Winters, Danny Scholl, Bill Callahan, George Irving and particularly Betty Garrett, who now finally achieved star status. Her chronicling of modern holiday priorities in "Yuletide, Park Avenue" was an early Christmas present, and she gave even more to Broadway history as she sang and gyrated through the crowning sendup of the Thirties South American craze, "South America, Take It Away."

But *Call Me Mister* was a Matterhorn rising from a flat, thinly populated plain. The 1945-1946 season played itself out without another revue of consequence.

The perennially running ice extravaganzas ran on at the Center Theatre, changing titles and some details but remaining essentially the same. This latest one, which opened on June 20, 1946, was called simply *Icetime*.

Then, on July 8, came *Tidbits of 1946*, yet another nailed-together vaudeville, this time with some fresh and talented young faces, including Joey Faye, Marais and Miranda and Muriel Gaines. It barely made it through one week, and was the last Broadway revue for a year-and-a-half.

But, as if need for quiet preparation time were the reason, the 1947-1948 season dawned to give revuers some hope for the future. Of the season's 12 new musicals, four were revues—two of them truly fine, full-scale Broadway productions. And if one of the others was a mess, the fourth gave promise.

The first concoction of the season was yet another black revue purporting to be Caribbean, as its title, *Caribbean Carnival*, indicated. It arrived on December 5, 1947 at the Playhouse, with Pearl Primus replacing the Katherine Dunham Dancers, to similar, disappointing results. The show left after 11 performances.

But then, the prospect brightened considerably, and with the appearance of the next two Broadway revues, a clear intimation of the future course of the form began to take shape. On December 11, 1947, *Angel in the Wings* opened at the tiny Coronet theatre. It was an intimate, unprepossessing revue that could just as easily have been staged in one of the small nightclubs that had sprung up during the war and were now proliferating. In fact, most of the personnel associated with *Angel in the Wings*—particularly its stars, Paul and Grace Hartman—were primarily associated with the cabaret scene.

But the Hartmans had also performed on Broadway, and they brought a pace and sensibility to the show that was pure theatre. And that made all the difference. The show was conceived for a small cast, headed by the Hartmans, who danced in their own satiric way and then proceeded to enter into sketches that centered mostly upon family life. Hank Ladd did some comic turns, most notably in a rowboat, looking for Florence, whom he had misplaced somewhere among the Thousand Islands. And then there was the dynamic and inimitable Elaine Stritch, who flattened Broadway with "Civilization," the one surviving song from the Carl Sigman and Bob Hilliard score. Written not for the show but for pop consumption, it was rushed in at the last minute when its "Bongo Bongo Bongo, I don't want to leave the Congo" refrain became a popular chant on radio. *Angel in the Wings* remained at the Coronet for 308 performances, thereby establishing the contemporary viability of the intimate revue.

A little over a month later, on January 15, 1948, *Make Mine Manhattan*, a big, bright and decidedly orthodox Broadway revue opened at the Broadhurst. Again, the right elements were all in place. Hassard Short directed, Max Liebman assisted. The music was solely by Richard Lewine, the lyrics and the sketches entirely by Arnold B. Horwitt, who had had a hand in the sketches for *Call Me Mister* .

Looking back on it now, the show seems fragile and temporary, a period piece about a Manhattan long since become little more than fondly remembered history. A square dance is held on Saturday night in an innocently safe Central Park; a sketch sends up the coming construction of the United Nations building; Rodgers and Hammerstein's *Allegro* is satirized; girls refer to their "gentlemen friends;" a Bronx boy relates, hilariously, his problems in taking multiple subways to keep a date with his girl in Brooklyn.

Make Mine Manhattan's strength lay in its deft touch and light heart. The pace was mercurial, the melodies melodious, the lyrics and sketches intelligent. A luminous young—and not so young—cast plunged headlong into the material, and at its comic peak were David Burns and the astonishingly talented Sid Caesar, who could seemingly conquer any accent, imitate any sound, dominate any sketch. *Make Mine Manhattan* was a smash hit, running for 429 performances.

That would have been enough for one season in the Forties, but in March, another revue, almost as impressive, almost as clever and just as expertly constructed, arrived at the Century. Produced by Arthur Schwartz, who, with Howard Dietz, supplied the music and lyrics, *Inside U.S.A.* borrowed only its title from John Gunther's recent best-selling account of the post-war American scene. The rest was pure Schwartz and Dietz, Arnold B. Horwitt, Arnold Auerbach and Moss Hart.

The cast was impressive. Beatrice Lillie and Jack Haley headed it, and they were ably supported by Thelma Carpenter, John Tyers, Louis Nye, Carl Reiner and Jack Cassidy. Dancer Valerie Bettis performed a moody Helen Tamiris ballet, and a hitherto unknown country monologist named Herb Shriner, in true Will Rogers style, strolled on alone before the curtain, commented on present-day happenings, and stopped the show.

Inside U.S.A. possessed a plenitude of other riches: Beatrice Lillie leading a madrigal group in Pittsburgh that sang about industrial pollution; Beatrice Lillie as a New Orleans Mardi Gras queen; Beatrice Lillie and Jack Haley as Indians in Albuquerque refusing to take the country back; Jack Haley cataloguing the charms and products of a long list of states, but concluding, musically, that "little old Rhode Island" is best, because "Rhode Island Is Famous for You,"; and John Tyers, in a hauntingly beautiful scene on the San Francisco waterfront, singing the show's melodious hit, "Haunted Heart."

Inside U.S.A. would be the last revue Schwartz and Dietz would write together, and it was a fitting and successful conclusion to a memorable creative collaboration. The show ran for 399 performances.

And so *Make Mine Manhattan* and *Inside U.S.A.*, two classic Broadway revues that reflected all the lessons learned through time, might have been the form's salvation. Except for the absence of bevies of showgirls, they were true replicas of the Broadway revue at its finest and exemplars of what it might do in the future.

But this was not to be. Something else happened in 1948 that would make this season not a rebirth, but the final season for multiple, successful Broadway revues. Television, denied to the public by World War II, came to stay in 1948. And, like the talkies in their early days, it turned to Broadway for its performers and material, and was, naturally, drawn to the two richest and most obvious sources: vaudeville and the revue. Vaudeville stocked some television variety shows, but the most popular attraction of the new medium was, ironically, the show most like a revue, because it was created and developed by a man whose schooling had been in revues, Max Liebman. That creation, *Your Show of Shows*, with Sid Caesar, Imogene Coca, Louis Nye and Carl Reiner, all veterans of Liebman's revues, seemed like a free evening of theatre, if you didn't mind the absence of color and cursing.

Its enormous success proved to be a mortal blow to the Broadway revue—although, like most mortal blows, it didn't fell its victim immediately, or even overnight. There were, in fact, new revues in the 1948-1949 season, one of which had producers who seemed intent upon making the same old mistakes. On September 9, Ken Robey and Stan Zucker, apparently uninformed about the recent burial of vaudeville, tried it again with *Hilarities*. Al Kelly, Sid Stone and Georgie Tapps were there from the past; Betty Jane Watson and singer Connie Stevens from the present, and dominating the proceedings was Morey Amsterdam, who also wrote his own material. *Hilarities* lasted a mere and deserved two weeks.

A week later, the Coronet had another tenant, much in the mold of its previous occupant, *Angel in the Wings*. *Small Wonder*, the new intimate revue, had music by Baldwin Bergersen and Albert Selden, lyrics by Phillis McGinley and Billings Brown, sketches by Charles Spalding, Max Wilk, George Axelrod and Louis Laun, and choreography by Gower Champion. Its sketches were bright, as were its young performers—Tom Ewell, Alice Pearce, Mary McCarty, Tommy Rall, Jack Cassidy and Joan Diener, notably among them. With these positives in place, it ran for a respectable 134 performances.

Gower Champion was, in fact, heavily involved with revues that season. His next and more challenging choreography job was with another intimate production which moved into the National on December 16, 1948. *Lend an Ear* was the brainchild of Charles Gaynor, who provided music, lyrics and sketches. The show had begun seven years before in Pittsburgh and had then traveled to Hollywood; consequently, it was highly polished and recommended by the time it opened in New York.

The cast of 21 included Yvonne Adair, William Eythe (who also produced) and Gene Nelson. But it also introduced the all-time Broadway bombshell, Carol Channing.

The show sent up psychoanalysts and gossip columnists and included a destitute opera company that, unable to afford an orchestra, spoke everything. But while these bonbons have probably melted in the heat of memory, *Lend an Ear* will forever be enshrined for its twenty-minute devastation of 1920s musicals, "The Gladiola Girl." Supposedly a lost road company finally coming home to Broadway (and not looking a minute older than it did in 1926), its cast, particularly Yvonne Adair and Carol Channing, tore into the tale of lounge lizards on a Long Island estate, with such songs as "Where Is the She for Me?," "A Little Game of Tennis," "In Our Teeny Little Weeny Nest" and the obligatory "Doin' the Old Yahoo Step."

"The Gladiola Girl" unleashed a nationwide revival of the Twenties, in fashion, on television, and in the next season on Broadway, as Yvonne Adair and Carol Channing repeated themselves in *Gentlemen Prefer Blondes*. *Lend an Ear* enjoyed a hugely successful run of 460 performances.

Elsewhere, the American musical marched on, with *Kiss Me, Kate* and *South Pacific* leading the way, while the revue foundered as the season of 1949-1950 began. Ken Murray had the audacity to bring his *Blackouts of 1949* in from its home at the El Capitan nightclub in Hollywood. Rumor had it that his main motivation was a television contract, which he eventually got. As for *Blackouts*, it was yet another variety show, with a few good looking showgirls thrown in for decoration. It parted from the formerly proud Ziegfeld after 51 performances.

More respectable was *Touch and Go*. It had begun as a student production at Catholic University in Washington D.C., where Walter and Jean Kerr were faculty members. They wrote the lyrics and sketches, Jay Gorney the music, Helen Tamiris the dances, and when the show came to the Broadhurst, its students were retired and replaced by a disciplined, mostly young cast of professionals, including Nancy Andrews, Helen Gallagher, Peggy Cass, Pearl Lang, Louis Nye and Mara Lynn. Witty and lovable, the show offered a takeoff on jungle numbers called "Gorilla Girl" and Hamlet as done by Rodgers and Hammerstein, with its title "Great Dane A'Comin'", and its featured song "You're a Queer One, Dear Ophelia." *Touch and Go* remained at the Broadhurst for 176 performances.

On January 17, 1950, Ray Golden and William R. Katzel tried once more to revive the big Broadway revue. They rented the Winter Garden for *Alive and Kicking*, which suffered from an embarrassment of riches in all departments, and a lack of cohesion as a show. Jack Cole danced up a storm and so did his dancers, including Gwen Verdon and Bob Fosse, while Bobby Van was the hoofer-in-charge. David Burns, Jack Gilford, Carl Reiner and Lenore Lonergan performed sketches by an army of writers that included I.A.L. Diamond, Henry Morgan, Jerome Chodorov, Joseph Stein and Will Glickman. Sammy Fain and Harold Rome supplied some of the music. But its parts didn't add up to any sort of sum, and the show closed after 46 performances.

Hard on *Alive and Kicking's* decline came *Dance Me a Song*, a Dwight Deere Wiman project that again threw a host of disparate talents together, including revue veterans James Shelton, Herman Hupfeld, Albert Hague and Vincente Minnelli and highly qualified writers George Oppenheimer, Marya Mannes and Robert Anderson. Jo Mielziner designed the sets, and the cast was largely composed of dancers, including Joan McCracken, Scott Merrill, Marilyn Gennaro,

Bob Fosse, Donald Saddler and non-dancers Marion Lorne, James Kirkwood, June Graham, and one spot of comedic brightness, Wally Cox. It, too, collapsed after 46 performances.

At least the Hartmans had the good grace to remain intimate and return to their first successful venue, the Coronet, with *Tickets Please*, Broadway's next revue. Possessed of no noteworthy music but a bright young cast that included an unknown Larry Kert, the charming little show remained in place for 245 performances.

By the 1950-1951 season, the writing on the wall had grown large and undeniable. Television had, for all intents and purposes, done away with the need for the really, really big Broadway revue. If further proof were needed, the lukewarm reception accorded the season's first two musicals, both revues and both attempts to prolong the past, provided it.

First, Michael Todd tried to capitalize on a good, wartime draw. Choosing as his star Lily Christine, possibly the most beautiful and classy stripper in the history of burlesque, he brought *Michael Todd's Peep Show* to the Winter Garden on June 8, 1950. It was a melange of Minksy burlesque, circus and vaudeville with a few sketches written by, of all people, Billy K. Wells, plus a few musical numbers composed by such stalwarts as Sammy Fain, Harold Rome, Jule Styne and—more for publicity than melody—the King of Thailand.

Hassard Short directed the overall production; Bobby Clark the sketches. Aside from La Christine, the cast was composed mostly of burlesque clowns, such as Peanuts Man, Bozo Snyder, etc. Lina Romay, Xaviar Cugat's bombshell, sang the songs, and Lily Christine took off more clothes than the license commission allowed. Todd met with them after opening night, modified the show somewhat and called the papers. Despite a drubbing by the critics, *Michael Todd's Peep Show* lasted for 278 performances. Skin was apparently still in.

Not so sanguine a result met Olsen and Johnson, who tried once more to bring their kind of patented insanity back to Broadway with *Pardon Our French*. The French part of the evening was given over to the busty and vigorously untalented Denise Darcel; Marty May was on hand to act as straight man to the zany stars, and Victor Young provided disposable music. It left the Broadway Theatre after 100 performances.

Yet another brave try at reviving the classic Broadway revue happened on December 14, 1950, when a group of veterans, including Harold Rome, Arnold Auerbach, John C. Wilson, Oliver Smith and Helen Tamiris, and performers Jules Munshin, Mary McCarty, Pearl Bailey, Gene Barry, Byron Palmer, Donald Saddler and Valerie Bettis, plus show girls, singers and dancers, arrived at the Mark Hellinger in *Bless You All*.

All the elements were there—some usable if not hummable music, good dancing, pretty girls, and sketches that sent up Tennessee Williams ("Southern Fried Chekhov"), the P.T.A., national presidential campaigns conducted on TV, and the Cold War. But the public wasn't interested. *Bless You All* barely made it through 84 performances.

It was a losing battle that even affected the intimate revue, which seemed ideally suited to its new venue, Off-Broadway. *Razzle Dazzle*, a revue largely devoted to sending up *All About Eve*, tried performing in the round at the Arena Stage and stayed in business for a mere week.

As more and more homes were now outfitted with television sets, TV variety shows proliferated, at no charge to viewers. Now all of Broadway began to feel the effects of the electronic enemy. Overall theatre attendance was down in the 1951-1952 season, during which only nine new musicals premiered, then a modern and depressing record.

But in a way, it was a season of recognition, too, during which the final categories of revues would be drawn and the last two big Broadway revues that could be classified as hits opened.

The first was the inspired creation of Betty Comden, Adolph Green and Jule Styne. Directed by Abe Burrows, *Two on the Aisle* paired Bert Lahr and Dolores Gray in a succession of fast paced sketches, songs and dances. The heavy production numbers and showgirl parades may have been missing, but Lahr and Gray and a supporting cast that included Elliott Reid and Colette Marchand worked the superior material at hand to the maximum. Lahr's routines included a hilarious session with a slightly punchy baseball great who, unable to understand that he's being interviewed on a children's TV show, insists on talking about his escapades with broads and booze. Gray was given one of the Comden-Green-Styne showstoppers, "If You Hadn't, But You Did," and the two brought down the house as old vaudevillians appearing at the Metropolitan Opera ("Catch Our Act at the Met").

Two on the Aisle remained at the Mark Hellinger for 281 performances; in the Twenties, Thirties and Forties, it would have run twice as long.

In contrast to it was the other blockbuster revue of the season, which arrived in April of 1952. Leonard Sillman's classic *New Faces of 1952* was a comparatively intimate revue, one of the last to play Broadway. It was in the mold of the five previous *New Faces*, but this time there was fresh and astonishing abundance in every department. For once, the group of composers, lyricists and sketch writers turned out inspired words and music, which was performed to the hilt and then some by a cast of new faces that included Virginia deLuce, Alice Ghostley, Ronny Graham, Eartha Kitt, Carol Lawrence, Paul Lynde, Robert Clary and Rosemary O'Reilly. The one familiar face onstage and on the creative staff was Sillman's sister, June Carroll, who wrote some of the revue's most lasting lyrics, all to music by Arthur Siegel—"Penny Candy," sung by her, about the loss of youth and simple fulfillment; "Monotonous," Eartha Kitt's sophisticated catalogue of conquests; and the exquisite ballad "Love Is a Simple Thing" sung by Rosemary O'Reilly. Ms. Carroll was also given Murray Grand and Elisse Boyd's "Guess Who I Saw Today?," one of the show's most long-lasting contributions to the cabaret circuit, a song whose greatest impact comes upon its first hearing, before the listener is aware of the punchline.

Comedy song honors clearly went to Alice Ghostley's chronicle of a disastrous date, set to music and lyrics by Sheldon Harnick, "The Boston Beguine." But there was plenty more: Ronny Graham's "Lucky Pierre" and "I'm in Love with Miss Logan" for Robert Clary, and his sendup of operetta ("Waltzing in Venice with you/Isn't so easy to do/If you should take one more step than you oughter/You will be doing the dance under water").

The sketches were at times masterful: Mel Brooks's sendup of *Death of a Salesman*, in which a pickpocket disowns his son for going honest; Ronny Graham's "Oedipus Goes South," a wild treatment of Truman Capote; and Paul Lynde's appearance, swathed from head to toe in bandages, reporting on his big game hunt in Africa.

John Murray Anderson directed at lightning speed, and this *New Faces* kept the Royale lit for 365 performances, after which it was filmed.

And that, absolutely, would be it for the revue as a potential big Broadway hit. Murray Anderson would come closest to prolonging its life during the 1953-1954 season with his *John Murray Anderson's Almanac*. Encouraged, no doubt, by his success with *New Faces*, the master revue director did score well in some departments. He introduced two new composing and lyric talents to Broadway: Richard Adler and Jerry Ross. He brought Sheldon Harnick along to once more produce a showstopping comedy number, this time titled "A Merry Minuet" that was anything but merry ("They're rioting in Africa, tra la la la la la...")

And he peopled his cast with winning comics—Billy DeWolfe, Alice Pearce, Orson Bean and, in her first appearance in America, Hermione Gingold, who thanked the country's citizens for placing a statue of Judith Anderson in New York Harbor. The singing tasks were handled by Carleton Carpenter, Tony Bavaar, Tina Louise and Nanci Crompton, and yet another major talent, Harry Belafonte, was introduced, singing his own calypso shout, "Hold 'Em Joe," which launched his meteoric career.

But, although Cyril Ritchard directed, and although the show contained one of the classic revue sketches of all time, "Dinner for One," in which Gingold has her butler set the table for herself and her four long-dead gentleman friends, there was a certain mustiness about the proceedings, including the resurrection of one of Anderson's beloved (by him) ballet ballads, "The Nightingale and the Rose," from a long ago *Greenwich Village Follies*. *John Murray Anderson's Almanac* stayed at the Imperial for 229 performances, which by 1953 was not enough to turn a profit.

In December of 1952, a year before Anderson's last effort to keep the revue alive, there was a similar attempt at a classy Broadway revue. *Two's Company* arrived with music by Vernon Duke, lyrics by Ogden Nash and Sammy Cahn, sketches by Charles Sherman and Peter DeVries, direction by Jules Dassin, choreography by Jerome Robbins and production supervision by John Murray Anderson. It came into the Alvin with a monster advance sale, occasioned by its star, Bette Davis. But even she seemed adrift in her inferior material, and the prodigious supporting talents of Hiram Sherman, David Burns, George Irving, Bill Callahan, Ellen Hanley and Maria Karnilova couldn't save a bad show. When the advance sales ran out, as they did within a few months, the revue closed after 90 performances.

The Ziegfeld Follies tried twice more, and failed ignominiously twice more—once in 1957, with Billy DeWolfe starring, and once in 1958, with six showgirls and Kaye Ballard, an effort that opened in Toronto and closed in Cincinnati.

No, for all intents and purposes, the Broadway revue, in its pure and largest and best manifestation, represented by its peak shows in the 1930s and 1940s, had passed into history, along with many of its creators.

But the revue form, itself, didn't depart. It merely metamorphosed. A new world, after all, demanded new forms. One of them had been evident as early as the end of World War II, when Edith Piaf had arrived in New York with a one woman show. Within months, Maurice Chevalier had followed. And now, in the 1950s, the floodgates opened. Beatrice Lillie, Anna Russell, Victor Borge, Yves Montand, Ethel Waters, Stanley Holloway, Eddie Fisher, Marlene Dietrich, Josephine Baker, Sammy Davis Jr., Judy Garland, Lena Horne, Barry Manilow, Mandy Patinkin, Shirley MacLaine, Patti LuPone, and various combinations of two or three stars gave staged concerts over the next 40 years. But that was what they were—staged concerts, and nothing more.

The intimate revue, which had refined itself, found a home, but not on Broadway. Off-Broadway was the venue for Ben Bagley's *Shoestring* series and the Ogden Nash-Vernon Duke *Littlest Revue* of 1955.

Other little shows originated out of town, and entered Broadway and Off-Broadway from places as close as the Catskills and as distant as New Zealand. With 1951's *Bagels and Yox* and *Borscht Capades*, the viability of Yiddish revues was established. Ten years later, in 1961, Chicago sent *From the Second City* to Off-Broadway for a long run. *La Plume de Ma Tante* originated in Paris; *Cambridge Circus* in London, *Wait a Minim!* in South Africa. *Double Dublin* made the trip from Ireland, and Maoris arrived with their revue, *Pacific Paradise*, in 1972.

In 1967, at Off-Broadway's Village Gate, the cabaret entertainment *Jacques Brel Is Alive and Well and Living in Paris*, which celebrated and consisted of the work of Belgian composer Jacques Brel, scored astonishingly, even journeying to Broadway for a brief stay in 1973 before embarking on an eternal world tour. The concept seemed to work, and so the composer revue was born. The very next year, the first of a batch of Noel Coward revues was whipped up Off-Broadway, followed by *Berlin to Broadway with Kurt Weill*.

Both succeeded, and Broadway producers, seeing a good, cheap moneymaker, leaped. *Rodgers and Hart* and its record 98 R&H hits was the first, followed by, among many, *Side by Side by Sondheim*, *Ain't Misbehavin'* (Fats Waller), *Sophisticated Ladies* (Duke Ellington), *Smokey Joe's Cafe* (Leiber and Stoller) and *Swinging on a Star* (Burke and Van Huesen).

In fact, on Off-Broadway, where life and productions are less expensive, the composer revue is still the revue of choice. *The Decline and Fall of the Entire World as Seen Through the Eyes of Cole Porter*; *Ladies and Gentlemen, Jerome Kern*, *Back to Bacharach and David*, *And the World Goes 'Round* and seemingly endless rummagings through Stephen Sondheim's trunk, closets and garage abound.

But, popular as they are, these revues still have more in common with concerts than with the great Broadway revue, of which there have been only two possible manifestations in the last decades.

Oh, Calcutta!, tacky to its core, and not very funny either, took the flash of flesh of the *Passing Shows* and *Artists and Models* to its logical extreme and, while doing so, proved that Jake Shubert, in spite of his horrific personality and habits, was a showman for more than his time.

Sugar Babies, for all its charm, humor and longevity, was basically a stripperless burlesque show, akin to the pastiches of the World War II era on Broadway.

No, the true Broadway revue has gone the way of unamplified voices and the classic pit band sound. It was television that did it in, and television continues to keep it safely buried, even though the variety show with all its good natured nonviolence has largely disappeared from the tube. What has replaced it in the public taste can only be achieved electronically, and this, more and more, has come to dominate the modern musical on Broadway. Threatened by films and television, the theatre is currently responding by trying to imitate films and television, a movement that has resulted in a kind of creeping depersonalization.

A pity, for pure theatre is the most personal and human of the performing arts, a refuge for the straightforward unfolding of stories, for communication and interaction among human beings in the here and the now. Until the 1950s, there was room in this equation for the Broadway revue, which, as the theatre matured, matured itself.

And in doing this, it took a long trip, from obscurity to faltering confusion, to fusion, to experiment, to spectacle, to intelligence, back to faltering confusion, on to experiment, and finally to obscurity. But along the way and for a long, rich time, it became the home of ingenuity, perception, contemporary reality and revelation, and, in lavish quantities, fun.

A Broadway without revues is an incomplete Broadway. And that's a loss. But who knows? Imagination has always been and always will be the lifeblood of art, and the possibility exists that somewhere, someone is searching for the chance to find a place between the corpulent and the compact forms of the present day musical theatre for a new/old genre, free of biography, liberated from plot, emancipated from overriding theme. And that will be, once again, and joyously, the Broadway revue.

Selected Bibliography

Abbott, George. *Mr. Abbott*, N.Y., N.Y.: Random House, 1963.

Anderson, John Murray, and Hugh Abercrombie Anderson. *Without My Rubbers*, N.Y., N.Y.: Library Publishers,1954.

Baral, Robert. *Revue*, N.Y., N.Y.: Fleet Publishing Corp.,1962.

Barrett, Mary Ellin. *Irving Berlin; A Daughter's Memoir*, N.Y.,N.Y.: Simon & Schuster, 1994.

Bordman, Gerald. *American Musical Theatre*, N.Y., N.Y.: Oxford University Press, 1978.

Burton, Jack. *Blue Book of Broadway Musicals*, Watkins Glen, N.Y.: Century House, 1952.

Carter, Randolph. *The World of Flo Ziegfeld*, N.Y.,N.Y.: Praeger Publishers, 1974.

Churchill, Allen. *The Theatrical Twenties*, N.Y., N.Y.: McGraw-Hill, 1975.

Clark, Norman. *The Mighty Hippodrome*, N.Y., N.Y.: A.S. Barnes & Co., 1968.

Cochran, Charles B. *The Secrets of a Showman*, N.Y., N.Y.: Henry Holt and Co., 1926.

Duke, Vernon. *Passport to Paris*, N.Y., N.Y.: Little, Brown, 1952.

Engel, Lehman. *The American Musical Theatre*, N.Y., N.Y.: CBS Legacy, 1967.

Farnsworth, Marjorie. *The Ziegfeld Follies*, N.Y., N.Y.: Bonanza Books, 1961.

Gordon, Max, and Lewis Funke. *Max Gordon Presents*, N.Y., N.Y.: Geis, 1963.

Gottfried, Martin. *Nobody's Fool; The Lives of Danny Kaye*, N.Y., N.Y.: Simon and Schuster, 1994.

Green, Stanley. *The Great Clowns of Broadway*, N.Y., N.Y.: Oxford University Press, 1984.

Ring Bells! Sing Songs! Broadway Musicals of the 1930's, N.Y., N.Y.: Galahad Books, 1971.

The World of Musical Comedy, N.Y., N.Y.: A.S. Barnes & Co., 1960.

Higham, Charles. *Ziegfeld*, Chicago, Ill.: Henry Rignery, 1972

Highland, William G. *The Song Is Ended: Songwriters and American Music 1900-1950*. N.Y., N.Y.: Oxford University Press, 1995.

Kahn, E. J. Jr.. *The Merry Partners: The Age and Stage of Harrigan and Hart*, N.Y., N.Y.: Random House, 1955.

Katkov, Norman. *The Fabulous Fanny*, N.Y., N.Y.: Knopf, 1953.

Jablonski, Edward, and Lawrence D. Stewart. *The Gershwin Years*, N.Y., N.Y.: Doubleday, 1958.

Mander, Raymond, and Joe Mitchenson. *Revue: A Story in Pictures*, N.Y. N.Y.: Taplinger Pub. Co,. Inc., 1971.

Marks, Edward B. *They All Had Glamour*, N.Y., N.Y.: Julian Messner, Inc., 1944.

McNamara, Brooks. *The Shuberts of Broadway*, N.Y., N.Y.: Oxford University Press, 1990.

Murray, Ken. *Body Merchant*, N.Y., N.Y.: Ward Richie Press, 1976.

Richman, Harry, and Richard Gehman. *A Hell of a Life*, N.Y., N.Y.: Duell, Sloane & Pearce, 1966.

Pollock, Channing. *Harvest of My Years*, Indianapolis, Ind.: Bobbs-Merrill Co., 1943.

Samuels,Charles and Louise.*Once Upon a Stage: The Merry World of Vaudeville*, N.Y., N.Y.: Dodd, Mead & Company, 1974.

Smith, Harry B. *First Nights and First Editions*, Boston: Little, Brown, 1931.

Stagg, Jerry. *The Brothers Shubert*, N.Y., N.Y.: Random House,1968.

Stein, Charles W. (Ed.). *American Vaudeville As Seen By Its Contemporaries*, N.Y.. N.Y.: Alfred A. Knopf,1984.

Taubman, Howard. *The Making of the American Theatre*, N.Y., N.Y.: Coward-McCann, 1965.

Toll, Robert C. *Blacking Up: The Minstrel Show in Nineteenth Century America*, N.Y., N.Y.: Oxford University Press, 1974.

Winer, Deborah Grace. *On the Sunny Side of the Street; The Life and Lyrics of Dorothy Fields*, N.Y., N.Y.: Schirmer Books, 1997.

Zeidman, Irving. *The American Burlesque Show*, N.Y., N.Y.: Hawthorn Books, 1967.

Ziegfeld, Richard and Paulette. *The Ziegfeld Touch*, N.Y., N.Y.: Henry N. Abrams, 1993.

End Notes

Introduction

1. Charles B. Cochran, *Secrets of a Showman*.
2. Noel Coward, in his preface to *Secrets of a Showman*.

Chapter 1

1. George C.D. Odell, *Annals of the New York Stage 1798-1821*.
2. Irving Zeidman, *The American Burlesque Show*.
3. *Literary Digest*, March, 1843.
4. E.J. Kahn Jr., *The Merry Partners: The Age and Stage of Harrigan and Hart*.
5. *ibid*
6. Quoted in Charles and Louise Samuels, *Once Upon a Stage: The Merry World of Vaudeville*.

Chapter 2

1. Samuels, *Once Upon a Stage*
2. *Ibid*.
3. *Ibid*.
4. Charles W. Stein (ed.) *American Vaudeville As Seen By Its Contemporaries*.
5. Robert Baral, *Revue*.

Chapter 3

1. Harry B. Smith, *First Nights and First Editions*.
2. Ziegfeld publicity for *The Red Feather*

3. *The New York Times*, July 9, 1907.
4. Guy Bolton and P.G. Wodehouse, *Bring on the Girls*.
5. Smith, *First Nights and First Editions*.

Chapter 4

1. Baral, *Revue*.
2. Marjorie Farnsworth, *The Ziegfeld Follies*.
3. Gerald Bordman, *The American Musical Theatre*.
4. Smith, *First Nights and First Editions*.
5. Farnsworth, *The Ziegfeld Follies*.

Chapter 5

1. Gerald Bordman, *The American Musical Theatre*.
2. Channing Pollock, *Harvest of My Years*.
3. Keenan Wynn, in a conversation with the author. Wynn swore that his father, Ed Wynn, overheard the exchange and reported it to him.

Chapter 6

1. Baral.
2. In Lee Davis, *Bolton and Wodehouse and Kern: The Men Who Made Musical Comedy*.
3. Jerry Stagg, *The Brothers Shubert*.

Chapter 7

1. Richard and Paulette Ziegfeld, *The Ziegfeld Touch*.
2. Norman Katkov, *The Fabulous Fanny*.
3. Stagg.

Chapter 8

1. *The New York Times*, September 23, 1921.
2. Quoted in Norman Clark, *The Mighty Hippodrome*.
3. *Ibid*.
4. Stagg.

Chapter 9

1. Ken Murray, *Body Merchant*.
2. *ibid*.
3. Quoted in Murray, *Body Merchant*.
4. Stagg.
5. Burns Mantle, *Best Plays of the Year, 1923-24*.
6. *ibid*.
7. Stagg.
8. Richard and Paulette Ziegfeld, *The Ziegfeld Touch*.
9. Murray.
10. *ibid*.

Chapter 10

1. Baral, *The Revue*.
2. Murray, *Body Merchant*.
3. Allen Churchill, *The Theatrical Twenties*.
4. Randolph Carter, *The World of Flo Ziegfeld*.
5. Burns Mantle, *The Best Plays of the Year, 1927-28*.
6. Richard and Paulette Ziegfeld.
7. Baral.
8. Deborah Grace Winer, *On the Sunny Side of the Street: The Life and Lyrics of Dorothy Fields*.
9. Baral.
10. Brooks McNamara, *The Shuberts of Broadway*.

Chapter 11

1. Stanley Green, *Ring Bells! Sing Songs! Broadway Musicals of the 1930's*.
2. Charles B. Cochran, *The Secrets of a Showman*.
3. *The New York Times*, June 4, 1931.
4. Quoted in Stanley Green, *The World of Musical Comedy*.
6. Richard and Paulette Ziegfeld.

Chapter 12

1. Burns Mantle, *Best Plays of the Year, 1932-33*.
2. *ibid*.
3. Stanley Green, *Ring Bells! Sing Songs!*
4. *New York Post*, October 1, 1933.

5. Stagg, *The Brothers Shubert*.
6. Vernon Duke, *Passport to Paris*.
7. John Murray Anderson and Hugh Abercrombie Anderson, *Without My Rubbers*.
8. William G. Highland, *The Song Is Ended: Songwriters and American Music 1900-1950*.
9. Quoted in Stanley Green, *The World of Musical Comedy*.

Chapter 13

1. Mary Ellin Barrett, *Irving Berlin; A Daughter's Memoir*.
2. Stagg, *The Brothers Shubert*.

INDEX

A

Aarons, Alex, 213
Abbott, George, 326
Abbott and Costello, 335
Aberdeen Proving Grounds, 149
Abie's Irish Rose (play), 182, 213, 227
Academy of Music, 35, 55
Actman, Irving, 322
Actors' Equity strike (1919), 157, 158, 159, 163
Adah Richmond's Burlesque Company, 65
Adair, Janet, 192, 219
Adair, Yvonne, 366
Adams, Franklin P., 194
Adams, Leslie, 308-9
Adams, Stanley, 326, 327
Adamson, Harold, 277, 285, 292
Adelaide and Hughes, 149
Adelphi Theater, 360
Adler, Larry, 302, 342
Adler, Richard, 371
Afgar, 208
Africana, 246
"African Fling, The" (dance), 33
"African Sailor's Hornpipe, The" (dance), 33
"Age in Which We Live, The" (sketch), 265
Ager, Milton, 163, 165, 265

Ahlert, Fred, 343
Ah, Wilderness! (O'Neill), 308, 314
"Ain't Misbehavin'," 263
Akst, Harry, 206, 250, 317
A la Carte, 248
Albee, Edward F., 52, 160, 190
Albertina Rasch Dancers, 227, 243, 247, 288
Algonquin Round Table, 194, 205
Alhambra Theatre, 104
Alice in Wonderland (Carroll), 134, 220
Alive and Kicking, 367
All About Eve (film), 369
"All Alone," 220
Allan, Lewis, 351
Allegro, 363
Allen, Florence, 216
Allen, Fred, 53, 192, 209, 218, 260, 279-80, 311-12
Allen, Lester, 173, 198, 213, 214
Allen, Vera, 320, 326
Allen Foster Girls, 262
Allez-Oop, 246
"All Girls Are Like a Rainbow" (production number), 170
All Star Jubilee, 115
"All the Stars and Stripes Belong to Me" (production number), 90
Allyson, June, 332
"Alone Together" (dance), 302, 305
Alphonso, King of Spain, 102

Alter, Louis, 248, 283
Althea, 180
Alvin Theater, 336, 347, 372
Amazons, The (Pinero), 60
"Ambassador's March" (production number), 90
Ambassador Theatre, 201, 295, 296, 340, 350-51
"Ambulance Chaser, The" (sketch), 255
American (newspaper), 201, 334
Americana (1926), 238-39, 246, 256
Americana (1928), 256-57
Americana series, 304
"American Eagles," 349
American Theatre (first), 41
American Theatre (second), 61, 72
American Tragedy, An (Dreiser), 361
American Way, The, 343
"America's Fighting Jack" (production number), 139
Amsterdam, Morey, 365
"Anatole of Paris," 340
Andersen, Hans Christian, 194
Anderson, John, 334
Anderson, Judith, 371
Anderson, Marian, 329
Anderson, Maxwell, 326
Anderson, Robert, 367
Andre Charlot's Revue of 1924, 208-9, 210, 222, 257
Andrews, Nancy, 367
And the World Goes 'Round, 374
"Angel Child," 186
Angel in the Wings, 362-3, 365
Angel Street (play), 355
"Ankle Up the Altar with Me," 276
Anna Held Girls, 81, 82, 85, 94, 101
Annals of the New York Stage (Odell), 28
Ansonia Hotel, 105
Anthony, Norman, 301
Antony and Cleopatra (Shakespeare), 131
Apollo Theatre, 213, 227, 254, 293
"April in Paris," 305-6
Arabian Girl and Forty Thieves, An, 74
Arden, Eve, 312, 314, 318, 323, 324, 341
Arena Stage, 369
"Are You Having Any Fun?," 336
Argentinita (dancer), 275, 347

Arlen, Harold, 274, 277, 278, 303, 304, 305, 315, 316, 326, 327, 328, 348
Armbruster, Robert, 231
Armstrong, Louis, 263
Army Emergency Relief Fund, 349, 350
Arno, Peter, 265, 291
Arnold, Edward, 285
Arnst, Bobby, 243
Arnstein, Nicky, 172
Aronson, Boris, 305
Aronson, Rudolph, 56
Around the Map, 129
Around the World, 101
Around the World in Eighty Days, 55
Art Hickman's Orchestra, 166
Artists and Models of 1923, 202-3, 204
Artists and Models of 1924, 219
Artists and Models of 1925, 228
Artists and Models of 1927, 249-50
Artists and Models of 1930, 277
Artists and Models of 1943, 353-54
Artists and Models series, 203, 217, 353
"Ashes" (sketch), 54
Astaire, Adele, 286, 287, 289
Astaire, Fred, 53, 287, 288
Astaire, Fred and Adele, 145, 148, 286, 288
As Thousands Cheer, 17, 307-10, 315 325
"As Time Goes By," 248
Astor Place Riots (1849), 31
Astor Theater, 219
As You Were, 162
At Home Abroad, 320-21, 326, 355
Atkinson, Brooks, 288-89, 331
Atta Boy, 149
Atteridge, Harold, 116, 118, 122, 128, 133, 139, 149, 166, 169, 174, 182, 192, 195, 208, 214, 230, 243, 248, 251, 259
Aubert, Jeanne, 295, 301
Auerbach, Arnold, 361, 364, 369
"Auld Lang Syne," 161
Auracher, Harry, 161
"Aurory Bory Alice," 235
Auto Race, The, 85
"Autumn in New York," 318
Avon Comedy Four, 160
Avon Theater, 72

Axelrod, George, 365
Ayer, Nat, 92

B

"Back Numbers in My Little Red Book," 186
Back to Bacharach and David, 374
Back to Methusulah (Shaw), 182
Bacon, Faith, 278
Bad Habits of 1926, 231
Baer, Bugs, 237
Bagels and Yox, 373
Bagley, Ben, 373
Bailey, Pearl, 369
Baker, Belle, 334
Baker, Edyth, 210
Baker, Josephine, 323, 324, 373
Baker, Phil, 167, 228, 243, 259, 277, 284, 304, 317, 346
Balanchine, George, 323, 342
Baldina, Maria, 122, 123
Balieff, Nikita, 181
Baline, Izzy. *See* Berlin, Irving
"Ballad for Americans," 334-35
"Ballad of Uncle Sam, The." *See* "Ballad for Americans"
Ballard, Kay, 372
Ballard, Lucinda, 342
Ballet Ballads, 191, 203, 218, 264, 372
"Ballet of 1830, The (as played for eight months at the Alhambra Theatre, London)," 104
Ballyhoo of 1932, 301
Balzac, Honoré de, 316
"Bamboo Babies," 229
Band Wagon, The, 285-89, 291, 294, 297, 302, 315
Bane, Paula, 355
Banjo Ingenues, 247
Banton, Trais, 208
Bara, Theda, 131
Bare Facts of 1926, 237-38, 241
Bare Facts of 1927, 245
Barker, John, 286, 288
Barnes, Djuna, 191
Barnum, P. T., 48, 75, 140, 189
"Barnum and Bailey Rag," 121
Barnum's American Museum, 32, 41

Barras, Charles M., 34
Barrie, Gracie, 306, 322, 326
Barrie, James, 257
Barry, Gene, 369
Barry, Philip, 245
Barrymore, Ethel, 254
Barrymore, John, 211, 221
Barrymores, 53, 160, 166, 171
Bartholomae, Philip, 158
Barton, James, 160, 214, 237, 282, 284, 353
Bashette, Billy, 139
Basselin, Olivier, 49
Bat, The (play), 169
Bat Theatre of Moscow, 181, 248
Bauer, Franklyn, 247
Bavaar, Tony, 371
Bayadere, La, or The Maid of Cashmere (ballet), 29
Bayes, Nora, 53, 82, 86, 91, 92, 93, 108, 122, 145-46, 168, 170, 290
Bean, Orson, 371
Beardsley, Aubrey, 174
Beaton, Betzi, 317
"Beatrice Lillie Ballad, A," 236
"Beautiful Girls," 191
"Beauty Contest, The" (production number), 213
"Because I Can't Tango," 117
"Because You're Just You," 141
Beck, Martin, 52
Beggar on Horseback (Kaufman and Connelly), 212
Beggar's Opera, The (Gay), 27
"Beggar's Waltz, The," 288
"Beginning of the French Revolution 1789" (production number), 195
"Behind My Lady's Fan," 219
Belafonte, Harry, 372
Belasco, David, 66, 71, 95, 105, 125, 145, 233, 262, 293
Bel Geddes, Norman, 302, 355
Belle of New York, The, 143
Belle Paree, La, 97-98
Belmont Theatre, 72, 238, 303
Belmont Varieties, 303
"Be My Little Baby Bumblebee," 101
Benchley, Robert, 194, 204-5, 209, 281, 292

Benét, Stephen Vincent, 191
Bennett, Wilda, 180
Benny, Jack, 168, 232, 277
Bergersen, Baldwin, 328, 365
Berkeley, Busby, 247, 259, 262, 264, 275, 283
Berle, Milton, 53, 303, 352
Berlin, Irving, 53, 92, 94-95, 97, 99, 101, 104, 120, 121, 125, 129, 131, 135, 142, 145, 147, 149, 154, 155, 156, 164, 165, 169, 178-80, 187, 193-94, 195, 203, 204-5, 220, 233,247, 265, 291, 308-10, 348, 349-50
Berlin to Broadway with Kurt Weill, 373
Berlo Sisters, 189
Bernard, Sam, 162, 180, 206, 290
Bernstein, Aline, 211
Berry Brothers, 284, 350
Bessie, Alvah, 222
Best Foot Forward, 345
Better Times, 189-90
Bettis, Valerie, 364, 369
Biche au Bois, La (ballet), 35, 36
Bickel, George, 96
Biddle, A.J. Drexel, 236
Biff! Bing! Bang!, 169
Big Show, 133
Bijou Dream Theater, 49
Bijou Theater, 144, 265
Billboard (periodical), 54
Billy Rose's Crazy Quilt, 284
Biltmore Theatre, 325
"Birds of Plumage," 195
"Birthday of the Dauphin, The," 171
"Birth of the Blues, The" (production number), 235
Bishop, John Peale, 191
Blackberries of 1932, 295-96
Blackbirds of 1926, 252
Blackbirds of 1928, 252-53, 259, 263, 275, 296
Blackbirds of 1933, 311
Blackbirds of 1939, 334
Blackbirds series, 311, 334
Black Bottom (dance), 159, 234, 266
Black Crook, The, 30, 34-37, 54, 55, 56, 57, 59, 61, 62, 63, 74, 84, 104
Black Crook Jr., 37

Blackouts of 1949, 366
Blackstone, Nan, 274, 276
Black Tuesday, 270
Blackwell, Donald, 280-81
Blake, Eubie, 186, 209, 251, 278, 281
Blane, Ralph, 325
Bless You All, 369
Blithe Spirit (Coward), 347
Blitzstein, Marc, 276, 328, 329, 351
Blonde Sinner, The (play), 240
Bloom, Rube, 334
Bloomingdale, Alfred, 352
Blossom Time, 182
"Blowing the Blues Away," 238
Blue, Ben, 336
"Blue Danube, The," 334
Blue Holiday, 357
Blue Jeans (play), 83
Blue Monday Blues (jazz opera), 188-89, 222
Blyler, James, 169
Boccaccio, Giovanni, 316
Bodenheim, Maxwell, 191
"Body and Soul," 279
Bohemians, Inc., 158
Bold, Richard, 175, 188
"Bolero" (Ravel), 292
Boley, May, 169
Bolger, Ray, 293, 294, 306, 315, 316, 342, 360
Bolton, Guy, 9, 72, 84, 99, 122, 141, 142, 145, 171, 238, 314, 328
"Bonus Blues, The," 180
"Booster's Song of the Far North, The," 235
Booth Theatre, 193, 253, 261, 333
Bordman, Gerald, 96, 121, 351
Bordoni, Irene, 140, 147, 162, 261, 274
Borge, Victor, 373
Borrah Minevitch and His Harmonica Rascals, 282
Borscht Capades, 373
"Boston Beguine, The," 371
Boston Ideal Opera Company, 57
Boston Traveler (newspaper), 54
Boucicault, Aubrey, 74
Boucicault, Dion, 38
Bourdet, Eduard, 240
Bowery Theatre, 30, 32, 44

Bowman, Patricia, 312, 317
Boyd, Elisse, 370-71
Boyer, Lucienne, 316
Boys and Girls Together, 343
Bradford, Perry, 259
Brady, Diamond Jim, 103, 116, 290
Brady, William, 259, 279
Braham, Dave, 44
Braham, Philip, 209, 229
Brahms, Johannes, 186
Brel, Jacques, 373
Bremen (ship), 216
Brennan, James, 167
Brennan, J. Keirn, 262
Brent, Romney, 222, 232, 260
Brian, Donald, 84, 130
Brice, Elizabeth, 112, 121, 142, 145,166
Brice, Fanny, 53, 95, 96, 100, 101, 131, 132, 140-41, 147, 156, 160, 162, 165, 171, 172-73, 184, 204, 207, 210, 211, 220, 247, 253, 263, 282, 283, 284, 312, 313, 323, 324, 351
Brice, Lew, 122
Bright Lights of 1944, 353
Bring on the Girls (Bolton and Wodehouse), 72
Brinkley, Nell, 87
"Britannia Rules the Waves" (sketch), 257
Broadhurst Theatre, 219, 231, 307, 335, 343, 350, 363, 367
Broadway Jones (play), 114
"Broadway Melody Gold Diggers of 42nd Street" (production number), 324
Broadway Nights, 264
"Broadway Reverie" (production number), 290
Broadway Sho-Window, 325
Broadway Theatre, 303, 341, 350, 369
Broadway to Paris, 108-9
Broadway Whirl, The, 170
Brockman, James, 146
Broderick, Helen, 206, 221, 286, 287-88, 303, 308-9
Brooks, Harry, 263
Brooks, Louise, 237
Brooks, Mel, 371
Broones, Martin, 243
"Brother, Can You Spare a Dime?," 304

Brother Rat (play), 350
Brougham, John, 29, 57
Broughton, Philip, 274
Broun, Heywood, 168, 189, 194, 291, 329
Brower, Frank, 30-32
Brown, Albert W., 114
Brown, A. Seymour, 92
Brown, Billings, 365
Brown, Joe E., 53, 174
Brown, John Mason, 231, 310
Brown, Lew, 140, 227, 265, 294, 306, 317, 345
Brown, Louise, 237
Brown and Henderson, 265
Brown and Watts, 174
Browne, Walter, 100
"Brown October Ale," 57
Brox Sisters, 180, 204, 220, 247-48
Bruce, Carol, 350
Bryan, Alfred, 166
Bryan, Vincent, 81, 84
Buchanan, Jack, 209, 229, 273
Buck, Gene, 106, 113, 121, 123, 126-27, 130, 147, 154, 156, 157, 163, 164, 172, 184, 207, 208, 213, 236, 289, 290
Buck and Bubbles, 281, 290, 291, 353
Buckingham, George Villiers, 27
Buckley Serenaders, 32
"Budweiser's a Friend of Mine," 81
Buffalo Bill (William Cody), 75
Bunk of 1926, 231
Bunty Pulls the Strings (play), 104
Burke, Billie, 114, 116, 125, 135, 155, 183, 236, 293, 311, 312, 322
Burke and Van Huesen, 374
Burkhardt, Addison, 85, 90
burlesque, 20, 21, 24-35passim, 45, 51, 53, 55, 59, 60, 63, 64, 65, 66, 90, 94, 103, 108, 211, 227, 278, 297, 324, 327, 331, 341, 348, 350, 368
"Burmese Ballet," 134
Burnand, F.C., 37
Burns, David, 363, 367, 372
Burnside, Richard H., 128, 129, 178, 183, 189, 190
Burr, Courtney, 305
Burrows, Abe, 370

Burton, Ralph, 182
Butterworth, Charles (Charlie), 238, 246, 302
Buy-It-Dear, 'Tis Made of Cashmere, 29
Buzzin' Around, 166
By Jupiter, 345
Byng, Douglas, 257
Byram, Al, 243
Byrnes, James, 144
Byron, Lord, 30
"By Strauss," 327
"By the Light of the Silvery Moon," 92, 94
By the Way, 230

C

Caesar, Irving, 147, 161, 186, 204, 229, 230, 236, 257, 265, 304
Caesar, Julius, 241
Caesar, Sid, 15, 341, 363, 365
Cafe Lido de Paris" (production number), 266
Cagney, James, 53, 254, 261
Cahill, Marie, 244, 315, 348
Cahn, Sammy, 372
Calahan, J. Will, 148
Caldwell, Anne, 120, 168, 218
Calkins, Florence, 296
Callahan, Bill, 361, 372
Calling All Stars, 317
Call Me Mister, 10, 361, 363
Calthorp, Gladys, 257
Cambridge Circus, 373
Camille (Dumas), 109
Campbell, James, 277
Campbell, Mrs. Patrick, 53
Camp Taminent, 340
Camp Upton, 149, 349
Canova, Judy, 317, 323, 324
Cansinos, 204
Cantor, Eddie, 53, 133, 141, 147, 156, 157, 168, 169, 182-83, 184, 207, 248, 263, 274
"Can't We Be Friends?," 261
Cape Cod Follies, The, 265
Capital theatre, 357
Capitan, El (nightclub), 366
Capote, Truman, 371
Captive, The (Bourdet), 240

"Carefree Cairo Town," 170
Caribbean Carnival, 362
Carle, Richard, 145, 170
Carmichael, Hoagy, 326, 327
Carmita (dancer), 316
Carncross and Dixey's Minstrels, 32
Carnegie, Andrew, 81, 105
Carnegie Hall, 189
"Carolina in the Morning," 193
Carpenter, Carleton, 360, 371
Carpenter, Constance, 229, 257, 261, 285
Carpenter, Thelma, 364
Carroll, Adam, 261
Carroll, Albert, 235, 254, 261
Carroll, Earl, 14, 15, 198-200, 203, 205, 215, 216, 228, 239, 240, 241-42, 246, 256, 263-64, 277-78, 291-92, 296, 303-4, 319, 341
Carroll, Harry, 118, 122, 165, 169
Carroll, June, 351, 370-71
Carroll, Lewis, 134
Carroll, Nancy, 195, 214
Carroll beauties, 201
Carter, Frank, 157
Cartier's (store), 281
Carty, Jim, 234
Caryll, Ivan, 109, 120
Casino de Paris theater, 231, 250
Casino roof theater, 74
Casino Theater (first), 56-66passim, 74, 75, 77, 82, 83, 90, 96, 114, 115, 166
Casino Theater (second), 292, 304, 305
Cass, Peggy, 367
Cassidy, Jack, 364, 365
Castle, Irene, 120, 131, 142, 250
Castle, Vernon, 90, 120
"Catch Our Act at the Met," 370
Catherine, 66
Catholic University, 367
Catlett, Walter, 141
Cato, Minto, 281
Cavendish, Charles, 289
Cawthorn, Joseph, 130
Cecil Mack Choir, 284
Center Theatre, 309, 326, 343-44, 350, 354, 362
Century Girl, The, 134-35, 139, 142

Index ≈ 391

Century Promenade theater. *See* Century Theatre Roof
Century Revue, The, 166
Century Theatre, 127, 134, 142, 146, 166, 182, 364
Century Theatre Roof, 161, 166, 174, 206, 211
Chamberlain, Neville, 329, 333, 335
Chamberlain Brown's Scrap Book, 296
Champion, Gower, 335, 365, 366
Chanfrau, Henry, 28
Channing, Carol, 366
"Chansonette," 208
Chaplin, Charlie, 73, 123, 132
Charig, Phil, 238, 246, 283, 291, 353
Charleston (dance), 219, 227-28, 234, 237, 246
Charlie (Pearl sidekick), 250
Charlot, Andre, 15, 16-17, 208-9, 272
Charlot revues, 208, 221, 229, 230
Charlot's Revue of 1926, 229
Charlotte (ice skater), 178
Charm School, The (play), 169
Charpentier (French boxer), 172
Chase, Ilka, 342
Chatelaine, Stella, 113, 117
Chatham Theater, 32
Chauve-Souris (1922), 181-82, 186, 193, 219, 220, 353
Chauve-Souris (1927), 248, 249
Chauve-Souris (1929), 259
Chauve-Souris (1943), 353
Chauve-Souris revue series, 284
"Cheerful Little Earful," 283
Cheer Up, 141
Chekhov, Anton, 181
Chester Hale Girls, 250, 251, 262, 264
Chevalier, Maurice, 373
Chicago Columbian Exposition, 58, 75
Chicago Musical College, 75
"Children of the Ritz," 333
Chinatown, 118
Chin-Chin, 119
"Chinese-American Rag," 162
Chodorov, Jerome, 367
Chopin, Frederic, 191
"Chop Stick Rag," 102
Christine, Lily, 368
Christy's Minstrels, 32, 33

Churchill, Stuart, 349
"Cigarettes, Cigars," 291
"Cinderella Brown," 275
Cinderella on Broadway, 166
"Civilization," 363
Claire, Ina, 53, 124, 125, 131, 145
Clarice, Mme., 98
Claridge Bar, 161
Clark, Bobby, 194, 220, 305, 317-18, 324, 335, 348, 350, 368
Clark and McCullough, 204, 305, 317
Clarke, Dorothy, 180
Clarke, Grant, 146, 165, 172
Clary, Robert, 370, 371
Clayton, Bessie, 66, 83, 92, 103, 108, 114-15
Clayton, Lew, 148
Cleary, Michael, 285, 296
Clorindy, or The Origin of the Cake Walk, 62-63
Club de Montmartre theater, 236
Cobb, Irvin S., 241
Cobb, Will, 81
Coca, Imogene, 15, 276, 291, 314-15, 317, 325, 330, 340-41, 357, 365
Cochran, Charles B., 15-16, 175, 208, 257-58, 272-74
Cochran, June, 222, 232
Cochran Girls, 257, 273
Cody, William (Buffalo Bill), 75
Cohan, George M., 77, 86, 91, 94, 121, 138, 145-46, 157, 159, 178, 219, 262-63, 270, 283
Cohan and Harris Minstrels, The, 94
Cohan Revue of 1916, The, 129-30
Cohan Revue of 1918, The, 145-46
Cohan revue series, 163, 201
Cohans act. *See* Four Cohans
Cohan Theatre. *See* George M. Cohan Theatre
Cohen, Alexander, 346, 353
Cole, Doris, 357
Cole, Jack, 352, 367
"College Boys, Dear" (production number), 139
College Girls, 94
Collier, William, 103, 121, 206, 244
Collins, Jose, 119, 199
Collyer, Dan, 42, 45

Colt, Ethel Barrymore, 293
Columbian Trio (act), 148
Columbia University Varsity Shows, 222
"Columbus and Isabella," 243
Comden, Betty, 255, 369-70
Comden and Green, 255, 369-70
"Come Down, Ma Evenin' Star," 103
"Come Hit Your Baby," 264
"Comes the Revolution!" (sketch), 301
Comic Supplement, The, 212
Commedia dell'arte, 26
Common Clay (Kinhead), 130
Compton, Betty, 238, 300
Comstock, Anthony, 24, 81
Comstock, F. Ray, 95, 122, 181
Comstock and Gest, 248
Concert Theatre, 346
Concert Varieties, 357
Connecticut Yankee, A, 9, 229
Connelly, Marc, 194, 212, 279, 284, 320
Connelly, Reg, 277
Connolly, Bobby, 312
Conrad, Con, 170, 204, 238
Conried, Heinrich, 81
Constitution Hall, 329-30
Continental Varieties, 316
Conversation Piece, 316
Conway, Curt, 346
Cook, Joe, 201, 344, 349
Cook, Joe, Jr., 349
Cook, Olga, 160
Cook, Will Marion, 63, 95
Coolidge, Calvin, 212, 214, 222, 254
Coots, J. Fred, 186, 219, 228, 229, 230, 232
Copacabana, 352, 353
Copley Theatre, 276
Cordelia's Aspirations, 45
Corey, Professor Irwin, 351
Corned Beef and Roses. See *Sweet and Low*
Coronet Theater, 362-3, 365, 368
Cort, John, 115
Cort Theatre, 239
Coslow, Sam, 219
Cosmo Vanities, 303
Costa, David, 36
Cotton Club, 252
Cotton Club revue (1927), 252

Coughlin, Charles, 318
"Countess Dubinsky," 313
Countess Maritza, 236
Courtneidge, Cicely, 230
Coward, Noel, 16-17, 209, 229, 257-58, 265, 271, 281, 284, 285, 286, 289, 291, 309, 316, 326, 333, 347, 349-50, 361, 373
Cowl, Jane, 131, 349
Cox, Wally, 368
Cradle Will Rock, The, 328
Craig, Helen, 325
Craig, Richy, Jr., 296
Craig's Wife (play), 240
Crawford, Clifton, 123
Crawford, Joan, 214, 309
Crazy with the Heat, 345
Creamer, Henry, 186
Creamer and Johnson, 248
Crichton, Kyle, 319
"Cricket and a Wonderful World," 320-21
"Crinoline Days," 193
Critic, The (Sheridan), 27
Crompton, Nanci, 372
Crooker, Earle, 285
Crouse, Russel, 326
Crumit, Frank, 167, 206
"Cuddle Up," 231
Cugat, Xaviar, 368
Cummings, Robert, 312
Cunningham, Arthur, 135
"Cup of Coffee, a Sandwich and You, A," 229
Cyranose de Bric-a-Bric, 66

D

"Daddy Has a Sweetheart (and Mother Is Her Name)," 106
Daily Mirror (newspaper), 241, 332
Daily News (newspaper), 242
Dairymaids, The, 83, 84
Dale, Sunny, 243
Daley, Cass, 324
Dali, Salvador, 355
Daly, Anna, 183
Daly, Augustin, 61
Daly's Theatre (London), 165

Daly's Theatre (New York), 61, 246
Damita, Lily, 304, 305
Dan Bryant's Minstrels, 33-34
"Dance Little Lady," 257
Dance Me a Song, 367-68
Dancing Ducks of Denmark, The, 75
Dancing Girls from the Empire Theatre, London, 85
"Dancing in the Dark," 288
"Dancin' to A Jungle Drum," 356
Dancrey, Anne, 114
Danse de Follies (nightclub), 126
Dan's Tribulations, 45
Darcel, Denise, 369
Dare, Danny, 260, 283, 344
Darewski, Herman, 162
"Darktown Poker Club," 117
Dassin, Jules, 372
Daughters of the American Revolution, 329
David, Lee, 245, 262, 264
David, Mack, 353
Davies, Marion, 129, 131-32, 142, 143, 145, 325
Davis, Benny, 139, 186, 206, 354
Davis, Bessie McCoy, 99, 101, 119, 142, 143, 158, 161, 293
Davis, Bette, 372
Davis, Eddie, 346
Davis, Jessie Bartlett, 58
Davis, Sammy, Jr., 373
Dawn, Hazel, 134, 206, 209-10, 232
Dazie, Mlle., 81, 86, 98, 122
de Angelis, Jefferson, 61, 83, 109, 139, 183
Dear Love. See *Artists and Models* (1930)
Death of a Salesman (Miller), 371
Death of Life in London, The, or Tom and Jerry's Funeral, 28
Debussy, Claude, 186
Decline and Fall of the Entire World as Seen Through the Eyes of Cole Porter, 374
De Cordova, Fred, 342
Deep, Deep Sea, The (Planche), 28
Deep Harlem, 257, 259
De Jacques, Eulallean. See Lorraine, Lillian

DeKoven, Reginald, 48, 57-58, 64, 76, 77
DeLange, Eddie, 278
Delf, Harry, 239
Delmar, Harry, 250
Delmar's Revels, 250
Delroy, Irene, 162, 247
deLuce, Virginia, 370
Deluge, The, 56
Delysia, Alice, 192-93, 208
DeMarcos, 350, 354
Demarest, William, 264, 292
DeMille, Agnes, 124, 302, 360
Dempsey, Jack, 172
Denny, Reginald, 160
Depew, Chauncey, 57, 81
Deppe, Lois, 253
Depression (1930s). See Great Depression
DeRose, Peter, 312, 313, 343
De Roze (magician), 316
Desert Song, The, 236, 360
Desire Under the Elms (O'Neill), 227, 240
Deslys, Gaby, 102, 114, 129
Desmond, Florence, 257
"Destiny" (production number), 218
DeSylva, B. G. (Buddy), 170, 172, 186, 188, 191, 198, 206, 213, 227, 294
DeSylva, Brown and Henderson, 227, 233, 254-55, 317
Deutsch, Janszieka and Rozsika. See Dolly Sisters
DeVries, Peter, 372
DeWolfe, Billy, 371, 372
Diamond, I. A. L., 367
"Diamond Horseshoe," 193
Dickson, Dorothy, 141
Diener, Joan, 365
Dietrich, Marlene, 373
Dietz, Howard, 244, 260, 261, 279, 286, 288, 302-3, 320-21, 326, 342, 364
"Digga Digga Doo," 252
Dillingham, Charles, 15, 102-4, 119-21, 127-28, 129, 130, 133, 134-35, 138, 140, 141, 142-44, 146, 150, 154, 159, 178, 185, 190, 205-6, 270, 277, 314, 315
"Dinah," 143

"Dining Out," 180
"Dinner for One" (sketch), 372
Ditrichsen, Leo, 115
Dixey, Henry, 53
Dixie to Broadway, 219-20, 252
Dixon, Harland, 129
Dixon, Mort, 283, 284, 295
Dixons (dance team), 294
Dockstader, Lew, 183
Dockstader's Minstrels, 98
Doc Rockwell, 264, 306, 355
Dodge, Roger Pryor, 283
Dodge Sisters, 262
Doing Our Bit, 142
"Doing the New York," 291
"Doing the Reactionary," 329
"Doin' the Chamberlain," 335
"Doin' the Gorilla" (dance), 246
"Doin' the Old Yahoo Step," 366
Dolin, Anton, 275, 355
Dolin, Gerald, 320
Dolly Sisters, 53, 99, 100, 103, 116, 121, 122, 130, 218
Dolores, (Ziegfeld beauty), 141, 142
Donahue, Jack, 165, 293
Donaldson, Walter, 193, 290
"Donkey Serenade, The," 208
Donlevy, Brian, 315-16
Donovan, Piggy, 154
"Don't Do the Charleston," 237
"Don't Send Me Back to Petrograd," 220
Dooley, Ray (female performer), 317
Dooley, Ray (slapstick female impersonator), 139, 147, 157, 165, 171, 172, 206, 213, 237, 256
Dooleys (act), 145
Doris Humphrey group, 304
Dos Passos, John, 191
Double Dublin, 373
"Doughnut Song, The," 161
Dova, Ben, 251
Dover Street to Dixie, 273
Dowling, Eddie, 156, 317-18
"Down By the Erie Canal," 121
"Down on the Farm," 189
Doyle, James, 129
"Do You Love Me?," 222
Dragonette, Jessica, 235
Drake, Alfred, 334, 340, 341, 342, 356

Drama Dept. (off-Broadway company), 310
Draper, Paul, 318, 346, 351
Draper, Ruth, 285
Dream Girl, The, 64
Dreiser, Theodore, 360
Dresser, Louise, 121
Dressler, Marie, 67, 74, 77, 108, 109, 169
"Drifting Along with the Tide," 173
"Drink," 356
Dr. Rockwell. *See* Doc Rockwell
Dr. Rockwell and Bobby Watson, 251
Dryden, John, 27
Dubin, Al, 229, 335, 342, 356
Duchamp, Marcel, 191
Dudley, Bide, 144
Duff-Gordon, Lady Lucille, 105, 120, 130, 132, 135, 158, 167
Dugan, William Francis, 240
Duggan, Thomas, 166
Duke, Vernon, 276, 291, 304, 305, 312, 313, 318, 323, 324, 326, 343, 372, 373
Du Maurier, George, 122-23
Dunbar, Dixie, 9, 316
Duncan, Isadora, 53
Duncan Sisters, 220, 325
Dundy, Elmer S., 78
Dunham, Katherine, 353, 357, 362
Durante, Jimmy, 306, 307, 326, 342
Duse, Eleanora, 53
"Dusky Debutantes," 330
"Dying Duck in a Thunderstorm, A," 174

E

Eagan, Jack, 141
Eagels, Jeanne, 206
Eagle Horse, Chief, 160
"Eagle Rock, The" (dance), 119
Earl Carroll beauties, 241
Earl Carroll Sketch Book, 319
Earl Carroll's Sketchbook, 263-64
Earl Carroll's Vanities of 1924, 38, 215, 216-17
Earl Carroll's Vanities of 1925, 228
Earl Carroll's Vanities of 1926, 239
Earl Carroll's Vanities of 1928, 256

Earl Carroll's Vanities of 1930, 277-78
Earl Carroll's Vanities of 1931, 292
Earl Carroll's Vanities of 1932, 303-4
Earl Carroll's Vanities of 1940, 341
Earl Carroll's Vanities series, 216, 217, 263, 304
Earl Carroll Theatre (first), 186, 228, 239, 241
Earl Carroll Theatre (second), 239, 246, 256, 292. *See also* Casino theatre (second)
"Easter Parade," 310
East Lynn (play), 274
Eastman, Max, 191
"East St. Louis Toodle-oo," 283
Eaton, Mary, 160, 165, 171, 184
Ebsen, Vilma and Buddy, 302, 312
Echo, The, 99, 154
Eddy, Nelson, 356
"Edinburgh Wriggle, The" (dance), 98
Edison, Thomas Alva, 41, 56
Edrington, William R., 199, 239, 241-42
Edwardes, George, 61-62, 165
Edwardes girls, 61
Edwards, Bobby (Robert), 158, 190
Edwards, Cliff (Ukelele Ike), 174, 248, 322
Edwards, Gus, 81, 86, 92, 96, 325
Edwards, Julian, 48
Edwards, Leo, 123
Edwards, Lou, 174
Ed Wynn Carnival, The, 163-64
Ed Wynn revue series, 164
Edyth Totten Theatre, 243
Egan, Pierce, 27
Egan, Raymond B., 150
"Eighteen Days Ago," 265
"Eight Notes," 180
"Eli Eli," 284
Eliscu, Edward, 274, 283, 284, 285, 344
Ellington, Duke, 252, 283, 357, 374
Ellis, Vivian, 230, 283
Elsie Janis and Her Gang (1919), 161, 181
Elsie Janis and Her Gang (1922), 180-81
Elsie Janis and Her Gang series, 186
Eltinge, Julian, 167, 192, 203
Emerson, John, 274
Emmett, Dan, 30-32
Empire State Building, 291, 294, 295

Empire Theatre, 85
Englander, Ludwig, 60-61, 63, 74, 83, 91
English Daisy, An, 83
E. P. Christy's Minstrels, 32, 33
"Ephraham," 101
Erlanger, Abe, 20, 71-72, 73, 78-80, 82, 84, 95, 96, 97, 99, 101, 103, 106, 112, 115, 116, 119, 122, 128-29, 130, 134, 173, 180, 230, 293, 296
Erlanger, Aline, 247
Erlanger's Theater, 72, 305. *See also* St. James Theater
Errol, Leon, 53, 99, 100-101, 103, 107, 112, 113, 117, 118, 124, 125, 126, 131, 134, 135, 140, 145, 146, 147, 180, 263
Erté (designer), 191, 207, 208
Escudero (dancer), 316
"Eskimo Blues, The," 235
"Esmeralda," 127
Ethiopian Serenaders, 32
Etting, Ruth, 247, 274, 290
Evangeline, 54-55, 57
Ever Green, 229
"Everybody Step," 180
Everybody's Welcome, 248
"Every Girlie Wants to Be a Sally," 170
"Everything in America Is Ragtime Crazy," 129
"Everywife" (sketch), 100
Everywoman (Browne), 100
"Evolution of Dancing, The" (production number), 109
"Ev'ry Time We Say Goodbye (I die a little)," 356
Ewell, Tom, 365
Ewing, Max, 254
"Exactly Like You," 275
Excelsior, 56
Eythe, William, 366

F

Fabray, Nanette, 344
"Fabric of Dreams" (production number), 206
"Face on the Dime, The," 361
Face the Music, 308
Fads and Fancies, 122

Fain, Sammy, 332, 334, 336, 343, 345, 367, 368
Fairbanks, Douglas, Jr., 309
Fairbanks, Douglas, Sr., 53, 309
Fairbanks, Madeline, 246
Fairbanks, Marian, 219
Fairbanks Twins, 147, 156, 169, 219, 235, 246
Fairchild, Edgar, 243
Fairchild and Rainger, 247
"Fairies at the Bottom of My Garden," 285
"Falling Off the Wagon," 301
Fall of Eve, The (play), 240
"Family Ford, The" (sketch), 165
Fanchon and Marco, 169-70
"Fancy Free" (ballet), 357
Fantastic Fricasee, A, 190
Farbares, Nanette (Nanette Fabray), 344
"Farljandio" (ballet), 185
Farrar, Geraldine, 102, 131
Farrar, Tony, 351
Fashions of 1924, 201
"Fatal Glass of Beer, The" (film short), 256
Fay, Frank, 148, 182, 186, 203, 250, 307, 353
Faye, Alice, 294
Faye, Joey, 362
Fears, Peggy, 215, 237, 243
Federal Theatre Project, 325, 328, 334, 335
Fetter, Ted, 276, 326
"Feudin' and Fightin'," 356
Fiddle-Dee-Dee, 66
Field, Cyrus W., 57
Fielding, Henry, 27
Fields, Benny, 189, 251, 354
Fields, Dorothy, 252, 275, 281, 282, 291, 306
Fields, Gracie, 347
Fields, Herbert, 142, 222, 273
Fields, Lew, 64, 65, 66-67, 77, 83, 90, 108, 115, 142, 170, 222, 252, 282
Fields, W. C., 53, 57, 121, 124, 125, 131, 140, 147, 156, 160, 162, 165, 171, 184, 188, 198, 212, 213, 256, 349
Fifty Miles from Boston, 86
Fillmore, Millard, 32

Financial Times (newspaper), 266
Finck, Herman, 129
Fine, Sylvia, 340
Finklehoffe, Fred, 350, 353
Fioretta, 263
Fireman Mose, 28
Fischer, Clifford C., 341, 346-47, 350
Fisher, Eddie, 373
Fiske, Mrs., 71, 254, 293
Fitzgerald, F. Scott, 187, 191
Fitzgerald, Zelda, 191
Fitzgibbon, Dorothy, 285
"Five A.M." (ballet), 323
Flaherty, Robert, 290
Flaming Youth, 187, 228
Fledermaus, Die, 102
Flippen, Jay C., 232, 245, 279, 354
"Florida Mammy," 229
Florodora, 62, 75
"Florodora Slide" (dance), 115
Fluffy Ruffles, 91
Flying Colors, 302-3, 305
Fokina, Vera, 178
Fokine, Michel, 178, 185, 237
Folies Bergere (Fischer U.S. production), 341, 346
Folies Bergere (Paris), 80, 114, 210, 262
Follies Bergere theater (New York). *See* Fulton Theatre
Follies of 1907, 80-82, 84, 85
Follies of 1908, 86-87
Follies of 1909, 92-94
Follies of 1910, 94-96. See also *Ziegfeld Follies*
"Follies of the Day" (newspaper column), 80
Follies of the Year, 80
"Follow On," 143
Fonda, Henry, 314
Fontanne, Lynn, 309, 350
Fools Rush In, 317
Forbes, Brenda, 341
Forbes, Peggy, 116-17
Forbidden Broadway series, 227
Ford, Corey, 302
Forde, Hal, 122, 218, 308
"For de Lord's Sake, Play a Waltz," 102
Ford Theatre, 32
"Forgive Us Odets," 330

Forrest Theatre, 315
"42nd Street's Gods, K. and E. and Jake and Lee," 130
44th Street Roof Theater. *See* Nora Bayes Theatre
44th Street Theatre, 108, 115, 159, 162, 284, 301, 345, 346
Forty-Five Minutes from Broadway, 77, 86
46th Street Theatre, 229, 278, 282, 331
48th Street Theater, 187, 322
49ers, The, 194, 208, 210
49th Street Theatre, 182, 220
For Your Pleasure, 351-52
Fosse, Bob, 367, 368
Foster, Stephen, 33
Foster Girls, 232, 264
Four Cohans, 43, 52, 73, 77 492, 58
Fox, George Lafayette, 55
Fox, Harry, 122, 129
Foy, Eddie, 53, 74, 97, 102
Foy, Eddie, Jr., 320
Foys act (Seven Little Foys), 73
Francis, Arthur. *See* Gershwin, Ira
Francisquay, Mlle., 30
Frank Fay's Fables, 182
Franklin, Harold B., 316
Franklin, Irene, 139, 174
Franklin, Malvin, 170
"Franklin D. Roosevelt Jones," 332
"Fraught," 351
Frawley, Paul, 180
Fred Waring's Glee Club, 356
Freed, Arthur, 167
Freedley, Vinton, 213
Freedman, David, 312, 315, 322, 323, 326
Freischutz, Der (Weber opera), 34
French, Harold, 230
French lesson sketch, 322
French Twin Sisters, 42
Friedlander, William B., 161
Friedman, Charles, 328, 332
Friend, Cliff, 169, 265
Friganza, Trixie, 104, 127, 264
Friml, Rudolph, 115, 172, 208, 222, 231, 236, 274
Frisco, Joe, 147, 163, 193, 256
Frivolities of 1920, 161-62

Frohman, Charles, 71, 73, 83, 138
"Frolicking Gods" (ballet), 185
Frolic Theater, 72
Froman, Jane, 312, 313, 342, 347, 354
"From the Plaza to Madison Square," 170
From the Second City, 373
From Vienna, 342
Front Page, The (play), 261-62
Fuller, Rosalind, 175
Fulton Theatre, 72, 101, 146, 182, 315, 319
"Fun to Be Fooled," 316
Furber, Douglas, 209
Furst, William, 63
Furth, Seymour, 81, 90
Fyleman, Rose, 285

G

Gaiety Girl, A, 61-62, 74, 75, 118
Gaiety Theater (New York), 72, 180
Gaiety Theatre (London), 62, 165
Gaines, Muriel, 362
Gallagher, Helen, 367
Gallagher and Shean, 185, 219
"Galli-Curci Rag, The" (dance), 148
Gandhi, Mahatma, 309
Garbo, Greta, 301
"Garden of Eden," 188
"Garden of Kama, The," 203
Garden of Paradise, The (Sheldon), 123
"Garden of Your Dreams, The," 147
Gardiner, Reginald, 320, 326, 327
Garland, Judy, 373
Garr, Eddie, 307
Garrett, Betty, 346, 351, 356, 361
Garrick Gaieties of 1925, The, 276-77
Garrick Gaieties of 1926, The, 232
Garrick Gaieties of 1930, The, 275-77
Garrick Gaieties series, 202, 221-23, 238, 276, 313, 328
Garrick Theater, 45, 86, 182, 221, 232
Gaston, Billy, 81
Gates, "Bet-a-Million," 78
"Gates of Elysium" (production number), 124
Gaxton, William, 346
Gay, John, 27

Gay, Maisie, 257
Gaynor, Charles, 366
Gay Paree (1925), 228-29, 230, 240
Gay Paree (1926), 240
Gay White Way, The, 82-83
Gear, Luella, 315, 335, 345
Geer, Will, 332
Genee, Adelaide, 85, 119
Gennaro, Marilyn, 368
Gensler, Lewis, 170, 301
"Gentlemen Prefer Blondes," 237
Gentlemen Prefer Blondes, 200, 243, 366
George, Grace, 53
George, Yvonne, 191
George M. Cohan Theatre, 161, 166, 180, 291
"Georgette," 191
George Washington Jr., 77
George White's Music Hall Varieties, 304-5
George White's Scandals of 1922, 187-88, 189
George White's Scandals of 1923, 198
George White's Scandals of 1924, 213-14
George White's Scandals of 1925, 227-28, 238
George White's Scandals of 1926, 233-35, 294
George White's Scandals of 1928, 254-56
George White's Scandals of 1929, 265-67
George White's Scandals of 1931, 293-94
George White's Scandals of 1936, 321-22
George White's Scandals of 1939-1940, 336
George White's Scandals series, 9, 38, 113, 187, 188, 201, 207, 218, 238, 255, 293, 304, 322, 374. See also *Scandals of...*
Gerber, Alex, 170
Gerry, Elbridge, 49
Gerry Society, 49, 52-53
Gershwin, Frankie, 257
Gershwin, George, 133, 147, 161, 164, 170, 173, 186, 187-88, 198, 205, 206, 213, 220, 222, 227, 231, 238, 257, 261, 264, 274, 284, 310, 326, 327, 334, 355
Gershwin, Ira, 188, 206, 213, 231, 238, 257, 274, 276, 283, 291, 310, 315, 316, 322, 324, 326, 327, 355

Gertrude Hoffman Girls, 228, 230-31
Gest, Morris, 161, 181, 193, 258-59, 294-95, 353
"Get Happy," 274
Get Together, 178
Geva, Tamara, 280-81, 302, 305
Ghostley, Alice, 370, 371
Gibson, Madeline, 257
Gibson Bathing Girls, 81, 82
Gideon, Melville J., 102, 250
Gielgud, John, 327
Gilbert, W. S., 42, 44, 48, 109
Gilbert and Sullivan, 356
"Gilding the Guild," 222
Gilford, Jack, 344, 367
Gillette, William, 38, 65
Gingold, Hermione, 371, 372
Girl Friend, The, 232
Girl from Utah, The, 130
"Girlies Are Out of My Life," 128
"Girl Is You and The Boy Is Me, The," 234-35
"Girl on the Magazine Cover, The," 129
"Girls of My Dreams" (production number), 165
"Girls of the Season" (production number), 214
"Girl's Trousseau, A" (production number), 130
Girofle-Girofla, 58
"Give Us a Viva," 351
Glad, Gladys, 290
Glad Hand, The, or Secret Servants, 65
"Gladiola Girl, The" (production number), 366
Glance at New York in 1848, A, 28
Glaspell, Susan, 191
Gleason, Jackie, 354
Glickman, Will, 367
Glimpse of the Great White Way, A, 108, 115
Glinka, Mikhail, 181
Globe Theatre (London), 26
Globe Theatre (New York), 102, 121, 129, 147, 148, 164, 171, 198, 237
Glorifying the American Girl (film), 293
"Glory of Sunshine," 229
"Goblins," 98
Goddard, Paulette, 237

Godfrey, John, 144
Goetz, E. Ray, 81, 84, 92, 127, 140, 145, 162, 170, 198
"Goin' Home Train," 360
Goldberg, Rube, 265
Golden, John, 102, 133, 141
Golden, Ray, 344, 367
Golden Gate Quartette, 352
Golden Theater, 250
"Gold, Silver and Green," 214
Goldwyn, Sam, 214
"Goodbye Becky Cohen," 95
"Goodbye Broadway, Hello France!," 139
"Goodbye to Dear Old Alaska," 191-92
Goodman, Alfred, 166, 192, 208, 229
Goodman, Benny, 355
"Goodnight Sweetheart," 277, 292
"Good Old-Fashioned Cakewalk" (dance), 115
Goodspeed Opera House, 10
Goodwin, J. Cheever, 54
Goodwin, Nat, 44
Gordon, Mack, 289, 291, 294
Gordon, Max, 11, 279-81, 286, 302-3, 332
Gordon, Waxey, 306
"Gorilla Girl," 367
Gorney, Jay, 218, 244, 264, 277, 291, 304, 344, 367
Gould, Jay, 170
Gould, Morton, 357
Grab Bag, The, 219
Grable, Betty, 307
Gracella and Theodore, 274
Grady, Al, 128
Graham, Irvin, 325
Graham, June, 368
Graham, Martha, 203, 204, 251, 306
Graham, Ronny, 370, 371
Graham, Sheila, 257
Grand, Murray, 370-71
Grand Central Station, 100, 134
"Grand Opera Ball, The" (production number), 189
Grand Opera House, 55, 61, 104
Grand Street Follies, The (1924), 211, 212, 221
Grand Street Follies, The (1925), 227
Grand Street Follies, The (1926), 235-36

Grand Street Follies, The (1928), 253-54
Grand Street Follies, The (1929), 261-62
Grand Street Follies series, 262
Granlund, Nils T. (NTG), 331
Grant, Bert, 166
Granville, Bernard, 107, 108, 119, 124, 125, 131, 161, 182, 201
Grattan, Harry, 140
Gray, Dolores, 355, 370
Gray, Gilda, 159, 170, 193
Gray, Lawrence, 295
Gray, Thomas J., 127
Grease, 17
"Great Dane A'Comin'," 367
Great Depression (1930s), 194, 261, 272, 275, 282, 289, 291, 292, 294, 302, 304, 306, 308, 313, 318, 324-25, 333, 354
"Greatest Battle Song of All, The," 128
Great God Brown, The (O'Neill), 237-38
Great Sandow, The, 75-76, 85
Great Temptations, 232
"Great Warburton Mystery, The" (sketch), 286-87
Green, Adolph, 255, 369-70
Green, Eddie, 296
Green, Howard, 222
Green, Johnny, 279
Green, Mitzi, 351
Green, Stanley, 333
Green, Sylvan, 321
Greenbank, Harry, 62
Green Bay Tree, The (play), 314
Green Mansions (resort), 328
Green Pastures (play), 281
Greenwich Village Follies, The, 158-59, 160
Greenwich Village Follies of 1920, The, 167-68, 264
Greenwich Village Follies of 1921, The, 174-75
Greenwich Village Follies of 1922, The, 190-92, 372
Greenwich Village Follies of 1924, The, 167, 203-4, 217-18, 230
Greenwich Village Follies of 1925, The, 229-30
Greenwich Village Follies of 1928, The, 251

Greenwich Village Follies series, 175, 190, 201, 230
Greenwich Village Nights. See *Greenwich Village Follies, The*
Greenwich Village Theatre, 158, 168, 190, 231
Greenwood, Charlotte, 104, 114-15, 193, 218, 243, 246
Greer, Jesse, 245, 250
Gregg, Norma, 248
Gregory, Lady, 293
Greneker, Claude, 214
Gresham, Herbert, 84, 86
Gresheimer, Frederick, 105-6
Grey, Clifford, 171, 209, 219, 230, 232, 233
Grey, William A., 239
Gribble, Harry Wagstaff, 203, 208
Grofé, Ferde, 188
Groody, Helen, 182
Gropper, William, 191
Gross, Milt, 344
Group Theatre, 297, 318
"Guess Who I Saw Today?," 370-71
Guild Theater, 275-76
Guinan, Texas, 115, 216, 245, 315
Gunther, John, 364
Gus Hill's Stars, 65
Gynt, Kaj, 246
Gypsy Baron, The, 360
"Gypsy Days" (production number), 258

H

Haaber, Louis, 334
Haakon, Paul, 320, 321, 326
"H-A-Double R-I-G-A-N," 86
Haenschen, Walter, 235
Haggin, Ben Ali, 141, 156, 165, 171, 203, 213, 242
Hague, Albert, 367
Haig, Emma, 143
Haile Selassie, 322
Hairy Ape, The (O'Neill), 182, 192
Hale, Binnie, 257
Hale, Chester, 218
Hale, Sonnie, 257, 273, 274
Hale Girls. See Chester Hale Girls
Haley, Jack, 229, 240, 350, 364

"Half-Caste Woman," 291
Hall, Adelaide, 252-53
Hall, Bettina, 260
Hall, Billy, 312
Hall, Owen, 62
Hall Johnson Choir, 357
Hallor, Edith, 140
Halperin, Nan, 186
Hamill, Stuart, 237
Hamilton, Morris, 239, 285
Hamilton, Nancy, 314, 333-34, 341-42, 360-61
Hamlet (Shakespeare), 26, 122, 367
Hammerstein, Arthur, 115, 206, 277
Hammerstein, Oscar, 70, 71, 72-73, 74, 81, 93, 97, 106, 115
Hammerstein, Oscar II, 272. See also Rodgers and Hammerstein
Hammerstein's 9 O'Clock Revue, 206
Hammond, Percy, 108, 262, 291, 303
Hands Up, 126, 127
Handy, W.C., 284
Hanemann, H.W., 274
Hanley, Ellen, 372
Hanley, James F., 172, 186, 213, 318
Happy Days, 159
"Happy in Love," 345
Happy Prince, The (Wilde), 218
Harbach, Otto, 115
"Harbor of Prosperity, The" (production number), 189
Harburg, E. Y., 264, 276, 277, 289, 291, 301, 304, 305, 312, 313, 315, 316, 326, 327, 328, 357
Harkrider, John, 237
Harlem Cavalcade, 347
Harlem Dancers, 256-57
"Harlem on My Mind," 310
Harlem Opera House, 61
Harling, Frank, 218
Harlowe, Richard, 58
"Harmony Boys from Demagogue Lane, The," 330
Harnick, Sheldon, 371
Harper, William, 132
Harper's Bazaar (magazine), 191
Harrigan, Ned, 39, 44-45, 57, 64
Harrington, Pat, 348
Harrigan and Hart, 39, 55, 64, 65, 77, 91

Harrigan Theater. *See* Garrick Theater
Harris, Henry, 101
Harris, Sam H., 138, 146, 178-80, 193-94, 262-63, 308
Harrison, Alfred, 141
Hart, Lorenz, 9, 133, 221-23, 276. *See also* Rodgers and Hart
Hart, Margie, 350
Hart, Moss, 308-10, 326, 327, 332, 343, 355, 364
Hart, Teddy, 314
Hart, Tony, 39, 44-45, 64
Hart, William S., 213
Hartman, Paul and Grace, 301, 346, 347, 362-3, 368
Hartnell, Norman, 257
Harvey, J. Clarence, 83, 105
Harvey, Morris, 206
Hassard Short's Ritz Revue, 218-19
Hats Off to Ice, 354
"Haunted Heart," 364
Havez, Jean, 96
Hawley, Joyce, 241-42
Hay, Mary, 162
Haydn, Richard, 341
Hayman, Al, 71
Haywood, Billie, 315
Haywood, Donald, 246, 296
Hayworth, Rita, 204
Hazzard, Jack, 191-92, 291
Healey, Eunice, 318
Healy, Betty, 243
Healy, Ted, 228, 243, 262, 284
Hearn, Lew, 258
Hearst, William Randolph, 66, 132, 242, 325
Heatherton, Ray, 276
"Heat Wave," 310
Hecht, Ben, 191, 355
Hecksher Theatre, 231
Hector's Dogs, 347
"He Hasn't a Thing Except Me," 324
Hein, Silvio, 81, 183
Held, Anna, 67, 75, 76-77, 80, 86, 91, 92, 96, 105, 115, 116, 157, 204
Helene and Howard, 10
Hellinger, Mark, 289
Hello Broadway, 121
"Hello Frisco Hello," 125

"Hello Hello Hello," 184
Hello, Paris, 101
Hellzapoppin, 331-32, 345, 352
Helter-Skelter, 66
Henderson, Ray, 191, 227, 294, 306, 321, 352
Henie, Sonja, 343
Henry, Grace, 239, 285
Henry's Harem (play), 240
Hepburn, Katharine, 314
Herald Square Theater, 74, 76, 83
Herbert, Victor, 48, 63-64, 77, 80, 91, 97, 109, 119, 131, 135, 141, 142-43, 144, 156, 164, 165, 172, 184-85, 207-8, 213, 274, 284, 360
"Here Comes the Yanks with the Tanks," 147
Herendeen, Frederick, 321
Herndon, Richard, 238
Hertz, Ralph, 116
Herzog, Arthur, 231
Hess, Cliff, 146
Heyman, Edward, 279, 312, 313
Hey Nonny Nonny, 296
"Hey There, High Hat," 317
Heyward, Dubose, 253
Hiawatha, or Ardent Spirits and Laughing Water, 29
Hickman, Art, 166
Hicks, Sue, 305
Higgledy-Piggledy, 67, 77, 80
Hilarities, 365
Hildegarde, 346
Hill, Billy, 313
Hill, J. Leubrie, 123
Hilliard, Bob, 363
Hip! Hip! Hooray!, 83
Hip-Hip Hooray, 128
Hippodrome (theater), 77-78, 80, 85, 90-91, 94, 97, 101, 119, 122, 123, 127, 128, 133, 141, 159, 178, 185, 189-90, 203, 266, 321, 344
Hirsch, Louis A., 85, 90, 101, 104, 123, 126, 131, 147, 184, 185, 191, 204
Hitchcock, Raymond, 53, 139-40, 145, 146-47, 160, 168, 171, 185-86, 218
Hitchy-Koo of 1917, 139-40
Hitchy-Koo of 1918, 146-47

Hitchy-Koo of 1919, 160
Hitchy-Koo of 1920, 168
Hitchy-Koo series, 185
Hitler, Adolph, 320, 333, 334, 340
Hit-the-Trail-Holliday (Cohan), 130
HMS Pinafore (operetta), 100
"HMS Vaudeville" (sketch), 100
Hobart, George V., 99, 112, 113
Hoctor, Harriet, 323
Hoey, Evelyn, 282, 305-6
Hoffa, Portland, 192, 260
Hoffman, Gertrude, 81, 108-9
"Hogan's Alley," 244
Hoity-Toity, 66
Hokey-Pokey, 103
"Hold 'Em Joe," 372
Holiner, Mann, 240, 284
Holland Tunnel, 86
Holloway, Stanley, 373
Holloway, Sterling, 222, 232, 276
Holman, Libby, 222, 244, 258, 260, 261, 279
Holtz, Lou, 128, 164, 173, 317, 346, 354
"Home, Sweet, Home," 141
"Home to Harlem," 306-7
Hooley's Minstrels, 32
Hooray for What!, 328
Hoover, Herbert, 308-9, 327
Hoover, Lou, 308-9
Hope, Bob, 53, 301, 323, 324, 326
Hopkins, Peggy. *See* Joyce, Peggy Hopkins
Hopper, DeWolf, 66, 139, 170, 183, 306
"Hoppy Poppy Girl," 162
Horne, Lena, 334, 373
Horwitt, Arnold B., 361, 363, 364
Hot-Cha, 293, 306
Hot Chocolates, 263
Hotel McAlpin, 112
Hotel Topsy Turvy, 74
"Hot, Hot Honey," 243
Hot Mikado, The, 348
Hot Rhythm, 278
Houdini, Harry, 73
"House I Live In, The," 351
"How About a Cheer for the Navy?," 349
Howard, Eugene, 104, 105, 255, 301
Howard, Joe E., 80
Howard, Leslie, 327

Howard, Tom, 203, 315
Howard, Willie, 104-5, 123, 134, 255, 294, 301, 313, 345, 346
Howard, Willie and Eugene, 53, 104, 115, 122, 134, 148, 169, 192, 193, 194, 233, 254, 266-67, 293, 294, 301, 305, 312, 322, 327, 336
"How High the Moon," 342
Howland, Jobyna, 105
"How's Chances?," 310
Howard Athenaeum theater, 48, 49
"How'd You Like to Be My Bow-wow-wow?," 85
Hoyt, Charles, 76
Hubbell, Raymond, 99, 103, 107, 112, 113, 122, 128, 133, 141, 146, 147, 189, 206, 213
Hudson Theater, 263, 334
Huey, Richard, 332
Huffman, J.C., 202, 208, 214, 230, 251
Hughes, Charles Evans, 132
Hulburt, Jack, 230
Humphrey, Moses, 28
Humpty Dumpty, 55
Humpty Dumpty Abroad, 55
Humpty Dumpty at Home, 55
Humpty Dumpty at School, 55
Humpty Dumpty in Every Clime, 55
Hupfeld, Herman, 232, 248, 279, 285, 304, 305, 326, 367
Hurly-Burly, 66
Hurok, Sol, 353
Hussey, James, 174
Huston, Josephine, 316
Huston, Walter, 168
Hutchins, Brice (Robert Cummings), 312
Hutton, Barbara, 310
Hutton, Betty, 341-42
Hutton, Ina Ray, 312
Hyde & Behman's theater, 48, 49
Hyland, Lily, 227, 235, 254
Hyson, Carl, 141

I

"I Am Only Human After All," 276
"I Can't Get Started," 324
"I Can't Give You Anything But Love, Baby," 253

"I Can't Give You Anything But Love, Lindy," 253
Icetime, 362
Ice Witch, The (play), 30
"I Could Go Home to a Girlie Like You," 128
"I Could Love a Million Girls," 79
"I'd Love to Waltz Through Life with You" (production number), 208
"I Donno What, The" (production number), 170
"I Do Not Care for Women Who Wear Stays," 158
I'd Rather Be Right, 328
"If a Table at Rector's Could Talk," 113
"If Men Played Cards As Women Do" (sketch), 205
"I Found a Four Leaf Clover," 188
"I Found a Million Dollar Baby (in a Five and Ten Cent Store)," 284
"If You Hadn't, But You Did," 370
"I Got a Right to Sing the Blues," 303
"I Guess I'll Have to Change My Plan," 261
"I Left My Heart at the Stage Door Canteen," 349
"I Like the Likes of You," 313
"I'll Lend You Everything I've Got Except My Wife," 96
I'll Say She Is, 210, 212
"I'll Sell You a Girl," 158
Illustrators' Show, The, 322
"I Love a Parade," 305
"I Love a Piano" (production number), 129
"I Love to Dance When I Hear a March," 219
"I'm a Crazy Daffydill," 101
"I'm a Dancing Teacher Now," 120
"I'm a Dumbbell," 180
"I'm a Gigolo," 273
"I'm an Anesthetic Dancer," 160
I Married an Angel, 332
"I Married a Republican," 332
"I'm a Vamp from East Broadway," 165
"I May Be Gone for a Long, Long Time," 140
"I May Be Wrong (But I Think You're Wonderful)," 265

"I'm Forever Blowing Bubbles," 160
"I'm Getting Tired So I Can Sleep," 349
"I'm Gonna Pin My Medal on the Girl I Left Behind," 147
"I'm in Love Again," 218, 230
"I'm in Love with Miss Logan," 371
Imperial Music Hall, 65
Imperial Theater, 295, 302, 372
"I'm the Hostess of a Bum Cabaret," 158
"I Must Have That Man," 252-53
"In Chi Chi Castenango," 344
Ingram, Rex, 332
"In Marbled Halls," 280-81
Innocent Eyes, 210
"In Our Teeny Little Weeny Nest," 366
Inside U.S.A. (Gunther), 364
Inside U.S.A. (revue), 10, 364
International Cup, The Ballet of Niagara and the Earthquake, The, 97
International Ladies Garment Workers Union (ILGWU), 328, 333
International Revue, The, 275
International Theater, 356
"International Vamp," 243
"Interplay" (ballet), 357
"In the Good Old Summertime," 143
In Town, 62
Investigation, 45
Invisible Brazilian Fish, 75
"I Oughtn't to Auto Anymore," 81
Irving, George, 361, 372
Irving, Washington, 38
Irwin, Charles, 258
Irwin, Flo, 293
Irwin, May, 53
Irwin, William (Will), 261, 283, 326, 345
"Isabella," 58
"Island in the West Indies," 324
"Isle D'Amour," 199
"It All Belongs to Me," 247
It Happens on Ice, 343-44
Itow, Michio, 186
"It's a Mighty Fine Country We Have Here," 346
"It's Getting Awful Dark on Old Broadway" (production number), 185
"It's Great to Be Alive," 306
"It's Moving Day Down in Jungle Town," 93

"I've Been to a Marvelous Party," 333
"I've Got to Get Hot," 322
Ives, Burl, 350, 356
"I Want a Daddy Long-Legs," 193
"I Want a Daddy Who Will Rock Me to Sleep," 158
"I Was a Florodora Baby," 165
"I Wish I Really Weren't, But I Am," 76
"I Wonder What's the Matter with My Eyes," 91
Ixion (Burnand), 37

J

Jack Cole Dancers, 346, 367
Jackson, Arthur, 155, 164, 173, 206
Jackson, Ethel, 84
Jackson, Joe, 122
Jackson, Tony, 128
Jacques Brel Is Alive and Well and Living in Paris, 373
Jaffe, Moe, 262
James, Paul (James Warburg), 261, 274, 276
Janet Sisters, 170
Janis, Elsie, 52, 53, 102, 135, 161, 180-81, 211, 221, 314
Janssen, Werner, 239
Jardin de Paris (roof theater), 79-80, 82, 83, 86, 92, 93, 95, 96, 101, 104, 112
Jarrett, Henry C., 35
Jazz Age, 187, 236, 241, 300
Jazzbow Girls, 247
"Jazz-Ma-Tazz," 147
Jazz Singer, The, 249
Jeans, Ronald, 229, 265
Jefferson, Joseph, 71, 273
Jefferson, Thomas, 327
Jerome, William, 81, 97, 108
"Jesse James Glide," 121
Jessel, George, 159, 195, 249, 282, 284, 350
Jessel, Leon, 181
"Jigaree, The" (dance), 128
Jinks, 115
John, Graham, 218, 230
John Murray Anderson's Almanac, 371-2
John Murray Anderson's Artists and Models, 38

Johns, Brooke, 207
Johnson, Albert, 286, 288, 308, 315
Johnson, Eddie, 344
Johnson, Haven, 315
Johnson, Hugh, 318
Johnson, Jimmy, 227, 259, 263
Johnson, Nunnally, 291
Johnson, Van, 325
Johnston, Arthur, 219
Johnstone, Justine, 120, 124, 129, 131-32, 144-45
Johnstone, Tom, 161, 210
Johnstone, Will B., 210, 274
Jolson, Al, 39, 53, 98, 168, 173, 192, 214, 249, 290
Jolson Theater, 183
Jones, Martin, 325
Jones, Sydney, 62
Jordan, Joe, 95, 258
Joyce, Carol, 231
Joyce, James, 316
Joyce, Peggy Hopkins, 142, 200, 201, 241
Joy Spreader, The (jazz opera), 222
Jubilee, 321
Judels, Charles, 107
"Ju-Jitsu Waltz," 81
Juke Box Saturday Night, 350
"Julia, Donald and Joe," 130
Jumbo, 133
"Jungle Jingle," 247
Justine Johnstone Girls, 144

K

Kahal, Irving, 345
Kahn, E. J., Jr., 39
Kahn, Gus, 128, 193
Kahn, Otto, 163, 233, 315
Kahn, Roger Wolfe, 257, 274
Kalmar, Bert, 164-65
Kalmar and Ruby, 169, 191, 206
Kane, Helen, 243
Karnilova, Maria, 372
Katherine Dunham Dancers, 357, 362
Katzel, William R., 367
Kaufman, George S., 57, 194, 205, 212, 260-61, 272, 286, 302-3, 326, 332
Kaufman, Harry, 340
Kaufman, S. Jay, 212

Kaufman and Hart, 343
Kay, Beatrice, 321
Kaye, Danny, 340-41
Kean, Betty, 304, 345
Keaton, Buster, 52-53
Keatons act. *See* Three Keatons
Keep 'Em Laughing, 347
Keep It Clean, 263
Keep Kool, 212
Keep Moving, 315
Keep Off the Grass, 342
Keep Shufflin', 263
"Keep the Home Fires Burning," 261
Keith, Benjamin Franklin, 48, 49-52, 53, 160
Keith-Albee circuit, 190
Keith's circuit, 51-52, 71, 134, 168
Kellerman, Annette, 124
Kellette, John W., 160
Kellogg, Shirley, 104
Kelly, Aethel Amorita, 119
Kelly, Al, 365
Kelly, Gene, 334
Kelly, George, 248
Kelly, Grace, 248
Kelly, Harry C., 92, 121, 135, 142, 143
Kelly, Kitty, 180
Kelly, Patsy, 264, 277, 302
Kelly, Paul, 274
Kelly, Walter C., 115-16, 134
Kenbrovin, Jean, 160
Kennedy, James, 321
Kent, Charlotte, 283
Kept (play), 240
Kerker, Gustave, 48, 63, 183
Kern, Jerome, 83, 91, 98, 99, 101, 109, 122, 130, 131, 141, 142-43, 144, 168, 171, 205, 220, 231, 238, 264, 292, 310, 328, 360, 374
Kerr, Geoffrey, 274
Kerr, Jean, 367
Kerr, Walter, 356, 367
Keystone Kops, 217
Kid Boots, 207
King, Allyn, 130, 140, 156, 160, 162
King, Charles, 90, 114, 121, 142
Kingsley, Sidney, 308
"King's New Suit of Clothes, The" (Andersen), 194

King Zany, 165
Kinhead, Cleves, 130
Kipling, Rudyard, 44
Kiralfy Brothers, 55-56, 57
Kirke, Hazel, 108
Kirkwood, James, 368
"Kiss Me Again," 143
Kiss Me, Kate, 356, 366
Kitt, Eartha, 370
Klaw, Marc, 20, 71-72, 73, 78-80, 82, 84, 92, 96, 97, 99, 101, 103, 119, 122, 128-29, 130, 134, 173
Klaw Theatre, 244
Klein, Manuel, 123, 127
Klein, Willie, 116-17
Knapp, Dorothy, 200, 201, 207, 216, 239
Knickerbocker Theatre, 122, 258
Knight, Fuzzy, 258
Koehler, Ted, 274, 278, 303, 304, 305
Kollmar, Richard, 345
Kosloff, Theodore, 123
Koster and Bial's vaudeville house, 74
Krazner, Kurt, 345
Kuhn, Fritz, 330
Ku Klux Klan, 220
Kuller, Sid, 344

L

Labor Theatre, 328
Ladd, Hank, 363
Ladies and Gentlemen, Jerome Kern, 374
"Ladies and Gentlemen, That's Love," 294
Ladies of Leisure (film), 307
Lady Alone (play), 241
Lady Be Good!, 174, 213, 248, 288
"Lady Fair," 208
Lady in the Dark, 343
"Lady of the Evening," 193
"Lady of the Lantern" (production number), 208
"Lady of the Snow," 230
Lady Windermere's Fan (Wilde), 58
Laffing Room Only, 356
LaGuardia, Fiorello, 316, 341, 348
Lahr, Bert, 53, 293, 304, 305, 315, 316, 322, 326, 327, 355, 356, 370
Lait, Jack, 186
Lambert, Edward J., 320

Lamberti, Professor, 341, 348
Lamb's Club, 278
"Lamplight," 315
"Land of Broken Dreams," 243
"Land of Mystery, The," 189
Land of Nod, The, 80
"Land Where the Good Songs Go" (production number), 142, 143
Lane, Burton, 277, 285, 292, 304, 356
Lang, Harold, 360
Lang, Pearl, 367
Langtry, Lillie, 53, 54
Lanin, Paul, 248
Lardner, Ring, 141, 185, 188, 194, 274, 315
LaRocca, Nick, 241
La Rue, Grace, 81
LaRue, Grace, 193, 251
Lasky, Jesse, 53, 101
"Last Roundup, The," 313
LaSueur, Lucille. *See* Crawford, Joan
Laugh Parade, The, 295
Laugh Time, 353
Laugh, Town, Laugh, 347
Laun, Louis, 365
Laurell, Kay, 124, 147
Laurence, Paul, 63
Laurence, Paula, 334
La Verre, Madelon, 166
Lawrence, Carol, 370
Lawrence, Gertrude, 209, 229, 275
Layton, Turner, 186
Lean, Cecil, 143, 210
Lecocq, Alexandre, 294
Lederer, George, 60
Lee, Gypsy Rose, 324, 335, 348, 350
Lee, Lester, 250
Lee, Sammy, 295
Leedom, Edna, 207
Leeds, Phil, 346296
Le Gallienne, Eva, 161, 181, 211
"Legend of the Cyclamen Tree, The," 171
"Legend of the Drums, The" (production number), 207
"Legend of the Pearls, The," 180
"Leg of Nations, The" (production number), 165
Lehac, Ned, 274, 285
Lehar, Franz, 84, 109, 229
Lehman, Herbert, 254

Lehmann, Liza, 285
Leiber and Stoller, 374
Lend an Ear, 366
Leonard, Benny, 149
Leonard, Helen Louise. *See* Russell, Lillian
Leonidoff, Leon, 275, 343, 356
LeRoy, Hal, 290, 291, 307, 318
Leslie, Bert, 127
Leslie, Lew, 219-20, 252-53, 275, 281-82, 283-84, 311, 334
Lester, Jerry, 341
"Let Cutie Cut Your Cuticle," 161, 170
Let Freedom Sing, 351
"Let's Do It," 274
Let's Face It, 345
Let's Go, 146
"Let's Put Out the Lights and Go to Sleep," 305
"Let's Take a Walk Around the Block," 316
Levey, Harold, 230
Levi, Maurice, 85, 92, 93, 99
Lewine, Richard, 363
Lewis, Ada, 45, 103
Lewis, Dave, 81
Lewis, Henry, 159, 162
Lewis, Morgan, 342, 360
Lewis, Sinclair, 325
Lewis, Ted, 156, 158, 160, 174, 191, 193, 243, 250, 273
Lewis, William, 285
Lewisohn, Jesse, 66
Lew Leslie's Blackbirds of 1930, 281, 283
Lexington Theatre, 149
Liberty Theatre, 72, 82, 155, 252
Lichtman, Nat, 344
Liebman, Max, 15, 340, 345, 350, 363, 365
Lief, Max and Nathaniel (Nat), 251, 285, 296
Life (magazine), 94
Life Begins at 8:40, 315-16
Life in New York, or Tom and Jerry on a Visit, 29
"Life Is Just a Bowl of Cherries," 294
Lightner, Winnie, 188, 198, 213, 229, 240, 250
Lightnin' (play), 169

"Lilies, The" (sketch), 99
Lillie, Beatrice (Bea), 209, 211, 221, 229, 236, 257, 261, 285, 305, 320, 321, 326-27, 333, 355, 364, 373
"Lily of Longacre Square," 147
"Limehouse Blues," 209
Limon, Jose, 304, 308, 342
Lincoln, Abraham, 32
Lindsay, Howard, 326
Lipsky, Nicholas V., 174
Literary Digest (magazine), 31
Little Duchess, The, 77
"Little Igloo for Two, A," 235
Little Johnny Jones, 77
"Little Love, a Little Kiss, A," 113
Little Nemo, 91
"Little Old Lady," 327
Little Show, The, 259-61, 263, 278, 279
Littlest Revue of 1955, 373
"Little Surplus Me," 360
Little Theatre, 206, 316, 342
Living Newspaper, The, 325
Livingstone, Jerry, 353
Lloyd, Harold, 213
"Loadin' Time," 321
"Lobster Crawl, The," 264
Locher, Robert, 167, 174
Lockhart, Gene, 231
Loeb, Philip, 222, 232, 244, 276, 286, 302, 315, 319, 332
Loebell, Marc, 254
Loesser, Frank, 322
Loew's circuit, 52
Logan, Ella, 317, 336, 345, 350
Logan, Stanley, 264
Lombardo, Carmen, 304
London Calling, 16-17
Lonergan, Lenore, 367
Lone Thief, The (play), 241
Long, Eleanor, 140
Long, Huey, 318
Longacre Theater, 351
Long Track Sam and Co., 189
Lonsdale, Frederick, 257
"Look at Them Doing It!," 120
"Looking at You," 273
Loomis Sisters, 304
Loos, Anita, 200, 274
Lord, Mindret, 325

Lorillard, Pierre, 57
Lorne, Marion, 368
Lorraine, Lillian, 92, 93-94, 96, 98, 100, 101, 102, 105-6, 107, 108, 112, 116, 119, 132, 144, 147-48, 162, 200, 215, 290, 319, 349
Lorraine, Ted, 166
Losch, Tilly, 257, 273, 286, 288
Lost Generation, 187, 300
"Lottie of the Literati," 325
Louise, Tina, 371
"Louisiana Hayride," 302
"Love Boat, The" (production number), 165
"Love Call, The," 194
"Love Is a Dancing Thing," 321
"Love Is a Simple Thing," 370
"Love's Awakening," 174
"Lovie Joe," 95
"Loving You the Way I Do," 278
Low and Behold, 314
Luce, Clair, 204, 236-37, 248
"Lucky Day," 235
"Lucky Pierre," 371
Luncki, Paul, 85
Lund, John, 351
Lunt, Alfred, 54, 350
LuPone, Patti, 373
Lusitania (ship), 138
Lyceum Theater, 201
Lydia Thompson and Her Imported English Blondes, 37, 61
Lyles, A., 246
Lynde, Paul, 370, 371
Lynn, Mara, 367
Lyon, Wanda, 139
Lyric Theatre, 77, 115

M

Macbeth (Shakespeare), 122
MacColl, James, 316
MacDonagh, Glen, 122, 140, 146, 168
MacDonald, Ballard, 165, 181, 198, 243, 245, 250, 283, 312
MacDonald, Jeanette, 190
MacDonald, W. H., 58
Mack, Cecil, 227
Mack, Willard, 172

Mackay, Ellin (Mrs. Irving Berlin), 220, 233
MacLaine, Shirley, 373
MacMahon, Aline, 211
MacMurray, Fred, 279
MacRae, Gordon, 360
MacReady, James, 31
"Mad About the Boy," 333
Madame Sherry, 97
"Madamoiselle," 90
Madden, Edward, 86, 90, 92, 166
"Mad Dogs and Englishmen," 285
Madison Square Garden Roof, 79
Madison Square Theatre, 57
Magidson, Herb, 256, 304
Mahoney, Will, 213, 264, 292
Maid in America, 121-22
"Maid of Gold" (production number), 207
Majestic Theater (old), 85, 95
Majestic Theatre (new), 243, 277, 306, 354
Major, The, 45
Major Barbara (Shaw), 130
Make It Snappy, 182-83
Make Mine Manhattan, 10, 363, 364
"Making of a Girl, The," 133
Malamute Saloon sketch, 348
Malin Studio Theatre, 346
Mam'selle Napoleon, 77
Mamzelle Champagne, 79
Manckiewiez, Herman, 212
"Mandy," 156, 349
Man from Mexico, The (play), 102
"Manhattan," 222, 232
Manhattan Vanities, 303
Manhatters, The, 246-47
Manilow, Barry, 373
Man in the Moon, The, 74
Mannes, Marya, 367
Mansfield, Richard, 64, 71
Mansfield Theater, 344
Mantle, Burns, 194, 244, 245, 300, 342
"Man Who Wrote the `Merry Widow' Waltz, The," 84
Marais and Miranda, 362
Moran & Mack, 218
Marbury, Elizabeth (Bessie), 122, 193
Marchand, Colette, 370

"March of the Toys," 144, 284
Marcy, Everett, 330
Mardi Gras, 364
Marie Dressler's All Star Gambols, 109
Marie Odile (play), 125
Marine Corps band, 63
Markert, Russell, 9, 263, 304, 306, 321-22
Markham, Pauline, 37
Mark Hellinger Theater, 369, 370
Markova, Alicia, 355
Marks, Edward B., 70-71
Marsh, Reginald, 191, 203, 204, 265
Marshall, Everett, 293, 294, 312, 317
Marshall, Henry, 101
Martin Beck Theater, 353
Marvelous Millers, 102
Marx, Chico (Leonard Marx), 210, 354
Marx, Groucho (Julius H. Marx), 210
Marx, Harpo (Adolph Marx), 210, 261
Marx, Zeppo (Herbert Marx), 210
Marx Brothers, 53, 168, 212, 262, 331
Mascagni, Pietro, 183
Mason, Jack, 122
Massey, Ilona, 352
Mata and Hari, 340, 356
Matthews, Jessie, 229, 257, 273, 274
Maul, Paul, 232
Maupassant, Guy de, 316
Maurice and Walton, 156
Mauritania (liner), 183
Maxine Elliott Theater, 344
Maxixe (dance), 116
Maxwell, Elsa, 330-31, 333
Maxwell, Vera, 99-100, 101, 108, 135, 142
May, Edna, 81
May, Marty, 369
Maya (play), 245
Mayer, Louis B., 332
Mayfair, Mitzi, 9, 290, 291, 317, 326
Mayfield, Cleo, 143, 210
Maytime, 141
May Wine, 321
McAllister's Legacy, 45
McCarthy, Joseph, 156, 164, 170, 207, 213, 289
McCarthy Sisters, 193, 235
McCarty, Mary, 365, 369

McCauley, Jack, 296
McColl, James, 349
McConnell, Lulu, 170, 282
McCoy, Bessie. *See* Davis, Bessie McCoy
McCracken, Joan, 368
McCullough, Paul, 194
McDonald, Grace, 334
McEvoy, J.P., 236, 238, 246, 256-57, 304
McGinley, Phillis, 365
McGowan, Jack, 198, 265, 303
McGrane, Paul, 350
McGuire, William Anthony, 161-62
McGunigle, Robert, 305
McHugh, Jimmy, 252, 275, 281, 282, 91, 306, 335, 342
McIntyre and Heath, 134
McLean, Ross, 294
McLellan, C. M. S., 129
McMahon, Jere, 355
McNulty, Dorothy (Penny Singleton), 296, 305
McPherson, Aimee Semple, 309, 313
McSorley's Inflation, or The McSorley's, 45
Mdivani, Alexis, 310
Mears, John Henry, 161, 170
Mecca (play), 169
Meet the People, 344
Meisner, Sanford, 222
Melba, Nellie, 293
"Melody Land" (production number), 247
"Memories of You," 281
Mencken, Helen, 240
Men in White (Kingsley), 308
Menken, Adah Isaacs, 30
Mercer, Johnny, 276, 304, 334
Merman, Ethel, 293, 294, 326, 348
Merrill, Gary, 350
Merrill, Scott, 368
Merry-Go-Round, 260
"Merry Minuet, A," 371
Merry Widow, The, 82, 83-84, 85, 121, 317
Merry Widow Burlesque, The, 84
Merry World, The, 232-33
Messel, Oliver, 257
"Metropolitan Nights," 120

Metropolitan Opera, 63, 93, 309, 370
Metropolitan Tower, 101
"Mexiconga, The," 336
Meyer, Joseph, 229, 283, 312
Meyers, George, 219
Michael Todd's Peep Show, 368
Michelena, Vera, 118
Middleton, Ray, 336
Midnight Frolics (1915), 126, 127
Midnight Frolics (1916), 130, 133
Midnight Frolics (1919), 160, 161
Midnight Frolics (1920), 163
Midnight Frolics (series of shows), 113, 126, 131, 141, 147, 156-57, 162, 166, 226
Midnight Frolics (theater). *See* New Amsterdam roof garden theater
Midnight Girl, The, 154
Midnight Rounders of 1920, The, 166
Midnight Rounders of 1921, The, 169
Mielziner, Jo, 260, 279, 285, 296, 367
Mikado, The (operetta), 166, 330
Miles, Carlotta, 210
Miles, William, 280-81
Miley, Bubber, 283
Millay, Edna St. Vincent, 191
Miller, Ann, 336
Miller, Arthur, 354, 371
Miller, Everett, 276
Miller, F. E., 246
Miller, Flourney, 281, 347
Miller, Henry, 53
Miller, Marilyn, 53, 119, 122, 123, 134, 148, 156, 157, 160, 165, 170-72, 183, 200, 215, 247, 308, 309, 310, 317, 324, 349
Miller, Woods, 321
Miller and Lyles, 232, 281
Mills, Florence, 219-20, 273
Milton, Billy, 317
Mimic World, The, 90, 174
Minevitch, Borrah, 282
Minnelli, Vincente, 303, 320, 323, 326, 367
Minsky, Harold, 15
Minsky Brothers (producers), 186, 313, 336, 348, 368
Minsky's theater, 303
minstrelsy, 20, 21-23, 25-26, 30-34, 35,

36, 42, 53, 55, 57, 59, 63, 85, 94, 95, 98, 121, 134
Miracle Woman, The (film), 307
Miranda, Carmen, 335, 336, 340, 344, 345, 347
Miss 1917, 113, 142-44, 154
"Miss Ginger from Jamaica," 81
Miss Innocence, 91-92, 105
"M-I-S-S-I-S-S-I-P-P-I," 140
Miss Manhattan, 74
"Mister Earth and His Comet Love," 96
Mistinguette, 172, 210
Mitchell, Frank, 266-67
Mitchell, Julian, 65-66, 80, 83, 84, 85, 86, 90, 91, 92, 93, 96, 103, 106, 112, 117, 122, 125, 128, 134, 140, 154, 161, 165, 212, 236, 237
Mitchell, William, 27, 29
Mizzy, Vic, 334
Mlle. Francisquay, 30
Mlle. Modiste, 119
Mlle. Niska, 319
Mme. Clarice, 98
Mme. Vestris and her troupe, 27
"(M-m-m-m,) Would You Like to Take a Walk?," 283
"Moanin' Low," 261
"Model Doddle," 219
Moffat, Harold, 260
Molnar, Ferenc, 276
Monaco, James (Jimmy), 108, 250, 290
"Mon Homme," 172, 181, 191, 210
"Monotonous," 370
Monroe, George, 118, 122, 123
Montand, Yves, 373
"Monte Carlo Town" (production number), 90
Monte Cristo, Jr., 149
Montgomery, Dave, 119
Montgomery, Robert, 231
Montoya, Carlos, 347
Moody, Richard, 57
Moon, George, 104
"Moonlight Kisses" (production number), 204
Moore, Florence, 275
Moore, Grace, 204, 220
Moore, McElbert, 230
Moore, Monette, 302

Moore, Victor, 246, 346
Moran, Ed, 146
Moran & Mack, 218, 239
Mordacai Lyons, 45
Morgan, Agnes, 227, 235-36, 253-54, 261
Morgan, Carey, 174
Morgan, Frank, 286-88, 296
Morgan, Helen, 227, 238, 290, 291
Morgan, Henry, 367
Morgan, J. P., 24, 57, 233
Moritz, Al, 357
Morosco Theater, 212
Moross, Jerome, 319
Morris, Daniel, 104
Morrisey, Harry, 266-67
Morris Gest's Midnight Whirl, 161
Morrison, Alex, 195
Morrissey, Will, 150, 166, 201-2, 263
Mose in a Muss, 28
Mose in California, 28
Mose in China, 28
Mose in France, 28
Moseley, Peggy, 294
Moss and Fontana, 282
Mostel, Zero, 346-47, 357
"Mothers o' Men," 258
"Motion Picture Glide, The," 118
Motzan, Otto, 133, 138
Moulin Rouge theater, 103, 105, 108. See also New York Theatre
"Mountain Greenery," 232
Mourning Becomes Electra (O'Neill), 297
"Mourning Becomes Impossible" (sketch), 303
movies. See talking pictures
"Mozambique," 281
"Mr. Gallagher and Mr. Shean," 185
"Mr. Gielgud Passes By" (sketch), 327, 355
Mr. Lode of a Coal, 95
M. Tillio and Mlle. Mitti, 171
Muddy Day, The, 45
Muir, Lewis, 92
Muldowney, John, 259
Mulligan Guard Ball, The, 44
Mulligan Guards' Chowder, The, 44
Mulligan Guards' Christmas, The, 44
Mulligan Guards' Nominee, The, 44

Mulligan Guards' Surprise, The, 44
Mulligans' Picnic, The, 44
Mulligans' Silver Wedding, 44
Mundy, Meg, 360
Munro, Bill, 158
Munshin, Jules, 361, 369
Murder at the Vanities, 304
Murphy, George, 291
Murphy, Owen, 174, 218, 230
Murphy, Stanley, 101
Murray, J. P., 289
Murray, J. Harold, 318
Murray, Ken, 319, 366-7
Murray, Mae, 87, 92, 93, 124
Murray, Ted, 354
Murray Anderson, John, 15, 158-59, 163, 167-68, 174-75, 191-92, 203, 218, 220, 229, 251, 264-65, 312, 315, 317, 319, 323, 333, 342, 352, 360, 371-2
Murray Anderson's Almanac, 264-65
Music Box Revue of 1921-22, The, 179-80, 182, 259, 349
Music Box Revue of 1922-23, The, 193-94
Music Box Revue of 1923-24, The, 204-5, 207, 208, 209
Music Box Revue of 1924-25, The, 220
Music Box Revue series, 218, 220, 229-30
Music Box Theatre, 178, 180, 193, 259, 261, 308, 310, 332, 333, 348
Mussolini, Benito, 322
"My Arab Complex," 317
"My Baby's Loving Arms," 156
"My Cozy Little Corner in the Ritz," 160
Myers, Henry, 238, 344
Myers, Richard, 246, 276, 304
"My Handy Man Ain't Handy No More," 281
"My Icy Floe," 235
"My Last Affair," 315
"My Man," 172, 253, 324
"My Rose of Spain," 243
Myrtil, Odette, 209

N

"Naked Truth, The" (sketch), 167
Namara, Marguerite, 314

"Nanking Blues," 167
Nash, Ogden, 296, 372, 373
Nathan, Alfred, 247
Nathan, George Jean, 199, 201, 325
National Theater, 360, 366
Naughty Marietta, 97
Naughty Riquette (play), 240
Nazimova, Alla, 53
Nazis, 334
Nazzaro, Nat, 239
Neagle, Anna, 257
Ned Wayburn's Gambols, 258
Ned Wayburn's Town Topics, 127, 258
Negri, Pola, 211
Neighborhood Playhouse, 211, 221, 235
Neilsen, Alice, 64
Nelson, Gene, 366
Nesbitt, Evelyn, 24, 73, 79
New Americana, 304
New Amsterdam roof garden theater, 79, 126, 133, 162, 184
New Amsterdam Theatre, 20, 73, 78, 82, 83, 84, 85, 97, 112, 113, 114, 117, 118, 120, 121, 126, 128, 132, 140, 145, 147, 148, 163, 164, 168, 170, 185, 213, 227, 247, 278, 285-86, 322
New Chauve-Souris, 294-95
Newcomers, The, 202, 313
New Deal, 332
New Faces of 1934, 314-15
New Faces of 1936, 325-26
New Faces of 1943, 351
New Faces of 1952, 10, 370-71
New Faces series, 202
New Glance at New York, A, 28
Newman, Alfred, 191
New Pins and Needles, 330
New Priorities of 1943, 350
"New Sun in the Sky," 288
New York Dramatic Mirror (periodical), 159
New Yorkers, The (1901), 242
New Yorkers, The (1927), 242-43
New Yorkers, The (1930), 242-43
New York Harbor, 94, 371
New York Observer (periodical), 49
New York Post (newspaper), 231
New York Public Library, 254

New York State Legislature, 245
New York Stock Exchange, 270
New York Telegram (newspaper), 212, 352
New York Theatre, 79, 84, 86, 91, 97.
    See also Moulin Rouge theater
New York Theatre roof theater. See
    Jardin des Paris roof theater
New York Times (newspaper), 37, 43, 57,
    59, 71, 103, 183, 216, 246, 331
"New York, What's the Matter with
    You?," 112
Niblo's Garden, 29, 34, 36, 37, 55, 56,
    63
Nicholas Brothers, 323
Nichols, Alberta, 240, 284, 311
Nic Nax of 1926, 239
Niesen, Gertrude, 323, 324
Nifties of 1923, 205-6, 209
Night in . . ., A series, 262
"Nightingale and the Rose, The"
    (Wilde), 191, 372
"Nightingale, Bring Me a Rose," 191
Night in Paris, A, 230-31, 243
Night in Spain, A, 243
Night in Venice, A, 262
9 O'Clock Frolic series, 162, 163, 169
9:15 Revue, 274-75
Nirdlinger, Samuel, 71
Niska, Mlle., 319
Nissen, Greta, 237
Noble, Ray, 277
"Nobody," 100
Nobody Home, 146
"Nobody Wants Me," 238
No Foolin'. See *Ziegfeld American Revue of 1926, The*
Nora Bayes Theatre, 144, 159
Norman, Karyl, 203
Norman, Lucille, 350
Norman, Marsha, 325
Norris, James, 276
Norris, Jerry, 283, 285, 305
Norvo, Red, 355
Norwith, Jack, 289
Norworth, Jack, 86, 91, 92, 93, 108,
    134, 144, 146
"Not As Good As Last Year," 255
"Not for All the Rice in China," 310
"Nothing But a Bubble," 94

"Nothing Naughtie in a Nightie," 214
Not So Long Ago (play), 169
Novello, Ivor, 209, 229
"Nubian Jungle Dance," 33
Nye, Louis, 364, 365, 367

O

Oakie, Jack, 210
Oakland, Vivian, 166
Oakley, Annie, 75
O'Brien, Chet, 317
Ochs, Al, 185
O'Connell, Hugh, 323
Odds and Ends of 1917, 144, 146
Odell, George, 28
O'Denishawn, Florence, 160, 168, 171
Odets, Clifford, 330
O'Donnell, Charles, 171
"Oedipus Goes South," 371
Offenbach, Jacques, 48, 294
Of Thee I Sing, 289, 297, 306
Of V We Sing, 346
Oh, Boy!, 141, 238
Oh, Calcutta!, 374
"Oh, How He Can Love!," 256
"Oh, How I Hate to Get Up in the
    Morning," 149, 349
Oh, Kay!, 236
Oh, Lady! Lady!!, 146
Oh! Oh! Delphine, 114
"Oh, That Beautiful Rag," 97
O'Keefe, Walter, 285
Oklahoma!, 332, 347, 352, 354
Olcott, Chauncey, 293
"Old Before His Time," 60
"Old Fashioned Cakewalk," 121
"Old Fashioned Garden" (production
    number), 160
"Old Joke Cemetery" (sketch), 192
Old Park Theater, 32
O'Leary, Tom, 217
"O Leo," 320
Oliver, Barry, 321
Oliver Twist (Dickens), 104
"Ol' Man River," 284
Olsen, Ole, 331
Olsen and Johnson, 331-32, 335, 336,
    345-46, 356, 368-9

Olson, George, 213
Olympia entertainment complex, 72-73, 74
Olympia Lyric Theater, 72-73
Olympia Music Hall, 72, 106
"Olympian Ballet featuring Thamara Swiskaia and Adolph Bolm, An," (dance), 132
Olympia roof garden, 73
Olympia Theatre, 55
135th Street (jazz opera), 188-89
"One Big Union for Two," 329
One for the Money, 333-34, 341, 360
"One Girl," 262
O'Neill, Eugene, 182, 191, 192, 227, 237-38, 245, 250, 254, 276, 308
O'Neill, James, 55, 71
"One Love," 278
One Touch of Venus, 353
"On My Nude Ranch with You," 296
"On the American Plan," 302-3
"On the Sunny Side of the Street," 275
On the Town, 357
On Your Toes, 323
"Ooh! That Kiss," 295
Operette, 333
Operti, G., 63
Oppenheimer, George, 247, 367
"O Promise Me," 58
Optimists, 250
O'Ramey, Georgia, 129
Ordway's Aeolians, 32
O'Reilly, Rosemary, 370
Origin of the Cake Walk, or Clorindy, 62-63
Orlob, Harold, 127, 147
Orpheum circuit, 52, 54, 65
Osterwald, Bibi, 360
Othello (Shakespeare), 131
Otvos, A. Dorian, 265
Our American Cousin (play), 32
"Out of Breath and Scared to Death of You," 276
"Overnight," 283
Over the River, 102
Over the Top, 144-45
Owney Geogheghan's Saloon, 40
Oxford, Earl, 316, 319, 322, 349

P

Pacific Paradise, 373
"Pack Up Your Sins" (production number), 193
Padilla, José, 232
Padlocks of 1927, 245
Palace Hotel, 118
"Palace of Beauties" (production number), 107
Palace Theatre (London), 76
Palace Theatre (New York), 52, 251
Pal Joey, 343, 344
Palm Beach Girl. See *Ziegfeld American Revue of 1926*
Palm Beach Night. See *Ziegfeld American Revue of 1926*
Palm Beach Supper Club, 236
Palmer, Bee, 193, 214
Palmer, Byron, 369
Palmer, Mrs. Potter, 75
"Panama Pacific Drag," 123
Panama Pacific Exposition, 118, 123, 129
Panic of 1893, 58-59
Pantages circuit, 52
Papa's Wife, 76
Parade, 318-19
"Parade of All Nations" (production number), 266
"Parade of the Wooden Soldiers," 181
Paradise roof garden, 73
Pardon Our French, 369
"Paree," 320
Paris, 274
Paris Bound (Barry), 245, 344
Paris Exposition, 73
Parish, Mitchell, 334
"Parisian Pierrot," 209
"Parisienne," 161
"Paris Is a Paradise for Coons," 98
Parker, Dorothy, 194, 291, 325
Park Theater, 182
"Parlez-moi d'Amour," 316
Parlor Match, A (Hoyt), 76
Parrish, Maxfield, 94
Parsons, Louella, 325
"Party's Over Now," 333
Pasadena Playhouse, 314

Pascal, Milton, 353
Pascaud (clothes designer), 208
Passing Show (1894), 59-61, 62, 65, 74, 104
Passing Show of 1912, 104-5, 114
Passing Show of 1913, 114-15
Passing Show of 1914, 118-19
Passing Show of 1915, 122-23, 125
Passing Show of 1916, 128, 132
Passing Show of 1917, 138-39
Passing Show of 1918, 148
Passing Show of 1919, 160-61
Passing Show of 1921, 168-69
Passing Show of 1922, 192-93
Passing Show of 1923, 194-95
Passing Show of 1924, 214, 215
Passing Show series, 114, 115, 123, 159, 166, 201, 208, 214-15, 228, 230, 374
"Pastie Parade" (production number), 217
Pastor, Tony, 40-44, 45, 48, 52-53, 54, 55, 61, 65, 70, 71
Patinkin, Mandy, 373
Patou (couturier), 208
Patricola, Tom, 214
Pavlova, Anna, 133, 293
Payne, Philip, 241, 242
"Pay the Two Dollars!" (sketch), 294, 305
"Peach Blossom Time" (production number), 189
Peanut Man (clown), 368
Pearce, Alice, 351, 365, 371
Pearl, Jack, 230, 250, 259, 275, 290
Pearl Harbor, 345, 346
"Peg o' My Heart," 113, 114
Pelham, Frank, 30-32
Pelham Naval Training Station, 146
Peluso, Tom, 296
Penner, Joe, 282
Pennington, Ann (Tiny), 112-13, 117, 124, 131, 142, 148, 154, 155, 159, 164, 173, 184, 188, 198, 207, 213, 214, 234, 247, 254, 255, 265
"Penny Candy," 370
"Pensacola Mooch" (dance), 96
Perelman, S. J., 284, 305
Perfect Fool, 180
Perkins, Bobbie, 232

Perkins, Ray, 251
"Peter Grimm" (sketch), 105
Peters, Paul, 318, 319
Peters, W. F., 123
Petit, Margaret, 175
Phillips, H.I., 312
Piaf, Edith, 373
Pic (magazine), 329
Pickens, Jane, 343
Pickens Sisters, 318
Pickford, Jack, 183
Pickford, Mary, 118, 123, 309
"Pickin' Cotton" (dance), 255
Pidgeon, Walter, 221
"Pied Piper of Harlem," 322
Pierce, Franklin, 32
Pierson, Arthur, 346
Pilcer, Harry, 129
Pinero, Arthur Wing, 60
Pink Lady, The, 97, 100, 107
Pins and Needles (1922), 181
Pins and Needles (1937), 17, 328-30, 332, 333
Pins and Needles (1939), 330
Pins and Needles (1940), 330
Pirates of Penzance, 42
Pittsburgh Symphony, 63
Planche, James Robinson, 27, 28, 29
Plantation Revue, 187, 252
Platt, Tom, 57
Playhouse Theater, 317, 362
"Play Me a Simple Melody," 120
Pleasure Bound, 259
Pleasure Seekers, The, 154
Plume de Ma Tante, La, 373
Pocohontas, or The Gentle Savage, 29
Poe, Edgar Allan, 203
Pokrass, Samuel, 312
"Polar Bear Strut, The," 235
Polk, James, 32
Pollack, Lew, 169, 174
Pollock, Channing, 123, 125, 172
Pollock, Muriel, 259
"Polly of the Follies" (sketch), 145
"Polly, Pretty Polly with a Past," 145
Polly with a Past (Bolton), 145
Polo Grounds, 94
Pond, James B., 259-60
Ponselle, Rosa, 53

"Poor Butterfly," 133
Poor Little Rich Girl, 222
"Poor Porgy," 321
"Poppyland," 161
Porgy (Heyward), 253
Porgy and Bess (opera), 321
Porter, Cole, 127, 160, 162, 167, 218, 220, 230, 264, 271, 273-74, 282, 326, 348, 355-6, 374
Posner, Lee, 296
Post, Wiley, 324
"Pour J'en ai Marre," 192-93
Powell, Eleanor, 250, 294, 304, 305, 320, 326
Power, Tyrone,, 314
Power, Tyrone, Sr., 293
Power of Darkness, The (Tolstoy), 162
Powers' Elephants, 189
Preisser, Cherry and June, 312, 323
"Pretty Baby," 128, 133
"Pretty Dance Is Like a Violin, A" (production number), 170
"Pretty Girl Is Like a Melody, A," 155, 193
Price, Georgie, 186
Price, Michael, 10
"Pride of the Claghornes, The," 287-88
Primrose Path, The, 99
Primus, Pearl, 362
Princess Theatre, 122, 141, 146, 150, 161, 162, 238, 328. *See also* Labor Theatre
Prince Tokio, 81
Priorities of '42, 346
Prohibition, 156, 158, 160, 161, 162, 170, 172, 180, 184, 187, 206, 214, 226, 242, 256, 271, 273
"Promenade the Esplanade," 243
Provincetown Follies, The, 321
Provincetown Players, 250
Provincetown Playhouse, 182, 321
Pulitzer Prize, 248
"Pull Your Strings," 219
Punch and Judy shows, 26
Punch and Judy Theatre, 194
Purcell, Charles, 149
Pushkin, Alexander, 181, 294
Puzzles of 1925, 221

Q

Quaker Girl, The, 104
"Quartet Erotica" (sketch), 316
Quedens, Eunice. *See* Arden, Eve
Queen's Lace Handkerchief, The, 56
Quo Vadis (Sienkiewicz), 66
"Quo Vas Iss?" (sketch), 66

R

Rabelais, François, 316
radio, 54, 226, 271, 275, 293, 295, 309, 332
Radio Aces, 350, 354
Radio City Music Hall, 9, 306, 309, 343, 357
Radio City Music Hall Rockettes, 263, 306
Raft, George, 245
Ragland, Oscar (Rags), 274, 331
"Ragtime Arabian Nights," 116
"Ragtime Carnival," 128
"Ragtime Jockey Man, The," 104
"Ragtime Minstrel Man," 90
"Ragtime Pinafore," 116
"Ragtime Pipe of Pan, The," 128
"Ragtime Suffragette, The," 113
Rain (play), 203, 206, 210
Rainbow, 262
Rainger, Ralph, 261, 274
Rall, Tommy, 365
Ralph Reader Girls, 251
Rambeau, Marjorie, 53
Ramblers, The, 236
Randall, Carl, 53, 124, 163, 180, 204, 285, 322, 345
Randolph, Forbes, 294
Randolph, William, Jr., 325
Rang Tang, 246
Rasch, Albertina, 279, 286, 290, 295, 302, 305, 343
Rascoe, Burton, 191, 352
Raskin, Harry, 218
Rathbone, Basil, 240
Rauh, Stanley, 239
Ravel, Maurice, 292
"Raven, The" (Poe), 203
Ray, Ina, 312

Ray, Kathryn, 216, 217
Raye, Martha, 317
Raye and Naldi, 345
Raymond Hitchcock's Pinwheel, 185-86
Razaf, Andy, 263, 281
Razzle Dazzle, 369
Read, Jessie, 156
"Rebecca of Sunnybrook Farm," 113
Rector's (restaurant), 113, 290
Red Feather, The, 77
Red Golden Crook, 37
Red Hot and Blue, 326
"Red Hot Stove Cabaret," 129
Red Mill, The, 119, 360
"Red Sails in the Sunset," 321
Reed, Florence, 145
Reeves, Richard, 350
Regay, Pearl, 188
Rehearsal, The (Buckingham), 27
Reichner, Bickley, 325
Reid, Elliott, 370
Reilly and the Four Hundred, 45
Reiner, Carl, 364, 365, 367
Reinhardt, Max, 114
Reisner, C. Francis, 139
"Reminiscent Rosy-Posy," 128
"Rendezvous Time in Paree," 335
Republic Theater. *See* Victory Theater
Reri (dancer), 290
"Rest Room Rose," 284
Reunion in New York, 342
Revel, Harry, 289, 291, 294
Revue of Revues, The, 101-2
Revue Russe, 193
Reynolds, James, 163, 167, 171, 185, 191, 204, 207, 217-18, 220, 229, 317
Reynolds, Robert, 330
Rhapsody in Black, 283-84
"Rhapsody in Blue," 284, 334
"Rhinestones of 1932," 308
"Rhode Island Is Famous for You," 364
"Rhythm," 326
Riano, Rene, 180
Rice, Edward E., 54-55, 58, 62
Rice, Elmer, 326
Rice, Gitz, 239
Richie, Adele, 61
Richman, Harry, 233-34, 235, 254, 275, 290, 291, 304, 305, 350

Rigoletto (opera), 309
quartet sketch, 301, 322
Ring, Blanche, 83, 170
"Ring Out Liberty," 139
Rio Rita, 253
Rip Van Winkle (play), 273
Ritchard, Cyril, 372
Ritz Theatre, 218
Roaring Twenties, 161, 187, 195, 228, 300, 355, 366, 370
Robbins, Jerome, 340, 357, 372
Robeldo, Julian, 175
Roberts, Lee J., 148
Robeson, Paul, 292
Robey, Ken, 365
Robin, Leo, 246
Robin Hood, 57-58
Robinson, Bill, 252, 253, 311, 348
Robinson, Earl, 351, 357
Robinson, Roberta, 286
Roche, Mary, 355
Rockefeller, John D., 24, 81, 309
Rockefeller, John D., Jr., 309
Rockefeller, Mrs. John D., Jr., 309
Rockefeller Center, 306, 326, 343
Rodgers, Richard, 9, 133, 222-23, 276
Rodgers and Hammerstein, 352, 360, 363, 367
Rodgers and Hart, 229, 231, 232, 276, 283, 284, 291, 321, 326, 328, 332, 373-4
Rodgers and Hart, 373-4
Rogers, Cynthia, 276
Rogers, Howard E., 166
Rogers, Will, 33, 53, 126-27, 130, 131, 139, 140, 147, 168, 180, 184, 185, 212, 324, 349, 364
Roly Poly, 108
Romay, Lina, 368
Romberg, Sigmund, 116, 118, 122, 127, 128, 133, 138, 141, 142, 145, 148, 149, 166, 182, 195, 210, 214, 219, 228, 231, 264, 321, 356
Rome, Harold (Hector Troy), 328-29, 332, 334, 348, 351, 361, 367, 369
Romeo and Juliet (Shakespeare), 131
"Room with a View, A," 257
Rooney, Pat, 354
Roosevelt, Eleanor, 316, 330, 333, 309

Index ☙ 417

Roosevelt, Franklin D., 306, 332, 361, 309
Roosevelt, Theodore, 81, 93, 107, 132
Rosalie, 157
Rose, Billy, 15, 229, 245, 250, 282-83, 284, 312, 321, 354-56, 357, 368
Rosebrook, Leon, 166
Rosenfeld, Sydney, 60, 82
Rosensteen, Irene, 170
"Rose of Arizona" (sketch), 232, 276-77
"Rose of Washington Square," 313
Ross, Don, 312
Ross, Jerry, 371
Roth, Lillian, 245, 256, 292
"Round the Opera in Twenty Minutes" (sketch), 60
Round the Town, 211-12
Rourke, Michael, 83
"Row Row Row," 108
Roxy Theater, 357
Royale Theater, 246, 279, 371
Royce, Edward (Teddy), 135, 165, 169, 171, 237
Rubens, Maurice (Maurie), 229, 230, 232, 250, 251, 262, 264
Ruby, Harry, 165
Rufus LeMaire's Affairs, 243
Runnin' Wild, 227
Ruskin, Harry, 265, 296
Ruskin, Robert, 265
Russell, Anna, 373
Russell, Lillian, 42-44, 52, 58, 61, 63, 64, 66, 71, 77, 103, 116, 183, 290
Russell, Rosalind, 276
Russian Art Players, 211
Ryan, Bennie, 154
Ryan, Colette, 188
Ryskind, Morrie, 170, 222, 238, 244, 258

S

Sablon, Jean, 335
Sachs, Dorothy, 334
Sacre Monte Gypsies (dancers), 316
Saddler, Donald, 368, 369
"Sadie Salome," 95
Sailor Beware (play), 313
St. Denis, Ruth, 53
St. James Theater, 305-6, 317, 341

"St. Louis Blues," 284
Sale, Chic, 139, 149, 160, 229, 240
Sally, 157, 170, 238
Salome, 93
"Salt of My Tears," 258
Sam H. Harris Theatre, 283
"Sammy," 143
Sam, Ted and Ray, 322
Samuels, Walter G., 258
Sanderson, Julia, 130, 168
Sands, Dorothy, 211, 235, 236, 254, 261
Sanford's Minstrels, 32
San Francisco, 118
San Francisco Exposition. See Panama Pacific Exposition
Santley, Joseph, 129
Sardi's (restaurant), 353
Satins, 166-67
Saturday Night (play), 240
Savage, Henry W., 82, 83-84
Savo, Jimmy, 210, 265, 277, 278, 318, 350
Savoy, Bert, 142, 167, 192
Savoy and Brennan, 192
Savoy Theater, 165
"Say It with Music," 180
"Say the Word," 285
Scandals of 1919, 113, 155, 173
Scandals of 1920, 164
Scandals of 1921, 173. See also *George White's Scandals of...*
Schaefer, Louis, 328
Scheff, Fritzi, 64, 102, 119, 143
Schenck, Joe, 135, 142, 143, 179, 293
Scholl, Danny, 361
Scholl, Jack, 278
"School Days" (sketch), 256
Schubert, Franz, 182, 235
Schultz, H., 85
Schumann, Robert, 235
Schwab, Charles M., 238, 243
Schwartz, Arthur, 235, 243, 258, 260, 261, 279, 286, 288, 302, 320-21, 326, 364
Schwartz, Jean, 81, 97, 102, 114, 148, 149, 160, 166, 169, 174, 182, 195, 208, 214, 243
Schwartz and Dietz, 260, 261
Scopes Monkey Trial, 222
Scott, Clement, 58
Scott, Hazel, 332, 346

Seabury Commission, 300
"Second Hand Rose," 172
Second Little Show, The, 278-79
Secret Service (Gillette), 65-66
Seeley, Blossom, 122, 127, 129, 189, 251
Segal, Vivienne, 142-43, 213
Selden, Albert, 365
Selden, Edgar, 81
Seldes, Gilbert, 191
Selwyn, Arch, 257, 316
Selwyns (producers), 170, 209
Selwyn Theater, 229, 247, 259, 272, 281
Sennett, Mack, 256
"Sentimental Me," 222
Sepia Guild Players Inc., 311
Set to Music, 333
Seven Little Foys, 73
Seven Lively Arts, 354-56, 357
Severn, Margaret, 167
Sex (West), 240
Shakespeare, William, 26, 38, 122, 131, 166, 333
"Shakin' the Blues Away" (production number), 247
Shanghai Gesture, The (play), 232, 233, 235
Shapiro, Irvin, 357
"Shavian Shivers," 276
Shaw, George Bernard, 130, 182, 276
Shaw, Neeka, 281
Shaw, Oscar, 130, 169, 204, 220
Shay, Dorothy, 356
Sheedy Agency, 52
Sheldon, Edward, 123
Sheldon, Gene, 354
Shelley, Frances, 274
Shelton, James, 314, 315, 340, 367
Shelton, Jerry, 352
Shelton, Yvonne, 143
Sheridan, Richard Brinsley, 27
Sherman, Charles, 302, 372
Sherman, Hiram, 332, 372
Sherman, William Tecumseh, 39
Sherry's (restaurant), 102
Sherwin, Manning, 231, 274
Sherwood, Benson J., 36
Shiebler, Howard, 321
Shimmy (dance), 148, 159, 214

"Shimmy Sisters, The," 148
"Shine on, Harvest Moon," 86, 91-92, 290
"Shine on Your Shoes, A," 302
Shipman, Helen, 161
Shoestring series, 373
Shoot the Works, 291
Shop Girl, The, 62
Short, Hassard, 179, 193, 204, 218, 229-30, 279, 281, 286, 288, 355, 363, 368
Show Boat, 17, 238, 245, 250, 253, 256, 272, 292, 307, 344
Show Is On, The, 326-27
"Show Me How to Do the Fox Trot," 120
Show of Wonders, The, 133-34
Show Time, 350, 353
Shriner, Herb, 364
Shubert, Jake (J. J.), 14, 15, 78, 114, 116-17, 123, 128, 130, 132-33, 135, 160, 161, 163, 168-69, 192, 195, 198-99, 202-3, 205, 208, 214, 215, 217, 219, 228-29, 230-31, 232-33, 240, 241, 248, 250, 262, 277, 286, 311, 312, 315, 350-1, 356, 374
Shubert, Lee, 78, 82, 114, 127, 130, 144-45, 214, 215, 304, 312-13, 314, 322, 326, 331, 340, 342
Shubert, Sam S., 78, 82
Shubert Alley, 311
Shubert building, 311
Shubert Gaieties of 1919, The, 159
Shuberts, the, 72, 78, 85, 90-91, 96-128passim, 133-34, 138-54passim, 157, 159, 160-61, 166, 168-69, 174, 182-83, 184, 193, 202-3, 208, 209-10, 210, 214, 228, 229, 232-33, 243, 245, 249-50, 251, 259, 262, 296, 311, 315, 320, 322-23, 327, 332, 335, 340, 342, 345-46, 350-51, 352, 353, 356
Shubert Theater, 168, 174, 181, 190, 203, 217, 250, 296, 304
Shuffle Along, 186, 246, 251
"Shuffle Your Feet and Roll Along," 253
Shutta, Ethel, 192
Side by Side by Sondheim, 374
Siegel, Arthur, 370

Sienkiewicz, Henryk, 66
Sigman, Carl, 363
Sillman, June, 314, 325, 331. *See also* Carroll, June
Sillman, Leonard, 15, 202, 244, 313-15, 317, 325-26, 330-31, 334, 351, 370-71
Silver, Abner, 186
Silverman, Sime, 121
Silvers, Sid, 228, 243
Simmons, Bartlett, 316
Simon, Robert, 235
Simpson, Harold, 206
Sinatra, Frank, 351
"Since My Mariutch Learned the Merry Widow Waltz," 85
Singer, Paris, 236
Singer Midgets, 315
Sing for Your Supper, 334-35
Singin' in the Rain (film), 255
Singleton, Penny (Dorothy McNulty), 296, 305
"Sing Me a Song with Social Significance," 329
Sing Out Sweet Land, 356
Sing Out the News, 332
"Sing Something Simple," 279
Sinner (play), 241
Sissle, Noble, 186, 209, 251, 347
Skelly, Hal, 282, 315
Skin of Our Teeth, The (Wilder), 347
Sklar, George, 318, 319
Slavin, John, 135
"Sleeping Beauty" (ballet), 133
Sloan, John, 191
Sloane, A. Baldwin, 158, 167
Small Wonder, 365
"Smile and Show Your Dimple," 310
Smile at Me, 319-20
"Smiles," 148
Smiles, 293
Smith, Al, 254, 294
Smith, Cyril, 321
Smith, Harry B., 57-58, 61, 63, 64, 74, 76, 77, 80, 81, 84, 85, 86, 91, 92, 93, 96, 99, 106-7, 112, 120, 127, 129, 201, 226
Smith, Irene, 92, 226
Smith, Joe, 239

Smith, Oliver, 369
Smith, Paul Gerard, 245, 265, 274
Smith, Robert B., 127
Smith and Dale, 160, 239, 347, 353
Smokey Joe's Cafe, 374
Smollett, Tobias, 27
Snapshots of 1921, 170
Snyder, Bozo, 368
Snyder, Ted, 97, 201
"Society Blues," 214
Society Circus, A, 78
"Society Circus Parade" (production number), 107
Society for the Suppression of Vice, 217
Society of Illustrators, 202, 322
Soglow, Otto, 322
Sokolow, Anna, 334
Solomon, Alfred, 81
Solomon, Edward, 44
"Somebody Loves Me" (production number), 213
Some Party, 183, 186
Something for the Boys, 348
"Something to Remember You By," 279
Sondheim, Stephen, 374
Song of Norway, 360
"Song of the Woodman," 327
Sons o' Fun, 345-46
Sophisticated Ladies, 374
"So This Is Paris," 133
Soul Kiss, The, 85
Sour, Robert, 279
Sousa, John Philip, 48, 63, 121, 128, 293
"Soused American Way," 340
"South American Way, The," 335
"South America, Take It Away," 361
"Southern Fried Chekhov" (sketch), 369
South Pacific, 366
Souvaine, Henry, 238, 244, 304
Sowing the Wind (Pinero), 60
Spalding, Charles, 365
Spanish Love (play), 169
"Spanish Shawl, A," 243
Sparks, John, 40
Sparks Brothers, 40
Spence, Ralph, 172
Spencer, Peter, 284
Spice of 1922, 186
Sporting Days, 90-91

Squatter Sovereignty, 45
"Stage Door Johnnies" (term), 62, 66, 74, 114
"Stairway to Paradise," 188, 198
Stalin, Joseph, 305
Stamper, Dave, 106, 113, 123, 126, 130, 131, 141, 156, 157, 164, 165, 169, 172, 185, 207, 213, 289, 321
Standard Theatre, 57
"Stand Up and Sing for Your Father," 170
Stanislavsky's Art Theatre, 181
Stanley, Jack, 192
Stanwyck, Barbara, 307
Star and Garter (1900), 348
Star and Garter (1943), 74, 348
Starbuck, Betty, 222, 232
Stars on Ice, 350
"Star Spangled Banner, The," 141, 326
Star Time, 354
"Stately Homes of England, The," 333
Stearns, Roger, 276
Steel, John, 155-56, 157, 165, 171, 193, 204, 207, 336
Stein, Gertrude, 187
Stein, Joseph, 367
Stept, Sammy, 304
Sterling, Andrew, 158
Stevens, Connie, 365
Stewart, Donald, 276
Stewart, Donald Ogden, 191
Stewart, Jimmy, 314
"Still Alarm, The" (sketch), 260-61
Stock Market Crash (1929), 249, 253, 272
"Stocks" (sketch), 266-67
"Stolen Bonds" (sketch), 256
Stolen Fruit (play), 240
Stolz, Robert, 291, 326
Stone, Ezra, 319, 350
Stone, Fred, 53, 119
Stone, Sid, 365
Stop! Look! Listen!, 129
"Story of a Fan, The" (production number), 189
Stothart, Herbert, 209
Stowe, Harriet Beecher, 235
Strange Interlude (O'Neill), 245, 250, 254, 255, 256, 276

Strauss, Johann, 48, 56
Strauss, Oscar, 109
Stravinsky, Igor, 355, 356
Straw Hat Revue, The, 340-41, 344
Streets of Paris, The, 335, 336, 341
Strictly Dishonorable (Sturges), 283
"Strictly Unbearable" (sketch), 283
Strike Me Pink, 306-7
strikes, 58-59
Strike Up the Band, 272
strippers, 38
Stritch, Elaine, 363
Stromberg, John, 48, 64, 66
Strut Miss Lizzie, 186, 187
Stryker, Muriel, 185, 207
"Student Robin Hood of Pilsen, The" (sketch), 231
Sturges, Preston, 283
Styne, Jule, 368, 370
Suesse, Dana, 313
Sugar Babies, 374
Sullivan, Arthur, 42, 44, 48, 109
Sullivan, Ed, 241, 345, 347
Sullivan, Frank, 296
Sullivan, Henry, 265, 285
Summer Nights, 62
Summurun (show), 114
Sumner, John S., 217, 242
Sun Agency, 52
Sunday, Billy, 140
"Sunday in the Park," 329
Sunkist, 169-70
Sunny, 157
"Sunny Disposish," 238
Sunshine Girl, The, 114
Sunshine, Marian, 98
"Sun Will Shine, The" (production number), 258
"Supper Time," 310
Suratt, Valeska, 83
Swanstrom, Arthur, 167, 174
Sweet and Low, 282-83, 284
"Sweetheart Lane," 191
"Sweet Italian Love," 97
"Sweet Music," 288
"Sweet So and So," 283
Swerling, Jo, 243
Swift, Kay, 261, 274, 276
Swinging on a Star, 374

Index ∞ 421

"Swing Low Sweet Harriet," 354
"Swing Me High, Swing Me Low," 96
"Syncopated Walk, The," 120
Syndicate, 71-72, 73, 78, 97, 296

T

Tabbert, William, 355
Taft, William Howard, 107
Take a Bow, 354
"Take Me Back to Philadelphia Pa.," 162
"Take Oh Take Those Lips Away," 207
talking pictures, 54, 226, 249, 256, 271, 275, 278, 296, 311, 365, 374
Talk of New York, The, 94
Tamale Brothers, 60
Tamiris, Helen, 364, 367, 369
Tammany Hall, 41
"Tango Footed Monkey" (dance), 115
tango palaces, 117, 118
"Tangorilla" (production number), 117
Tanguay, Eva (I Don't Care Girl), 93, 95, 168, 219
Tannen, Julius, 239
Tapps, Georgie, 256, 365
Tashman, Lilyan, 135
Tattle Tales, 307
Taylor, Deems, 99, 154, 357
Taylor, Irving, 334
Taylor, Laurette, 114
Taylor, Zachary, 32, 117
"Teach Me to Dance Like Grandma," 257
televison, 54, 365, 366, 368, 374
Tellegen, Lou, 123
Tempest, Florence, 98
Templeton, Fay, 53, 66, 103
"Ten Cents a Dance," 291
"Ten Minutes in Bed," 283
Tenniel, John, 134, 220
Terris, Dorothy, 175
Terris, Norma, 230
Tester, Ruth, 279
Texaco Fire Chief radio hour, 295
"Texas Tommy Swing" (dance), 101
Thailand, King of, 368
"That Colored Jazzboray" (dance), 167
"That Lost Barber Shop Chord," 238
"That Old Fashioned Garden of Mine"

(production number), 208
"That Peech-a Reeno, Phil-i-Peeno Dance," 139
"That's the Kind of Baby for Me," 141
"That Stupid Melody," 245
Thaw, Harry K., 24, 79, 241
Theater Comique, 44-45
Theatre Guild, 182, 221-23, 235, 250, 297, 318
Theatre Union, 318
"There'll Always Be an England," 355
"There's a Broadway Up in Heaven," 320
"These Pretty Fine Depths" (sketch), 211
They All Had Glamour (Marks), 70-71
"They Call It Dancing," 180
"They Didn't Believe Me," 142, 143
"They Didn't Know What They Were Getting" (sketch), 222
They Knew What They Wanted (play), 222, 227
"They Knew What They Wanted Under the Elms" (sketch), 227
"Thief in the Night," 321
Third Little Show, The, 284-85, 286
This Is the Army, 349
"This Is the Army, Mr. Jones," 349
"This is the Missus," 294
"This Time Must Be the Last Time," 349
This Year of Grace, 257-58
Thomas, John Charles, 114, 122, 123
Thomas, Olive, 124, 131-32, 158, 183, 290
Thompson, Fred, 209
Thompson, Frederic, 78
Thompson, Hal, 283
Thompson, Kay, 314
Thompson, Lydia, 37
Thompson, Randall, 235-36
Three Bobs, 189
Three Keatons, 44, 52-53, 73
Three Musketeers, The (operetta), 222
"Three Musketeers, The" (sketch), 276
"Three O'Clock in the Morning," 175
Three's a Crowd, 279-81, 286, 302
Three Stooges, 336
Three to Make Ready, 360-61
"Three White Feathers," 333
"Thrill Is Gone, The," 294
"Thrill Me," 301
Thumbs Up!, 317-18, 348

"Thunderbird" (ballet), 178
"Ticket for the Ballet," 355
Tickets Please, 368
Tick-Tack-Toe, 162
Tidbits of 1946, 362
Tierney, Harry, 133, 140, 156, 164, 170, 207, 213
Tiffany's (jewelry store), 253
Tiller Girls, 206, 213, 227, 257
Timber, Sam, 232
Timberg, Herman, 162, 264
Times Square Theatre, 170, 186, 209, 278
Tinney, Frank, 53, 102, 103, 112, 113, 121, 135, 142, 149, 215-16, 241
Tin Pan Alley, 113
Tiomkin, Dmitri, 290
Tip Tap and Toe, 345
Tis of Thee, 344
"Tobacco Juice" (sketch), 320
Tobacco Road (play), 308, 314, 320
Tobias, Charles, 332
Tobias, Harry, 169, 245
Todd, Michael (Mike), 15, 348, 368
Todd, Mildred, 331
"Toddlin' Along," 274
"Tokio Blues," 220
Tolstoy, Leo, 162
Tom and Jerry, or *Life in London*, 27
Tombes, Andrew, 142, 185, 247
Tonight at 8:30, 326
"Tonight or Never," 277
Tony Pastor's Minstrels, 42
Tony Pastor's Theatre, 43-44, 48, 49, 97, 101
"Too, Too Divine," 276
Toot Sweet, 150, 201
Topics of 1923, 208, 210
Top Notchers, 347
Top of the World, The, 85
Topsy and Eva, 325
Tosca (opera), 93
Touch and Go, 367
Tours, Frank, 98
Tovarich (play), 327
"Toy Clog Dance," 144
Tragedy of Tragedies, or *The Life and Death of Tom Thumb the Great* (Fielding), 27
Trahan, Al, 279

Treacher, Arthur, 282, 352
"Treasurer's Report" (sketch), 205, 209, 238, 302
Treat 'Em Rough (play), 240
Trent, Jo, 246
Trentini, Emma, 53, 64
Trial Marriage (play), 241
Triangle Theater, 237, 245
Trilby (Du Maurier), 123
Trip to Chinatown, A, 57
Trip to Japan, A, 94
Trip to Venus, A, 58
"Trombone Jazz" (dance), 148
Tropical Revue, A, 353, 356
Troy, Hector. *See* Rome, Harold
Truex, Ernest, 53, 285
"Tsin," 167
Tucker, Sophie, 92-93, 119
Tufts, Sonny (Bowen Charleton Tufts III), 331, 334
"Tulip Time" (production number), 156
"Tum on and Tiss Me," 164
Turgend, Harry, 216
"turkey" companies, 37-38
"Turkey Trot" (dance), 113, 114, 117
Twelfth Night (Shakespeare), 26
Twentieth Century Fox, 191
"Twentieth Century Rag," 116
Twenty Million Frenchmen, 273
Twirly Whirly, 66
Two for the Show, 341-42
Two on the Aisle, 10, 370
Two's Company, 372
Tyers, John, 364
Tyler, Jeanne, 335
Tyler, John, 32
Tyler, Royall, 38
Tyrolese Minstrel Family, 30

U

Ulric, Lenore, 221, 233, 245, 261
Ulysses (Joyce), 316
"Uncle Tom's Cabin," 235
Uncle Tom's Cabin (Stowe), 235
"Under the Bamboo Tree," 143
Union Square Playhouse, 51
Union Square Theatre, 71
United Artists, 179

Unter den Linden, 129
"Up Among the Chimney Pots," 274
Up and Down Broadway, 96-97
Up in Central Park, 360
"Up, Up, Up, in My Aeroplane," 94
Urban, Joseph, 56, 123-24, 125, 129, 131, 134, 140, 142, 144, 147, 160, 163, 165, 167, 171, 236, 239, 247, 290, 291, 293, 294, 312, 315
U.S. Army, 349, 350
U.S. Army Air Corps, 349
U.S. Navy, 349

V

Valaida (performer), 284
"Valencia," 232
Valentino, Rudolph, 53, 123, 211, 303
Vallee, Rudy, 293, 294, 322
Van, Bobby, 367
Van, Billy B., 229
Van, Gus, 135, 142, 143
Van Alstyne, Egbert, 91, 128
Van and Schenck, 156, 157, 165, 171, 206
Vanderbilt, Gertrude, 92
Vanderbilt, William K., 57
Vanderbilt Revue, 282
Vanderbilt Theatre, 325
Vanities of 1923, 199-201, 202
VanLoane, Paul, 350
Vanna, Della, 230
variety, 20, 25-27, 34, 35, 36, 41, 43, 45, 49, 50, 51, 53, 55, 57, 59, 60, 62, 63, 103, 117, 347, 350, 367, 374
Variety (periodical), 52, 121, 171, 199, 203
vaudeville, 45, 49-66passim, 74, 78, 85, 94, 106, 108, 109, 115, 117, 118, 122, 131, 166, 174, 178, 184, 190, 193, 201, 210, 229, 232, 251, 262, 284, 296, 303, 316, 325, 341, 342, 346, 347, 350, 352, 353, 354, 357, 362, 365
Vavra, Valma, 276
Veiller, Bayard, 108
Velázquez, Diego, 204
Velez, Lupe, 293, 306, 307
Velie, Jay and Janet, 219

Veloz and Yolanda, 250, 352
Verdon, Gwen, 367
Vestoff, Valodia, 175
V for Victory, 346
Victoria Theatre, 70, 73, 74
Victory Theater (Republic Theater), 73
Victrola (phonograph), 189
Vienna State Opera House, 288
Villa, Pancho, 131, 132
Village Gate cabaret, 373
"Virginia Jungle Dance, The," 32-33
Virginia Minstrels, 30-32, 33
Virgin Man, The (Dugan), 240
Voegtlin, Arthur, 123
Vogues of 1924, 209-10
Volga Sisters, 347
Volney, Maurice, 104
Volpone (play), 245
Volstead Act. See Prohibition
Von Tilzer, Albert, 140
Von Tilzer, Harry, 96
Voyage of Suzette, The, 58

W

Wagner, Jerome, 215-16
"Wagon Wheels," 313
Wait a Minim!, 373
Wake Up and Dream, 272, 273-74
Waldorf Hotel, 161
Wales, Prince of, 156
Wales Padlock law (New York State), 245
Walk a Little Faster, 305-6
Walker, Esther, 149
Walker, George, 95
Walker, James J. (Jimmy), 238, 300, 316
Wall, Harry, 284
Wallace, Beryl, 319
Wallace, Edgar, 181, 293
Wallace, Oliver G., 167
Wallack's theater, 74
Waller, Thomas (Fats), 263, 374
Walsh, Mary Jane, 332
Walt Disney, parodies of, 314
Walter, Serge, 254, 261
Walters, Charles, 314, 319, 325, 326
Walters, Lou, 352, 353-4
Wanamaker's (department store), 276

Wanger, Walter, 145
Warburg, James. *See* James, Paul
Ward, Aida, 253
Warfield, David, 66, 192
Waring, Fred, 356
Warner, Genevieve, 130
Warner, Jack, 249
Warner Brothers, 350
Warners Theatre, 249
Warren, Harry, 283, 284, 295
Warrior's Husband, The (play), 314
Wars of the World, 119
Washburn, Grace, 98
Washington, George, 309, 313
Washington, George Dewey, 307
Washington, Ned, 311
"Washington Square," 162
"Was Mrs. Macbeth Really Sleeping When She Took That Famous Walk?," 166-67
Watch Your Step, 120, 121
Waters, Ethel, 246, 281, 284, 308, 310, 320, 321, 353, 373
Watson, Betty Jane, 365
Watson, Harry, Jr., 96, 100, 107
Watson Sisters, 149
Watteau, Antoine, 163
Watts, James, 174
Wayburn, Ned, 90, 101, 104, 115, 126, 127, 130, 131, 142, 144, 147, 154, 165, 168, 184, 236, 258
"Way Down Yonder in New Orleans," 186
Weatherly, Tom, 259-60, 279, 285, 322
Weaver, Alice, 201
Weaver, Doodles, 344
"Weaving My Dream," 184-85
Webb, Clifton, 127, 162, 260, 280-81, 302, 305, 308, 309, 320
Weber, Joe, 64, 65, 67, 77, 83, 84
Weber, Rex, 304
Weber and Fields, 64-66, 77, 91, 103, 108, 259, 306
Weber and Fields Music Hall (first), 64, 66, 74, 80
Weber and Fields Music Hall (second), 108. *See also* 44th Street Theatre
Weber's Music Hall, 83, 84
Weidman, Charles, 304
Weill, Kurt, 373

Weitz, George. *See* White, George
Welch, Elizabeth, 252
Weldon, Francis, 203
Welles, Orson, 333, 351
Wells, William K. (Billy K.), 233-34, 250, 255, 265, 266-67, 304, 321, 368
Wenrich, Percy, 183
"We're Cleaning Up Broadway," 237
"We Sing America," 330
Weslyn, Louis, 166
Wesner, Ella, 42
West, Mae, 103, 168, 174, 240, 254
West, Paul, 81
"Western Union," 233
Westley, Helen, 191
Weston, Lucy, 87
Whalen, Grover, 276, 316
"What a Beautiful Face Will Do," 219
"What a Village Girl Should Know," 219
"What Can You Say in a Love Song?," 316
"What Did Annie Laurie Promise?," 219
"What Is There to Say?," 313
"What Is This Thing Called Love?," 273
"What'll I Do?," 205
What Price Glory? (play), 227, 240
What's in a Name?, 163
"What's My Man Gonna Be Like?," 282
Wheatley, William, 34-35
Wheaton, Anna, 104, 169
Wheeler, Bert, 207, 350, 353
Wheeler, Betty, 207
Wheeler and Woolsey, 207
"When a Pansy Was a Flower," 283
"When I'm Looking at You," 147
"When Johnny Comes Marching Home from College," 90
"When Knighthood Was in Flower," 214
"When My Baby Smiles at Me," 158
"When Tetrazinni Sings High F," 90
"When the Shaker Plays a Cocktail Tune," 237
"When Yuba Played the Tuba Down in Cuba," 285
"When Ziegfeld Follies Hit the Town," 145
"Where Can He Be?," 288
"Where Is the She for Me?," 366

Where's Your Husband? (play), 240-41
Whirl-i-Gig, 66
Whirl of Society, The, 154
Whirl of the World, The, 115-16
White, E. B., 291, 296
White, Frances, 157, 160
White, George, 9, 14, 15, 113, 124, 142, 154-55, 163, 164, 165, 174, 184, 187-88, 192, 195, 198, 213-14, 227, 233-35, 241, 254-56, 265-67, 293-94, 296, 304-5, 321-22, 335-36
White, Helen, 116
White, Stanford, 24, 66, 79, 241
Whitebirds, 252
White Cargo (play), 199, 240
White Crook, 37
White Deer, Princess, 160, 169
White Fawn, The, 37
"White Heat," 288
White Horse Inn, 326, 343
"White House Glide, The" (dance), 115
Whiteman, Paul, 188-89, 198, 207
Whitford, Annabelle, 81, 82, 92, 93
Whiting, Jack, 317
Whiting, Richard, 150, 155
Whitlock, Billy, 30-32
Whitney, B.C., 164
Whitney, Nina, 321
Who Cares?, 278
"Who Dat Say Chicken in Dis Crowd?," 63
Whoop-Dee-Doo, 66
"Who Paid the Rent for Mrs. Rip Van Winkle When Rip Van Winkle Was Away?," 290
Whorf, Richard, 317
Who's Who, 330-31
Wilcox, Ruth, 265
Wilde, Elizabeth, 325
Wilde, Oscar, 58, 191, 218, 264, 372
Wilder, Thornton, 347
Wild West Show, 75
Wilk, Max, 365
Williams, Bert, 73, 95, 96, 99, 100-101, 107, 108, 112, 117, 124, 131, 141, 156, 184
Williams, Frances, 233-34, 254, 266-67, 315, 316, 353

Williams, Hannah, 282, 283
Williams, Harry, 91
Williams, Herb, 320
Williams, Hugh, 321
Williams, Tennessee, 354, 369
Wills, Nat M., 112, 113, 128
Wilson, Edmund, 191
Wilson, Imogene, 215-16
Wilson, John, 123
Wilson, John C., 369
Wilson, Teddy, 355
Wilson, William J., 116
Wilson, Woodrow, 132
Wiman, Dwight Deere, 259-61, 279, 285, 367-68
Winchell, Walter, 241, 276, 332, 345
Windsor Theater, 72
Wine, Women and Song, 350-1
Winninger, Charles, 146, 160, 165, 170
Winsome Widow, A, 103-4, 105
Winter, Winona, 170
Winter Garden theater, 97-98, 101, 104, 107, 114, 115, 116, 117, 118, 119, 122, 128, 132, 133, 139, 142, 148, 149, 154, 161, 166, 169, 182, 193, 203, 210, 214, 232, 240, 249, 251, 312, 315, 319, 321, 322, 332, 346, 367, 368
"Wintergreen for President," 306
Winters, Lawrence, 361
Wirtz, Arthur, 343
Within the Law (Veiller), 108, 114
"Without the Girl—Inside!," 83
"Without the Law" (sketch), 108
Wizard of Oz, The (play), 119
Wodehouse, P.G., 72, 84, 99, 141, 142, 171, 238, 328
Wolf, Rennold, 123, 125
Wolfe, Thomas, 211
Wolfson, Martin, 211
Wood, Peggy, 121
"Wood Alcohol Blues," 170
"Woodman, Woodman, Spare That Tree," 101
Woods' Museum and Menagerie, 37
Woodward, Matt, 81, 85
Woolf, Walter, 166, 195
Woollcott, Alexander, 159, 179, 183, 204, 257

Woolley, Monty, 279, 305
Words and Music (1917), 145
Words and Music (London), 333
"Working for the Pictures," 118
Works Progress Administration (WPA), 325
"World Is Going Shimmie Mad, The," 157
World of Pleasure, A, 128, 129, 133
World's Fair (Chicago; 1933), 348
World's Fair (New York; 1939-40), 332-33, 335, 341
World War I, 292, 349
World War II, 333, 340, 345, 365, 373
"World Weary," 257
Worth, Billie, 355
Wright Brothers, 94
Wynn, Ed, 53, 117-18, 124-25, 132, 142, 163-64, 180, 198, 219, 265, 295, 307, 343, 347, 352
Wynn, Keenan, 334, 341
Wynn, Nan, 355

Y

"Yaller," 279
"Yama Yama Man, The," 143
Yankee Circus on Mars, A, 78
"Yankee Doodle Blues," 186
Yansci, Jenny. *See* Dolly sisters
Yellen, Jack, 265, 321, 336, 343, 345
Yip-Yip-Yaphank, 149, 156, 179, 349
"You Are My Rainbow," 191
"You Better Go Now," 325
"You Cannot Make Your Shimmy Shake on Tea," 156
"You Can't Stop Me From Loving You," 284
"You'd Be Surprised," 156, 159
"You Forgot Your Gloves," 285
"You Made Me Love You," 290
Youmans, Vincent, 231, 262, 264, 274
"You Naughty, Naughty Men," 35-36
Young, Joe, 295, 311
Young, Victor, 311, 369
"Young King, The" (Wilde), 264
Youngman, Henny, 350
"Young Man's Fancy, A," 163
"You-oo Just You," 147

"You Oughta Be in Pictures," 313
"You're a Builder Upper," 316
"You're a Queer One, Dear Ophelia," 367
"You're Lucky to Me," 281
"You're My Everything," 295
Your Show of Shows (television series), 341, 365
"You've Always Been Along With Me," 361
"You've Got Your Mother's Big Blue Eyes," 135
"Yuletide, Park Avenue," 361
Yvain, Maurice, 172

Z

Zeidman, Irving, 30
Ziegfeld, Florenz, 9, 10, 14, 15, 66, 67, 74, 75-77, 79, 80-82, 83, 84-85, 86-87, 90, 91, 92-96, 97, 98-101, 102-4, , 109, 112-14, 115, 116, 117-18, 119, 120, 121, 123-27, 129, 130-32, 133, 134-35, 138, 140, 141, 142-44, 146, 148, 150, 154-58, 160, 161, 162-63, 165-66, 167, 168, 169, 170-73, 174, 179, 183-85, 188, 189, 191, 192, 195, 198, 199, 200, 201, 203, 204, 205, 206-8, 210, 212-13, 214, 215-16, 222, 235, 236, 238, 239, 240, 241, 242, 247-48, 251, 253, 263, 264, 266, 270, 273, 282, 290, 292, 293, 296, 306, 311, 312, 322, 344, 348, 352
Ziegfeld, Florenz Patricia, 135
Ziegfeld American Revue of 1926, The, 236-37
Ziegfeld Follies (final), 10, 13
Ziegfeld Follies of 1911, The, 99-101, 116, 154
Ziegfeld Follies of 1912, The, 104-5, 105, 106-8
Ziegfeld Follies of 1913, The, 112-14, 117, 199
Ziegfeld Follies of 1914, The, 117-18
Ziegfeld Follies of 1915, The, 20, 121, 123-25, 127, 154
Ziegfeld Follies of 1916, The, 130-32, 133, 134

Ziegfeld Follies of 1917, The, 140-41, 313
Ziegfeld Follies of 1918, The, 147-48, 149
Ziegfeld Follies of 1919, The, 155-56, 157, 158, 159
Ziegfeld Follies of 1920, The, 164-66
Ziegfeld Follies of 1921, The, 92, 170-73, 210
Ziegfeld Follies of 1922, The, 184-85, 188, 206
Ziegfeld Follies of 1923, The, 157, 201, 206-8
Ziegfeld Follies of 1924, The, 212-13, 215-16
Ziegfeld Follies of 1926, The. See Ziegfeld American Revue of 1926, 'The
Ziegfeld Follies of 1927, The, 247-48
Ziegfeld Follies of 1931, The, 289-91
Ziegfeld Follies of 1934, The, 312-13
Ziegfeld Follies of 1936, The, 321-22, 332-24
Ziegfeld Follies of 1943, The, 352
Ziegfeld Follies of 1957, The, 372
Ziegfeld Follies of 1958, The, 372
Ziegfeld Follies series, 33, 38, 55, 66, 92, 99, 103, 105, 113, 115, 117, 120, 123, 125, 126, 131, 141, 142, 145, 147, 149, 155, 156, 158, 160, 165, 168, 184, 190, 193, 198, 201, 204, 207, 212, 213, 215, 217, 236, 237, 251, 278, 286, 290, 311, 312, 324, 349, 352
Ziegfeld girls, 76, 86, 118, 125, 126, 156, 184, 207
Ziegfeld Girls, 162, 163
"Ziegfeld Rag," 130
Ziegfeld's Midnight Frolic (1927), 184
Ziegfeld's Midnight Frolic, (1921) 180, 183. *See also* Midnight Frolics
Ziegfeld Theatre, 239, 291, 311, 354, 357, 367
Zimmerman, J. Frederick, 71
"Zing Went the Strings of My Heart!," 318
Zinkeisen, Doris, 257
Zorina, Vera, 350
Zucker, Stan, 365
"Zulu Hop" (dance), 116

About the Author

❦

Lee Davis is a biographer, journalist, playwright, musical theatre historian and consultant, stage director and educator.

He is the author of six books: *Bolton and Wodehouse and Kern: The Men Who Made Musical Comedy*; *You Gotta Have Heart* (an autobiography of and with theatre composer and lyricist Richard Adler); *MGM: When the Lion Roars* (contributor); *Natural Disasters: Man-Made Catastrophes and Environmental Disasters*; *Assassination* (adapted into a four-part television series, featuring Mr. Davis as a narrator, for the History Channel) and *Scandals and Follies: The Rise and Fall of the Great Broadway Revue*. He has contributed essays to a number of CD booklets, including the Elektra-Nonesuch recording of *Girl Crazy* and the Roxbury recreation of *Oh, Kay!*, featuring Dawn Upshaw.

His theatre pieces include five revues: *Of George We Sing (A Gershwin Revue)*, *Jerome Kern: The Touch of His Hand*, *Broadway by the Book: Musicals with a Literary Heritage*, *Let's Misbehave: The World, the Words and the Music of Cole Porter* and *Noel Coward: A Talent to Amaze*.

He has written narrations for Kitty Carlisle Hart and others at various Jerome Kern and P.G. Wodehouse celebrations at such venues as Town Hall and the Morgan Library, and appeared as a panelist at *Encores! Great Musicals in Concert* at New York's City Center. He served as a consultant on Swedish Television's *P.G. Wodehouse: The Man and His Work*, and BBC Bristol's *P.G. Wodehouse on Broadway*, and appeared as an interviewee on a BBC three-part broadcast concerning the correspondence of P.G. Wodehouse. In March of 1998, he appeared on a panel and was an active participant in the four-day Gershwin Centennial Celebration at the Library of Congress.

A lecturer on the American Musical Theatre at Long Island University's Southampton Campus and Suffolk Community College, the producer and narrator of *The American Musical Theatre*, broadcast over WPBX-FM, Southampton, N.Y., a constant contributor to *Show Music Magazine*, and a theatre critic for several Long Island newspapers, Mr. Davis currently makes his home in Westhampton, New York.